Polygamy

Published in cooperation with the
William P. Clements Center for Southwest Studies
Southern Methodist University

Polygamy

An Early American History

Sarah M. S. Pearsall

Yale

UNIVERSITY PRESS

NEW HAVEN AND LONDON

Published with assistance from the income of the Frederick John Kingsbury Memorial Fund.
Published with assistance from the Annie Burr Lewis Fund.
Published with assistance from the foundation established in memory of
Calvin Chapin of the Class of 1788, Yale College.

Yale University Press books may be purchased in quantity for educational, business, or promotional use. For
information, please e-mail sales.press@yale.edu (U.S. office) or sales@yaleup.co.uk (U.K. office).

Set in Fournier MT type by IDS Infotech Ltd.
Printed in the United States of America.

Library of Congress Control Number: 2018962621
ISBN 978-0-300-22684-3 (hardcover : alk. paper)

A catalogue record for this book is available from the British Library.

This paper meets the requirements of ANSI/NISO Z39.48-1992 (Permanence of Paper).

10 9 8 7 6 5 4 3 2 1

To Teddy

Men and women find universally, (however the fact may be concealed,) that their susceptibility to love is not burnt out by one honey-moon, or satisfied by one lover. On the contrary, the secret history of the human heart will bear out the assertion that it is capable of loving any number of times and any number of persons, and that the more it loves the more it can love. This is the law of nature, thrust out of sight, and condemned by common consent, and yet secretly known to all.

John Humphrey Noyes, "Bible Argument"

Contents

Acknowledgments

"This work hath taken up more than *twelve* years. What a length of time, and painful drudgery, to make yourself at the last stage of life ridiculous!" So smirked James Penn, a 1781 critic of a book about polygamy in *Remarks on Thelyphthora*. *This* work did not take quite that long, and I hope I'm not yet at the last stage of life. Still, many individuals and institutions contributed to making the research and writing of this book a great joy, with only occasional painful drudgery. I'm delighted to thank them here.

I've been lucky to be able to rely on generous financial support. A British Academy Small Grant was critical in allowing me to pursue research in early stages. I also benefited greatly from a year of leave supported by a National Endowment of Humanities Long-Term Fellowship at the Newberry Library; a term of leave supported by the Centre for Research in the Arts, Social Sciences, and Humanities (CRASSH) at Cambridge University; and another year of leave from a senior fellowship at the Clements Center for Southwest Studies at Southern Methodist University. Cambridge University History Faculty also helped with sabbatical as well as sustaining research support. Thanks especially to Tony Badger and Gary Gerstle, both Paul Mellon Professors of American History; Lawrence Klein, chair of the History Faculty; and Phil Allmendinger, head of the School of Humanities and Social Sciences, all at Cambridge University.

The musty air of libraries and archives is to me intoxicating, a gateway to new worlds. For supplying me with my fix, I thank many institutions and the helpful staff in them. I have relied on two great British library systems: those at Cambridge University and Oxford University. In the Chicago area, I relied on the extraordinary Newberry Library (and its Illinois Interlibrary Loan system), as well as Northwestern Libraries. I also used repeatedly the rich collections at Yale University, especially the Beinecke Rare Book and Manuscript Library, and Harvard University, especially Houghton Library. The staff at the well-stocked Southern Methodist University libraries were unfailingly sweet, and I thank Russell L. Martin III in particular for pointing me in the direction of some key texts at the DeGolyer Library. I also appreciated the interlibrary loan system there. Other wonderful repositories for material included the John Wesley Powell Library of Anthropology at the Smithsonian; the Archivo General de Indias; the British Library; the National Library of Scotland; the John Carter Brown Library at Brown University; the state archives for Massachusetts, Connecticut, and New Hampshire; the Boston Public Library; the Merrimack County Probate Department; Connecticut Historical Society; Swem Library, William and Mary College; the Virginia Baptist Historical Society at the University of Richmond (and many thanks to Lori Gates Schuyler for arranging my stay there); Glasgow University Archives; and the LDS Church History Library, Church of Jesus Christ of Latter-day Saints. I have also benefited from numerous online and electronic databases. I am also grateful for permission to republish some of the material found in two articles: " 'Having Many Wives' in Two American Rebellions: The Politics of Households and the Radically Conservative," *American Historical Review* 118, no. 4 (October 2013): 1000–1028, and "Native American Men—and Women—at Home in Plural Marriages in Seventeenth-Century New France," *Gender and History* 27, no. 3 (November 2015): 591–610.

I have also been so delighted with the insights of audiences, as well as genial hosts, at many institutions at which I have presented material. In the United States, I have gained much from lectures at the University of Utah, Yale University, the University of California–Berkeley, Southern Methodist University, and the University of Alabama, as well as at the Washington, D.C., Early American Seminar; the American Origins Seminar, Early Modern Studies Institute at the University of Southern California–Huntington Library; the Rocky Mountain Early American Seminar; the Boston Area Early American History Seminar; the Newberry Library Early American History Seminar and the Fellows' Seminar; and the Omohundro Institute of Early American History and Culture Colloquium. Special hats off to Andy Graybill, Heather Kopelson, Eric Hinderaker, Robin Einhorn and Mark Peterson, David Blight, Rick Bell and Holly Brewer, Peter Mancall and Carole Shammas, and Ron Hoffman. In the United Kingdom, I thank seminar organizers, and participants, at the University of East Anglia; the Institute of Historical Research, University of London; Nottingham University; Sheffield University; Warwick University; Oxford University (Rothermere American History; Eighteenth-Century British

History; and From Restoration to Reform); and Cambridge University (World History; Multidisciplinary Gender Studies; Comparative Social and Cultural History; American History; The Eighteenth Century). I appreciate comments from students and others at History Society talks at Murray Edwards, Robinson, and Gonville and Caius Colleges at Cambridge as well as the History Society at the North London Collegiate School, lectures to sixth-form students at Robinson, and the Cambridge Rotary Club. I also gained much from presenting at l'Université Paris 7 Diderot, so thanks to Marie-Jeanne Rossignol. Dr. Charlotte Lerg, my impressive former undergraduate, sent a timely invitation to speak at the Westfälische Wilhelms-Universität Münster, where a great audience welcomed me. She and her mother, Sabine, also arranged a special tour of Stadtmuseum Münster with Dr. Bernd Thier, from whom I learned a great deal about the (Ana)Baptists.

To enter so many areas new to me, as I have in this book, has been an engrossing but daunting challenge. I could not have managed it without the insightful, expert readings of individual chapters by these generous colleagues: Seth Archer, Juliana Barr, Kathleen DuVal, Amy Erickson, Sylvia Frey, Kathryn Gleadle, Sarah Barringer Gordon, Emma Griffin, Joel Isaac, Margaret Jacobs, Daniel Livesay, Rowena McClinton, Margaret Newell, Matthew O'Hara, Benjamin Park, Dylan Penningroth, Ann Marie Plane, Bianca Premo, Edward Rugemer, Brett Rushforth, Elena Schneider, Susan Sleeper-Smith, Christina Snyder, Laurel Thatcher Ulrich, Lee Palmer Wandel, Ruth Watson, and Elizabeth Wright. Brian DeLay not only read the whole manuscript but did so with his trademark combination of critical brilliance and generous encouragement. I am abidingly grateful.

An invigorating manuscript workshop at the Clements Center brought many other excellent readers. The Clements Center, beautifully codirected by Neil Foley and Andrew Graybill—though actually run, as they would be the first to admit, by the exceptional Ruth Ann Elmore—was a terrific place to finish writing this book, not least because of my lovely fellow Fellows, Aimee Villarreal, Sarah Rodríguez, and Tommy Richards. Two remarkably talented historians, Anne Hyde and Alan Taylor, gave me the benefit of their critical readings, as well as their encouragement: what gifts. I also gained much from the comments of the other astute readers at the workshop: Lindsay Chervinsky, Stephanie Cole, Paul Conrad, Edward Countryman, Neil Foley, Andy Graybill, Ben Park, Tommy Richards, Sarah Rodríguez, Joshua Tracy, and Aimee Villarreal. Ed also went out of his way to welcome a fellow sojourner, even dancing at a powwow with me. At SMU, David Meltzer gave me his useful anthropological perspective.

Although I admit that I cursed them at the time, I am grateful to Harvard's history graduate school requirements, which made even U.S. Americanists show reading proficiency in two foreign languages. This background helped to give me sufficient courage to take on early modern Spanish and French texts. I have not always been the most graceful translator, but I have sought help from people who are. On this point, thanks especially to Betsy Wright and Bianca Premo, who introduced me to the online Spanish dictionary database RAE-NTLLE. Neil Wright generously and unblushingly translated an array of saucy Latin for me.

For providing specific references or images or answering pestery queries (in some cases more than once), thanks to all the readers just mentioned as well as: John Bishop, Joe Brandão, Holly Brewer, James Brooks, Kevin Brousseau, Trevor Burnard, Kate Carté, Emily Clark, David Costa, Barbara De Marco, Konstantin Dierks, Alexandre Dubé, Sunday Eiselt, Garrett Fesler, Kathleen Flake, Vic Gatrell, Allan Greer, Matthew Grow, Ron Hoffman, Mandy Izadi, Marjoleine Kars, Cynthia Kierner, Sarah Knott, Allan Kulikoff, Jan Lewis, Sally Mason, Kate Masur, Sara McDougall, Sarah Meer, David Meltzer, Bob Morrissey, Brittany Chapman Nash, Louis Nelson, Simon Newman, Jeani O'Brien, Susan Pearson, Mark Peterson, Helen Pfeifer, Bianca Premo, Andrew Preston, Robert Preucel, Jenny Pulsipher, Richard Ross, Hamish Scott, Scott Stevens, David Hurst Thomas, Sam Truett, Felix Waldman, Danny Wasserman-Soler, and Betty Wood. Ruth Watterson and Zoe Waldman, cheerful research assistants, helped out at the start and at the end.

Since I started this book, I've worked at three universities; in each of them, colleagues have indulged me by talking—probably more than they wanted—about polygamy. At Northwestern, I learned much from conversations with Susan Pearson, Kate Masur, Sarah Maza, Peter Carroll, Dylan Penningroth, Butch Ware, Nancy MacLean, Ed Muir, Ethan Shagan, Dyan Elliott, and subsequently from Deborah Cohen and Caitlin Fitz. At Oxford Brookes University, I appreciated time with Joanne Begiato, Tom Crook, Anne-Marie Kilday, Alysa Levene, Glen O'Hara, Jane Stevens-Crawshaw, and, above all, Erik Landis. I also thank faculty at Oxford University, especially Kathryn Gleadle, Pekka Hämäläinen, Joanna Innes, Stephen Tuck, and Patricia Clavin, as well as visiting Harmsworth Professors Linda Kerber, Peter Onuf, and Phil Morgan.

My colleagues at Cambridge are just the right combination of encouraging and bracing. I have especially benefited from conversations about the book with Andrew Preston, Betty Wood, Gary Gerstle, Joel Isaac, the late Michael O'Brien, Helen Pfeifer, Amy Erickson, Ruth Watson, Andrew Arsan, Joya Chatterji, Chris Clark, Larry Klein, Nick Guyatt, Renaud Morieux, Rachel Leow, Peter Mandler, Ulinka Rublack, Alison Bashford, Shruti Kapila, John Thompson, Melissa Calaresu, Mary Laven, David Maxwell, Sujit Sivasundaram, Magnus Ryan, Bronwen Everill, and Emma Spary. I'm also grateful for my fellow Fellows at Robinson, especially the other historians, David Woodman, Amy Erickson, Deborah Thom, and Mike Shin. Many of my students have also followed me into the unfamiliar worlds into which I journey, and I have been buoyed by their enthusiasm and curiosity. I am especially grateful for the astute reading of the manuscript by a most talented undergraduate (now postgraduate), Ella Sbaraini.

One dear departed mentor, Alfred Young, entered my dreamscape to remind me that to see encounters only from one perspective was meshugga. Ron Hoffman was another wise, generous, humane mensch whose passing saddens me profoundly. The loss of those two wonderful men, as well as two other terrific colleagues and friends, Jan Lewis and Leonard Sadosky, makes the world feel poorer. Still, their warmth and wisdom continue to radiate, from their scholarship as well as from cherished memories.

Chris Rogers, my editor, shaped beautifully while also accepting my vision here. I am thrilled to have an editor who *edits*, with grace, enthusiasm, and intelligence. Adina Berk and Karen Olson have also been so helpful, as has mapmaker Bill Nelson, proofreader Erica Hanson, and indexer Alexa Selph. Dan Heaton was an exemplary manuscript editor who much enlivened the process of checking editorial changes. Had I known that two such gifted historians as Kathleen M. Brown and Sarah Barringer Gordon were the initial readers for the Press, I would have quaked in my boots. That both were positive meant a great deal. Still, even Sally's little pink highlighter is formidable, and both historians greatly improved the text with critical readings. Kathy Brown and an anonymous reviewer later read the completed manuscript and gave insightful feedback. I am so grateful. All of these people made the book better. The errors remaining are of course only the fault of ridiculous me.

Glenys Denton, Mary Smith, and many others at Robinson College have made daily life pleasurable over the past several years. I am also grateful to Liz Partridge, Liz Haresnape, and Mike Weaver of the History Faculty. I am aware of how much real labor underpins my privileged Cambridge life, and I am so thankful for those who do it. Charley Marshall took me on a stakeout in Utah, and also sent me home with High West; thanks, Charley! We so enjoyed getting to know our neighborly neighbors in Dallas: the Lujans, the Arnolds, the Kays, Haley Phelps Montanaro, and Susan Fletcher and John Garrigus (and It's OK), who made a year in a city we'd never been a great delight. I have also had the good fortune of being part of writing groups (or at least solidarity groups for those trying to write), mostly by distance. I gained much from confabs with Elena Schneider (who helped pull me, stumbling, across the finish line) and Molly Warsh; with Ben Irvin; and with Joya Chatterji. Their sympathy from afar kept me going in lonelier months. A writing group in person, with Margaret Jacobs and Seth Archer, in which we actually exchanged work, was even more fun.

Margaret Jacobs, as well as David Blight, both became accidental but welcome mentors when each came to Cambridge as the Pitt Professor of American History. Their humane understanding and wisdom have inspired me. Gary Gerstle warned me the last stage was tough, and his admirable backing kept me going through it as through much else. Ari Kelman swooped in like the fifth-best local firefighter that he could have been, to quell burning anxieties in that last push. For many years, in his gallant way, Hamish Scott has given useful advice on my "marriage project" over lovely dinners. Sally Mason and the late Ron Hoffman have been generous, sympathetic, and fun. Andy Graybill and his tolerant and delightful spouse, Jennifer Ebinger, welcomed us graciously to Dallas, and transformed the last stage of writing into one of productivity and pleasure. With characteristic sharpness, Andy also summarized the book in a memorable fashion (!). The dazzling Jane Kamensky provided excellent advice and sustaining support, not to mention yummy meals. Marvelous Andrew Preston has made everything better since we first became colleagues in 2012.

I inadvertently stopped my awe-inspiring teacher and friend Laurel Thatcher Ulrich in her tracks in Cambridge, England, in 2004 when I said I was planning to write my next book on polygamy. We ended up approaching the topic from different vantage points, and I have been so grateful for her advice. She has been my guiding star since I first read her books. Pauline Stone Pearsall and John Rogers have also talked with me in wonderfully engaged ways about Latter-day Saint polygamy, and much else besides. So glad to have them in the family. Amy Gambrill has always believed in this project, and in its author; Mange, we'll always have Paris. Emma Griffin and I have swapped cakes, chat, and sympathy for decades. All of them have kept me going.

My generous grandparents Ira and Ella Meyer lived married monogamy for more than sixty-five years, so I witnessed early on what its joys can be. By contrast, my fierce feminist mother, Marilyn Pearsall, was never a conformist. I can thank her more than anyone for teaching me early on that lifelong monogamous heterosexual marriage is hardly inevitable. Although she passed away just as I was finishing this book, her loyal affection and intellectual iconoclasm have left an indelible mark on me, as well as on my brilliant siblings, Anthony and Cornelia Pearsall. This little sister still hopes to catch up to them both. In the meantime, I delight in their own fascinating constellation of interests. Peter Kail took it in his stride that he had a wife transfixed by polygamy. I'm so glad for his friendship. Michael Gould has lit up my life in all kinds of ways. I appreciate them all profoundly. My work on this book has coincided with another, much more impressive production of about twelve years, a source of inexhaustible joy (and hugs), with only occasional painful drudgery: my son. He and I are often ridiculous together, and I couldn't be more grateful.

Polygamy

Introduction

Contrary to popular opinion, American polygamy did not start with the Mormons. Before Europeans arrived, North America was largely polygamous. In polygamy's unexpected and mostly unknown trajectories over the centuries, there is a rich, unsettling story of conflicts over American marriage, gender, and sexuality. This book is about intimate choices: falling in love; becoming a second or third wife; keeping a marriage going, or leaving it. It is also about public actions by colonies, states, and religious institutions, because marriage, whether monogamous or polygamous, unites the personal with the political. This history provides a novel perspective on power in early America, as seen through households, which is where most people actually lived. The view starts small, but in the end, it encompasses worlds. Polygamy controversies place us amid major events in early America because such clashes were about the organization and governance not just of households but of societies, nations, and empires.

Sometimes those debates began with the quiet murmuring of women in the woods, as in 1627, just outside the beautiful, ancient pueblo of Taos in what is now New Mexico. Five women had just been listening to the Franciscan friars preaching, as usual, that it was better for husbands "to leave off having many wives, as was their custom before they were baptized." The friars assured their audience that the torments of hell awaited women and men who undermined the holy sacrament of monogamous marriage. These ominous warnings echoed in the head of one woman as she went about her daily chores. She had lived a long time, remembered how it was in the adobes before the friars had lodged there. The world seemed different now, but

Taos Pueblo, 1880. The J. Paul Getty Museum, Los Angeles. John K. Hillers, North Taos Pueblo, New Mexico, 1880, Albumen silver print, 20.6 × 30.6 cm. Courtesy of J. Paul Getty Museum.

some things didn't change. Women still had to find the wood to light the household fires. So off she went with four other women, who talked as they collected and carried kindling. Steering the conversation to husbands—easy to do in a group of wives together—this experienced woman shared her thoughts. "It was better," she declared, "to follow the custom of marriage as in their heathenism" when men "had many wives."[1] The other women did not entirely agree.

In the midst of their spirited conversation, out of "a clear, tranquil sky," a bolt of lightning flashed, striking the woman who dared to espouse polygamy. It killed "that infernal minister of the devil in the middle of those good Christian women who were resisting her evil doctrines." This episode apparently confirmed for the wives what the Franciscans already believed: the "truth of the holy Sacrament of matrimony." Yet just as this woman had not accepted what the missionaries preached, many other Indians probably drew a radically different conclusion from her electrifying death. Like the Franciscans, they likely interpreted lightning as a sign from the heavens. Yet they might well have assumed that the gods plucked this respected leader up in glory, not anger, thus confirming the righteousness of what she taught. The same event could look so different, depending on the viewpoint. The four women who reported it may have wondered themselves if she was right. Still, that they publicized their disputes with her suggests that there were conflicts within indigenous communities, even among women themselves, about this strange, exclusive kind of marriage: indissoluble lifetime monogamy.[2]

Why in the world would a woman defend "having many wives"? Was she an "infernal minister of the devil," as this Franciscan writer called her? Was she a "duped drudge," which is what a lot of other European observers (and subsequent scholars) termed a plural wife? Was she, as one later periodical had it, a mere "martyr to unbridled lust"?[3] She was none of these things. She was a canny observer, a teacher, and a rebel, resisting Spanish colonialism as surely as the insurgents in the Pueblo Revolt, which took place at Taos and other pueblos some fifty years later. The friars knew she was trouble—and competition. They called her a "sorceress," termed her advice a "sermon" and her ideas "doctrines." These words imply that they saw her as a formidable rival for the hearts, minds, and spirits of the people of the pueblo. That even supposedly peaceful missionaries recorded with joy the sudden, shocking death of a woman who advocated alternative forms of household organization shows how much people in early America cared about marriage—even when they had never entered into it themselves. For a woman to condone plural marriage threatened them. In their stories, the friars sought to dismiss her and to deny her testimony. In this book, I do the opposite.

Defiant defenses of plural marriage are worth taking seriously, even when—indeed, especially when—they puzzle us so much. They open up new ways of understanding early America and its complicated colonial legacies. Polygamy—marriage with multiple spouses—factored into all kinds of encounters between many people—Native Americans, Europeans, and Africans, among others—in the contacts that gave rise to the modern United States. Why and how did women and men both champion and contest plural marriages in what is now the continental United States? To answer this question is to elucidate some key and often overlooked dynamics, and the roles women and men played in early American life. Marriages and households were central arenas for complicated and brutal confrontations. Debates, fights, and even massacres roiled what now seems a placid and settled issue, marital monogamy.[4]

Polygamy's surprising history tracks through many indigenous communities, numerous colonies, and into the new American nation. Many key touchstones of American history, those that fill most standard textbook accounts, appear here: the Pueblo and other revolts against the Spanish, Catholic missions in New France, New England settlements and King Philip's War, the entrenchment of African slavery in the Chesapeake, the Atlantic Enlightenment, the American Revolution, missions and settlement in the West—and East, and the rise of Mormonism. Polygamy illuminates these well-known episodes and processes in unanticipated ways. Disagreements over polygamy did not end in the colonial period. In 1852, the Church of Jesus Christ of Latter-day Saints officially announced the doctrine of plural marriage.[5] In 1856, the Republican Party declared its commitment "to prohibit in the Territories those twin relics of barbarism—Polygamy, and Slavery." Although it is more famous as an antislavery statement, this platform also sought to eradicate the plural marriages of the Latter-day Saints in Utah Territory.[6] That opposing polygamy was such a high priority in the new party's platform, right up there with opposing slavery, is clear evidence of the importance marriage had assumed as a national issue by the 1850s, when the present story (largely) ends. Like the chronology, the geography is also broad. Although polygamy in modern imaginings seems western, the story of American polygamy reaches from the Atlantic to the Pacific.

All that said, at least five reasons might be suggested for why this book shouldn't exist. First, everyone knows the Mormons instigated polygamy in America. This was patently not the case—there was plenty of polygamy before that—and there was even more imagining, thinking, and writing about polygamy in the early modern era. Second, polygamy seems so outlandish that if it did flourish in early America, it might be more polite not to mention it. I take that sense of alienation not as a barrier to discussion but as an invitation to explore why so many of us find this form of marriage so disturbing. What tales have been told about it over many centuries, and how have they shaped our sense of the matter, even today? (Also, should we still believe them?) Third, polygamy is marginal, a minor matter, not worth our time. In fact, polygamy has been a practice of millions of people, and it was also an issue in major rebellions, wars, enlightenments, as well as, of course, the history of one of America's major religious groups, the Mormons. Investigating polygamy, taking this oblique angle, illuminates all kinds of important American histories. Fourth, the story of polygamy deals with sex, and of course scholars, students, and readers of history are too high-minded to be interested in *that*. You can determine for yourself the validity of that claim.

Fifth, it is impossible to tell a tale that centers on early modern women, many of whom were not literate. There are no sources, right? The following eight chapters refute this point—as does the story of the Taos woman.

For the friars in New Mexico, that the wicked witch was dead was a marvel, a reason for "good Christians" to ring the bells and share the story. What started as women friends chatting in the woods became an international sensation, witnessing God's abiding presence even amid American "savages." Alonso de Benavides, the Franciscan custodian of the New Mexico missions, wrote and published his account in 1630 for the edification of Catholics everywhere. For him, it showed that God was working on the side of Christians—and monogamy, and Franciscans, and Benavides himself (who, as it happens, was angling for a promotion to bishop). Friars such as Benavides publicized their American successes in part to mark their territory against other missionary orders. Since Philip IV of Spain had bankrolled their efforts, they also wanted to assure the government that their missions could bring in revenue. Therefore the account was published in Spanish, but also in French, German, Dutch, and Latin. It was so popular that its author published a revised version four years later, presenting it with a flourish to the pope himself.[7]

Men like Benavides told tales about other people's marriages in part to highlight the challenges facing Christians around the world. Narratives about defenses of polygamy, as well as its practice, filled the shelves of European libraries in the early modern period. Most of them concerned people beyond Europe, but some were closer to home. One episode in particular singed itself onto European consciousness: the rebellion of John of Leiden and his radical Protestant Anabaptists against Catholic authorities in the German city of Münster in the 1530s. The same kind of learned, pious Catholic who could have read Benavides' *Memorial* would probably have already read about the outrageous events at Münster, which became synonymous with religious insubordination. John and his followers there rejected the authority of the Catholic Church, championing an extreme Protestantism. These insurgents reportedly sought to instigate a reimagined society based on the Old Testament, including the ancient patriarchal practice of polygamy. (Our information about them comes from their enemies, so it is difficult to know exactly what they did.) Catholic authorities crushed the rebellion, torturing and killing John and two fellow leaders in a massive public spectacle. They put their bodies in cages on the church of St. Lambert as a

The three cages that held John of Leiden and two other rebel leaders, still hanging on the church of St. Lambert, Münster, Germany. Courtesy of Rüdiger Wölk, Münster.

warning to others (the cages are still there). They then recounted sensational tales about the practices of these militant Protestants. Even as critics declared, "It is better to pass over these matters in silence than to offend modest ears," lists of John of Leiden's wives, and ever more lurid accounts of his plural marriages, appeared in cheap pamphlets and expensive histories that circulated in many countries and languages.[8]

According to his detractors, John of Leiden created an elaborate system by which he had sex with each wife in succession. When it was her turn, a wife "entered the bathroom, washed, doused herself in perfume, and put on a purple garment of cotton." Then two older women helped to instruct her, as "her hair was pulled back with gold, her temples were adorned with fragrant wreaths, her womb was concealed with a silken loin cloth, her two breasts shone out through the thinnest muslin and, to summarize, everything that could stimulate sex was provided." "In this way," the author of this Catholic history of the events at Münster concluded, "the king indulged in the foul pleasures of his lust." (Perhaps by this point, a few readers did too, since this description reads much like sixteenth-century pornography, printed in Latin to prevent impressionable people like children, servants, and wives from reading it.) John of Leiden thus showed himself to be a base seducer, no "king" at all. His followers were equally lascivious: "Raging with unbridled wantonness, everyone was now carried away with obscene lechery, and they were set ablaze with such promiscuous lustfulness that no restraint was kept on their prodigal sexuality." In other words, radical Protestantism was smoking hot and dangerous, unleashed in lewd acts and insurrection.[9]

The salacious description of polygamy in Münster confirms what many people still think: that polygamy, unlike monogamy, is merely about sex and "promiscuous lustfulness." It is not. It is a form of marriage and therefore, like monogamy, a matter of public concern structuring societies, cultures, and lineages. Sometimes marriage leads to sexual abandon; sometimes, as some married people will tell you glumly, it has the opposite effect. Marriage brings states, religious authorities, communities, and families into the most intimate of realms, legitimizing children and ordering and transmitting property and inheritance. It shapes gender, race, and rank. It has therefore been critical to the exercise of religious, state, and colonial power. When John of Leiden and his fellow leaders supposedly instigated polygamy, they were not just showing off their masculine potency or indulging themselves in carnal pleasures, though some may have been doing both of those things. They were also enacting a Protestant recasting of marriage. This reconfiguration removed its status as a sacrament even as it also celebrated married life as no longer the inferior counterpart to the idealized celibacy of priests, monks, and nuns. Even the most holy Protestants could—and should—be married. To adopt plural marriages, if indeed the Münster rebels did, was to depart even more dramatically from Catholicism. It was a self-conscious method of returning to Old Testament worlds in which great patriarchs had more wives than one.

Spicy tales of sexual depravity among people so committed to Christian beliefs that they died for them make clear that marriage was a central arena in which to hammer out religious differences. To broadcast John of Leiden's polygamy, as critics did repeatedly, was to imply that religious nonconformists were also revolting perverts, insatiable for both power and flesh. The "Anabaptist madness" rang most clearly in accounts of its women, duped and disturbed by violent passions. "They were so deranged, so unbalanced, so driven by frenzy that they . . . surpassed the Furies," their prayers echoing like "the voices of a thousand pigs grunting at the same time."[10]

Catholic critics used these words to construct a landscape of monstrousness around polygamy and religious difference. Radical Protestantism transformed men into filthy beasts, women into snorting sows. These distorting and damning images of gender and sexuality, of loins and lusts, underpinned larger ideas about religion and politics.

The Protestant Reformation made "matrimony . . . an acute issue" at the same time that "monogamy-preaching Europe was suddenly conscious of being a small enclave surrounded by a polygamy-permitting world." These two streams, of Reformations and global encounters, sometimes ran together and sometimes crisscrossed; taken together, they increased the political importance of marriage. The Protestant rejection of marriage as a sacrament launched novel ways of considering how households might be organized. From the sixteenth century on, polygamy conjured up mysteries for many Protestants who sought to align their societies with Old Testament values, as the Münster rebels purportedly did. How could a form of marriage practiced by holy patriarchs like Abraham and Solomon and nowhere explicitly condemned in the Bible (Old Testament or New) no longer be acceptable for godly people? Had God changed his mind about it (impossible!), or had these ancient polygamists had a special dispensation, no longer available? This theological conundrum vexed many, and a few edgier Protestants from the sixteenth century on, at least, thought it pointed to a viable Christian endorsement of polygamy.[11]

Yet arguing for polygamy was incendiary stuff, in part because monogamy had long distinguished Christians in Europe, demarcating them from Jews and Muslims, many of whom did allow plural marriages. As Christians moved out across the world, monogamy—and Europeans' sense of its superiority—took on renewed importance. Commitment to monogamy informed the Christian mission around the world over many centuries. Polygamy provided Europeans with an excellent method by which to judge differences between cultures around the globe as well as within their own worlds. In an era when Europeans roamed and sought new dominions across the globe, polygamy appeared over and over in their judgments on other people. European and American interest in plural unions marked literally thousands of sources: from descriptions of travel and exploration to theological and political tracts to letters and arts. Scholars have considered these representations of polygamy, but mostly in a way that focuses only on theory and only on Europe.[12]

Until now, there have been no books on early modern American polygamy. Although people literally died over polygamy and what it represented, few studies grapple with the vexed, shifting, and complicated nature of disputes over marriage in North America from the sixteenth century to the eighteenth. With a few noble and notable exceptions, most studies of early American colonialism have treated disputes over marriage and especially polygamy as something like mere local color in the background of a heady borderlands drama. In several cases, though, differing ideas about households were not the backdrop for the drama; they *were* the drama. Households were political units, as well as politicized markers of civility and authority, in the period from 1500 to 1800, whether for Native Americans, Africans, or Europeans. Marriage controversies are thus an exceptionally useful way to survey busy hubs of intersectionality, crisscrossing gender with racial, ethnic, religious, and other identities and ideals. Many scholars have focused on interracial sexual relations. Standardizing marriages in terms of who could marry whom was a central means of asserting dominance, but, though far less noticed, so was limiting the form unions could take.[13]

Colonial and imperial powers monitored and established family norms, winding monogamous Christian marriage, progress, and civility together so tightly that they have yet to be unspooled. Marrying the "right" way helped to affirm those who had authority as deserving of such power. Early modern global encounters transformed the "problem of polygamy" in substantive ways so subtle that it takes a long historical view to see them. At the start of this period, polygamy was a problem because it seemed un-Christian, even anti-Christian, the practice of heathens and infidels. By the end, it was more often cast as backward and barbaric, the practice of the inherently depraved. There were continuities: authorities asserted that the practice of polygamy, among other things, justified ferocity, against both individuals and ways of life. Yet there was also change. As scholars observe, "The modern world is filled with—one could say it is constituted by—things said to be primitive, traditional, and backward. Distinguishing these qualities and marginalizing them is endless, highly politicized work." Constructing racial groupings depended in part on having already forged categories like "polygamy" and "monogamy."[14]

This book, then, offers a broad history elucidating what has seemed a much shorter and more contingent history of Mormon controversies in the nineteenth-century United States. Historians of the debates around

Latter-day Saints have argued that condemnations of polygamy stemmed in part from its perceived violations of republican principles. In this view, it offended American sensibilities because it deprived women of consent, denied them the right to loving marriage, and transformed husbands into tyrants. Such unequal marital structures seemed at odds with republican virtues of contract, equality, and rights. This argument acknowledges, correctly, that marital and political structures are intertwined. However, it underplays the power of what polygamy represented, over a long time period indeed. After all, great minds of every century, the architects of those movements that textbooks call Reformation and Enlightenment and Revolution and the Women's Rights Movement, pondered polygamy. Women and men sat at their desks, and laid in their beds, and wondered about it. It was a useful thing "to think with," furnishing an opportunity for writers to raise issues around marriage, households, and sex. These early modern encounters preceded the nation of the United States of America; they did not follow from its republican origins, though they continued to shape the American republic.[15]

Investigating the history of polygamy also reveals something about the American present. This trajectory allows us to see hidden structures, what I call the infrastructure of monogamy, or a system of two-by-two domestic organization so embedded as to render itself virtually invisible. The whole point of infrastructure is that no one is supposed to have to think critically about it; it just underpins the world as we know it. This is what marital monogamy does in the United States, though its persistence, in the face of so many other changes or alternative possibilities, seems rather remarkable and worthy of attention. A lot has changed in the history of marriage. In American colonies and states, it used to be nearly impossible to get a divorce. Until far more recently, marital monogamy also meant one man plus one woman (a definition depending on both sexual and gender binaries). However, despite so many other shifts, that infrastructure of monogamy remains foundational—as a legal and organizing ideal, anyway. All too many examples in public and private life provide daily proof of the challenges and fantasies of truly exclusive monogamy for many. After all, in societies in which polygamy was permitted, it was never the only form of marriage, or even the predominant one. In such places, monogamy and polygamy coexisted as acceptable forms of union; such societies had a more capacious definition of marriage. Many people, over many centuries, worked hard to segregate systems allowing only monogamy, deemed noble and civilized, from systems permitting polygamy, rendered tawdry and barbaric. This book does not adhere to these loaded, often xenophobic distinctions; instead, I interrogate the forces required to embed the infrastructure of monogamy. I also consider what legal marriage has done, and who has benefited most from it.[16]

For many, polygamy and bigamy continue to flag sexual and domestic disorder. In the landmark 2003 U.S. Supreme Court ruling in *Lawrence v. Texas,* which overturned state laws against sodomy, the dissent offered by conservative justice Antonin Scalia invoked the danger of the slippery slope from that practice to any number of others, including "bigamy, same-sex marriage, adult incest, prostitution, masturbation, adultery, fornication, bestiality, and obscenity," fretting that "every single one of these laws [against such practices] is called into question by today's decision." Polygamy and perversion have thus long been twinned. Then, as now, allegations of polygamy often accompanied accusations of what were seen as other forms of sexual disorder, including same-sex relations. The counterintuitive early modern claim was that having many wives actually increased sexual desire in husbands. As a result, polygamous men's uncontrolled sexuality spilled over into seduction, adultery, assault, even what one eighteenth-century writer termed "that passion which nature disallows," homoerotic desire. At the same time, polygamy supposedly left wives restless and longing. As one writer inquired in 1781, "If a woman will not be *satisfied* with her *own* husband, is it more likely that she *would* with an eighth or a sixteenth *share* of him?" In these imaginings, wives turned to adultery, prostitution, and same-sex love, too. The claim then was that polygamy inexorably led to other sexual practices, condemned by many. Indeed, polygamy can still seem subversive—some have even called it queer—even as it can also seem the most rigidly hetero of heteronormative forms, privileging heterosexual, masculine desires.[17]

So you may now be wondering: how did a nice historian like me come to write a book on something so seemingly debauched? Let me be clear: I have no personal investment in polygamy. My interests are purely historical. First, in the midst of same-sex marriage debates, and statements like Scalia's, I wondered why people got so upset about what they perceived as other people marrying the wrong way. Why have some people felt so threatened by other people's marriages? Why has marriage seemed so foundational to the social and political order? Polygamy seemed a useful way to access this issue. Second, I wanted to understand better how different ideas about marriage, and the women and men in them, came into contact and conflict in early modern global encounters. Concerns about polygamy seemed to indicate deeper anxieties about living amid diversity. "If you want to locate the hegemonic home of liberal logics and aspirations," one theorist advises, "look to love in settler colonies."[18] Love in settler colonies presents rich pickings for figuring out the complex politics of households and societies. Third, I became fascinated by what life might have been like for people, especially women, in this unfamiliar domestic arrangement. Why would women have agreed to live this way?

What I found was that plural wives were not simply victims, even as their lives so easily support a feminist critique of profoundly inegalitarian household practices. Many plural marriages have and do involve the grotesque exploitation of women, another reason most Americans continue to believe they should not be legalized. Polygamy has had so many disadvantages for women that they hardly need rehearsing. It seems uniquely patriarchal and unfair to wives, all of whom are supposed to serve the husband. It also seems likely to lead to women's smoldering resentments and jealousies, and chaos and dissipation of resources for everyone. It has mostly been grossly unequal, since it is almost always one man with many wives (polygyny), and only rarely the reverse (polyandry). Yet if polygyny oppressed women—which it did and which it does—early modern monogamy also had its shortcomings. Euro-American laws of this era enshrined inequalities. Most women forfeited property rights at marriage. They also had little access to divorce. If they did divorce, they lost rights to their children. In European colonies, the ideal for wives was cheerful obedience. In the nineteenth century, Elizabeth Cady Stanton, that great campaigner for women's rights, contended, "Until men and women view each other as equals, marriage will be in most cases a long hard struggle to make the best of a bad bargain." Stanton, along with fellow campaigner Susan B. Anthony, supported plural wives in Utah in their struggles, partly because they saw *all* American marriage forms as bad bargains for women. Many women in systems of allegedly exclusive monogamy also suffered from being perceived as "nasty wenches," not fit for civilized marriage, thus sexually available to men. Poorer women, especially women of color, often did not benefit from systems centered around an ideal of monogamy at least sometimes subverted by a grimmer reality of adultery and sexual violence.[19]

In systems of exclusive monogamy, there were also challenges for married women. In theory, a monogamous husband gave his one wife all his attention. If she was married to a good man, then this could be a welcome situation. If he was not so good—unpleasant or drunk or adulterous or violent—there was no possibility of escape, either temporary or permanent. One nineteenth-century woman reported the astonishment of a Pacific Island woman at monogamy: " 'It is a very good custom to have but one wife, provided the husband loves her; but if he does not, he will only tyrannize over her the more.' " A monogamous household also meant no fellow wife to care for the household, to help cultivate and prepare food, or to take care of children while the other cooked or processed fur or collected firewood. In some cases, as among Cherokees, a husband might marry sisters and move into their house. Such a system gave wives networks of task sharing, and dynamics could be as harmonious as any other family relations, which is to say involving affections *and* rivalries. To buy into the notion that plural wives spent all their time obsessing about sexual jealousy, instead of being busy with their own concerns, is, once again, to put men at the center of women's lives. Women's lives and relationships with one another are richer than that. Monogamy—not polygamy—might mean isolation, separation from family and kin into a husband's community, and exhausting domestic burdens for a woman to juggle all on her own.[20]

Even if the husband was a model one, being the only wife meant that every night together could bring the possibility of *another* pregnancy. Alas, one does not have to look far in early America to find examples of women whose repeated childbearing literally killed them. One such woman was Martha Jefferson, whose fine, loving husband, the American Revolutionary patriot and third U.S. president, Thomas, continued to have sex with her even as each pregnancy and birth damaged her more. For virtually the entire ten years of their marriage, she was either pregnant or nursing, giving birth no fewer than six times. She died shortly after the sixth. She was thirty-three. As one scholar has put it, "The terrible predicament the Jeffersons, and other couples, faced—marriage with no birth control—pitted Jefferson's own sexual desires against Martha Jefferson's health, and Martha lost." She was hardly the only early American woman who lost. Her enslaved half-sister, Sally Hemings, did too, though in different ways. Hemings became a life partner to Jefferson, but never a recognized legal wife, in part because enslaved people could not legally contract marriages. Since Jefferson and Hemings never married, their children, deemed illegitimate, were not recognized as his heirs. Marriage made the difference here. Yet neither Martha nor

Sally had much control over the timing and spacing of sex—and births. Polygamy was one way to secure such spacing, though it did not always work this way in practice. Anthropologists tell us that women who chose plural marriages have tended to have fewer babies. In other words, in a world of unreliable birth control options, plural marriages offered a different way of directing sexual energies, a form of family planning. In most cases, husbands and wives were also fathers and mothers, and this other set of relationships mattered, too.[21]

This book centers on how people have defined polygamy; it is also about how polygamy has defined people, both individually and as nations. Polygamy has never been legal in the United States or indeed most of Europe. It is therefore necessary to move beyond what those laws defined as marriage, since such a move would exclude the marriages of most Native American and African-American people as well as many others, including Mormons. There was diversity between places, and people without legal authority were constantly involved in the process of defining marriages. However, the emphasis here is on marriages recognized by all in them—and by others in the community or religious life—as marriages. I focus on controversies surrounding the public practice, advocacy, or defense of plural unions, where the spouses all knew about one another, and where at least a large portion of the community regarded it as a marriage, with attendant rights, obligations, and inheritance. Many other forms of unions could resemble polygamy, but I focus only on the most publicly acknowledged sort so that I can cover a broad span of times and places.[22]

This book considers "polygamy"—that shorthand for lawless, wanton marriage—as a symbol, but it is also, as much as possible, about plural marriages. Imagined "polygamy" and lived plural marriages were separate and distinct, but they often merged in the texts remaining. It is possible to write a history of polygamy as an idea with little consideration of lived plural marriages. Actually, that's what all previous book-length histories of early modern polygamy have been. It is not possible, however, to write a history of American plural marriages without also confronting polygamy as an idea, because sources of the era mingled the two indiscriminately. This book contends therefore with both of them, though sometimes the tilt is toward polygamy as a theoretical or symbolic system (as in Part Two here). There was also considerable variety in plural marriages, and in this book I try to recover that diversity.[23]

To approach the texture of plural marriages, especially among people who left no written sources, is challenging. There remain many intangibles, and there are limits to what I, or anyone, can say. Still, there are flashes and glimmers in many sources, even if some of them—dictionaries, pots, needles, even teeth—are somewhat improbable. I have read tens of thousands of pages of material because polygamy appears often only in scattered references. These traces mark travel journals, eyewitness testimonies from rebellions, legal documents, missionary accounts, dictionaries, diaries and letters, newspaper and magazine articles, maps and city directories, treatises and tracts, novels and stories, and histories from the period. Where possible, I have consulted sources in their original languages. In French and Spanish, the same word, *femme* or *mujer*, can mean woman or wife, so context is vital. Indigenous languages are also revelatory. One word in seventeenth-century Miami-Illinois, *kissabamigouta*, means "a wife separated from her husband who does not wish to see him anymore even though [they are] in the same village." This word, while capturing what might be seen as a universal, also gives insight into the specifics of divorce and female agency in the seventeenth century. Material items and archaeology help to fill in blanks generated by the lack of written sources; this book owes much to the patient work of archaeologists. It turns out that pots and dictionaries are considerably more provocative—even occasionally sexier—than you might first think. By the time you have finished Chapter 2, and learned what both double-headed key motifs and *sousoupihe-poutinghi* mean, you will understand this point better.[24]

The relative richness of extant sources for particular areas, and an attempt to cover wide swaths of what is now the continental United States, drove the choices of particular examples. These boundaries were not the same in the early modern era, though, so the book does not rest strictly within continental U.S. borders but crosses the St. Lawrence River into what is now Canada, the Rio Grande into Mexico, and indeed the Atlantic Ocean itself. The method is also a little unusual. Each chapter covers particular polygamy controversies in a roughly chronological narrative. There is not a central cast of characters or location because the history of polygamy radiates broadly. Rather, there is a shared set of concerns and arguments animating the specific contours of individual contexts. The sheer variety of those times and places builds to demonstrate how much marriage controversies reveal about American life and politics. By the end, major national debates over polygamy in the nineteenth century look different because of what has gone before. In keeping with a book about the early modern, I take as a method what was called in Dutch Golden Age art "tot lering en vermaak": for learning and pleasure. The Dutch meant the presentation of a moral message in an accessible form. There is much that is deeply distressing here. I have not shied away from the sex, violence, and gross inequalities that underpin this subject. I attend to them not to sensationalize, but because I hope you will find this book an absorbing account from which you will also learn something.[25]

This tale covers more than puritans and planters, though they appear here. Early America, vast and unwieldy, was more enthralling than those stereotypes. This world was diverse, not limited to English speakers or elite lawmakers, but vital all the same. A Native American wife living and loving along the St. Lawrence River in the first years of French colonization; an enslaved African, transplanted to Virginia, despairing over his situation; a dissenting New Englander fighting with his neighbors; a young woman running away from her husband: what do they all have in common? On the face of it, not a lot; it's a varied group of protagonists. At another level, much unites them. They were all at the center of polygamy controversies, revealing the complex lines of authority linking households to larger politics. They also demonstrate how choices about marriage, gender, and sexuality were central to, and affected by, other major changes, from colonialism to slavery to revolution to religion. All kinds of people had a stake in polygamy: sometimes living it, other times defending it, sometimes arguing against it. People denounced polygamy for worthy reasons, and less impressive ones. Defenders of polygamy were a mixed bunch, too. There were heroes and villains on both sides. But mostly there were just ordinary women and men, in all their sweaty, full-bellied humanity. They struggled to manage the disconcerting changes affecting their world, and they often did so in the ways most familiar to them: through lovers, spouses, children, and families. This perspective moves intimate motivations of actors to center stage, thus arguing for the fierce politics of the domestic.[26]

This voyage to early modern America won't be easy, and it might get a little mucky. Blood, colostrum, and other sticky bodily fluids smear these family stories. Even the Pilgrims in Plymouth, the Franciscans in California, and the Mormons in Utah were messier than the textbooks would have you believe. The marriage plot here provides neither a clean nor a happy ending. A turbulent journey, from sixteenth-century Europe to the nineteenth-century United

States, with a lot of stops—in Amerindian wigwams, West African compounds, American bedrooms, and many other locations—awaits. There are sweet affections and tender heroics here, but there is also troubling carnage and lingering misery. Although populated with husbands and lots of wives and children, the tales that follow are not cozy little ones behind white picket fences. They are squalid and brutal, at times, because so was early America. Americans fought then, as now, over marriage, sex, and men's access to women's bodies, as well as over race, religion, resources, and difference. Noseless faces, heads on poles, bodies missing testicles, and many other horrors line the route. The long trajectory of polygamy both disturbs and dazzles. It flashes in a tranquil sky, illuminating in brilliant, jagged streaks a dark history of America.

PART ONE

Colonial Clashes

1. "Una Casa, Dos Mujeres"

The woman dusted off her hands and stood up. She had just painted a double-headed key motif on the pot, an old, old Pueblo pattern revitalized in the dramatic new worlds of the 1680s. She and her family had taken refuge in the mesas above the pueblos and built a new home there. Along with other weary refugees, they were creating something of which to be proud. It was challenging, as they did not even speak the same language. Still, they all understood what they had done, and why it mattered. They could freely "follow the custom[s] . . . as in their heathenism." They answered to no one but themselves. She could finally limit backbreaking labor in the cornfields as well as the bloody, messy work of eviscerating deer, turning their heavy bodies into clean hides. Instead, she could lavish time and attention on this beautiful, useful vessel. Since these refugees did not leave written records, this artist remains anonymous. Still, she left her mark on the world. What she painted was an ancient design, one even her grandmother would have thought old-fashioned. Still, turned to new purposes, it was now fresh and provocative. Although she did not know it, she, and thousands like her, had achieved the most successful rebellion against colonial rule in North America in the seventeenth century. They had vanquished the Spanish and driven them out. Even when the Spanish returned more than a dozen years later, it was to a different world, and a new colonial situation. This woman was one of the rebels of the Pueblo Revolt.

In August 1680, after years of relentless tribute and slaving demands from the Spanish, church repression of local religions, and drought and depopulation, a majority of Pueblo Indians in a variety of locations launched

Unknown artist, tall-necked Kotyiti glazed polychrome. The double-headed key motif appears in darker color along the top lip. Catalogue no. 29.0/3144. Courtesy of Division of Anthropology, American Museum of Natural History. Photo kindly supplied by Robert Preucel, Brown University.

a coordinated rebellion against Spanish authority. It was a success of major proportions. Po'pay or Popé, a spiritual leader who had previously been punished for practicing ancient rituals, was its leader, rallying others to his cause of overthrowing the Spanish and returning to the traditional ways in language, in religion, in plural marriage. It resulted in hundreds of deaths, including those of more than twenty Franciscan friars. Insurgents ransacked and burned houses, churches, and fields. They also supposedly defecated on an altar, and hacked the arms off of a statue of St. Francis, while also contemptuously wearing priestly vestments. All this activity seemed to be directed only at the Spanish, by angry men.[1] There was indeed fury here, but the rebellion was also about a realignment of communities of Native women and men in novel ways. Focusing on polygamy allows these larger communities to come into view better.

Far away on the other side of that northern border of New Spain, another rebellion launched with too many wives and one headless friar. In 1597 in the town of Tolomato, in what the Spanish called *La Florida* (now most of Florida and Georgia, as well as parts of South Carolina and Alabama), a Franciscan friar, Pedro de Corpa, had attempted to prevent the recently elected *mico mayor* (or paramount chief), Don Juan, from being married to more than one woman. According to Guale Indians from numerous towns, as well as a subsequent Franciscan historian, "the having of many wives" was a central reason for the rebellion. De Corpa had warned the baptized Don Juan that "since he was a Christian, he should live as a Christian and not as an infidel." What De Corpa meant was that Don Juan should not continue to practice polygamy. Don Juan did not take kindly to this admonition. Indeed, he and his followers, "faulty as he was in the same libidinous vice," expressed their disagreement with blood. They beheaded the friar. Another mico taunted the Spanish, displaying the hat of his village's friar, boasting that it was all that was left of him.[2] By the end of the revolt, five missionaries were dead and a sixth taken into captivity. It took several years of coercion, burnings of homes and fields, and enslavement to return even to a troubled equilibrium.

Polygamy, then, was a symbol, a practice, and a rallying cry in two rebellions in the far north of New Spain: the Guale Rebellion of 1597 and the Pueblo Revolt of 1680. Taking it seriously helps us to see these two formative events of Spanish colonialism in North America—and elsewhere—differently by highlighting relations among Native Americans, especially in terms of gender and rank, and not just between Native Americans and the Spanish. Usually, polygamy has been seen simply as an anti-Spanish provocation, but it was in fact a method by which Native Americans signaled to one another. While both Europeans and Native Americans laid claims to "traditional marriage," such assertions obscured the fact that in some cases they were doing something novel, specific to the cultural encounters of the early modern period. Spanish sources emphasized unchanging lifelong sacramental marriage against what they saw as the equally entrenched lack of respect for that institution by Native Americans. Such characterizations, which assumed a static worldview on both sides, should not be read as fact. Forms of households, and their meanings, were changing in the early modern period: in Europe, in Native America, in the places where they met. For Native Americans enduring the significant upheavals of colonialism and epidemics, certain household practices took on new importance. Polygamy indicated complicated political maneuvers, not just traditional practices or personal indulgence. Some Native men emphasized having many wives as a way to unify disparate peoples, to broker new alliances, to reorient household labor toward new economies, and to establish leadership in volatile situations.

Guale and Pueblo Indians were utterly distinct in terms of their social and marital organization. Yet there are parallels between these rebellions. Indeed, one helps us to see the other more clearly. Both involved conflict with Franciscans, highlighting the creative responses of indigenous people to the pressures of colonialism. The typical scholarly understanding is that by rebelling, Pueblos were attempting to "restore a traditional social and religious order" against the imposition of Spanish control. The desire for polygamy seems incidental or merely symptomatic of a larger yearning to go back to how things were, before the modernizing monogamous Christianity of Europeans.[3] Such a reading is understandable but not satisfactory, especially for the women involved. Far from implying simply a return to tradition, the schemes of rebels had the potential to effect a profound transformation in existing cultures, in terms of gender. This process was directed at unifying diverse peoples, in novel ways. After all, as the story of the 1627 Taos "sorceress" demonstrates, there was diversity of opinion even between wives from the same pueblo. Yet unity and rebellion prevailed because there was also shared anger. Households became twisted into complicated and brutal masculine power plays, as the missionaries found when they lost their hats—and their heads.

"Bad Weeds"

Conquests built on reconquests. To understand why monogamy mattered so much in the Spanish Empire, it helps to start in Spain itself. Spain, a union of many regions, was novel itself in this period. Spain was also launching its global empire in this period, and both empire building and state building coincided with a new, intimidating emphasis on Catholic orthodoxy. Jews, Muslims, and, soon, Protestants were all to be excluded from Spanish society, though Jews and Muslims had lived peaceably in many Spanish regions for centuries. Christian authorities forced baptisms on reluctant Jews and Muslims, transforming them into *conversos* (converted Jews) and *Moriscos* (converted Muslims). After the Protestant Reformation began in 1517, Catholic powers also worked hard to eradicate this new heterodoxy. Throughout the sixteenth century and beyond, the Spanish Inquisition pursued those who did not adhere to Catholic orthodoxy, or who continued to practice Jewish or Muslim religions. Some fled; some continued to elude authorities; some were punished, ending their lives in galleys or worse; some resisted. In 1568, there was a rebellion of Moriscos in Alpujarras, the mountainous region outside

Granada. Angered by recent repressions, converted Muslims called for "traditional" cultural practices: rejecting the Spanish (Castilian) language, resuming typical dress, destroying churches, and targeting for attack priests and Franciscan missionaries. That year also saw the commencement of another revolt against Spanish Catholic rule, in the iconoclastic Protestant rebellion of Dutch Calvinists in the Spanish-ruled Netherlands.[4]

Instilling marital monogamy became a major concern for secular and religious authorities in sixteenth-century Spain and its empire as part of this drive for orthodoxy. Households were central arenas for the attempts to eradicate religious subversion, whether Muslim, Jewish, or Protestant. Muslims and Sephardic Jews, in Spain and elsewhere, had practiced polygyny for centuries. Muslim men had long been considered sexually licentious by Christian authorities, in part because of practices such as polygyny and cousin marriage. After 1492, households became even more fiercely politicized spaces, especially in Granada and its environs, as Catholic authorities transformed, as one scholar has phrased it, "difference into deviance." Muslim practices, including plural marriage, worried many. As a contemporary noted of Moriscos, "in secret they taught and indoctrinated one another in the rites and ceremonies of the Mohammedan sect." Christian authorities feared what happened behind closed doors, where they imagined (sometimes rightly) that the façade of Christianity was thrown off, and hennaed brides married men in polygamous configurations. One of those most active in tightening the regulations against Moriscos that led to the Alpujarras uprising was Pedro Guerrero, archbishop of Granada from 1546 to 1576. He was also one of the most significant figures in the Council of Trent, which hammered out the policies of the Catholic Reformation in opposition to the Protestant threat. It was at this council that bigamy was declared anathema. Polygamy worried Catholic authors. One of them argued that, by allowing Muslim populations to grow faster than any others, it would make them pernicious and hardy "bad weeds," ready to choke the pure flowers of Christian Spain. The leader of the Alpujarras rebellion, Aben Humeya, married three women in the course of the uprising, so that polygyny and political subversion became enmeshed.[5] This connection of polygamy and revolt only confirmed the suspicions of those who fretted over perverse practices occurring within households, away from the eyes of Christian authorities. For many Spaniards, this revolt, and that of Dutch Calvinists, demonstrated the power of heresy, nurtured in the home, in prompting rebellions.

For those inclined to suspect perversity, there was much to fear. The Spanish Inquisition also emphasized monogamy, targeting Jews, Muslims, Protestants, "sodomites"—and bigamists. The violation of monogamy, previously a minor and rarely prosecuted secular offense, became a heresy, fiercely pursued. In the region of Castile, almost as many convicted bigamists as heretics were sent to serve as galley slaves. Part of the concern over marriage, and many bigamy cases, turned on the fact that even among orthodox Catholics, early modern Spanish marriage law was itself not clear-cut. One scholar has observed that through the early modern period, there was "a notable evolution in the legal and moral consideration" of cohabitation, sex, and marriage, as well as "a great deal of confusion" over them. Secular Spanish law allowed cohabitation, prostitution, and consensual sex between single men and women. Laws regulating marriage and sexuality were changing in just this period, yet orthodoxy became increasingly important for Spanish Catholic authorities eager to assert dominance at home and abroad.[6]

These legacies of monogamy continued to resonate powerfully in American settings. Historians largely agree that the ferocious culture of the Reconquista, and the persecution of Jews and Muslims, provided the crucible in which Spaniards hammered out their policy toward non-Christians. These concerns remained important even on the frontiers of New Spain. It is then little wonder that household difference so quickly became deviance in the Americas. Orthodox practices of marriage continued to be a way of establishing and maintaining authority and old world order. Of course, celibate missionaries, those preaching and enforcing monogamy, could not demonstrate it themselves. Franciscan missionaries were the most "confrontational" in their approach to Jews and Muslims in Spain. They were also leaders in Spanish America. Franciscans helped to pass the first laws against polygyny and divorce in the New World. In 1530, a royal *cédula* declared that any Christian Indian who married a second time while the first spouse was alive would be punished; in 1551, this law was extended to all indigenous Americans, even non-Christians. Polygamy continued to frustrate Spanish authorities in sixteenth-century Mexico. Part of the difficulty in eradicating plural marriages was precisely their linkage with leadership and status. For instance, in precolonial Mexico, one of the best-documented examples of Native polygyny, a *tlahtoani*, or leader, who had many wives also had diplomatic links to different territories through these wives, positive ties that ameliorated the often violent acquisition of tribute states. In addition, women were major economic producers; they wove cloth, the most valuable trading commodity. Such wives often had a hierarchy themselves: from a first highly ranked wife down to, in some cases, additional captive wives. Captive taking among a great number of Native American nations depended on integrating women and children into captor households. Women often entered as "chore wives." Plural marriage usually brought a family many children, who provided labor and increased kinship networks. In other words, across large portions of Native North America, powerful men both proved and increased their might by establishing families with multiple wives.[7]

Little wonder, then, that polygamy became a leitmotif in Spanish stories of Native perversion—and subversion. The narrative line went like this: a turn to highly public sexual indulgence (including polygamy) among baptized Christians (whether Morisco or Native American) went hand in hand with their leaving mission areas, their desecrating sacred goods (symbolic of their contempt for the sacraments, including marriage), and ultimately their rebellion. It is difficult to reconstruct what Guale and Pueblo people made of Spanish practices around marriage. The lack of divorce must have seemed a bad idea, likely to lead to violent strife. The fact that no Spaniard could have more than one wife may have made them seem weak. The hypocrisy of leaders, who preached celibacy and monogamy but lived outside of them, must have been striking.

"Being a Bad Christian"

Guales called him *Mico Santamaría*, or Chief Holy Mary, though he called himself Pedro Menéndez. He was the first governor of Florida, the descendant of men who had assisted in the Catholic reconquest of Granada.[8] He landed in Guale territory in the 1560s. The name the Guales gave him indicates how these Muskogean speakers integrated this Spanish interloper into their own busy system of chieftancies and alliances. Micos, or leaders, ruled their world, in centralized towns with thousands of residents. Guales lived in a "kind of a confederacy," with large individual towns linked. Language, custom, and trade united these towns; so did kinship and marriage. Rank divided Guales, though, into highly stratified communities, with elites jealous of their privileges. Such was true through most of these related lands in the broad territory of Florida. A mico managed each town in a top-down fashion, with a mico mayor, or paramount leader, the head of all the micos and their lands. Leader of leaders was a fiercely contested position, triggering conflicts.

Indeed, in Guale cultures, "competition between chiefs, often resulting in small-scale warfare" was common, frequently revolving around women. In Guale political systems, there were commanding micos and submicos. They demanded tribute and labor, and they used force and violence to obtain them. If slave women did not come to dance when asked, micos could punish them. Micos could also order other men to break the arms of people who resisted orders to work. These were not leaders with whom to trifle. Spanish sources omit the ways that these rivalries over women influenced the internal politics of the Guale confederacies, so we have few primary sources detailing them. However, they did have an impact if the neighbors of the Guales, the Powhatans to the north, are reliable analogues. These northern neighbors furnish useful and roughly contemporaneous parallels for the ways that these contests over women worked in loose confederacies of highly stratified societies. Early English observers noted the ubiquity of such fights over women in Powhatan cultures. In 1612, William Strachey mentioned that Powhatan had deposed another local leader, because he "had stollen away a Chief woman from Opechankeno, one of Powhatans brothers." A few decades later, Edward Bland recorded local memories of the "King of the Pawhatan," who, on greeting "the King of the Chawan" with a hug, suddenly strangled him over "a yong woman that the King of *Chawan* had detayned of the King of *Pawhatan*." One archaeologist has contended that in the wake of colonial contacts, chiefdoms such as the Guales were not simply "highly centralized political entities" but were actually "cross cut by factional groups and competing interests." That there must have been major political debates comes through in evidence of council houses, or *buhíos*. One buhío could evidently hold two thousand individuals.[9]

Yet these authoritative rulers depended on connections to women, and could be women themselves. Guales probably identified Menéndez through his links to Santa María partly because of his allegiance to Catholicism but also because connections to women were vital to their own micos. They may have imagined that his devotion to Mary stemmed from his filial piety to her as his sacred ancestor; they had their own. As one friar observed in the early seventeenth century, leaders established their position "with the succession not coming by way of the male, but rather the female." A mico obtained rank first from matrilineal lines of inheritance: often as the child of the mico's sister. In testimony before Spaniards, Guales went out of their way to

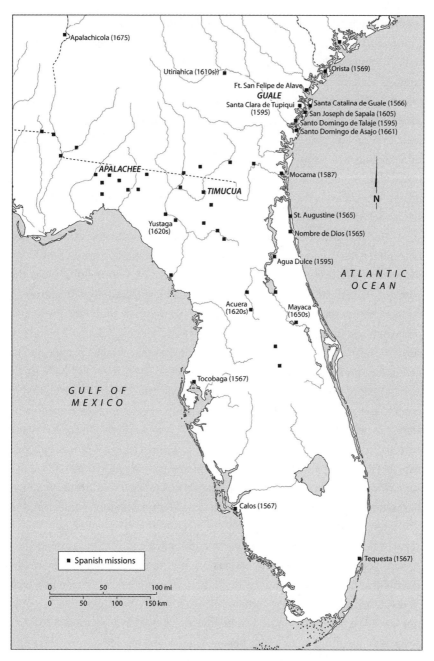

Map of seventeenth-century Florida. Cartography by Bill Nelson.

The labels on the map:

Apalachicola (1675)
Utinahica (1610s)
Orista (1569)
Ft. San Felipe de Alava
GUALE
Santa Catalina de Guale (1566)
Santa Clara de Tupiqui (1595)
San Joseph de Sapala (1605)
Santo Domingo de Talaje (1595)
Santo Domingo de Asajo (1661)
APALACHEE
TIMUCUA
Mocama (1587)
N
Yustaga (1620s)
St. Augustine (1565)
Nombre de Dios (1565)
Agua Dulce (1595)
ATLANTIC OCEAN
Acuera (1620s)
Mayaca (1650s)
GULF OF MEXICO
Tocobaga (1567)
Calos (1567)
■ Spanish missions
Tequesta (1567)
0   50   100 mi
0   50   100   150 km

establish their maternal connections. In the late sixteenth century, one man, Francisco, took pains to establish that his mother was an "india principal," or noble woman, related to micos; so did a woman in the early seventeenth century, Catalina Valdés, granddaughter of an "india principal, cacica [female mico] de Escamacu." Women could also be micos, or as the Spanish had it *cacicas* (the feminized form of *cacique* or male ruler). In 1598, there were at least two *cacicas,* one in charge of the region of Nombre de Dios and the other ruling the region of Acuera. An early-seventeenth-century account noted that women were not generally permitted in the buhío for counsels unless "the cacica is the one in charge and the lord of the land. And then she sits alone on her seat."[10]

Matrilineal lineage was a necessary but not sufficient condition for becoming a mico. The sources of a mico's power remain opaque, but probably included ritual, access to trade goods, hospitality, and household. Does the name of "Chief Holy Mary" signify more than just the attempt of natives to connect him to the women in his lineage? That they called him by a woman's name may also indicate their sense that he was not quite a full man. He did not seem to have a wife (or wives): odd behavior. In other words, he appeared to lack a key prerogative of elite masculine power, even if he did have guns, horses, swords, fancy clothing, and other powerful objects. The ability to control the productive and reproductive labor of women was a marker of status, as well as a way of maintaining it. Wives were significant for many reasons, not least because they managed food provision. Women and men usually labored separately, though in complementary ways, in their daily activities. Women's efforts included ensuring adequate food and drink: planting, harvesting, preparing, cooking. Women's connection with food comes through in a late-sixteenth-century engraving of neighboring Timucuans, showing a regal bride, an india principal, on her way to marry a mico. She is attended by several young women, holding baskets of fruit, to indicate both the symbolic fruitfulness of this union and the literal bounty provided by women as wives. When friars tried to get one Indian to leave his wife, he replied that he could not leave her because then he would have no one to provide food. Women's work was integral to men's well-being. A mico who needed to provide hospitality for many people needed strong women's hands to do so.[11]

As a result, micos, though few others, practiced polygamy. Florida society was highly ranked, and polygamy was reserved for the elite. Sometimes a mico married sisters. It is likely that this form of plural marriage

Theodor de Bry, "The queen-elect is brought to the king." A Timucuan royal bride is carried to her wedding. Like her ladies-in-waiting at right, she is adorned with beads on neck, arms, and legs, though she also has elaborate body paint. Printed in Jacques le Moyne de Morgues, *Brevis narratio eorvm qvae in Florida Americæ provĩcia Gallis acciderunt* (Frankfurt: J. Wecheli, 1591), plate 37. Courtesy of Library of Congress.

resulted in wives of roughly similar status. Often, each wife had her own household, and the mico would visit them in turn. Yet plural marriages were also consistent with differential status between wives, and the use of coerced labor. Senior wives of micos would have had a great deal of status, resting in part on their ability to command the labor of other women, some of them probably enslaved. Enslaved women may well also have been secondary wives. Timucuan neighbors also had a system in which micos presumed sexual access to women. A 1613 Timucuan confessional included a question for micos about whether they kept a slave as a mistress.[12] "Mistress" in Spanish could also mean "consort" or "spouse" in Timucua. Such a question implies a polygamous relationship. These relations demonstrated the potency of the male head of household, and they also increased the number of children: another source of labor and kinship connections.

Polygamy was one of many practices the Florida missionaries were keen to curtail. Converting the Native people to Christianity was of paramount concern. The first Franciscans arrived in Florida in 1573. By 1575, they had succeeded in baptizing a Guale mico and his wife. Despite this early triumph, though, the Franciscan mission soon sputtered. It gained momentum again only with a new set of enthusiastic arrivals in 1595; shortly thereafter, in 1597, a new governor, Gonzalo Méndez de Canzo, also arrived. Energetic new administrators in both religious and secular life brought increased tribute demands, increased surveillance, and what one scholar terms "heavy-handed Spanish control." Franciscan surveillance indeed became heavy-handed. Their confessional implies that they were asking all kinds of Native people detailed questions about intimacies. They posed questions of women and men, single and married, about, for instance, whether they had displayed their naked bodies in order to arouse lust. They also asked about whether they had touched themselves sexually in the company of others, in a shared bed or bath. They inquired, too, about "acts against nature" by both men and women. They fretted about sexual relations with spousal relatives. They asked men whether they had been with "two sisters" or other men, or even if they had simply desired to be. They demanded such things of women, too: "Woman with woman, have you had sex as if you were a man?"[13]

This enhanced attempt at control over every aspect of Native life partly drove the 1597 conflict, but there were other issues. After killing the Franciscans, rebels under the command of its leader, the would-be mico mayor Don Juan, "began to exchange wives." So declared Luis Jerónimo de Oré, the Peruvian Franciscan scholar who visited Florida in the aftermath of the Guale Rebellion, thus linking the locals' murderous violence with their domestic disarray. On hearing of the massacres of the friars, the new governor, Méndez, swiftly sent soldiers and began taking testimonies. He ordered the burning of homes and crops. Meanwhile, Don Juan and his supporters fled west, staying far from the missions until 1601. At that point, Méndez brokered an agreement with the mico of the town of Asao, Don Domingo, to lead an assault on them. These forces managed to kill Don Juan, and Don Domingo became the new mico mayor of Guale territory. Thus was this conflict ended—at least for a while.[14]

Polygamy was a factor in this rebellion, but not quite in the ways that have been assumed. Scholars have long acknowledged the importance of polygamy as an anti-Spanish action, noting that the Franciscan attempt to restrict it was the "incendiary spark" that provoked rebellion. Most have also noted anger over missionary restrictions on movements and behavior, interference in lines of inheritance, and unhappiness with Spanish tribute demands. Yet here, as elsewhere, the rebellion was as much about relations *between* Indians as it was an act of subversion of Spanish authority. More recent work has emphasized these linkages more, sidestepping polygamy as a major factor.[15] In fact, taking polygamy seriously helps us to see indigenous dynamics more clearly.

The protection of households was a vital prerogative for micos, whose power depended in part on hospitality and tribute. Yet colonialism had begun to put pressure on these systems. In Guale cultures, as in Powhatan ones, a leader who attempted to interfere with the domestic practices of another leader might find himself in a fatal embrace or on the receiving end of a vicious blow from a *macana* (stone axe). The Florida friars learned this lesson the hard way. Part of Don Juan's willingness to use violence stemmed from the violation of his household offered by the Franciscans, since it was critical for him to show other Indians that he was not letting his domestic life be ruled by other men. Violence here was a language communicating not only to the Spanish but also to Guale audiences.

Such demonstrations of authority took on particular force in this period because of other underlying changes wrought by the Spanish presence. Although population loss was more limited among the Guale than among some other Native American people, thanks to the geography of Florida and the relative dispersal of its population across the landscape, there was still decline. New infectious diseases affected the population, as did novel dietary practices: there was increased corn production and consumption at the expense of other sources of food such as fish. This shift was not salutary, either in terms of nutrition (with carbohydrates replacing protein) or in terms of the repetitive, static work needed to obtain the food. It made the population more vulnerable to disease. For some, colonialism literally brought diarrhea and death.[16] This demographic loss probably increased rivalries between men, who had to compete for wives to have children.

These changes also altered tribute patterns and the division of labor by gender. Micos had long received tribute, but it was limited and diverse. The Spanish demanded corn for tribute, and a lot of it. Such requirements, unpopular in an array of locations, had probably begun to transform Guale labor arrangements based on gender roles. Traditionally, women worked in the fields, especially in planting and harvesting. With the advent of new demands, the agricultural labor of women became even more critical, and likely sharpened competition for female laborers among Guale elites. It may also have meant that such women had to work even harder. Some men, especially "commoners," had to start doing what had traditionally been "women's work": basic agricultural labor.[17] The sting of this gendered humiliation may have prompted them to join in conflicts, to fight the Spanish and their allies.

This shift in labor practices etched itself onto Guale ceramics, crafted by women, as simplification in such patterns may have been the result of women no longer having as much time to produce complex designs. These changes in work structures, as well as population loss and a decline in indigenous religion, seem to have altered the ability or desire of women to pass on and replicate traditional ceramic designs. Christianity may have had an impact here. The Spanish governor described one of those female micos, Doña María, as "a good Christian Indian" married to a Spaniard. Other women also adopted Christianity. They therefore perhaps had less interest in replicating patterns associated with older religious sensibilities. Oré, the Franciscan scholar, described the 1570s to the late 1590s as a tense period during which nonconverts "persecuted" converts.[18] Were some of these converts women, perhaps even potential wives of Don Juan and his coconspirators? We know that some powerful Guale women, including Doña María, married Spaniards in Catholic ceremonies. At one level, such was to be expected, since marriage was a traditional way of cementing political allegiances. Yet did Spanish desires for indigenous wives mean further rivalries, further pressuring already strained relations among high-ranking indigenous men?

The Spanish saw an elite jealous of privilege, arrogant polygamous micos ready to crack the limbs of those who did not work for them. They imagined these characteristics to be timeless. Yet this situation may have been partially a result of relatively recent political reconfigurations, ones resulting in an indigenous elite ruling with a heavier hand themselves. Anthropologists have wondered whether early Spanish colonialism increased "social differentiation."[19] It seems to have done so in Florida. The rebellion of Don Juan may have been partly about his determination not to let the Spanish and their allies dictate his household relations because such connections, and the work of his wives, supported his standing in the eyes of other Guale people. His seemingly anti-Spanish stance may have been a way for him to demonstrate his power to other Guales. The 1597 conflict may have been more about indigenous rivalries, with anti-Spanish sentiments only incidental to shifting politics especially among elites. In other words, the Spanish became pawns in a game between Guales.

Indigenous leaders also competed for tribute. Tribute was such an important issue in the 1597 uprising that the Spanish actually altered their policies as a result. The uprising led to a modification of tribute requirements: the Spanish waived it entirely for micos who remained loyal to the crown. This alteration resulted in a transformation of a per capita labor system into one of labor service, one that favored Native leaders. In other words, the Spanish presence increased the resources of the already powerful. The protection of polygamy is consistent with a general guarding of chiefly status. One seventeenth-century poet, highly critical of "savage" Floridians, nevertheless noted that the mico was "so poised / that one will never, ever see him / eat too much, or with mouth open." Indeed, "discretion keeps his passions in check [and] he gives no signs of showing weakness."[20]

Micos were expected to restrain themselves in some respects, but the rewards for those of such high rank were many. Privileges included royal seating, special titles, even separate graves. In the buhío, "they have its seats placed around with great order and arrangement, with the one belonging to the principal chief being the best and the highest. . . . No one is permitted to approach this one except with the greatest respect [and] fear." Privileges showed in language: "They have particular terms of respect and courtesy that they use, as is the case among us with [expressions] such as Your Grace, Your Lordship, and Magistrate. These have not been found along any other nations." Even the graves of micos were "kept . . . separate from the rest and all on the highest hills." In their 1613 confessional, friars demanded of indigenous women: "Have you decorated yourself with evil intent so that someone desires you and has you?" Where the Franciscans saw women trying to seduce men into sin through their beads and paint, though, women might instead have been using elaborate body decoration to showcase their elite status. After all, in that image of the bridal procession, the bride and her attendants, elites themselves, were all covered in elaborate beading, from heavy necklaces down to anklets. Only the bride herself had a tattooed or painted body; pictures of micos also highlighted that only the mico and his wife (or wives) could style themselves in this way. Another visiting friar, Andrés de San Miguel, related that both women and men stained themselves with red ocher, and that "some wear strings of beads on their wrists, upper arms, knee, and ankle for grandeur." Such embellishments were probably as much or more about status as about possible carnal desires. Indeed, one mico mayor showed San Miguel his well-provisioned house which had "maize and some Castilian hens," as well as "two wives" who wore "deerskins in place of the common dress . . . for grandeur."[21]

Once the Spanish arrived in number, Guale wives and husbands started to use clothing other than deerskin and beads "for grandeur." They began wearing Spanish clothing to show their status to other Indians. As one scholar has observed, Native elite use of Spanish clothing not only collapsed distinctions between indigenous and Spanish elite but also "widened the distance between lords and vassals." Another mico and his wife encountered by San Miguel not only were Christians "who spoke the Castilian language very well" but also "dressed well in the Spanish manner." When the mico's wife "went out she wore a cloak like a Spanish lady." Guale commoners could not afford to deck themselves like Spanish ladies and gentlemen, as this clothing was costly. Guales used political alliances, through marriages such as that of Doña María to a Spaniard and through baptisms that linked them to Spaniards as for this mico and his wife, in part to gain access to Spanish trade goods, including iron tools, guns, and clothing. The Spanish governor praised the female mico of Nombre de Dios for providing gifts, many of them Spanish, to other Guales, in order to win them over to a Spanish alliance. Guale politics involved gift giving and tribute, and the Spanish and their things became part of these politics. Contemporaries and scholars have noted that rebels in 1597 took the clothing and other goods of the friars in part because of a general desire for European items. That anti-Indian poet of the seventeenth century imagined that if Florida natives were asked why they had converted to Christianity, that they would reply, "If we accepted / the law of God, the cause was the clothes."[22]

We don't know whether Don Domingo, the mico mayor who killed the rebellious Don Juan in 1601, adopted Christianity for the clothes, but he probably dressed in expensive Spanish garments. We know he was baptized, spoke Castilian, and remained a vital ally of the Spanish. Yet his differences with Don Juan may have had little to do with his devotion to Santa María or even his pro-Spanish sentiments. Indeed, what the Spanish saw as a rebellion against them may actually have been a dispute between micos, in which the Spanish became embroiled. For although he benefited royally from vanquishing Don Juan and obtaining a system of tribute that favored rulers like him at the expense of other Indians, he does not seem to have been the staunchest of Christian monogamists. According to Oré, during the revolt, many women and men who had previously been married in Christian ceremonies left their spouses and found new ones; these unions were not Catholic ones. It was not only husbands who did so; Oré reported that Christian wives had departed the missions with "infidels," bearing "two or three children" in the period from 1597 to 1601. One such violator of monogamy was Don Domingo, who had taken his sister-in-law as a non-Christian wife, living with both sisters, having four children with his first wife and three with her sister. Such sororal polygamy may have been a way for Don Domingo to demonstrate his authority among the dispersed Indians who had fled west after the initial massacres; he was showcasing his power. From the Franciscan perspective, by living with his new wife, the mico was engaging in an unholy combination of polygamy, incest, and cohabitation. Don Domingo was willing to try to please the friars, but only up to a point. He assured the friars that he saw "the evil I have done." He also promised them that, though the sister-in-law should continue in his house, that he would no longer have sex with her. The friars were not pleased, but in the fragile postrebellion world, they were also unwilling to upset the equilibrium.[23] So Don Domingo continued to live with his second wife/sister-in-law. The sources do not reveal whether he kept to his promises of sexual abstinence.

The fragility of conversion enterprises on these peripheries of New Spain meant that missionaries often had to live with situations they did not condone, as the Spanish had to fit into indigenous practices more than they would have liked. For all the deleterious effects of colonialism on Florida's Native people, and there were many, this was still Indian country, and the Spanish had to play by Native rules. Oré conceded that getting Indians to return to their Christian wives required "more work than if they had to be newly converted." Confounded by Don Domingo's intransigence in marital matters, friars asked him to send the second wife to her father's house, urging that "the reformation should start with him." For them, the leader was the most important role model for monogamy. In fact, all that happened was that the second wife moved into her own house with her three children. This compromise represented what one scholar has called a "colonial bargain" that involved "a degree of native political and cultural autonomy in exchange for a grudging consent." Other Guales, identifying a typical arrangement for elite plural marriages (in which each wife had her own house), complained that, in changing "una casa, dos mujeres," or "one house [and] two wives," for "two houses," he was still just living as an "infidel." By this point, the first, Christian, wife had died, so locals urged the mico to make the situation right by marrying (in the church) the sister-in-law. The friars were still not happy with that proposed solution, as it smacked of prohibited marriage on grounds of incest. The sister-in-law took her sister's children into her house, in keeping with Guale tradition. The friars forbad the mico to go there. He complained that "he had no relatives and that he would die of hunger if that woman would not give him [food] to eat." As we have seen, food provision by wives was critical, but he also may have imagined that the friars would be more willing to accept claims of economic hardship than those of sexual, marital, or political deprivation. They were not, finally taking a hard line. One friar offered bleak prophecies: the mico would suffer in hell, "being a bad Christian." The friars also ominously predicted that he or the sister-in-law would die within a month.[24] It was a source of wonder and conversions when she indeed died within twenty days. Such miracles, like the lightning strike of the Taos woman who preached against monogamy, offered an otherworldly means of solving a worldly problem.

The use of plural marriage even by this Christian mico demonstrates the continued strength of Native practices, and the expectation that even friars might allow variations of Christian monogamy. It also shows the continued importance of rank and status among Guale people. The Spanish presence, both religious and secular, put new pressures on political, economic, spiritual, and social structures, forcing a variety of transformations. Novel systems of tribute redirected the labor of women and men in novel ways; religious and rank distinctions became particularly pressing. Attention to the Guale Rebellion also clarifies that messages of violence and grandstanding were often directed at other indigenous people, not just the Spanish.

"They Should Leave the Wives Whom They Had Taken in Holy Matrimony"

Po'pay evidently did not even want to hear the name of Santa María; he exiled her and all the saints. In 1680, he "came down . . . proclaiming through the pueblos . . . that they should burn all the images and temples, rosaries and crosses, and that all the people should discard the names given them in holy baptism and call themselves whatever they liked." He also apparently enjoined the men that "they should leave the wives whom they had taken in holy matrimony and take any one whom they might wish." Their language was also to change: "They were not to mention in any manner the name of God, of the most holy Virgin, or of the Saints. . . . They were ordered likewise not to teach the Castilian language in any pueblo and to burn the seeds which the Spaniards sowed and to plant only . . . the crops of their ancestors." Another Native man confirmed this testimony, declaring that Po'pay had "ordered . . . that they instantly break up and burn the images of the holy Christ, the Virgin Mary and the other saints . . . and they burn the temples, break up the bells, and separate from the wives whom God had given them in marriage and take those whom they desired." Another man relayed a report that "the Indians . . . have said that the Indian who shall kill a Spaniard will get an Indian woman for a wife, and he who kills four will get four wives, and he who kills ten or more will have a like number of wives." One scholar has suggested that the rebels, in making this offer, were replicating "an indigenous pattern: Spanish men . . . would die, while their spouses and children were assimilated by marriage and adoption into victorious Indian families."[25] Yet this testimony specifically notes that it is Indian women, not Spanish ones, who were to become the plural wives of successful warriors.

All this testimony would appear simply to indicate a powerful indigenous desire to return to a precolonial world, to hack away at St. Francis's arms and all his powers. Presumably, such calls would have appealed to many unhappily married husbands and wives. Yet it is necessary to be cautious, as the kinds of claims in this revolt echo with those of many others recorded with horror by the Spanish. Indeed, many of the aspects considered central and specific to the Pueblo Revolt, including the defilement of sacred objects, the murder of missionaries, and the calls for rejection of Spanish Catholic culture and its use of Castilian and sacramental monogamy, were all issues in both the Alpujarras rebellion of 1568 and the Guale Rebellion of 1597. It is difficult not to draw the conclusion that the clerk-mediated witness statements from the Pueblo Revolt refracted earlier rebellions, so closely do they align in outlook. It is also unclear how far we can trust the testimony of informers threatened with torture.[26] Since Po'pay was long dead by 1693, it was easy to scapegoat him, in ways that may or may not have reflected the actual situation of 1680 itself. It is hard to know from the limited sources surviving; many were destroyed in the Pueblo Revolt or later. However, putting together archaeological evidence with textual accounts, flawed as they are, allows us to move past the old interpretations of this conflict which center so much on Spanish men. Instead it is possible to witness that relations between indigenous people, revolving around rank and gender, were vital here.

Pueblo Indians lived in a diversity of pueblos, or towns, across hundreds of miles. They spoke many languages from four major language families. They also had distinct economies, cultures, and alliances. Some large pueblos, such as Taos, Pecos, and Picurís in the north, were thriving centers of commerce and life, with populations of more than two thousand individuals. They had long been deeply enmeshed with their neighbors. Every autumn, Apache hunters brought loads of bison to these towns, for them to be processed, broken down into meat and hides, and traded with interior pueblos. Apaches carried away agricultural produce and other goods in exchange. This largely peaceful trade was critical to both sides. Archaeological sources indicate that "Apaches de Navajo" (as the Spanish called them) resided in the Chama Valley, near these major northern pueblos, in the seventeenth century.[27] Other pueblos had very different relations with neighboring Apaches (diverse themselves). Indeed, Apaches moving from the west and south raided southern pueblos such as Piro, Tompiro, and Tewa in the 1670s, leaving them virtually depopulated, as their traumatized residents fled.

In normal circumstances, intermarriage helped to knit together these diverse locations. Over the course of the sixteenth and seventeenth centuries, given population decline, there was considerable flux in political alliances. Marriage here, as elsewhere, was a key part of the larger Pueblo consolidation. Marriage was also a mark of maturity for men and women, and a groom and his family exchanged gifts with the bride and her family, with most matches matrilocal (requiring the husband to join the bride's family and community). For all except high-ranking older men, monogamy was the usual form of marriage. As in many other Native cultures, polygamy existed as an option only for the most elite, reserved for what one scholar has termed "seniors" or political and spiritual leaders who supported large households.[28] As elsewhere, polygyny was as much about economics as it was about sex. It was also about the establishment of rank within and between Native communities. The practice of plural marriage, very selected, marked certain members of society as elite and born to be such. In general, by this era, Apache societies, as opposed to Pueblo ones, both were more martial (heavily dependent on raiding and horses) and had different systems of marital organization. Polygyny based on a man's personal capacities as a warrior, raider, and controller of horses, rather than on established elite rank as a leader or priest, was more common among Apache and related people than among Pueblo Indians.[29]

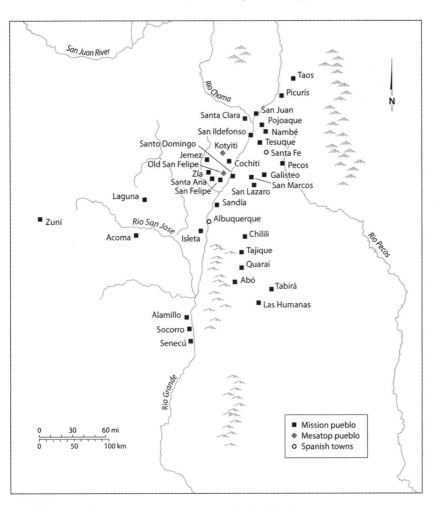

Map of seventeenth-century New Mexico. Cartography by Bill Nelson.

Yet the wider landscape was changing. Colonialism was pernicious, and it is easy enough to believe that most indigenous people hated it. As in Florida, tribute demands, from Spanish church and state, worsened Pueblo life in virtually every town. Spanish demands for hides for trade led to increased specialization between villages, as some struggled to provide these hides. Others paid in corn, and colonialism brought again a narrowing of nutritional range as more corn was grown and consumed. Here, too, the effects were not salutary. There was a decrease in life expectancy and a deterioration of maternal and infant health, which left populations more vulnerable to epidemics. There was also an increase in heavy and repetitive labor for both women and men. Physical activity centered on processing hides, harvesting corn, and literally bearing burdens. More adult men were carrying heavy loads across the landscape, and more older women were working with hides relentlessly. This onerous work left such clear marks on the damaged bodies of both women and men that it is perceptible to archaeologists today. Yet it had different effects on them. Women's work became more focused on processing hides, and more women, including older ones, were now forced to do it. Men often had to move long distances, and to carry a lot when doing so. As archaeologists observe, "A consequence of the reorganization of labor was that *men's and women's lives diverged* significantly in the colonial period."[30]

Much of this toil by indigenous women and men was forced. Older, more limited systems of captivity, centered around women and children incorporated into households, became a full-scale system of slavery, ensnaring men as well as women and children into systems of backbreaking exploitation. Spaniards made use of bound laborers in novel ways. Women and children remained enslaved and subordinate, not becoming incorporated as fully in the household as had at least sometimes been the case before the Spanish had arrived. In a 1633 case, friars complained that the governor ordered the taking of Native children "as if they were yearling calves or colts. . . . These children he has placed in permanent bondage, taking them away from their fathers or mothers." By 1680, more than half of Spanish households had at least one slave. The Spanish demanded more and more slaves, and not just for domestic service. Spanish ambitions to mine silver in Mexico, down a long dusty road leading past the pueblos, meant many Pueblo and Apache Indians were forced to provide this arduous and dangerous form of labor. The uptick in mining in the decades after 1650 increased vicious raiding and slave trading in this wider area. Even friars complained that governors "made opportunity to send, apparently in the service of his Majesty, squadrons of men to capture the heathen Indians to send to the camp and mines of El Parral to sell." There were complaints about the capture of Indian girls "about nine or ten years of age" taken from their families. In one case, the girl's mother and uncle, the head of the pueblo, were able to buy the girl back, but the witness who recounted this story lamented that they had suffered "a great tyranny," especially since the raiders charged as much to ransom this little girl as they would have for "an Apache woman." Spanish labor systems also meant that men were enslaved in large numbers, a major shift. Part of what may have disturbed many Pueblo men in the period before the rebellion was that they were drafted into the silver mines, thus forced into the lowly position of slave, like women or children. Such humiliating inversions of gender and age likely enflamed tensions. Men probably also felt frustrated at their inability to protect wives and children from raiding and slaving and were thus responsive to calls for insurrection. Gender and rank, then, were critical to slavery and its overthrow. This system of slavery, and an ever greater use of horses, led to "a sharp rise in violence and militarism" in Apache and other groups in the vicinity. Spanish slave traders also used Pueblo allies to raid neighboring Apache communities, breaking apart relations. Yet the residents of those northern pueblos stood fast with Apache allies, resisting Spanish attempts to make them raid for Apache slaves.[31] These Pueblo Indians were leaders in the revolt.

Po'pay's calls for polygamy for successful rebels were designed to appeal especially to men disaffected by these pernicious reorientations of labor. His promises would have democratized polygamy for such men, making it accessible to warriors, not just established leaders. He was directing his message at "common" Indian men, not just Spaniards. He was not suggesting a return to precolonial worlds, even though his vision deliberately capitalized on anti-Spanish nostalgia. He was offering instead something novel couched as a return to a timeless past: that a man who showed martial ability in a single war—but who perhaps lacked elite family connections, gifts for brides, important kinship ties, or indeed any other sign of rank and status—could gain a marital prerogative traditionally associated with leaders. It opened up polygyny to men who were not "seniors," so that leadership status came to those who may well have lacked any such credentials previously. In Florida, polygamy was about maintaining and bolstering a hereditary elite; here it was about upending hereditary rank, making polygamy more widely accessible for those with martial prowess. This appeal was predicated on masculine solidarities in war trumping older forms of privilege based on lineage and kinship. Arguably, it would have increased the incidence and possibly the challenges of polygamy for women, but it may also have seemed a useful form of protection for families.

This democratizing appeal to men seems to have resonated powerfully in a time of great economic hardship and increased slavery. Po'pay was promising that effective warriors against the Spanish could themselves become leaders. Such rulers were exempt from paying tribute and from slavery for themselves or their families; indeed, they received tribute and commanded

slaves. For those who had suffered what one scholar terms the "violent discipline" of the tribute and slaving systems, Po'pay was turning the world upside
down, vowing to make aggrieved providers of tribute and their fellow captives
into recipients of them.[32] To hold out the domestic, sexual, and financial benefits of plural marriage to men who endured the humiliation of control by the
Spanish as well as economic deprivation and even slavery of the decades
before the revolt was partially about conjuring up precolonial situations, in
which the church did not control unions. However, it was also about promising resources and status to men who lacked both, and about unifying
increasingly martial Apache communities with Pueblo ones.

In fact, Po'pay's demands were as much pro-Apache as they were anti-
Spanish. Indeed, as with the Guale Rebellion, what has long been cast simply as
timeless resistance by indigenous people was a more complicated situation,
about indigenous relations as much as colonial ones. A reorientation to this new
form of polygamy spoke as loudly and eloquently to more ancient rivals and
allies as it did to the Spanish. After all, the practice of plural marriage existed
among neighboring Athapaskan groups, such as the Apaches and Comanches,
not just in visions of the past. Before the rebellion, following his whipping for
spiritual crimes, Po'pay had taken refuge in the northern pueblo of Taos, where
he met with disaffected war captains, some of whom had been living among the
Apaches. At least some Apaches supported Po'pay and his fellow rebels,
working together against the Spanish. Po'pay's promise to provide four wives
for four dead Spaniards may have been a way of appealing to Apaches, as well
as to war captains among the Pueblo, whose status would have been enhanced
by this populist polygamy. Adopting polygamous marriage would have brought
the people of the Pueblos much closer to neighboring Athapaskan societies. In
other respects, such a realliance of indigenous rivals seems to have occurred, as
after the rebellion, some Pueblo groups, with Spanish arms, began to commit
raids on other pueblos in what one scholar terms "mobile equestrian units."[33]
Po'pay's assurance of providing multiple wives to successful rebels would have
substantially altered traditional Pueblo cultures.

Po'pay was able to unite disparate groups in effective ways. However,
the revolt was never uncontested among the peoples of the pueblos. He
allegedly killed his own son-in-law, the governor of the Pueblo of San Juan,
to prevent him revealing the revolt. Was his daughter on the side of her
husband, too? Although scholars acknowledge that the Pueblo Revolt was
the most successful rebellion in New Spain in this period, they also

emphasize that Pueblo political union almost immediately fell apart, devolving rapidly into civil war, tyranny, and chaos. They also note that Po'pay himself was removed as leader and died in 1681, following unhappiness with his overbearing demands.[34] There was not complete unity ever, perhaps for understandable reasons, given the nature of Po'pay's plan.

If we start to see Po'pay not as the leader of a united pan-Pueblo confederation but as a politician who made specific populist promises designed to appeal to certain segments of Pueblo society, then our readings of this rebellion change. Perhaps at least some of those Pueblos who leaked news of the rebellion to the Spanish may have been among those who rejected Po'pay's particular brand of leadership and alliances. In this case, they should not simply be dismissed as treacherous collaborators with imperial overlords. After all, Po'pay's vision was not especially sustainable or stable. It would have required either ongoing war to obtain female captives who could become secondary wives, or severe internal tensions between warriors competing over women. There would probably have been a lot of frustrated men, left without wives at all. Traditional elites, those who had status already, would have been unlikely to support that increased competition for wives and power.

How did the wives themselves feel about this plan? It is so difficult to access the perspective of the women here that few historians have even made the attempt. Yet how can we tell this story fully without its women? There is no way that this successful and large-scale work of rebellion and confederation, which survived many years beyond Po'pay's demise in 1681, could have succeeded without significant ongoing support from both men and women. This rebellion was the fruit of ongoing efforts to unite disparate people, and it transformed Pueblo lives, but not in quite the ways Po'pay had imagined. Pueblos never did jettison the language or produce of the Spanish, and monogamy and ultimately Catholicism came to be more, not less, important. Po'pay's promises might not have seemed terribly appealing to many women. For women, it might have looked like exchanging servitude to the Spanish for a similar status among the Pueblos. It seems doubtful that women would have embraced the chance to be trophies of war, as wives or slaves (or both). Yet changing the world as they knew it likely appealed to them, for other reasons. After all, they too had endured forced labor, tribute, and violence before the revolt. Their mothers and grandmothers had to work in fields and in processing hides in ways previous generations had not.

Women had other reasons to loathe the Spanish. Numerous Hopi oral traditions, for instance, indicate that Spanish priests exacted tribute and slave labor, including sex work, from them. One priest, called Tutaachi, or "Dictator," apparently forced men to collect water far away so that the priests had unfettered sexual access to their wives, mothers, daughters, and sisters. In 1661, there were accusations that one friar had "taken" the wife of an Indian man and also had had sexual relations "with more than twenty Indian women." In another case, the governor tried to take legal action against a friar accused of "the execrable crime of forcing a woman, cutting her throat, and burying her." The governor noted that he wanted to stop the friar from striking again. He also wanted to prevent the Indians there from killing the friar in anger and "revolt[ing], as they did upon another occasion because of an event like this."[35]

Women and men had reasons to revolt—and to rebuild in new ways, despite the many challenges of doing so. They found new solidarities in the wake of the rebellion in 1680. One archaeologist has termed this process "Pueblofication" or, elsewhere, the "creation of tradition." There was always a diversity of opinions and approaches, but the majority worked for unification during and after the revolt. We have no direct Spanish accounts for a dozen years after the revolt because they had been so effectively vanquished.[36] To understand this period, we must rely on material sources and oral traditions. Both suggest that the majority of Pueblos, women and men, were disaffected with the Spanish and indeed accepted and fostered basic principles of Pueblo resistance and confederation. They also continued to ally in many cases with Apaches. It is helpful here to separate the means from the ends. Po'pay's end was the achievement of transformed, autonomous Pueblo societies. His means were violently anti-Spanish appeals to martial prowess and new forms of gender and status allied with Athapaskan practices. Many of the people of the pueblos rejected those methods. Yet other efforts to achieve solidarity—including architecture, ritual, and material culture—may have succeeded among communities made new but rooted in tradition. The Spanish returned in 1693, true enough, but it was to an altered landscape, one that endured for centuries. We might say that Po'pay did not entirely succeed, but other Indians, women and men, did.

To understand better a wider group of participants, not just a few leaders on whom the Spanish focused, it helps to turn to material culture. After the revolt began, women and men left their old towns and founded new ones, what one scholar has called "sanctuary cities." Going to safe spaces on the tops of mesas, they built new communities. Such was not easy work, transporting building materials, as well as food and water, to inaccessible locations. It would have taken a lot of people pulling together and even more load carrying. But now they carried burdens to reconstruct their own lives. These villages united diverse refugees, who spoke distinct languages. So the new settlement of Patowka included Towa-speaking people from Jemez Pueblo, but also Keres speakers from Santo Domingo Pueblo, and even Navajos. They worked to understand one another and to rebuild—ironically probably using Spanish as a lingua franca. In these new towns, including nearby Kotyiti, building took the form not of Spanish mission styles but of a dual-plaza form that made reference to, but did not replicate, precolonial indigenous architectural forms. Jemez people had long had an open-plaza style of urban design, but this bounded dual-plaza form was probably adopted from the other Pueblo people who joined them in the period immediately following the revolt. It was probably related to ritual and social organization in terms of moieties and balance. People sought spiritual and social equilibrium in these new places. They used old forms in new ways, reimagining and indeed creating communities. Lines of continuities joined with innovative styles and religious orientations to create novel forms, ones presumably designed to appeal to larger audiences.[37]

Women also painted their support for unity on the ceramics they made. On the pots they crafted, they began to employ an archaic double-headed key motif, which originated around 1400, fell into disuse until the mid-seventeenth century, and then became a unifying rebellion-era motif across a range of Pueblo communities. When women and men carried water and food in these pots, they thus also carried messages of confederation in the very designs of the vessels. Women also stopped making Spanish-style glazeware and instead returned to older matte ware, with Kachina, or Native religious, motifs. Individual pueblos, new and old, began to trade eagerly with one another, much more in the years following the revolt than in those preceding it.[38] Women and men may not have agreed with the means proposed by Po'pay and other leaders, and they never did take up polygamy in any great numbers. Instead, they worked in their daily lives to create new kinds of solidarities in the wake of the removal of the Spanish. The rebellion was a catalyst for a broader Pueblo cultural unification. Builders, migrants, artists, and traders—women and men—all joined in these endeavors. This quiet work of building new communities mattered as much as the bloody conflict.

This revolt also resonated throughout the wider region, which underwent transformations in this period. The Pueblo Revolt was part of a larger period of unrest in which gender and marriage were at the center. After the revolt, there was yet another significant rebellion against the Spanish in Nueva Vizcaya to the south and east of the Pueblos, so that some scholars see the whole period as a single larger Great Southwestern—or Northern—Revolt. The Tarahumaras and others who revolted were in contact with the Pueblos and knew of their successes. When rebels were recruiting others, they apparently taunted men who refused to join by asking whether the Spanish were their husbands, a seventeenth-century way of saying they were the bitches of the Spanish conquerors. One account related that the leader of the "Yepómera" was angry that a friar refused to let him have three wives. One Jesuit history of the rebellion emphasized the impossibility of eradicating the two great Indian vices: drunkenness and polygamy. Its author singled out one Tarahumara "sorcerer," or spiritual leader, for encouraging polygamy and orgies and rejecting Catholic monogamy: a new wrapper for an old package.[39] As elsewhere, polygamy was both a powerful European shorthand for lawlessness and a way for Indian men to make claims to power and leadership. These scattered references also suggest that continued controversies over clashing systems of marriage, between groups such as the Apaches who were practicing polygamy and slave trading and raiding and others who were not, animated the larger uprisings. These great shake-ups of the late seventeenth century demonstrate the ways that new worlds, out of old forms, were emerging across the wider landscape.

To confront this broad region and its material remains is a way to move beyond Spanish sources, which naturally only ever draw attention to the leaders, the men, and the centrality of the Spanish. Looking at these rebellions across the Southeast as well as the Southwest, and even in Spain itself, it is possible to see the connections relentlessly drawn between polygamy, desecration, and violence. Polygamy symbolized anarchic rebellion by men who refused to accept such Spanish mores as monogamy. At the same time, calls for, and practices of, polygamy illuminate the gender dynamics at play in these transformative moments across a much broader space. Larger communities, including women and children, may not have imprinted themselves on those Spanish sources, but they counted. Our image of these indigenous rebellions has been fed by Spanish texts complicit in their repression and often echoing old themes about polygamy. This view remains too often only one of angry indigenous warriors attacking meddling missionaries, amid landscapes shot through with blood, fire, and slavery. Fixed there by Spanish sources, those rebels seem locked in a bleak diorama of Christianity, monogamy, and colonial conquest on the one side and ancient and unchanging indigenous practices on the other. Appeals to traditional ways, directed at Europeans, appear to issue from a place of dark nostalgia wrought by the horror of colonial existence as well as ruthless coercion and slavery. But the role of "having many wives" in these uprisings demonstrates that indigenous people, women and men, were responding to colonialism's damage in creative and complicated ways, in ways destructive but also constructive.

New peoples emerged out of the fiery crucible of colonialism and rebellion. Florida micos suavely spoke Castilian and donned elegant Spanish cloaks to communicate their elite status to other Indians. In the world of the pueblos, women and men built dual-plaza places of refuge and crafted and traded new kinds of goods. If men there successfully defeated and drove off the Spanish, women flooded in to rebuild their shaken world. Many of those ancient pueblos, as at Taos, are still standing. Free from Spanish demands, perched on their mesa tops, artists could paint rock art as well as ancient motifs of Kachinas and dual-headed keys. This beautiful land was theirs again, and they could fashion it as they wished. Looking back, they looked forward. Helping daughters, sisters, and nieces to cast pots and to paint them with messages of solidarity, such women did the work of successful rebellion as surely as Po'pay and his war captains did.

2. "Poligamie/Nintiouiouesaïn"

Makheabichtichiou was blessed with courage, an agile tongue, the respect of his people—and three wives. Paul Le Jeune, first superior of the Jesuits in New France in what is now Canada, in the 1630s, praised him for all these qualities but the last. Thanks to his talents, Makheabichtichiou became leader or "capitaine" of *la Petite Nation*, a collection of Algonquin and Innu (or Montagnais) refugees clustered together north of the St. Lawrence River in a difficult period of reconfiguration following epidemics and war. Eager to further trade and diplomatic ties with the French, he converted to Christianity, establishing an alliance with the Jesuits (or Black Robes), who welcomed him warmly. Makheabichtichiou agreed to renounce all the customs that the Jesuits condemned: "that he would never give eat-all feasts, that he would not summon the Sorcerers to treat him in his sicknesses, that he would no longer believe in dreams, and that he desired to be baptized and to believe what the French believe." This offer showed just how courageous he was, because it demonstrated his willingness to compromise many sources of political authority. Feasts where leaders furnished hospitality, thus demonstrating the prosperity of their households, were important markers of status. The connections nurtured by "sorcerers," animal spirits, and dreams also enhanced the ability to lead. Still, Makheabichtichiou made clear his readiness to depart from the dreamscape of Bear and Beaver, the Algonquin way of life. He was such an enthusiastic convert that he even proclaimed the "wonders of our Holy doctrine, preaching it publicly."[1]

Here, then, was sweet triumph for the Jesuits. It had not been an easy mission. Le Jeune and others found this new land forbidding, its people disconcerting. Indeed, Le Jeune termed the Native house in which he had wintered "a dungeon which had neither lock nor key." The guard was "the cold, the snow, and the danger of getting lost in these great woods": pressing fears for inexperienced French travelers. To ward off the bone-chilling cold, a huge fire burned, leading to roasting heat and choking smoke that burned eyes and lungs, what Le Jeune, in sardonic reference to Christian saints, called "martyrdom." Then there were the dogs, "great and in great number," hungry, smelly dogs, scampering on people and things, thrusting their wet noses into any dish of food. Le Jeune complained that he could not even stand up in these suffocating, stinking houses packed with the bodies of men, women, children, and dogs: "Consequently you must always lie down, or sit down upon the ground, the usual posture of the Savages." In other words, this Frenchman felt compelled to lower himself to fit in this new kind of household. Yet such "martyrdom" seemed worth it when Makheabichtichiou turned to Jesus. Schooled in hierarchy, Le Jeune assumed that the conversion of this bold capitaine would effect the Christianization of his whole people. For all their learning, how little those Black Robes knew sometimes![2]

No sooner had Makheabichtichiou shown himself a good Christian in so many ways than the Jesuits' hopes started to unravel. He agreed to everything they wanted—with one critical exception. He "kept all the commandments, except that one about having only one wife." His obdurate refusal to renounce his three wives prevented his baptism and, in Jesuit eyes, rendered the whole mission a failure. It was a crushing blow, experienced repeatedly in the colonial period. Across numerous locations in colonial America, as we have seen, missionaries kept meeting powerful Native men who professed belief in Christ and his church yet who would not give up polygyny. Such "gave us all some trouble," as Le Jeune later phrased it.[3] These leaders saw no incompatibility between being a Christian and being married to more than one wife. They saw both as possible sources of authority, ones to be nurtured in periods of political and economic trauma. To comprehend why Makheabichtichiou would not relinquish his wives is to learn more about the complex interplay between colonialism and marriage.

One plural marriage and its four spouses illuminate in ways rarely possible the transformative dynamics in both Native communities and colonial confrontations, for this one time and place but also for many others in New France and elsewhere in the Americas. Historians of such encounters, following the missionaries, have usually focused less on how such plural marriages seemed to people like Makheabichtichiou and his wives than on how they seemed to people like Le Jeune and the missionaries: an "obstacle," a "target," "disorder," and "savagery." Much more can be said on the Indian side of this history. While early feminist accounts of these encounters argued that polygyny was one of many native "freedoms" given up with conversions, more recent work has argued that women converted to Catholicism in part to escape polygyny. Even historians who disagree about how "Frenchified" Natives did or did not become in New France agree that polygyny was an oppressive regime propelling women into Christianity and a European way of life. Sometimes it was, but that is not the whole story. Plural marriages were part of a larger system organizing indigenous households and labor. Women like Makheabichtichiou's wives, and many others, linger too often in the background, emerging from the shadows only when they become involved with European men in interracial relations and *métissage,* or mixed-race unions. Although historians have recently emphasized the need to understand indigenous dynamics on their own terms, indigenous gender and sexual relations remain opaque.[4] In addition, what have been called "gender frontiers"— the meeting of distinct systems of organization of lives and labor of women and men—existed not just between Europeans and Native Americans but also among Native Americans. Despite recent work on the significance of "*nindoodemag,* or kinship networks," there has been little work on Native households themselves and how much they influenced political decision making and colonial encounters.

Households represented a focal point of power and labor. Women's work made households for men, whether in marriages singular or plural, so men protected them fiercely. Gender made a difference; rank and age did too. For women, marriage and household regimes, whether plural or otherwise, involved hierarchies and services: whether to a husband, a fellow wife, a sister-in-law, or a mother-in-law. Senior members of households, men and women, could and did threaten and enact violence against junior members, whether in singular or plural unions. They often did so to protect larger systems: of labor, of reproduction, of kinship lines. Violence and the threat of it kept individuals in check in myriad ways. These household systems were not static, though. New pressures of colonialism reshaped them in this period. The refusal to give up plural marriage was here, as elsewhere, not a reflection of a timeless clinging to tradition. Rather the importance of family and indeed plural marriages amplified because of colonial catastrophes. Reorientation to markets for fur led to environmental depletion and dramatic political reconfigurations as well as war. Epidemics of European diseases also uncoiled themselves with deadly force into these already struggling communities, disproportionately destroying the most vulnerable: children. These population losses meant that plural marriage became a vital way to rebuild. The analysis here tracks several possibilities for a man's refusal to renounce his wives, ones relating to love, lust, pride, violence, and family. Comprehending this decision in its full context illuminates much about a changing landscape and also about family and its critical importance to Indian leaders and politics. It also reveals a frankly startling amount about what one contemporary observer called "the beast with two backs"—and, improbably, love itself.[5]

"I Love Only One"

Colonialism brought new encounters as well as pressures. Amerindians like Makheabichtichiou and French sojourners like Le Jeune found themselves among people more confounding than any they had ever met, at points of unique vulnerability for them both. Each man was a consummate diplomat and knew how to move cautiously among strangers, to bend in new postures in disorienting, sometimes hostile lands. Both were canny and cosmopolitan, adroit at wrapping their tongues around unfamiliar words and making themselves understood, whether through word or gesture. Native Americans and French men came together in these novel encounters, mostly with peaceful intentions, but also wary and armed: men like Makheabichtichiou with arrows and arquebuses, men like Le Jeune with quill and paper. Each kind of tool shaped the encounters themselves, as well as the ways they have been narrated. Like many officials who left abundant writings about people who left none, Jesuit missionaries such as Le Jeune recorded in order to obliterate much of the behavior that they were observing. They wrote about polygamy and divorce because they wanted to replace them with lifelong monogamy or, better yet, celibacy.[6]

After all, ending infractions of the sacrament of monogamous Christian marriage was part of the Catholic global mission. Early modern Jesuits around the world, in the courts of Kongo and Mughal and Native American rulers, spent a lot of time arguing for perpetual Christian monogamy, even for kings: a message rarely greeted with much enthusiasm. They also wrote about it. From the early 1630s to 1658, Utopian visions of Jesuits and Ursulines fueled missionary work along the St. Lawrence. The French state was also

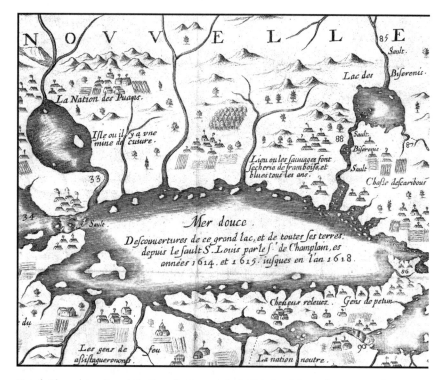

Detail, Champlain, *Carte de la Nouvelle-France* (1632). This detail from a larger map of la Nouvelle France shows the "Petitte nation des Algommequins" on the right-hand side,

regulating marriage in novel ways, to encourage marriage and reproduction at home and in the colonies. In the wake of sixteenth-century Wars of Religion and the presence of Protestants (Huguenots), the establishment of Catholic colonies took on particular force. French Catholic missionaries did not find it easy to assert their teachings about marriage and other matters, for many reasons, not least the difficulties of learning Native languages and ways. The Ursuline mother superior, Marie de l'Incarnation, in her mission in Canada, complained that Amerindian languages made her feel like "stones were rolling around in my head." Yet she and others persevered. Jesuits wrote reports home (edited before publication); they also wrote dictionaries for each other to help new missionaries. The former source has been used a lot, the latter rarely. These dictionaries capture extraordinary information, even as they also expose French judgments and incomprehension.[7]

This very complication of language highlights the complex, fluid nature of identities in seventeenth-century Native America. Algonquian is a very

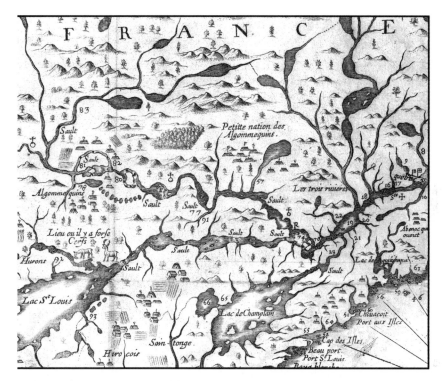

northwest of Trois Rivières. Samuel de Champlain, *Carte de la Nouvelle-France* (Paris: Faicte . . . par le sieur de Champlain, 1632). Courtesy of John Carter Brown Library, Brown University.

wide linguistic designation. It includes many people, such as those in the wider areas of the Great Lakes and north of the St. Lawrence River. A contemporary map shows the northern regions. The focus here is on three distinct linguistic subgroups in those regions: Algonquin / Algonkin (of the Ottawa River valley), Innu (or Montagnais), and Miami-Illinois. Each linguistic subgroup included smaller entities identified specifically by the French, such as the Peoria Illinois. There was considerable variety within and between them; the Miami-Illinois were the most hierarchical with the most established practices of polygamy. Still, it is possible to identify a shared set of beliefs about gender and households, which marked them out from neighboring ones such as the Haudenosaunee (or Iroquois) or the Wendat (or Wyandott or Huron). The exigencies of a harsh northern climate and limited resources had long shaped the nature of family and community life among such people. Outside of the abundant summer season, groups needed to be small in order for resources in a given area to support all of the people in them. These entities were not nation-states in a European sense. They were also not tribes. Rather, they were fluid social networks, structured by kinship ties, organized around villages, and linked though language, culture, and marriage. In part, family connections profoundly shaped identities and made marriage a vital means of linking communities. Indeed, one scholar of these kinship networks has contended that marriage was "a crucial institution."[8]

Marriage was indeed crucial: to Makheabichtichiou, to his wives, to his community, and to his Jesuit teachers, among others. In the course of his many conversations with the Jesuits, Makheabichtichiou defended his practice of marriage. He contended: "Of the three women I have married, I love only one, whom I wish to keep with me." Indeed, he claimed that he had sent the other two away, but they had returned despite him. The Jesuits emphasized the need to have only one wife. *Loving* only one wife might have been Makheabichtichiou's version of Christian monogamy: a surprisingly modern version of marriage in which affection was the defining aspect. Yet it also raises an important and understudied issue: the meanings of marital love in this time and place. To learn more about love, it is helpful to start with marriage, and more particularly the dynamics of polygyny.[9]

Polygyny existed across a range of Algonquian peoples, as suggested by the Jesuit translation dictionaries. The earliest, a 1662 Algonquin one, includes such phrases as "I have two wives" and "the wife (or wives) of my husband." It even includes the word polygamy: "poligamie/nintiouiouesaïn." These phrases reappear in other Algonquin sources, as well as Innu and Miami-Illinois ones, for the entire period. The nature of such plural unions depended on the relationship between husband and wives, but also between wives. Households could take different shapes. Sometimes a new couple lived with the husband's parents, at least for a while. It probably would have been a mother-in-law and sisters-in-law, then, who initiated a new wife into the ways of that household, clan, and community. Such initiations could be gentle. They could also be harsh, because these households were places of productive labor, and the senior matron of such a household was as much a strict manager of labor and economics as a motherly figure. In a culture in which sibling relations were paramount, households often depended on brothers setting up households together, with wives who married into those families. In this case, the wives of the brothers might exert control over a new bride. Sometimes the couple lived alone, sometimes with the family. Sometimes a woman became a second or third wife, joining other adult women in a larger household.[10]

The nature of such plural unions depended much on the relationship between the women in them. It is helpful to distinguish sororal polygyny from other kinds. Among Illinois people, especially, it was possible for two (or more) sisters to marry the same man. One writer, Charlevoix, observed, "A plurality of wives is allowed of . . . and it is common enough to marry all the sisters; this custom is founded on a persuasion, that sisters must agree better than strangers. In this case all the women are upon an equal footing; but amongst the true Algonquins there are two orders of wives, those of the second order being the slaves of the first." While this point may have been an exaggeration, it does seem that for nonsisters, the first wife enjoyed considerable status, while subsequent wives, some of whom may have been "chore" or captive wives, had less. The distinctiveness of Illinois cultures might be related to an upsurge in captive taking and slavery in those areas in the late seventeenth century. One Illinois dictionary gives the phrase "to be a second wife; that's bad."[11]

Regardless of their origins, however, plural marriages and divorces reveal, unexpectedly, the importance of love. In some cases, the first wife had a senior position but was also, interestingly, assumed to be the most loved. It is hard to know exactly what *love* meant, but this is a rare glimpse into it. One dictionary provides the phrase for "the first wife who is most loved." Another includes the single word for "first and most loved wife who is mistress of all," as well as the word for "the other wife, like the second, a term of contempt." Such phrases indicate status differentials between the wives. Internal rank could matter a great deal. There is also evidence of the jealousies that might be expected. The phrase for "I am the second wife" is linguistically similar to "I look upon him with jealousy, hate." They also suggest, though, that it was not always the first wife who was the most desired, as implied by the related words for jealous or jealousy and "she prevents him from going to her rival, to his second wife." One phrase is "she is one of his/my wives whom he/I love[s] the most." These phrases suggest a choice: that husbands, like Makheabichtichiou, might love one particular wife, not necessarily the first, but the one with the greatest compatibility.[12]

Ironically, divorce, too, reveals something about love, because not loving could spell the end of a marriage. Since, as elsewhere, a marriage, whether single or plural, carried significant political, diplomatic, economic, and social weight, its severance was a moment of potential social and economic disruption, to be carefully managed. Yet it seems that both men and women could terminate a marriage if they no longer loved each other. Mutual choice appears in phrases such as "the spouses left each other." Sometimes it was the man who ended it, with more than one dictionary offering such phrases as "the wife that I have left" and "I change my wife." Some of these entries linked to phrases for "woman chaser." It is possible, though, also to witness female agency in instigating separation and divorce: phrases such as "she does not love her husband" or "the wives do not love their husbands so they have separated." Some went even farther, offering such choice vocabulary as the single Illinois word *kissabamigouta,* which meant "a wife separated from her husband who does not wish to see him anymore even though [they are] in the same village." Such phrases, stressing the necessity of marital love, indicate something emotionally dynamic and even familiar and modern. By contrast, the Jesuits did not prioritize love in this way. Love was an ideal, but its disappearance (or nonappearance) was no justification for ending a marriage. Missionaries wanted to ensure that Makheabichtichiou was legally and religiously married only to one wife, that he had sex only with one wife, that he recognized only those children born to that one wife as legitimate. Love between spouses, their mutual pleasure in each other, was secondary. For Algonquin and Innu and Miami-Illinois peoples, it was primary. So although seventeenth-century Native Americans could marry in ways that seem oppressive and archaic, they could also marry in ways that seem egalitarian and modern.[13]

Mutual love was the ideal. That other forms of marriages existed—ones involving less love than perhaps duty or labor or obligations—is clear. Yet the idea that both husband and wife should feel love, that not loving each other could end a marriage, was the dominant ideal, even among the more hierarchical peoples in the Great Lakes region. One of the more freethinking French observers of this period, Baron Lahontan, noted the contempt in which Native people held Europeans with their strange, striking attachment to perpetual monogamy even when a marriage was loveless and conducive only to unhappiness. While Lahontan was using such claims to critique French practices, there may have been some truth to them. After all, European marriage likely seemed restrictive. Lahontan noted that "these People cannot conceive that Europeans, who value themselves for their abundance of sense and knowledge, should be so blind or ignorant as not to know that Marriage is for them a source of Trouble and Uneasiness." He contended that Native Americans "consider it as a monstrous thing to be tied to each other without hope of ever being able to break the knot." According to Lahontan, whatever counterarguments Europeans presented, Native Americans held "firmly and unmovingly" that such absurd practices of marriages meant that "we [Europeans] are born in slavery and deserve nothing other than servitude."[14] In Native eyes, then, at least according to Lahontan, marriage in the wrong way could make both women and men dupes and slaves, deserving of contempt: a neat parallel, and upending, of European notions.

"I Burn with Lust"

In his conversations with Le Jeune and others, Makheabichtichiou apparently never offered the most obvious explanation for plural marriage that might be expected: sex. Le Jeune did, though. He contended that the problem lay in the sins of lust and pride. Le Jeune wrote that Makheabichtichiou had a "soul almost of flesh," a phrase as elusive in French as it is in English. Le Jeune implied that Makheabichtichiou's impulses were carnal, not spiritual, and that it was an "effort" of some "difficult[y]" to rise above them. Another priest, Father Buteux, reported an incident in which Makheabichtichiou was involved in a near-murder of a Frenchman. Buteux noted that Makheabichtichiou "did not conduct himself in this matter as he should have done." Buteux added that Makheabichtichiou "has great power over his people, but very little over himself; he makes mistakes, and then he acknowledges them; he sees that what we teach is best,—he says so to everyone, yet meanwhile he does not give up his three wives."[15] Buteux echoed Le Jeune: Makheabichtichiou lacked self-control.

Lack of control over sexual desire might help to explain Makheabichtichiou's reluctance in part because, ironically, men like him were in fact expected to refrain from sex so often. Lahontan declared, self-servingly, that Indian women preferred French men as lovers because French men were "less concerned about conserving their vigor," a suggestion that Native men might have viewed ejaculation as a way of draining strength. Beyond this claim, men were expected to avoid procreative sex at certain periods because nursing mothers were not supposed to get pregnant. In a land so forbidding as these northern ones, people there, who managed to grow and hunt a lot of food but who always faced uncertainties and privation, privileged the needs of their children. Mothers nursed babies for two to three years. If a mother's milk stopped flowing because she became pregnant, it could endanger the child. So husband and wife were also expected to avoid having sex during this period. As one French observer (among many) noted: "When the women are nursing, their husbands do not ordinarily have commerce with them. As they have several [wives], they manage it easily." To give up wives could have meant, for a rule-abiding husband, two to three years without procreative sex. Makheabichtichiou might well have found this prospect less than enticing.[16]

On the other hand, two to three years without procreative sex did not mean no sex at all. Jesuits were keen to eradicate these nonprocreative behaviors, so they identified them, in Latin, thus leaving an astonishing record in those old dictionaries. While we do not know, will never know, how much these words matched practice, they convey a considerable range of sexual actions and understandings. There was looking and touching: "I look at the woman with lust, I gaze at her genitals"; a person could also "touch her breasts so that they swell." There was more than one way to say something like "she lies naked, legs apart." A speaker could say "I touch her shamelessly." A man could "make himself erect by touching himself," but it could also be done by someone else: "I pull on his penis with great force so that he reaches orgasm." There also seems to have been sexual penetration from behind, probably of the anus, in a word for "a woman taken from the rear, but preserving her vessel."[17] At least some of these phrases do not indicate gender, and could imply either same-sex intimacies or those between women and men.

Many terms for nonprocreative sexual activity invoke an ideal of mutuality—of affection in marriage, for example, or consideration for nursing mothers. Evenhandedness in terms of male and female sexuality show up in the recorded interests as well as actions of these unions. Women and men apparently both freely spoke about sexual matters: "These vile and infamous people pronounce the names of the private parts of man and woman" grumbled a shocked Le Jeune, aghast to find them "very lewd, both men and women." He complained that though young women were "modestly clad," "their language has the foul odor of the sewers." Dictionaries and gendered grammar also suggest certain equalities. Women as well as men could own and express sexual longings. A man might say, "I burned with the heat of wicked desire," while a woman could say, "I burn with lust." One dictionary conflated polygamy and prostitution but indicated that women and men could both be "prostituted/have many spouses." Both were assumed to show arousal "with genitals swollen." Another word implies mutual masturbation or possibly orgasm: the Jesuits translated it as mutual sin and defilement. A man could touch a woman's genitals, and a woman could touch a man's. There was a word, *sousoupihepoutinghi*, for "when two people suck each other's private parts."[18]

Acknowledgment of desires experienced by both women and men appears in other sources. Makheabichtichiou's great Algonquin rival, Pigarouïch, balked at monogamy in a more explicit fashion than Makheabichtichiou ever did. After giving many arguments against monogamy as a system, he finally asked the Jesuits whether he might agree to monogamous marriage, but still keep his options open in terms of sex with other women. He said he understood that in general, he should not, but "if the women seek me, shall I do wrong to yield to their desire?" The Jesuits replied that such an act of selflessness would of course be very wrong, but his question suggests a wider acknowledgment of female agency in initiating sex. So too do words in Algonquin dictionaries such as the woman who "provoke[s] lust by baring [her] breasts." Although the priests described all these activities in terms of sin and wickedness, there is little sense that these Native Americans did so.[19] Lust might help to explain Makheabichtichiou's choices, but it is unlikely to have been the only, or even the main, motivator.

"You Forbid Me to Kill"

"I do really wish to embrace your belief," promised Makheabichtichiou to Le Jeune, "but you give me two commandments which conflict with each other; on the one hand you forbid me to kill, and on the other you forbid me from having several wives; these do not agree." This puzzling statement is the closest thing to an explanation from Makheabichtichiou himself. There are several ways to interpret this enigma. There is a good chance that Makheabichtichiou was teasing the Jesuits. Even the articulate Le Jeune was impressed by his wit and fluency, demonstrated in frequent sparring with the French. Verbal dexterity was a chief criterion for leadership: "All the authority of their chief is in his tongue's end; for he is powerful in so far as he is eloquent." Le Jeune also rued that this "nation" was so "given to sneering and bantering," their time "passed in eating, laughing, and making sport of each other, and of all the people they know." Indeed, he admitted in frustration, "I could not know when they were speaking seriously, or when they were jesting."[20]

Was Makheabichtichiou jesting? Much to the embarrassed dismay of the Jesuits, his community valued mockery, and used it notably in relation to gender and domestic relations. Le Jeune observed elsewhere, for instance, that for a man to do what was perceived as "women's work" prompted derision on the part of other Algonquin men: "They would make fun of a man who, except in some great necessity, would do anything that should be done by a woman. Our Savage, seeing Father de Noüe carrying wood, began to laugh, saying: 'He's really a woman,' meaning that he was doing a woman's work." One dictionary included a word which meant "I mock him, fart in his nose several times," an act which combined ridicule and aggression. Laughing at someone from another culture indicates the power Native men possessed, and there is every possibility that Makheabichtichiou was making fun of Le Jeune and the other earnest missionaries.[21] Indeed, another meaning of *hardi*, the word used by Le Jeune to describe Makheabichtichiou, was "impudent."

Still, as it often does, this playfulness underscored a serious point, a conundrum that vexed missionaries across the world. It was one thing to steer men away from polygamy when they were not (yet) practicing it; it was quite another to end it when it meant dissolving a household—a critical political and economic unit—and removing a husband and father from wives and children. Makheabichtichiou was sage enough to know that this kind of rupture disturbed his Jesuit teachers. He was making clear what the stakes were here. There is another, more cynical explanation. He may have been dodging and ducking the issue. His supposed enthusiasm for this new religion may have been a method for this skilled politician to ingratiate himself with the French by feigning interest without any intention of full conversion. Closer relations with French missionaries might have been a politically and economically savvy move for a leader like Makheabichtichiou. After all, only Christians were allowed to buy guns from the French, and they also got a discount on other trade goods.[22] Being a Christian mattered to material, not only spiritual, well-being.

Still, it is possible that Makheabichtichiou might have meant his enigmatic statement literally, in two different ways. He might have been alluding to the fact that if he sent his wives away, amid what was a full-blown demographic crisis of the 1630s, it might have been a virtual death sentence. War had taken over his world, and turning his wives away might have made them vulnerable. Stemming from ancient enmities, wars took on new and horrific force due to the pressures of colonialism. The fur trade with Europeans had altered the environment dramatically and rapidly. By the 1630s, beaver, which had always been hunted, was virtually exterminated because of the European trade. This disappearance affected not only the environments and economic prospects of the Algonquin and the Innu but of the neighboring Wendat and the Haudenosaunee. Looking for new sources of fur, these long-standing indigenous foes moved into new areas, a situation that led to increasingly vicious fights over hunting territory. Survival rested in forming alliances, and a sense of urgency prompted closer relations with the French in the 1630s. In 1638, Le Jeune reported that under Makheabichtichiou's leadership, "a band of Montagnais and Algonquins . . . had encamped near us during the winter." This brief statement, seemingly innocuous, reveals a lot. While the Algonquin and Innu had long been political allies, they would not usually have camped together. Makheabichtichiou was seeking to forge an alliance between those remaining Algonquin and the Innu. While alliances of hungry refugees were not uncommon, it was unusual for a group such as this one to stay together over the winter. Usually, even bands of Algonquin split apart over the winter, spreading out so as not to overtax natural resources. For two distinct groups to remain together, and near the French, suggests desperation. Its causes may have been political (to avoid Haudenosaunee raids), or economic (sharing or trading for food with the French), or both. In any case, Makheabichtichiou may have been suggesting that if he no longer protected his wives in his household, that they would have been cast adrift, without resources, and prey to warriors and captivity in dangerous times.[23]

A second possibility—over which Makheabichtichiou felt conflicted—has to do with customs. He might have meant that he was literally permitted to kill his wives if he chose. Indeed, as both a "capitaine" and a husband, he had the power to do so legally, at least in certain highly controlled circumstances. Leaders such as Makheabichtichiou had the power of life and death over war captives; husbands had similar powers in other circumstances. To understand this point, it is crucial to explore more about Algonquin marriage in general and the authority it bestowed on men. In these cultures, wives generally moved away from family, patterns known as patrilocal or virilocal, and this separation from kin could make them vulnerable. Linguistic sources confirm what has been a matter of speculation. One dictionary gives a word for a wife living with her husband's family. A 1662 Algonquin dictionary records ways to say "wife of my country," distinct from a wife of other countries. Dictionaries gave phrases, spoken only by wives, such as: "I am married outside my country, into another nation." One phrase in a dictionary signified, "I am outside my country, my village," and as a related phrase,

"You do not treat me like a relative." There is also a way to describe a "foreign woman married into this country."[24] These foreign-born wives could pay a high price for a system dependent on their abilities to connect larger networks through their bodies and their babies.

In cases of adultery, Algonquin husbands and indeed other family members had power of life and death, or at least of brutal punishment, over straying wives. Evenhandedness and liberal sexual policies did not extend to adultery by wives; even their own families could sanction violence against them in such circumstances. One early French observer in the Acadian area contended that although polygynous wives did not evince jealousy of other wives, by contrast, married men "are jealous; and if the wife be found making the beast with two backs she will be put away, or be in danger of being killed by her husband." Another traveler reported, "If any Woman defile her Marriage-bed, the Husband cuts off her Nose, or an Ear, or gives her a flash in the Face with a stone Knife; if he kill her, he is clear'd for a Present which he gives to her Parents *to wipe away their Tears*." Another Frenchman noted of the Great Lakes region, "The woman cannot at her own whim abandon her husband, since he is her master, who has bought and paid for her; even her relatives cannot take her away from him; and if she leaves him custom authorizes him to kill her, without any one blaming him for it. This has often brought on war between families, when [relatives] undertook to maintain the husband's right when the woman would not consent to return to him."[25] In other words, murder of an adulterous or departing wife might be forgiven, even by her own natal family (at least in some cases).

A wife's adultery could prompt extreme violence sanctioned by family and community, even if it stopped short of murder. The dictionaries corroborate claims of travel writers who reported that these wives or their lovers in Illinois country had their noses or ears or the crowns of their heads cut off. A single word among the Illinois conveyed the following: "Go get my wife and bring her to me, will she nill she, she is following another whom she loves." Such a word indicates a refusal to accept that a wife might love another. "Will she nill she," that is, with or without her consent, chillingly hints at coercion and implies, at least, the threat of violence from a larger community. So does the single word for "wife who leaves her husband and goes with another so that her husband threatens to cut off his nose." In this case, the person at the receiving end of physical punishment was the lover. Sources also suggest that, especially among the Miami-Illinois, adulterous wives were punished through horrific gang rapes, organized by the husband and tolerated by the community. In such moments, "her cries are futile." Indeed, such occasions seem to have been a horrendous form of male sociability.[26]

Historians have puzzled over the shocking brutality of these punishments for adultery, especially in cultures in which women appear to have had some degree of sexual autonomy. Some have contended that it was only captive wives who endured this degree of violence. It is true that captives did indeed suffer much. They had no rank, at least not initially. For instance, an early observer in the St. Lawrence River area, Pierre Biard, reported that when a Frenchman tried to stop an Indian man from beating his wife, the Indian, affronted, demanded: "How now, have you nothing to do but to see into my house, every time I strike my dog?" Biard summarized: "The comparison was bad, the retort was keen." But this "bad" comparison may reflect the fact that the word for "dog" was generally the same as that for "slave." This man's wife may also have been his slave. There has been little work on captivity in early moments of encounter in the St. Lawrence River area, but the Jesuit accounts make clear that it was part of life. Among the neighboring Wendat, the Jesuits recorded that a man poisoned himself because "his wife had been taken away from him." The context suggests that she had been taken captive.[27]

Yet there is limited evidence to suggest that it was exclusively enslaved women who faced fierce punishments for adultery. In part, the extreme violence of Illinois men may have been because of the greater likelihood that these wives were captives, but even this point is not clear. As we have already seen, even nonenslaved wives were often at some distance from natal kin. Sources imply that violence and its threat surrounded women, enslaved or otherwise, who violated household norms. Indeed, archaeologists have identified a high degree of cranial trauma among reproductive-age women in some of these areas going back centuries. These findings led them to argue that the likeliest explanation is that such women were survivors of spousal abuse—or abuse from other wives, though they may also have been captives. The fact that such bodies seem to have been accorded no special treatment in burial suggests that these forms of violence did not mark permanently altered status. In other words, it was not necessarily a population of women with a distinct status who suffered aggression. Rather, there was an endemic if low-lying level of violence against reproductive-age women that put them, as these scholars conclude, "in harm's way."[28]

Jesuits did not approve adultery, but they also did not approve punishments for it involving rape, disfigurement, or murder. So when Makheabichtichiou declared that he was forbidden to kill his wives, yet could not get rid of them, he may have been serious. Christianity may well have liberated some wives who found themselves on the receiving ends of brutal force, as captives or adulterous wives or both. As one scholar has noted, "In marriage coercive authority, elsewhere so weak in Algonquian society, stiffened." Makheabichtichiou's marriage, as with many, brought tensions between his need for authority as a householder and leader and the softer texture of affections and shared parenting.[29]

"His Proud Spirit"

Husbands like Makheabichtichiou defended their households because households provided power on every level. While Le Jeune deplored Makheabichtichiou's carnal tendencies, he conceded that the main problem was actually "his proud spirit." Pride was an aspect of being both a husband and a leader; they enhanced each other. A husband's status depended on the work his spouse(s) did. Indeed, one dictionary offered a single word for "I make him his house, he is my husband." There was a corresponding single word for "this is my wife, she makes my house, she gives me a place to live, she cares for me, she gives me food." For women, marriage meant work and children. Ideally, it also meant love, but it definitely included productive and reproductive labor. For men, marriage meant ideally love but also certainly having a home and children and the chance to offer hospitality to others which depended on the work of a wife—or of wives.[30]

"To live among us without a wife is to live without help, without housekeeping, always a vagabond." So declared Makheabichtichiou's rival Pigarouïch, who also wavered in his commitment to Christianity. Both men fretted that their status might be diminished by monogamy. To have no wife was to be a socially, economically, and politically disadvantaged man, a "vagabond" without a household of his own. Pigarouïch worried explicitly over the consequences of giving up multiple wives (an arrangement available to, and desirable for, a powerful healer) should his sole wife, by choice or necessity, leave him. A man who lost his wife, whether through divorce, captivity, or death, might literally become a vagabond, moving between other men's households. He would be cut off from a major source of strength and status. He would no longer be able to offer hospitality to visitors, ambassadors, and trading partners, a vital necessity for doing business in this world. He would become dependent on the hospitality of others, losing his social, economic, and even political position. Dictionaries reveal that it was possible to be a vagabond not only among strangers but also among one's own people. To be a "vagabond, without place, without fire" was a way of stating contemptuously in seventeenth-century French that a man had absolutely nothing. Such a man had no wife, no family, no home.[31]

Polygamy, then, was insurance for leaders. Men with high rank could not afford to become vagabonds in their own communities; it would have cost them not just personal happiness but political standing. A leader's exalted position depended on being a householder, on having a wife or wives who could "make their homes." Children also enhanced his status, and were thus more of a necessity than a luxury. Yet in the 1630s, times were perilous. Wars had intensified, thus increasing the likelihood of losing a spouse to capture. After all, to steal the wife of a leader was an aggressive political act. So one dictionary gave the phrase for "I marry his wife, I steal her away from him." An Innu dictionary offered: "I take by force the goods, the wife of others." It is unclear whether the goods include the wife, or whether the goods and the wife were both stolen. A third and fourth posed the question: "Have you ravished the wife of others?" One word in this phrase, *mingano,* was also a word in the phrase "to be a second wife." Such a point suggests that stolen wives—captives—and second wives might have been one and the same. The uptick in violence provoked by colonial rivalries over trade might have made such kidnapping of wives more common, a thing to be particularly feared in this period.[32]

At the same time, colonialism also increased the economic importance of households. Households generated resources, largely through women's work. Among the Algonquian-speaking peoples in general, women and men had distinct roles in the household economy. Women managed households. One early Jesuit summarized the gender division of labor: "The women know what they are to do, and the men also; and one never meddles with the work of the other." He noted, "Men go hunting, and kill the animals; and the women go after them, skin them, and clean the hides. It is they who go in search of the wood that is burned."[33] The preparation of anything that could be sewn, cleaned, cooked, or burned: such was the province of women. Days could be long, as wives and other women in the household worked together to collect wood; to grow, harvest, and prepare food; and to produce and

Front and back of Canadian Skin Shirt ("A Match-coat from Virginia of Deer-skin"), 1656. Courtesy of Tradescant Collection, Ashmolean Museum, University of Oxford.

repair clothing, housing, and other items. This labor is on display in one rare Native tunic, apparently the oldest surviving Indian skin garment, now in a museum in Oxford, England.

Fashioned from caribou skin, decorated with fringes and dyed porcupine quills, this long elaborate shirt would have been worn by a man—but created and sewn by women. To craft such a tunic would have required frost-drying the caribou skin, treating and softening it into workable fabric, collecting and dying porcupine quills, and sewing it all with sinew thread. The tunic has been mended, to fix a slash in the left chest area "perhaps sustained in fighting," a hardly unlikely event in this area in the seventeenth century. Makheabichtichiou may well have worn a similar tunic himself.[34] This elaborate garment would have showed the wearer's status: that he had talented artisans at home to make it for him.

The fur trade, and this tunic, bolstered the status of men, yet they were possible only with the sustained background labor of women. Discussions of the early fur trade focus on the men: European traders who bought the furs and indigenous men who did the hunting, which required considerable work and skill. However, households, not simply individual hunters and traders, underlay this commerce more broadly. Beaver and other furs are called "raw" materials, yet they required processing before they could be shipped. It was women who did this hard grind. Women retrieved and eviscerated animals in all weathers. They scraped away flesh with serrated bone knives. They cleaned the fur (and sometimes even chewed it to soften it). The processing time was limited; if furs were left untreated, they decomposed into worthlessness. So when winter hunts brought in lots of animals, women had to work long hours to ready them for trade. Anthropologists remind us that in predominantly hunter-gatherer societies, "A hunter who is not attached to a gatherer is a hungry man; a man who catches [animals] will have a pile of rotten flesh on his hands (and no clothing on his back) if he cannot find a woman who will process his catch."[35]

Yet Native American men in the seventeenth century wanted more than just clothing on their backs, even those elegantly decorated with colorful porcupine quills. Before French colonies, and even in their early years, complex ritual governed the fur trade among Native Americans. For instance, hunters carefully disposed of beaver bones in rivers or fires, not letting their hungry dogs gnaw at them. They apparently believed that the souls of slain beaver returned to see how they were treated, and, if thrown to the dogs, they would alert other beavers not to let themselves be caught. Bear bones and offal received even greater respect. The flesh of bear, and to a lesser extent beaver, were prized foods. Beaver, bear, and other furs also made warm winter clothing and embellishment.[36] This small-scale economy of fur, bound by ceremony, had been sustainable for centuries.

However, colonialism transformed the hunt and the fur trade. Native hunters scrambled to capture as many animals as possible, ignoring older niceties and rapidly depopulating beaver. They wanted guns, kettles, beads, and other items. If they killed a lot of animals at once, they also needed a lot of women to transform them into furs ready for trade. In other times and places, such a situation resulted in an increase in polygamy. It is difficult to know with certainty for this early period, but it is likely that reorientation to European markets, and a new emphasis on furs as commodities, not simply useful objects and status markers, also increased the importance of polygamy. Status depended even more dramatically on the work wives did.[37]

Marriage thus became even more important as a way of enhancing the economic and political power of men's status. As one anthropologist has observed, "it is virtually impossible to talk about marriage without also talking about social hierarchy." Marriage was critical for Algonquin (and other) leaders, especially self-made ones like Makheabichtichiou. Le Jeune contended that he had not inherited a position as a "capitaine." Rather, he had gained this position through his own actions, in a time of considerable flux and political reconfiguration. He seems to have been able to unite Algonquin and Innu peoples, which was unusual. He was also an astute diplomat, involved in negotiations with French officials (for instance, offering them a Haudenosaunee captive woman to cover the loss of three Frenchmen). His three wives both demonstrated and augmented his authority as a leader. While he seems to have been willing to compromise some aspects of his power (the feasts, the dreams), he may have felt that giving up his wives was a step too far. Marriage made possible political authority for men among Algonquin, Innu, and other peoples.[38]

Native men depended on the work their wives did. Pierre Biard explained why Native leaders were so loath to give up polygyny. He noted that it was "not because of lust (for this nation is not very unchaste) but for two other reasons." First, Biard explained, they sought "to retain their authority and power by having a number of children; for in that lies the strength of the house. Second, Biard continued, "is their entertainment and service, which is great and laborious." He concluded: "Now they have no other servants, slaves, or mechanics but the women. These poor creatures endure all the misfortunes and hardships of life." Female drudgery was a common trope for travel writers, a way of castigating indigenous men for laziness and tyranny. Such accounts should not be read literally. However, undeniably, women did a lot of work in these households. One word among the Innu summarized the conflation of the subordination of many women: *nitichkouemak*, which could be translated as "my daughters/girls, my wives/women, my servants." The labor of women, as providers of both hospitality and children, was highly significant in supporting "authority and power" and "the strength of the house." "Having a number of children" mattered a great deal, too.[39]

Although Jesuits labored to eradicate polygamy, their presence, along with that of other French settlers, may have had exactly the opposite effect. It was not simply that natives ceaselessly maintained the tradition. Polygamy may well have increased in importance. Novel economic orientations toward markets as well as political reconfigurations, such as that witnessed by a nonhereditary leader who united two disparate groups, may have disposed some men more strongly to polygamy. Men were looking for ways to shore up their position in moments of overhunting and uncertainty. Warfare and an increase in female captives may also have meant more households with one husband, many wives. Certainly, polygamy was defended aggressively throughout the seventeenth and eighteenth centuries, notably in Illinois country as well as along the Mississippi.[40]

"The Relatives of the Man"

Makheabichtichiou seems to have been willing to go along with the Jesuits in many things, but choice about his wives may not have been his to make. Le Jeune expected that this leader could decide for himself about his spouses. If he consented to giving up two wives, he could be baptized. But Le Jeune's position presupposes that the only or indeed the main actor in these households was the husband, and that the individual patriarch acted as he wished. In many French households, such indeed was the ideal (though not always the case). Yet it is unlikely to have worked the same way among Makheabichtichiou's people. This marriage was a crowded one. There were four adults in it, and many more children, and in-laws, and relatives. Taking these other participants seriously as actors, considering their motives and interests, allows us to see the ways in which even a powerful leader was still constrained by larger structures of households, economies, and kinship. It shows the enormous importance of family.

Alas, Le Jeune is a poor guide to these other voices; he did not even record the names of Makheabichtichiou's wives. There were so many tongues wagging in this time and place, yet in the sources, so few of them belong to indigenous women. This is unnatural. The women who were so central to making households are not represented fully. We must return, then, to Makheabichtichiou's words. He claimed to Le Jeune that he loved only one of his wives, the most recent, and that he had tried to send the other two away, to "their own country." However, they came back. He claimed that he hoped that one day he could make them go back to their own country. The one he said he loved had been baptized a Christian. This baptism flags a set of sources which, triangulated, gives us more information than we might have expected about Makheabichtichiou and his wives—including, astoundingly, all of their names. They were: Kanerouik, Ousaoumoukoueou, and Oupououkoue. Records suggest that the Christian and third wife, whom he married in 1637 and said he loved, was Oupououkoue; she was later listed as a godmother with the Christian name of Monique. When Makheabichtichiou sent Kanerouik and Ousaoumoukoueou away, they had returned, unbidden, and would not be dismissed, or so Makheabichtichiou and Le Jeune claimed. We also have evidence from Le Jeune that two of these wives were with him on a trip that proved fatal to him, and that they returned to the Algonquin "very wretched."[41]

Being "from another country" could mean any number of things. It could imply that they were from different clans of the same Algonquin band of la Petite Nation. Indeed, baptismal registers identify both Kanerouik and Oupououkoue, the third wife, as from la Petite Nation, though this designation is vague. It might mean they were now identified as la Petite Nation but had not started life this way. How the French saw *pays,* nation, was not how the people of the clan of the crane or the beaver saw it. The name of Kanerouik seems different from the names of the other wives; it sounds more like a Haudenosaunee name than an Anishinaabe one. Perhaps Kanerouik was a captive wife. We don't know, but it's plausible. We know that Makheabichtichiou had earlier offered a captive Haudenosaunee woman to the French, so such women were part of his world. The Jesuits claimed of this time and place that "many a young man will not hesitate even to marry a captive, if she is very industrious; and thereafter she will pass as a woman of his country."[42]

We do not know how industrious these three wives were; we do not know much about them at all. Yet the baptismal records reveal a few facts. They show first that although one wife did convert to Christianity, the other two did not. Whatever Makheabichtichiou's ambitions might have been, two wives would not accept baptism. Here, then, were two plural wives not so keen to escape oppressive polygamy that they were willing either to convert to Christianity or to renounce their husband, despite Jesuit and indeed their own husband's apparent desires for them to do so. This situation was not unique. Another husband in a plural union reported that although one wife was baptized, the other wife was "cold towards the faith," but he did not "wish to repudiate" her, a possible echo of Makheabichtichiou's domestic arrangement.[43] Records also show that indigenous naming practices continued, even though French Christian names also appear.

That two of Makheabichtichiou's wives refused to be baptized suggests their agency. This lack of embrace of Christianity, as well as

Makheabichtichiou's own reports, might also suggest that they did not wish to end their polygamous marriage. In these early years of encounter, and in the lands of the Algonquin and the Innu, women seem to have felt ambivalence about plural unions. Perhaps it is fairer to state that some women rejected them, but others benefited from, or at least accepted, them. Among the Innu, some women refused to be secondary wives; dictionaries offered phrases such as "I do not marry a married man" and "I will not marry a man who already has a wife." This rejection demonstrates that some women did not wish to live in plural unions as secondary wives. Yet it also suggests that women in Innu cultures had a choice. It may be as much of a rejection of being a secondary wife as a plural one, given the often subordinate status of secondary wives. It may be additional, not first, plural wives who found monogamy or even celibacy more appealing (in the ways historians have noted); after all, they tended to be lower in the household hierarchy, especially if they had entered as captives. First or senior wives usually managed the household. For first wives, but not for subsequent ones, plural marriage may have had costs, but it would have also enhanced their own status and the productivity of their household. For others, quite simply, family mattered more than marriage or the individual. Polygamous unions created children, united clans, furthered diplomacy, and enhanced economic units of the households. Such goals may have made polygamy acceptable for some, especially when it involved sisters who stayed together and built their own household. Like men, women gained status and children by being married. Also, the relations between wives, who worked together on a daily basis and with the husband frequently away for hunting or war, may have been at least sometimes positive. Whether they liked each other or not, they often had to work together: to feed their children and their selves; to clothe and warm everyone in cold winters; to keep life going. One word that a wife could use for "the other wife of my husband" also meant "my companion." This word could imply service, but it also implies roughly equivalent rank, as well as friendship and familiarity.[44]

Women also helped to take care of one another's children. Biological motherhood was probably less important than a relationship of mothering. In the Miami-Illinois language, the word for "mother" could also mean "maternal aunt." It could even mean all female descendants of a maternal uncle. These linguistic conflations suggest the close connections that could exist between these female relatives. A child might address as "Mother" a considerable range of female relations. In Miami-Illinois cultures, there may have been a greater possibility of such mothering relations among wives who were also sisters. Sibling relations were highly significant, and sisters may have shared labor as well as affections for children of a household. Kinship evidently shaped even the afterlife. Le Jeune worked hard to convince Makheabichtichiou that it was impossible that good and bad people in the same family could go to the same place after death, thus implying that Makheabichtichiou and his compatriots believed exactly that.[45]

Family relations could ameliorate even captivity. A wife such as Kaner-ouik, who might once have been captive, might well have been integrated through marriage, passing for "a woman of his country" and gaining status. Incorporating foreign wives was common in patrilocal cultures like those of the Algonquin and Innu. Children in plural unions do not seem to have had a hierarchy based on their mother's status, as in some other polygamous cultures. Rather, each probably had a position based on sex and age in relation to sisters and brothers, because sibling relations mattered so much. Kinship terminology picked out distinctions in the sex and age of siblings in careful ways. Having many siblings was an advantage; children in larger households enjoyed the connections, though also of course suffered the rivalries, of having many siblings. They also had a wide range of kin opportunities from which to draw in life.[46]

Such family relations were critical. Indeed, it was a grave insult, "vox injuriosa," to call someone an orphan. In centering abandonment, "orphan" dripped contempt, but it was not a literal truth. This word implied that no one cared about that person, who therefore lacked any meaningful ability to mobilize kinship, property, or affection. Family links, when acknowledged, conferred status, constrained behavior, and structured society. The extended family supported, though also exerted pressure on, individuals, women and men. One French observer contended that brothers had a say in a sister's choice of husband, as did fathers and mothers. In a marriage, such family involvement meant that the woman could appeal to her brother and her parents if the marital situation turned out not to be to her liking.[47]

Family interventions could be profound and violent. If a husband died before the marriage was consummated, this same French observer claimed, "the women are to be pitied, for the relatives of the man continually reproach her with his death." Such a widow had to wait to remarry, and if she married too soon, her former in-laws had the right to kill her. Another French traveler, Nicolas Perrot, concurred: "If the husband dies, the wife cannot marry again unless the man is one to the liking of the mother-in-law, and after two years of mourning." Indeed, the widow had to accept the choice of new husband by her parents-in-law "without the power to refuse him—for the parents of the deceased are masters of her body." Yet conversely, a widower had also to observe two years of mourning and to take a new wife chosen by his mother-in-law. If he did not abide by these rules, the costs were high for his new wife: "If he disobeyed this rule all the relatives of his deceased wife would heap a thousand indignities on the woman whom he had taken without such consent; and if he had two wives, they would do the same to the other one." Perrot claimed that the brothers and cousins of the deceased wife might even "carry away his new wife and violate her; and this act would be considered by disinterested persons as having been legitimately perpetrated": another community-sanctioned gang rape of a wife (not an enslaved one), another show of force between men over the larger household unit and its sanctity.[48] Women paid an unduly heavy price for the violation of household order, but both women and men lived under the power of this larger unit and its inexorable demands. Makheabichtichiou may have been constrained by the desires of his wives or his or their families; he emphasized that they did not do as he wished, refusing to return to their own country.

Children may also have affected this situation, and there were many of them here. At least one child of each wife received baptism, so even if two wives were never baptized, each one of them apparently agreed to having children baptized. Le Jeune told stories in which husbands and wives disagreed about this decision. He recounted one situation in which a man had to convince his wife to baptize their ailing son, as she worried that it would prove fatal (since so many recently baptized children died). Somewhat miraculously, according to Le Jeune, following the baptism, the son was finally able to nurse and became "fine-looking and plump, the joy of his parents, and the admiration of those who saw him in his sickness." Baptisms may have seemed another form of insurance for families in peril. The first baptism of any of Makheabichtichiou's children took place in 1635. This baptism was of an older boy, listed as ill, so perhaps a somewhat desperate measure. No further baptisms took place until 1638, suggesting that it may have taken years to persuade wives to allow them. There might have been other reasons for the hiatus, but other baptisms did occur in this period in this area. With Kanerouik, Makheabichtichiou had at least two baptized children.

With Ousaoumoukoueou, Makheabichtichiou had one baptized child. With Oupououkoue, he had two baptized children, one of whom died within a year. Three other children died whose mothers are not listed. One adult son later died without baptism "like a dog," according to *Jesuit Relations*. The relatively advanced ages of one son (born around 1615) suggests that Makheabichtichiou was middle-aged by the 1630s. Kanerouik had apparently had a child in 1623 and another in 1637, a fourteen-year span suggesting that she was also probably in or near her thirties in 1638.[49]

At least one of these mothers, possibly all of them, had buried a child; so had the father. The deaths read in the register neutrally, but each line witnessed a beloved child gone, a family and community struck by grief, and, in the long-term family strategy, a line of kinship extinguished. It mattered both emotionally and materially for fathers and mothers, for uncles and aunts, for brothers and sisters, for others in the household and beyond. They may simply have been unlucky, but the 1630s were a peculiarly perilous era. In just five years, there were four major epidemics in this area. In 1634 there was measles, in 1636 influenza. The epidemic of 1637 cannot be identified, but it was often fatal. The worst scourge of all came in 1639: smallpox. Almost every year another wave of disease engulfed people and killed thousands; children were the most vulnerable. Such epidemics also wreaked havoc on food supplies, as they often struck in summer and early autumn: just at harvest time when able bodies were needed most. Even those who did not fall ill were too busy tending the sick and dying to gather and store vegetables, fruit, and seeds, nor could they dry out and preserve meat brought in from hunting parties—if those parties could even go out in the first place. The result then was hunger and, as a consequence, further vulnerability to disease, which is partly why epidemics nipped at the heels of epidemics. Le Jeune summarized: "These poor people do not know to what cause to attribute the mortality among them." Later that year, one Indian came to ask the French why they survived when his people "were becoming visibly depopulated." Makheabichtichiou himself reported that his compatriots blamed the Jesuits for disease, but claimed that he had told them, "No harm could happen to us than is [already] happening every day, for we are dying every moment."[50]

In the 1630s, devastation sounded in so many ways: war whoops, the firing of arquebuses, the gasping breaths of a child trying to suck air into little lungs, the dreadful silence of a small lifeless body. Parents could never fill the void. But they could offset the stillness of death with sounds of life, the insistent cries of a newborn, squalling against the harsh light and cold of the world. With their tiny fingers and milky heads, babies joined families who greeted them with love and joy, even when their mothers were captives or otherwise subordinate. Children were precious. When Le Jeune asked Pigarouïch about worries over whether adultery might compromise paternity, Pigarouïch scoffed: "You have no sense. You French people love only your own children; but we all love all the children of our tribe." Jesuits were not especially delighted with this evenhanded love for the young. The Jesuits wanted children to leave family and go to school, so they hardly applauded what they termed "the extraordinary tenderness that savage women have for their children."[51]

Such remarkable maternal affection comes through even in simple stories. In 1634, Le Jeune reported the funeral of an eight-month-old boy, Pichichich, who had, in his illness, been baptized and named Adrian after his French godfather. Although Le Jeune emphasized the actions of the child's father, Tchimaourineou, in fact, his entire extended family brought him for burial: "His Father did not fail to bring the body, having with him eighteen or twenty Savages, men, women, and children." Such women and men included his mother, Matouetchiousanouecoueou. The softest beaver furs and expensive imported linen swaddled the body of this "poor little child." At the moment of lowering the small coffin into the ground, "his mother placed his cradle therein . . . and soon after she drew some of her milk in a little bark ladle, which she burned immediately." Le Jeune puzzled over why she had done so. "A woman answered me that she was giving drink to the child, whose soul was drinking this milk. I instructed her upon this point, but I still speak the language so poorly that I scarcely made her understand me."[52]

Despite the difficulties of communication, what comes through in these gestures is the "extraordinary tenderness" of a heartbroken mother whose last act for her baby was to ensure that he had mother's milk even when he could no longer suckle. It was also an important ritual and performance of grief. At the funeral, the Jesuits rejoiced in the timely baptism of Adrian and the progress of the faith, so that "this little Canadian angel," as Le Jeune called him, could "fly to heaven." His death did not matter so much to them; what counted was his everlasting life through baptism. Others felt differently; his own father wavered about Christianity. His mother, Matouetchiousanouecoueou, saw Pichichich given milk for an afterlife populated by family members and animal spirits, in a place reachable through dreams and signs. As other women sighed, contemplating the horrors of their times, the warm, insistent tug of a baby's mouth at the breast could keep them grounded. It provided a sort of weary hope, even when other children, other family, had "flown to heaven," to the world of dreams and spirits. Such women might well have included Makheabichtichiou's own grieving wives, who had also mothered his children. To see plural marriages only in terms of jealousy, to assume that the sexual attention of husbands was women's highest or only interest, is to miss what might have been a greater priority for these tender "savage women": their children.[53]

War's menacing efficacy radiated so far beyond the actual deaths in combat, removing young men disproportionately from families as well as communities. Many women wanted to be wives and especially mothers; it became increasingly difficult for them to be either without men. War altered the tenor of such household relations. Simple demographics, a sex ratio in which women came to outnumber men greatly, cannot explain the complicated individual decisions that people made about marriage and children. Yet the terrible circumstances wrought by the wars of colonialism may have made polygamy especially attractive: for men, but also, perhaps, for women. It enhanced their chance of being part of a household and, more particularly, their chance of being respected mothers in those households, even if they had started as captives or secondary wives. It gave them a form of security and caretaking for children, as too many around them perished.

Women who endured these disasters were strong. They were not deluded or too oppressed to comprehend their own grim realities, whatever travelers and visitors may have asserted about their "drudgery." Women may have chosen to share a husband because even a half or a third of a husband could give them full children, households full of children. This choice may not have been the preferred one; consider those dictionaries which showed women stating: "I do not marry a married man." Still, even being a second or third wife might have seemed preferable to being no wife at all. Makheabichtichiou himself reported to the Jesuits, "Since I have been preaching . . . that a man should have only one wife I have not been well received by the women; for, since they are more numerous than the men, if a man can only marry one of them, the others will have to suffer. Therefore this doctrine is not according to their liking." The women may have found it particularly galling that a man with three wives should have been preaching against polygamy. On the other hand, his sense of the demographics suggests more than simply disaffection with a hypocritical leader. Despite the assumptions of historians about women's desire to escape polygamy, it may not have been so simple.[54]

What is clear is that in every area of life strictly under Makheabichti-chiou's control, he did what Jesuits wanted. However, he seems to have been constrained in ways beyond his control when it came to his family life. Even for this leader, all the power was not his; it was shared with his wives, his children, his relatives, his extended family. Such larger entities structured, cushioned, and constrained individuals in these cultures.

"Fort & Hardi"

The tale of one husband who would not—or could not—give up his wives demonstrates the awesome power of the family in indigenous leadership, politics, conversion, and colonialism. Living as purportedly celibate men among men, Jesuits almost willfully ignored the significance of ties to women and children. As men like Le Jeune recorded their mounting frustrations with men like Makheabichtichiou, they failed to see the larger networks that both buoyed up and limited even a powerful leader like him. To their minds, if he did not choose to cast aside wives and children to be legally monoga-mous, then he did not deserve baptism. This exclusion surrounded even powerful, otherwise Christian men like Makheabichtichiou. Missionaries and many others underplayed the power of households and the women in them in almost every kind of source they left; even their drawings failed often to include women, as in the otherwise vividly illustrated Codex Canadensis. In this codex, there were beautiful images of "capitaines" with potent political symbols of peace pipes and spears. Yet there were no Native families depicted and only one Native woman; these leaders were here, as elsewhere, weirdly detached from the households on which their power actually depended.[55]

Although Jesuits and others saw it merely as an "obstacle" to converting Indians, polygamy was here, as elsewhere, a political choice for men. Polygamy was critical to rank and status as well as to gender. Yet its presence also reveals something of the emotional tenor of life as an indigenous person surviving colonialism. Allegedly archaic practices like polygamy could go together with progressive practices such as an emphasis on love and even mutual sexual pleasure in marriage. Still, love did not mean liberty. Families limited the options of individuals, even powerful ones like Makheabichtichiou. House-holds helped individuals survive colonial catastrophes, but it also held them in

Capitaine de la Nation

Louis Nicolas, Codex Canadensis, ca. 1700. This "capitaine" is depicted holding and smoking the calumet, or peace pipe, a potent political symbol. He also holds a spear. He is adorned and decorated in ways indicating high rank. Courtesy of Gilcrease Museum, Tulsa, Oklahoma.

check in particular ways. Marriage shaped the nature of colonialism. This particular Jesuit mission, and many others elsewhere and later, failed, largely because of plural unions. Without this "obstacle," the story of these encounters would have been different. There were many reasons for the refusal of these powerful leaders to give up their wives. There may also have been good reasons that their wives also did not choose monogamy and Christianity. At the same time, colonial encounters also reshaped marriages. Colonialism changed so much: politics, economies, environment, and demographics. All of these factors amplified the importance of women's labors, productive and reproductive. These sea changes propelled new situations in even what seemed like the timeless institution of polygamy.

Violence accompanied these transformations. On a diplomatic trip among the Wabanaki, attended by at least two of his wives, Makheabichtichiou was killed, dying unbaptized and far from his own people. "Behold the end of those who shut their ears to the voice of God who is calling them," intoned Le Jeune portentously when he wrote of this death. Le Jeune also declared Makheabichtichiou's whole family "ruined," his returning wives "wretched." Le

Jeune's language echoed, probably deliberately, a passage from the sixth chapter of Luke: "But he that heareth, and doeth not, is like a man that without a foundation built an house, . . . and immediately it fell; and the ruin of that house was great." For Le Jeune, the death of the unbaptized patriarch, who heard but did not convert, "ruined" the whole family.[56] This "savage" had refused to the bitter end to bend to French colonial household practices.

However, the story does not, cannot, end with a bleeding husband or smug Jesuit pontifications. It is time to still the ever-wagging tongues and quills of men. In the quiet, there is the soft crunch of women's feet on the snow. Along the frigid horizon, two huddled figures, two "wretched" wives, come into view, trudging slowly. It was winter. It would not have been an easy trip. Together, though, they did not get lost in these great woods, despite the cold and the snow. Kanerouik might have offered a steadying hand to Ousaoumoukoueou when she stumbled in the deep banks—and vice versa. They may have had babies on their backs or in their bellies, bodies coursing with blood and milk to nourish children. Although women traveled light, they carried a lot with them. Yet the likelihood is that at least some of these women's children were in the care of other mothers, elsewhere. Those networks of family would have influenced, limited, and helped them, even as they seemed to be lone figures on the white horizon. These two women probably left the Wabanaki in shock and grief, but they faced forward, insistently heading home. They had survived violence, their husband shot and killed. Yet they were not ruined, nor did they disappear, as so many have claimed Indians did. They were widows now, but still connected to each other: by children, by household, by labor, perhaps by love. Le Jeune shut his own ears to these voices. He did not see—or chose not to see—the everyday heroics and endurance of polygamous wives and their children. For Le Jeune, Makheabichtichiou was a person abounding in courage, "fort & hardi." He was. But Kanerouik, Ousaoumoukoueou, and Oupououkoue, surviving widows and mothers, were, too.

3. "Christians Have Kept 3 Wives"

Colonial wars created strange households. Two suffering wives found themselves living in the same tight space, jostling with babies, bedrugs, and stockings. Normally, both were privileged women, mothers of beloved children, respected members of their communities. They would not ordinarily have lived in the same house. In the close-knit chaos of these temporary quarters, though, the situation was different. Each saw the other up close and personal. They were so jammed up together that each could feel the warm breath of the other, smell the other's sweat, hear the other's snores at night. Neither was happy about it. Both had similar concerns: protecting their children, families, and communities in a time of war. However, shared interests did not forge affections. The two women loathed each other for personal reasons, as they squabbled over resources and authority in a time of flight and confusion. They also loathed each other for political reasons, as enemies in a war that devastated the homes of both. One was the war captive of the other.

The captor was Weetamoo, sachem, or leader, of the Pocasset, who came from the coastal area of what is now southern New England. The captive was one of New England's most famous: Mary Rowlandson. Their confrontation was about a war—King Philip's War, to use the name the English applied to the sachem—in 1675–76. Yet it was also about a clash between forms of household and political organization, and the painful human encounters that welled up from colonial confrontations. Placing marriage at the center of this story illuminates how individual husbands and wives navigated changes and continuities in seventeenth-century New

England. For colonists, polygamy had been a distant, exotic practice, known mainly through the Old Testament. For Indians, polygamy had long been an elite practice, and became only more so under pressures of colonialism. Marriage and households were, as elsewhere, key arenas for governance and the demonstration of authority, as well as for fierce conflicts over it. These intimate encounters vexed, and transformed, both sides.

Although often marginalized even in accounts of the war, Weetamoo was one of the most important women in seventeenth-century New England and arguably its most powerful female leader. Arms heavy with bracelets of alternating dark and light wampum, earrings gleaming under powdered hair, she was so prosperous and commanding that she appeared in the pages of numerous English accounts as the "proud dame" who struck fear into the hearts of settlers. One New England author described her "as Potent a Prince as any round about her, [who] hath as much Corn, Land, and Men at her Command" as did King Philip—or Metacom—himself. In fact, this same author claimed that when Metacom considered launching an attack on the English in 1675, his first action was to secure Weetamoo's vital support. Metacom knew that without it, war against the English would be impossible. Once the fighting began, she "had greater Success than King *Philip* himself." Even discounting that this New England author might have been implying, in a classic gendered insult, that Philip's leadership wasn't as impressive as that of a woman, other sources echo this assessment of her strength. One recent account of the war, which ended with great losses for both sides but victory for the English in 1676, notes, rightly, that the war "is better described as a multitribal Indigenous resistance movement during colonial expansion, a complex series of alliances forged by multiple leaders including Metacom and Weetamoo."[1] At the least, as shorthand for a resistance movement advanced by many indigenous women and men, we might stop calling it King Philip's War and start calling it Metacom and Weetamoo's War. After all, as even enemies recognized at the time, no Weetamoo, no war.

Yet Weetamoo, this powerful leader, was the third of three wives of Quinnapin, himself the sachem of the Narragansetts. This situation is unexpected. Secondary plural wives were often less powerful than the first one. As one English observer framed it in the 1620s, wives beyond the first one could be like "servants and yeeld a kinde of obedience to the principall [wife], who ordereth the family, and them in it." This point may be overdrawn, but still it was generally the case for Algonquian people that the first wife was the senior one, and most likely to be the manager of the household. For one woman to be both a sachem and a third wife was rather unusual. However, this particular secondary wife was a commander and a manager herself, one who gave "severe" orders to Mary Rowlandson and others. This exceptional marital situation reveals a people in flux, coping with colonialism in creative ways. It illuminates the complex dynamics of rank and gender among indigenous people in terrains that were shifting in terms both of borders and of complex intercultural relations.[2]

New England settlers also wondered about polygamy in these changing worlds. Their beloved Old Testament celebrated the successes of holy polygamists, including Abraham, David, and Solomon. Yet God apparently no longer allowed polygamy. How could this change be explained? Did the ancient patriarchs have a special dispensation, no longer available except perhaps to those who were unaware of their sin? How could Christians account for such change over time? Protestants, especially Calvinists, tried to hew closely to the Old Testament. They were the people of the Book, in the mocking words of one critic, "new men, with the scriptures much in mouth and hand." These issues did not remain theoretical; they affected the laws and practices of New England inhabitants. As ministers and others wrestled with these thorny issues, New England settlers also confronted the lived realities of plural marriages. They knew from travel literature that Indians practiced "polygamie," but soon they found themselves existing amid it. It unsettled a bit, this vivid, living polygamy. Yet English responses could be more muted than we might have expected of such puritanical folk: another surprise.[3]

Could polygamists be blessed? Wattapahtihinnit, a Wampanoag living in what is now Martha's Vineyard and contemplating Christianity, wondered about this question; John Cotton, New England minister, did, too. Natives and settlers, women and men, also pondered how their households could best support their authority, as well as the good order and hierarchies of society more broadly. Individuals questioned how marriage was supposed to work: for themselves, their families, their communities. They also made choices about marriage in order to respond to changing environments and priorities. Here, as elsewhere, polygamy could seem both a means of unleashing disorder and a way of containing it. It provoked many questions.

Did seventeenth-century New Englanders have more questions than other people, or did they just record them more frequently? Either way,

Native Americans and settlers alike seemed to ask questions about everything. In part, people of the Book, with scriptures in hand, mulled over its meanings. Settlers wondered, debated, and bickered over the Bible and much else; so did Native Americans. Questions could serve many purposes. They expressed the fundamentally apprehensive and searching quality of reformed Protestantism in New England. They were a teaching tool. They highlighted varieties of opinion and forced elucidations, sometimes highlighting conventions. They needled hypocrisies. In other words, questions could speak truth to power. Keeping a record of them was a way of taming the more awkward ones and of ensuring that subsequent generations knew that the right had been pursued, even if not always followed. Studying the questions people asked in the past helps us to see how the world looked to them, as women and men struggled to make sense of their changing times.

Both sides can seem immutable and even monolithic in these encounters: anxious English Christians obsessed with God's laws and their own elusive righteousness, Native Americans shielding ancient traditions and possessions in the face of European invasion. Yet in fact, both sides were full of questions and in transition, even their seeming timelessness a product of their times. The seventeenth century was a period of innovation and change, in part because of colonialism and the problems of governance it provoked. There has been a great deal of vital work over the past twenty years on Metacom and Weetamoo's War, one of the most studied of early America's fierce wars. Marriage and gender in New England's indigenous and borderlands encounters in the seventeenth century have also received considerable attention. However, there has as yet been no account of the war centering marriage and households. Dropping down into one polygamous household allows us to see the context and its dynamics with greater clarity. The particular era in which New England leaders crafted their laws affected the settlers, as they struggled to ensure that Old Testament laws underpinned dynamic colonial societies. The changes wrought by colonialism, as well as creative responses to it, also come through, as Native communities had altered in terms of rank and political organization. Both societies centralized, and the political economy shifted. It is helpful, then, to dive deep into understandings of marriage and polygamy on both sides, starting with theories of polygamy and moving to the practice of it. These critical conflicts between marital and social systems, and people, played out as much in women's cramped sleeping quarters as in swamps with lead shot whizzing past.[4]

"All Ye Patriarcks Did Sin Against God in Their Polygamie"

"You may well thinke that all ye Patriarcks did sin against God in their polyg-amie, but yet you never read, that their consciences were troubled about it, or [that] God did punish [them] for it." This theological conundrum occupied many authors, including John Cotton, one of New England's founding ministers. How was it that behavior acceptable "in old times of ignorance," such as polygamy, should not be so now? How could modern people account for this shift? Cotton pondered the issue in a sermon he delivered at Boston's First Church, probably in the 1640s. Cotton was "teacher" at this church, a prestigious position he held until his death in 1652. He had been a major figure even in old England. Educated in that hotbed of reform Emmanuel College, Cambridge University, Cotton became a minister in East Anglia, the region most noted for its fiery Protestants. At his church in Boston, Lincolnshire, Cotton proceeded to reorganize liturgy to reflect his reformed beliefs. When John Winthrop departed England with the Massachusetts Bay Company in 1630, Cotton preached the farewell sermon. This high-profile activity brought him to the attention of that scourge of the puritans William Laud. When the summons to the Court of High Commission came, Cotton, along with his pregnant wife, Sarah, fled to Boston in New England in 1633.[5]

Some of the most heated Protestants such as the Cottons crossed the frigid ocean to create a pure and gathered church, forging what one scholar calls a "puritan Atlantic." In the words of Cotton's own 1640s catechism, this church in New England was to be a "Congregation of Saints joyned together in the bond of the Covenant." New England was a place of religious experi-mentation and Utopianism, and multiple attempts to put the law of the Old Testament, unperverted by "papist superstition," into modern legal and social realities. The Old Testament patriarchs were in many respects moral exemplars for these settlers. Indeed, one historian of seventeenth-century New England has noted, "The Abraham of the Old Testament resonated deeply with English men in the New World, as he embodied the ideal of the householder-patriarch." Yet there was a stumbling block here: Abraham was a householder-patriarch who lived in a plural union.[6] It took some of the most elaborate reasoning to make sense of these complications. Polygamy raised theological, as well as legal, conundrums, so it received attention.

The vast majority of reformers of Cotton's era favored monogamy as the building block of society. Still, there was a variety of opinions about polygamy. Two sixteenth-century controversies involving the complicated

[Unknown], John Cotton[, Senior]. Although the sitter is not formally identified, it was probably John Cotton. The learned minister, his library behind him, is here represented as "the man of the Book," with even his collar echoing the pages of the Bible itself. Courtesy of Connecticut Historical Society.

marital and inheritance needs of two rulers, Henry VIII of England and Philip, Landgrave of Hesse, brought these issues to the forefront. A number of leading Continental theologians, including Martin Luther, Martin Bucer, and others, argued that it would be better for Henry VIII to have two wives rather than to divorce Catherine of Aragon. There was an even clearer statement in a similar situation for Philip of Hesse, in which Luther, Bucer, and Melanchthon allowed that bigamy might be acceptable, noting: "what was permitted concerning marriage in the law of Moses [the Old Testament] is not forbidden."[7]

The problem of polygamy also vexed Anglophone reformers including William Ames, another Cambridge-educated East Anglian, whose work on conscience was among New England's "standard manuals for Calvinist theology." There was general accord on the two central reasons for marriage:

"the first end is the begetting of children, the second end is a remedie against lust." Most writers focused on Adam and Eve, who became one flesh: "Polygamie is contrary to the first institution of God, for God made one man and one woman, and not one man and two women." Polygamy was thus a "sinne against the first institution and law of Marriage." Scholars also emphasized the injunction in Leviticus (18:27) ordering that a man should not take a sister as a plural wife. Most agreed that this rule was against multiple wives, not literal sisters as wives. Reformers also gestured to society, history, and nature in ways that would reappear in centuries to come. For Ames, only three of the eight reasons given for polygamy's unlawfulness had explicit backing from biblical verses, an unusually low number for theological tracts of the era. Ames contended that polygamy was a "sinne against the law of nature and right reason," against both instinct and "conjugall affection." He also argued that fowl were monogamous, so humans should match "brute beasts." Polygamy also subverted the proper care of progeny and broke the golden rule. Another reforming author, John Weemes, also stacked up reasons relating to nature and society, defining polygamy as "a middle sinne betwixt fornication and adultery, less then adultery, and greater then fornication."[8]

"The Ancient Fathers Were Generally Polygamists"

The polygamous patriarchs haunted these defenders of monogamy. According to Ames, "Those ancient Fathers, who married more Wives then one, cannot bee excused, unless they had some singular dispensation." But did they? For all his certitude about polygamy, Ames was not sure: "Wee cannot affirme any thing for certaine, then that God tolerated some such things in them." The polygamy of the blessed patriarchs also gnawed at John Weemes, who noted that they "through a general custome thought it no sinne" which "extenuated the sinne." He had to concede that "the Prophets spake little or nothing against polygamie, as they did against adultery." Like Ames, he also left the issue open: "None could ever shew this dispensation." He contended that it was not a "sinne pardoned" but merely among those "*sinnes passed by.*" When the Old Testament patriarch David was forgiven for adultery, "he got pardon likewise of his polygamie which he knew not to bee sinne." For Weemes, it was not *knowing* its wickedness that made the difference. He concluded that "Polygamie was a sin of ignorance." Yet ignorance could no longer excuse: "If a man should marry moe wives at once now, it should be flat adultery." Yet fancy rhetorical footwork did not entirely solve the problem. Indeed, polygamy was so vexing that it appeared even in texts which had virtually nothing to do with marriage, including one arguing for the necessity of war against the king in 1642. The author, John Goodwin, contended that when a good man committed a bad act, his character did not make the behavior acceptable. In the same way, "The ancient Fathers were generally Polygamists; yet the plenty of their practise is but a defective proof of the lawfulnesse of Polygamy."[9]

One author undaunted by patriarchal polygamy was the poet John Milton. It is one of the delicious ironies of the history of marriage that the author most associated with the tale of Adam and Eve, the biblical account used to justify indissoluble monogamy and so dazzlingly portrayed by him in *Paradise Lost,* argued in favor of both polygamy and divorce. He did not live long enough to publish his views on polygamy, but he explicated them thoroughly. That only two should become one flesh held no weight. Milton contended that the polygamy of the blessed patriarchs was proof of its righteousness: "Polygamy is either marriage or else it is whoredom or adultery. . . . Let no one dare to say that it is whoredom or adultery—respect for so many polygamous patriarchs will, as I hope, stop him!" Patriarchs whom God "loved supremely" could hardly be dismissed as "whoremongers and adulterers," their progeny rejected as "bastards." After all, how could it be that "so many men of the highest rank sinned throughout so many centuries" or that "God would have endured it in his own people?" Milton also pointed to the silence of most of the rest of the Bible: "Absolutely no trace of the reproving of polygamy is seen in the whole law . . . not even in all of the prophets, although these were . . . constant reprovers of the people's vice." There was also no New Testament condemnation: "How can an act be dishonourable or base which even under the gospel . . . is prohibited to no one?" Even if few at the time read this defense, these kinds of arguments pricked at those who defended monogamy.[10]

So we return to John Cotton—and his sermon. What made the "Patriarcks" different from Christians in seventeenth-century New England? For Cotton, as for Weemes, the Old Testament figures committed merely "a sinne of ignorance." Since modern Christians should know better, though, the practice of polygamy now would provoke "a sting in o[u]r Conscience." How was such a thing possible? In a different sermon, Cotton made clear the issue: despite being "defiled with Polygamie," David was at peace because it was no sin for him. By contrast, when David committed adultery and murder, acts he knew to be wrong, "then the [joy] of Gods salvation was dampened in him." It was knowledge that "pricked" him and made these actions sinful, a problem for Christians. What such an understanding suggested, though, was that polygamy was not intrinsically sinful, or damning in its very nature. It may have been defiling, but God's blessing could still attend those who practiced it. That is where it was a real problem. Ardent reformers, ever mindful of "the *corruption* that is in the *naughty heart* of Man," knew that women and men needed marriage as one of the central "remedies against lust."[11]

Old Testament backing for marital and sexual law can seem clear-cut and unchanging, but it actually represents an innovative theological legalism, specific to its time and place. Those who created New England's legal codes were busy "new men," seeking to create societies more consonant with "Moses his Judicials," or Old Testament law, in a style of jurisprudence one scholar has termed "Mosaic legalism." Starting in the late sixteenth century and continuing until the mid-seventeenth century—just the period of New England's settlement by the English—theorists sought to distinguish perpetual and unchangeable law from laws specific to particular periods and people, for example the ancient Jews. New England settlers were among the most enthusiastic in seeking to "build a bridge between the world of the ancient Jews and of early modern Christians." Putting Old Testament laws into practice was not a simple process, though. After all, there were three kinds of law stemming from the Old Testament. First, there was the moral law, perpetual and immutable, expressed in the Ten Commandments, binding to Jews and Christians alike, forever. Second, there was ceremonial law, ordinances (such as avoiding pork) specific to the time and place of ancient Israel. Jesus had fulfilled the law and negated the need for such ceremonies. In some cases, such as divorce, he had specifically condemned existing laws, so ceremonial laws could—and should—be ignored. Finally, there was judicial law, which should shape civil society. This last category provoked the most questions, as Protestants disagreed over its status. Some reformers argued that nonceremonial Old Testament policies supported the moral law. Indeed, Cotton's draft of a consideration of "how far Moses Judicialls bind Mass[achusetts]" opened with the following key question: "whether we as X[Chris]tians or as people of god, are not bound to establish the Lawes & penalties set down in the script[ure]. as they were given to the Jewes." According to another seventeenth-century minister, Charles Chauncy, the "judicials of Moyses, that are appendages to the morall law," were, like the moral law itself, "grounded on the law of nature," thus "immutable and perpetuall."[12] What did Cotton and Chauncy mean? To understand better such high-flown legal theology, it helps to turn to something a little more down to earth.

"The More Any Law Smells of Man the More Unprofitable"

If one man held another man's erect penis in his hand, was it "sodomy," or did there have to be "penetration of the body"? If the second man then ejaculated ("contactus et fricatio usque ad effusionem seminis"), did that make it sodomy? If the acts occurred "with frequencie and long continuance with a high hand," did that constitute sodomy? If the only witness to these acts was one of the men involved, and the other man denied it, was a conviction possible, in a legal system that generally required two witnesses? Was it permissible for a godly magistrate to extract a confession using "racks, hote-irons, etc"? Could women, too, commit sodomy? These questions, and the effects of "the sinfull, base, cruell lusts of the profane," preoccupied people in Plymouth colony in 1642, despite the busy pamphleteers and distracting turbulence in Britain that same year. Ministers including Charles Chauncy parsed these points with precision, leaving a remarkable record in William Bradford's *History of Plymouth Plantation*. Although such minute analysis by New England's learned heads is a surprise, the answers mattered, as at least one man's life was in the balance. A sodomy conviction carried a death sentence. The questions were also significant because a people who did not adequately follow God's law could all be destroyed, as Sodom and Gomorrah had been, "because the land is defiled by shuch sins, and spews out the inhabitants."[13]

Despite all these questions, in fact, all three ministers agreed on the fundamentals in this so-called "case of buggerie." A set of shared beliefs shaped New England laws on these matters. "Sodomy," once established, was "against the light of nature . . . to be punished with death." All concurred on key points because Old Testament texts seemed to condemn "men lying with men." Passages most notably in Leviticus, cited by Plymouth, Massachusetts, Connecticut, and New Hampshire colonies, condemned this behavior as an "abomination." For New England settlers, specific injunctions to the ancient Jews to avoid these activities remained relevant. It was therefore straightforward to make New England law consonant with these precepts, and every colony did. While they defined sodomy differently, it was everywhere in New England a capital crime, though rarely enforced. In total, for all the fierceness of laws, two men were executed for sodomy in all of seventeenth-century New England, though many more trials revolved around the accusation.[14]

John Cotton himself was a chief shaper of Massachusetts law codes, and Old Testament precepts informed them. As Cotton phrased it, "the more any Law smells of man the more unprofitable." Judicial laws were to be "a fence to the morall law." For these lawmakers, antisodomy laws were judicial, not ceremonial, bolstering the moral law. On the more radical end, both Cotton and New Haven Colony opted for a remarkably broad interpretation of sodomy that went beyond penetration, incorporating even sexual intimacies between women. The 1641 Body of Liberties, a draft law code authored by Cotton, defined sodomy as "carnall fellowship of man with man, or woman with woman," though in the actual code of 1648, sex between women was omitted. The radical New Haven Colony, in typical fashion, went even farther, defining virtually any nonprocreative sex, including sex between women and masturbation "in the sight of others" as sodomy.[15] For Cotton and others, these interpretations were necessary to make New England legislation consonant with Old Testament regulations.

Given this emphasis on the continuities between ancient Jewish laws and modern New England ones, and their codification, the problem of polygamy pinched and rubbed at men like Cotton. Polygamy could not be relegated to ceremonial laws, such as keeping kosher, which could and should be ignored. It was also not part of the moral law since it could hardly be construed to be ideal in perpetuity. Yet Old Testament practices would seem to endorse it. The Ten Commandments did not forbid polygamy (or, in fact, "sodomy"), and there were no specific injunctions against it in either the Old or New Testament. This situation made polygamy distinct from, say, the intermarriages of "heathen" with Christians. This case, covered by John Cotton in his draft document on "Moses Judicialls," showed how New Testament reconsiderations could overturn Old Testament injunctions. In the time of the ancient Jews, "if a man did marry a heathen not of the tribes of Israell," he was "bound to put her away & her children." Yet Paul had transformed this policy by advising specifically in 1 Corinthians 7 that a man married to an unbeliever should not put her away. In the same way, Cotton, bringing the issues into contemporary times, wrote, "We cannot put away indians." Yet Cotton and others never drew the obvious link: modern practices of polygamy might be acceptable in certain contexts. Still, the precedent seemed to be there: even polygamists could be blessed, especially if they saw no sin in what they did.[16]

However, what if sin grew so great that the land, like Sodom and Gomorrah, "spewed" out its defiled inhabitants and returned it to its original people? Success depended on the good behavior of settlers, which is partly why strict laws against activities such as sodomy underpinned these colonies. Events of the 1630s and 1640s, especially the well-known trial of Anne Hutchinson and the less well-known one of Ann Hibbens, circled around gendered threats to household and social stability. Accused of insubordination to her husband and others, Hibbens defended her lack of wifely obedience by citing a passage about Old Testament polygamy in which God ordered Abraham, "In all that Sarah [his first wife] hath said unto thee, hearken unto her voice," specifically in taking Hagar as a second wife. To the horror of New England authorities, she argued that husbands should thus "hearken unto" their wives, too. Writers connected modern women's subversion of authority with that ever-haunting hotbed of polygamy and radical Protestantism under John of Leiden: Münster. "See the impudent boldnesse of a proud dame. . . . She vented her impatience with so fierce speech and countenance," bellowed John Winthrop in his 1644 history of the Hutchinson affair. Such behavior meant "the Tragedy of *Munster* . . . gave just occasion to feare the danger we were in." In that city, "they also grew (many of them) very loose and degenerate in their practises (for these Opinions will certainly produce a filthy life by degrees)." Others such as Cotton also invoked the notorious Münster Anabaptists as well as the English Familists, both radical religious dissenters accused of polygamy and other carnal sins. He railed that Hutchinson's rejection of orthodox beliefs on the resurrection of the body would inexorably lead to "all promiscuous and filthie cominge togeather of men and Woemen."[17] In fact, such "filthie cominge togeather" did not come from the actions of women like Hutchinson, Hibbens, and others; it came from Cotton's own son.

"What Must a Man Doe When His Wife Goes from Him?"

John Cotton had long fretted about the possibility that parents in New England might "suffer their children to degenerate." He was right to worry. His own son and namesake, another Harvard-educated minister, married

Joanna Rosseter, a surgeon-midwife, in 1659. He became the promising pastor of the church in Wethersfield, Connecticut, in 1660. The details of what happened there remain elusive, but it did not end well. Cotton, Sr., had apparently possessed "an insinuating and melting way in his preaching." Was the son, too, blessed with a seductive tongue, now deployed for baser purposes? It seems so. He also got into fights. His home parish, the First Church in Boston, excommunicated him in 1664 for his "lacivious uncleane practises with three women" and his "horrid lying to hide his sinne." Cotton lost his Wethersfield pulpit and his reputation. He ended up taking up the only position he could get, disdained by most: missionary to the Wampanoags on isolated Martha's Vineyard. He worked with Thomas Mayhew, the missionary already there (with whom, inevitably, he also fell out). His wife joined him on the island, though she may not have been happy about it. He himself lamented the "vilenesse of my heart and Life" and worked hard to overcome them. He studied for over a year with Indian tutors so that by 1666, he was able to preach in their language, not his.[18]

What Cotton called "my dreadfull fall" was in some senses a fortunate one for posterity because it generated exceptional sources. Cotton kept a diary in the early 1670s in which he recorded both the questions Natives asked him and a basic dictionary of Wampanoag words. The vocabulary lists lacked the depth of those revealing Jesuit ones; still, they, along with the questions, provide as close as we can get to the voice of indigenous people in this area in this pivotal era. Among those Wampanoag words he recorded were those for "wife," "husband," "marry," and . . . "adultery" (a vital word for translating the Ten Commandments). Cotton lived amid a community of praying Indians. Dutifully noting the names and questions of the local people, Cotton thus captured a snapshot of societies in flux, pulsing with tensions. These questions focused on theology and biblical interpretation, but they also display profound disharmony over marriage, leadership, and colonial relations.[19]

Cotton recorded questions, not answers. We don't know how he responded or even why he kept this journal of questions. Did he imagine that future missionaries would find it useful? Was it a way to remember? Like the settlers, Wampanoags puzzled over the meanings of the Bible. They asked: "What is it to lift up the soule to God" and "What may a man have in his heart to fit him to receive the Lord's supper?" and "Who sinned first Adam or Eve?" They also wondered how to align their domestic lives with what the Christians preached. "What must a man doe when his wife goes from him?" queried one

Wampanoag man called Nicodemus. What choices did a husband have if his wife, who may not have been a Christian, ended the marriage, in ways time-honored among Wampanoags? Divorce was suddenly no longer an option, even for someone married to an unbeliever. Cotton, no stranger to domestic tumult himself, would have counseled that such a man must do what his own betrayed wife had done: forgive and reconcile. Indeed, some time later, Cotton helped two unhappily married couples do exactly that. Cotton noted that "there was an uncomfortable difference broken forth between Robin & his wife, & the like betweene George & his wife." The Christian names of the men reveal that they were converts, and Cotton's diary indicates that they were recent ones. In the case of Robin, there is no mention that his wife had also converted. Their differences might therefore have been about Christianity. However, George's wife had also just converted, so there may be other reasons. In this case, recourse to the minister might have been a new way to settle disputes. In the old way, such quarrels might have led to divorce. Instead, as Cotton recorded, "by Gods blessing upon my Counsell to them, they were both comfortably reconciled, acknowledging mutually their faults, & promising to live better together for time to come." "Uncomfortable differences" could become "comfortable reconciliation." "Mutual comfort" was a marital ideal among reform Christians. One widely read writer, Thomas Gataker, used *comfort* repeatedly in his 1620 tract on marriage. He lamented unhappy unions: "What a wretched and lamentable case is it then, when she that should be a comfort, proveth a discomfort." However, comfort and marital equilibrium could prove elusive. Others wondered whether there were any situations in which a separation or even a divorce might be warranted. Another man, Mahquian, asked Cotton a few months later: "What may separate man & wife?"[20] The range of possibilities had suddenly narrowed for Wampanoags.

"I Am No Adulterer, Keepe But One Wife"

Marriage was a personal challenge for some; it could also be a political one. Mayhew effected one Native polygamous marital reconciliation that provoked considerable resentment and raised major questions about leadership. Apparently, one wife had "Justly and publickly [and before(?)] the sachim & people of the place . . . thrown away" her husband, a sachem himself. The cause was his "fornication." This last word suggests that the other woman was unmarried, and indeed after the wife left him, he "had lived for many months" with his new lover. However, the wife had changed her mind, announcing that, despite his relations with another woman, "she loved him againe." Here, as in the world of Makheabichtichiou, it is possible to see how important—indeed, how much more important—love was for these Native Americans than it was for their European teachers, who, even if they argued for marital comfort, privileged law and duty over affection and pleasure. Once the wife took him back, "they were admitted to live as man & wife together," presumably thanks to Mayhew and his efforts.

Whatever the domestic choices of husband and wife, for a sachem, marriage was also a highly political matter. This reconciliation was unpopular: "The body of the Indians did manifest their dislike of it." Indeed, even one enthusiastic convert, Hiacoomes, pointedly raised a biblical passage, just after this controversial marital settlement. He asked, "What is the meaning of Deu:24:1:2:3:4?" This Old Testament passage outlined how a man might divorce a wife, which Christians like the Cottons had determined had been overturned by Jesus' teachings. Yet there was a sting in the tail since this passage concluded, "Her former husband, which sent her away, may not take her again to be his wife, after that she is defiled; for that is abomination." According to the word of God, postadultery reconciliation was an "abomination." It is hard to escape the conclusion that Hiacoomes was querying whether the sinning husband was "defiled," not worthy of being taken back into the arms of his wronged wife. Hiacoomes and others were therefore questioning the authority of the sachem, whose leadership, like his marital reconciliation, roused discontent.[21]

Why did so many Wampanoags "dislike" this marital reconciliation? It's hard to say exactly. Did they side with an aggrieved wife against a transgressing husband, worried that she had been pressured by Mayhew to take him back? Had the husband left the new partner pregnant or otherwise vulnerable? Were there diplomatic implications to these marriages? Why had another sachem and the people been involved in the first place? Regardless, marriage was an important alliance of a powerful man and woman . . . or women. The intervention of ministers did not always soothe the dissatisfaction they unleashed. That the "sachem" and "the people" had been involved in the original separation suggests a level of community involvement in the end of a marriage. This sachem, though a praying Indian, did not give up his other wives, which may begin to explain the "dislike" many felt. In this increasingly turbulent atmosphere, there was anger at Mayhew's involvement. Mayhew had intervened in the marriage(s) of a sachem, and pressures had been exerted on the wife to take him back. This aspect may have weakened the sachem's political standing. When a leader could not manage his own household, how could he lead his people? As we have seen in other settings, households underpinned leadership. Elsewhere, Cotton, himself no fan of Mayhew, observed: "Here the Indians, as they had Many times formerly, soe now they complained greatly for want of rulers according to the manner of [Christ]ians, much disliking Mr M's Compelling them still to owne the present sachem." Mayhew's continued support for this sinning sachem tarnished them both. The continued and problematic practice of plural marriage, when the ministers preached monogamy, undermined the authority of the sachem even among those who were "Non-praying" Indians. Political resentments centered on household choices, here as in many other times and places.[22]

Shortly after this unpopular reunion in April 1671, questions about marriage exploded. Wattapahtahinnit twice asked loaded questions about the practice of polygamy by converted Indians. He asked first, in April: "I am no Adulterer, keepe [b]ut one [wife] steale not etc what lacke I [to] be happy?" Linking adultery and polygamy as infractions of Christian monogamy, he wondered why comfort remained elusive, when he was living a de facto Christian life. The next month, he asked more pointedly: "How shall I know I [se]rve God, seeing I that am a Non-praying man never had but [1] wife, & some that are x[Christ]ians have kept 3 wives?" Here was the problem in starkest terms. Wattapahtahinnit had not converted to Christianity, yet he was a monogamist, with moral standing among Christians from his marital choice. Meanwhile, there was a high-ranking convert to Christianity who evidently would not give up his three wives. We have seen similar situations in other cultural settings. In all of these cases, "murmurings" among the community surrounded the continued practice of polygamy by elite men who converted to Christianity, thus indicating complicated vectors of both rank and gender in these moments of conversion and ongoing polygamy. Questioning personal choices among leaders was a useful way to needle hypocrisies among those in authority.[23]

The chorus of protests, framed merely as questions and requests for biblical clarification, grew. A number of men inquired pointedly about the nature of sin, quoting passages about "unclean spirits." One wondered, "Can a good man at any time desire to sin?" Another asked: "Are sinners in heaven?" Another was even more specific: "whether any man [that] hath committed Adultery may goe to heaven?" Another, not converted, sought clarification of two passages in Proverbs that focus on sin and hypocrisy in ways that seem barbed. The first was Proverbs 30:12: "There is a generation that are pure in their own eyes, and yet is not washed from their filthiness." Such a passage was an excellent way to highlight the hypocrisy of leaders who claimed to be pure and Christian but were anything but. The other was Proverbs 22:14: "The mouth of strange women is a deep pit; he that is abhorred of the LORD shall fall therein." This statement is puzzling, but it is difficult to avoid the conclusion that its use here made a political point. Knowing that the Bible was beloved, at least some Wampanoags weaponized it against erring leaders and unpopular ministers. These questions may have been barbs against John Cotton, who had himself fallen into that "deep pit."[24]

There were a lot of stresses and strains rising in these communities in 1671. Biblical passages and questions about hypocrisy and abomination emerged from a larger nexus of anger at English Christian practices. They focused some of the outrage that many felt about the presence of, and their treatment by, the English—and the praying Indians who defended them. The nature of such criticisms comes through in other questions. One Wampanoag queried Mayhew's purchase of Indian property and his perceived exploitation: "whether it be a Righteous thing for Mr M: to buy away soe much of the Indians lands?" Another asked about English lack of hospitality even to Christian Indians: "Why doe not English church men let In[dian] church men rest in th[eir] houses, seeing th[ey] must all rest with God?" Indians were expected to welcome English visitors to their households, but the English did not apparently do the same. Hospitality was a political necessity, and sign of leadership, for Wampanoag rulers. English failures in this area were more than rude; they were political catastrophes, worrying signs of their complete disrespect even for Christian Indians. Had Mayhew or Cotton personally failed on this point?[25]

"Scorn" heaped on leaders was a potent political force, as indicated in other sources. An earlier observer of neighboring Narragansett people, Roger Williams, translated indigenous words including *Nummeshannánantam* and *Nummayaôntam*, "*I scorne, or take it [in] indignation.*" Williams related that "this is a common word" in both peace and war. Evincing surprise that unclothed, seemingly uncivilized men should be so vain and easily offended, Williams observed that "their spirits in naked bodies [are] as high and proud as men more gallant." Williams declared that the "sparkes of the lusts of pride and passion, begin the flame of their warres. . . . This mocking (between their great ones) is a great kindling of Warres amongst them." Tensions continued to spark in the early 1670s, smoldering around Christianity, family, and politics. That there were differences between those who had converted and those who had not is clear in questions to Cotton such as: "Is it lawfull for praying Indians to Incourage those [who] doe not pray to God?" These differences could rip families apart. John Wanna converted to Christianity "with teares trickling downe his cheeks," and the rest of his family, including his daughter-in-law Naomi, did, too. However, Naomi's father, Tuchpoo, "a great Enemy to praying to God," as Cotton noted, "advised his daughter ag[ain]st it, but she would obey God rather then man." We do not know if Tuchpoo cut his daughter off, but his continued resentment against the English and their Christianity probably contributed to his taking up arms against the English in 1675. He might have echoed the Narragansett whom Williams had earlier reported: "There is not roome for so many": *Noonapúmmin autashéhettit.* This bloody conflict over room, land, and resources exploded for him and many others in 1675, led by the married leader, Metacom.[26]

"A Sachim *Will Not Take Any to Wife but Such an One Who Is Equall to Him"*

Metacom worked hard to rally a range of allies among other Native people. Marriage strengthened his ability to do so. What does centering marriage reveal about the trajectories of both Metacom and Weetamoo? Although no one seems to have noticed it, Metacom himself likely had more than one wife. One settler reported that at the beginning of August 1676, both Quinnapin, Weetamoo's husband, and Metacom "had a wife & Child killd but they use to have more then one." This acknowledgment of polygamy by both sachems goes along with recognition of the familial costs of war. Marriage linked Metacom and Weetamoo, and this alliance became critical. Metacom married Wootonekanuske, the sister of his brother Wamsutta's wife, Weetamoo. Weetamoo was therefore twice over Metacom's sister-in-law, as the sister of his wife, and the wife of his brother. Wamsutta, or Alexander, was an ally to Metacom, though he died well before the war began. Sibling relations were vital. These interlocking links formed a chain that became unbreakable. Weetamoo maintained the personal and political loyalties forged by this sibling marriage crisscross long after Wamsutta's death. Metacom and Wootonekanuske, Weetamoo's sister, had at least one son. Wootonekanuske's indigenous name indicates a continued refusal to accept Christianity; the fact that the son's name was not recorded (and therefore was probably not a familiar one to the English) suggests that even if Metacom—or Philip—had willingly taken an English name, his wife and son had not been baptized.[27]

This pair of unions also implies a considerable level of intermarriage among political elites, part of the drive for consolidation in this period. The nature of leadership and communities shifted, and the level of intermarriage in this sibling double marriage makes this shift plain. Sachems were usually male, and they claimed sachemdom partly through lineage. To preserve rank distinctions, they generally married daughters or sisters of other sachems. As an English sojourner put it, "A *Sachim* will not take any to wife but such an one who is equall to him in birth, otherwise they say their seede would in time become ignoble." Such women could occasionally become sachems themselves, but they too claimed power through kin connections. Lineage priorities may have been shifting in this period, and maternal, as well as paternal links, could matter.[28] The emphasis on lineage further suggests a consolidation of the position of the elite, here as elsewhere.

The position of sachem required not only being born to it but also earning it. Leaders had to show courage, wisdom, and eloquence. They needed "melting and insinuating" ways, just as English leaders did. They also had to demonstrate their ability to mobilize others. One of the most fundamental ways to do so was through an established and extensive network of kinship. Leaders also needed to furnish hospitality, demonstrating command of a strong and productive household. Having many wives who planted and harvested corn and other crops and who performed many other critical labors enhanced the ability of the household to furnish hospitality and to generate household wealth. As one English observer had it, "for where are most women, there is greatest plenty." For all these reasons, sachems practiced plural marriage, thus marking them out from other Indian men, who generally did not.[29]

Status distinctions—between elite, even royal, people who practiced plural marriage and commoners who did not—became more salient in the seventeenth century. Native Americans in this area faced a range of immense pressures including catastrophic loss from epidemics. There were knock-on

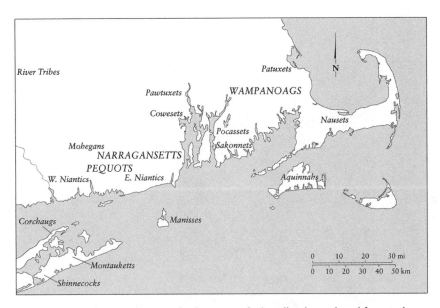

Map of seventeenth-century New England. Cartography by Bill Nelson, adapted from Andrew Lipman, *The Saltwater Frontier: Indians and the Contest for the American Coast* (New Haven: Yale University Press, 2015).

effects, as groups sought tributaries and to a lesser extent captives to rebuild devastated communities. There was thus also an increase in wars, as people competed over hunting territory (increasingly important for the international fur trade as well as subsistence and local exchange). They also developed rivalries over access to European trade goods, including guns. The fur trade depended on the labor of women, as did trade in corn, and there was commensurate increase in the use of plural marriage among elites. Altogether, there was a consolidating tendency in the period of the sixteenth and seventeenth centuries.

As in other settings, ambitious men seeking to unite disparate peoples in times of uncertainty often used plural marriage to demonstrate and to bolster leadership credentials to other indigenous people. It was also a powerful message to Europeans, with their tedious insistence on Christian monogamy: this leader would not live by their rules. The Mohegan leader Uncas exercised just such a challenge from the 1630s on. Uncas was an ambitious sachem of the Mohegans in what is now southeastern Connecticut. He worked hard to consolidate his position in this volatile period, resisting colonialism in a variety of ways, including in his married life. He was a committed, and highly

[Unknown American], *Native American Sachem*, ca. 1700. Although the portrait is stylized, this unidentified sachem shows marks of leadership, including the alternating light and dark wampum so prized in this era. Photography by Eric Gould, courtesy of the Museum of Art, Rhode Island School of Design, Providence.

strategic, polygamist. His first marriage was to the sister of the late sachem; his next wife was the widow of another sachem. Roger Williams observed that this second marriage was a major reason that Uncas "hath drawn all the scattered Pequots to himself." Indeed, unusually, he married at least six or seven women, all from leading families. As one scholar of Uncas has noted, "this extraordinary series of marriages to some of the highest-ranking women . . . was an important part of Uncas's efforts to legitimize his claims to leadership." When these ambitions were not fully realized, Uncas allied himself to the English. Still, he did not become a monogamist. His marriages extended his network; gave him access to tributaries, workers, and trade; and strengthened lines of elite kinship.[30]

Uncas's trajectory illustrates a wider move toward consolidation in Native communities in the seventeenth century. Faced with political realignments forced by colonialism, indigenous communities clustered together, increasing the power of their often polygamous leaders in ever more hierarchical societies. This shift in rank organization marks burials. From the 1620s to the mid-eighteenth century, burials bunched together, in much more systematic ways. The graves themselves, lined with goods meant to accompany the deceased into the afterlife, show notably increased stratification between individuals in them. One Narragansett cemetery in Rhode Island, in use in the 1660s and 1670s, shows distinct clustering, as well as carefully staged burials with consistent positioning of corpses to the east. Archaeologists believe that this deliberate design shows the power of one lineage "claiming exclusive access to land, corn, and other resources," perhaps even making "a symbolic declaration" of political solidarities against other groups. These polities competed relentlessly: for access to trade, for tribute, for captives, and for dominance. Weaker groups paid tribute to stronger ones, again heightening a tendency to hierarchy, between groups as well as within groups. In such circumstances, as another archaeologist points out, "the 'managerial' role of the sachem became increasingly important," and members of this leading family shared in this power, thus "exacerbating social division already sharply drawn."[31]

Relations of rank, then, took on new significance in this period. The political force of "scorn" in Native communities indicates not simply the timeless nature of indigenous people, their naked pride, but something distinctive about those relations in the wake of the crisis of colonialism. Williams contended even as early as the 1620s that the "sparkes of the lusts of pride and passion, begin the flame of their warres." If such an observation held true in the 1620s, it became even more relevant by the 1670s, after another fifty years of pressure. One historian of Metacom and Weetamoo's War has summarized, "Philip made it clear that affronts to his authority were his chief complaint." English disrespect for Native communities, along with other factors such as material grievances and an uptick in Indian slavery, helped to provoke the war ("Why doe not English church men let In[dian] church men rest in th[eir] houses?"). However, war was also about fierce protection of status within indigenous communities: both by particular polities such as the Narragansett and the Pocasset, but also by an ever more distinctive elite determined to demonstrate its importance to the "ignoble." Their leadership was under threat from shifting political and material realities, so they were working hard to shore it up. Sachems did so through polygamy as well as wars.[32]

Status distinctions shifted in this era; so did gender ones. Weetamoo's own position, along with those of other female sachems, such as Awashunkes of the Sakonnet, demonstrate this change; there seem to have been fewer female sachems before this era, as well as after it. This situation probably reflects the loss of many men, due to war, as well as changing political landscapes. Graves also suggest haunting absences among the living. In that orderly Narragansett cemetery, there were double the number of females as males, and virtually no young men, thus demonstrating a "community under stress." Those strains also marked the pages of one of the most remarkable sources on early American polygamy and Weetamoo herself: Mary Rowlandson's captivity narrative.[33]

"My Master Had Three [Wives]"

Deer blood boiled in the stomach of the animal itself struck Mary Rowlandson as thoroughly repugnant. Yet her captors "ate it sweetly." When Rowlandson dipped the pot in which she carried communal water into the kettle in her own household, the women there were disgusted at her "sluttish trick." Women confronted the household practices of other women and found them deeply wanting. Although few have lingered on it, Rowlandson's account is a remarkable window onto Native practices of plural marriage and domestic life. While Rowlandson knew that it was a useful shorthand for savagery, her treatment of plural marriage was surprisingly evenhanded. Other contemporaries thundered much more: "The customs and manners of these Indians were, and yet are, in many places, very brutish and barbarous in several respects, like unto several savage people of America. They take many wives." Rowlandson noted simply that her master had three wives, though she used a less neutral term for them. She also observed that he moved between them, sometimes staying with one for weeks at a time. Eager to emphasize that her own virtue was never compromised, Rowlandson may have chosen not to linger on any possible "lust" motivating this husband. Still, she addressed all three wives on their own terms, and she did not take the easy opportunity to condemn the system. Of the youngest wife, Rowlandson merely noted that she had two babies, while the English captive actually wrote positively about the oldest of the three wives. This unnamed wife promised to feed Rowlandson. Rowlandson also described one winter episode in which this senior wife laid a bedmat down for an exhausted Rowlandson, and tucked her in "with a good

Rugg," or blanket—"the first time," Rowlandson noted in grateful astonishment, "I had any such Kindness shewed me." Plural wives appeared, then, in unexpected ways. Yet Rowlandson pointedly denounced the "proud gossip," Weetamoo. Their relations were deeply strained, and Rowlandson recounted several points when Weetamoo, enraged, turned on her.[34]

Anger often springs, snarling, from vulnerability. Worried mothers holler loudest. Weetamoo's flashpoints of fury illuminate the cracks that threatened to split her world apart. Emerging from intimate, quotidian encounters, they reveal a people in crisis. Relations between wives, and the nature of this plural marriage, demonstrate one such point of fragility. Rowlandson saw threats and violence and shouting. Behind these actions, though, lay grief, anxiety, and affection. She was also witnessing self-sacrifice by a mother and leader. As we have seen, high-ranking Weetamoo first married Wamsutta, or Alexander, the brother of Metacom. Weetamoo's loyalty to Metacom, as her brother-in-law, and to Wootonekanuske, her sister, remained arguably her most important connections, more significant than ties to any of her husbands. Sibling relations were fundamental in such communities, even as marriage forged significant connections. When Wamsutta died, she subsequently remarried Petananuet (Petonowowett, or Peter), though it is unclear exactly when. However, this marriage became a problem by 1675; at that point, Petananuet wished to side with the English. It is hard to know whether their political differences followed from their personal ones, or the reverse. Either way, Weetamoo was one of those wives who left her husband. Perhaps with the intervention of her family, she chose a new husband, Quinnapin, sachem of the Narragansett.[35]

Yet Quinnapin already had two wives, as Weetamoo would have known. Usually, the first wife was the highest ranking.[36] Weetamoo was willing to take the role of a third wife, as this alliance was politically important. Such a decision suggests a level of diplomatic desperation, as well as a possible willingness to sacrifice herself for her people and their enduring ties to the Wampanoags. It meant that the Pocassets and the Narragansetts would work together with the Wampanoags to vanquish the English. These political exigencies may not have entirely smoothed the complicated personal dynamics between the wives, though. Weetamoo joined this family only in the summer of 1675, not so many months before Rowlandson's capture in February 1676. To Rowlandson, the "proud gossip" Weetamoo seemed imperious and demanding. Rowlandson's language about Weetamoo echoed that used about Anne Hutchinson: "See the impudent boldnesse of a proud dame. . . . She vented her impatience with so fierce speech and countenance."[37] For Rowlandson, Cotton, and others, women were supposed to show neither "proudness" nor "impatience." In stepping beyond these gendered bounds, Weetamoo was, like Hutchinson, showcasing her elite status. She was a political leader, recognized even by the English as a "sachem" and a "queen." Naturally, she spent time, "as much time as any of the Gentry of the land," in such tasks as "powdering her hair, and painting her face, going with her Neck-laces, with Jewels in her ears, and bracelets upon her hands."[38] Such conspicuous ornamentation informed the world, and her fellow wives, of her prosperity and lineage.

The other wives may have resented this high-ranking addition to the household. Is this why the senior wife went out of her way to ally with Rowlandson, to thwart the authority of this imperious secondary wife? Or were there political motivations here, too? Pulling a blanket over a shivering captive may have been simply an act of warm humanity in wartime. However, it may also have been a quiet act of personal and political insubordination against both Weetamoo and Quinnapin, akin to the "murmurings" about the Christian sachem's polygamy earlier. Historians of this war have identified intergenerational disputes between younger Native men, who more glibly called for war, and older ones, who did not. Perhaps this "older" wife, in publicly siding with Rowlandson against the other wife of her husband, was also indicating her preferences for an English alliance. There may also have been generational shifts between elite women. Such complications between generations, as with Tuchpoo and Naomi, show how colonialism and war could rend Native families. Households mattered to male authority; they were also meaningful for female authority. This particular household symbolized the alliance of Pocassets and Narragansetts, supporting the Wampanoags. For this union to appear weak was unacceptable. The behavior of captives reflected on captors.[39]

Anxieties and performances of power often centered around food. When Rowlandson served Weetamoo and Quinnapin some prized bear meat from the same plate, Weetamoo would eat nothing but one bite fed directly by her husband. Etiquette demanded nothing less. Rowlandson was chagrined by such niceties. In another, more dramatic episode, a hungry Rowlandson, after eyeing up the "Corns and Beans" in a neighbor's house, wolfed down a piece of boiled horse's foot at another neighbor's wigwam. She also snatched a half-gnawed piece of it out of a captive child's mouth there, wiping away the slobber and gobbling it herself. When Weetamoo heard about these transgressions, she was furious. She berated Rowlandson for having "disgraced My Master with begging," threatening that "they would knock me on the Head" if it happened again. Weetamoo was concerned about herself and her larger household appearing powerful. Household dynamics were a public matter for sachems as for English leaders. An inability to control a captive, who went begging and grabbing, did not reflect glory on the larger unit. It suggested that they were not feeding Rowlandson, a serious breach of that important political virtue of hospitality, required even toward a captive. It also implied a larger general problem of food supplies.[40]

Hunger haunted everyone, and it made people mean. As Rowlandson noted, the destruction of Indian food was a deliberate wartime strategy: "It was thought, if their Corn were cut down, they would starve and die with hunger: and all their Corn . . . was destroyed." However, Rowlandson declared her amazement that she "did not see . . . one Man, Woman, or Child die with Hunger." She was horrified by their willingness to eat not only boiled deer blood but meals even less palatable to her: "They would pick up old bones . . . and boyle them, and drink up the Liquor . . . and eat them." Rowlandson declared her admiration for the God who supplied these Indians, so that they always had food, even in the worst times. She did not mention the women who worked so hard, seeking, boiling, and harvesting anything remotely edible, even "the very Barks of Trees" to ensure the survival of their children and their people.[41]

Women also gave up food for the greater good. The teeth of skeletons in that orderly Narragansett cemetery illustrate that sacrifice, even before the war began. Naturally, everyone there had poor dental health (it was the seventeenth century), but women's teeth were worse, revealing bouts of malnutrition. This situation probably reflects partially the physical demands of pregnancy and nursing, but it also implies women's more limited access to—or sacrifice of—high-nutrition food, just as with Weetamoo and the bear meat. Women suffered more from the privations that still affected even the prosperous individuals found in those graves. Still, appearances mattered even when hunger chased; ritual had to be followed, and protocol observed. Weetamoo may have been pregnant or nursing a child, and in urgent need of protein, fats, and calories. Yet she denied herself that bear meat delicacy because doing so mattered more to her than sating her own fierce hunger. Little wonder she was appalled by the weakness of a woman who stole the food out of a child's mouth.[42]

Rowlandson's seeming indifference to children consistently rankled Weetamoo. In yet another incident, Weetamoo became enraged at Rowlandson over an apron, reflecting larger economic exigencies. Metacom's "Maid" came into Weetamoo's household, carrying a child who might well have been Weetamoo's own niece or nephew. She asked Rowlandson for "a piece of my Apron, to make a flap for it." Rowlandson refused. Weetamoo ordered her to hand it over. Rowlandson stood her ground, getting into a fight with the maid. Weetamoo raised a stick against her, but Rowlandson stepped out of the wigwam before it could strike her. However, this stick, which Weetamoo may have intended only to scare this belligerent captive, had the desired effect. Rowlandson capitulated and handed over the entire apron. This action from Weetamoo indicates again her concern for Wootonekanuske, Metacom, and their household. It also reflects her sense that a captive had better adhere to her wishes; to disrespect her mistress was unacceptable.[43]

This fracas over a piece of cloth also indicates larger issues over economics and trade. Cloth was one of the goods for which New Englanders traded; so were fur and wampum, the shells that formed a kind of political and economic currency among indigenous people. Even before English settlement, there were probably shifts in these areas. The abundance of shells for wampum in what is now Rhode Island and Connecticut had likely increased territorial disputes, as different polities competed for access to these coastal areas and their rich troves of wampum shells. The acceleration in the fur trade had also exacerbated tensions. There was a system of alliance between groups with access to fur (usually farther inland) and wampum (coastal), and this situation contributed to consolidation of certain polities, as suggested by the graveyards including the Narragansett ones. In the seventeenth century, with shifting alliances, many leaders used wampum to broker allegiances and, as one scholar has it, "wampum production soared, and various groups, both Native and European, struggled for control of wampum production and distribution." It also shifted the balance of labor within households, as seen in the previous chapter, as women devoted ever more time to processing furs. This economic shift again promoted an ever more hierarchical society, in terms of both rank and gender. Yet there were also novel pressures in the middle of the century, as the fur trade declined in many areas (due to overhunting and population pressures from European settlers) and also due to shifts in wampum.[44]

Wampum was a vital commodity in these indigenous communities, important for political, diplomatic, and economic reasons. Rowlandson

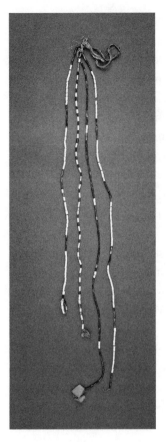

These necklaces of wampum show the light and dark beads which characterized New England in the seventeenth century. Courtesy President and Fellows of Harvard College, Peabody Museum of Archaelogy and Ethnology, PM 46-78-10/28122.

reported that Weetamoo's main "Work was to make Girdles of Wampom and Beads." Only elites could produce wampum, and it traditionally circulated only among sachem families, often as a form of bridewealth with which the groom's family paid the bride's. Weetamoo's labor in making girdles of it, then, held symbolic importance, both demonstrating and augmenting her status, as did her wearing of wampum. Distributing hospitality in the form of both wampum and European goods was also a central way to ensure political loyalties. Wampum also cemented alliances between distinct polities. So Weetamoo's labors were also directed at consolidating political alliances, both among the Pocasset and the Narragansett and with others. Wampum also had economic importance, as a form of currency that was traded with other groups, especially for European goods.[45]

Wampum's usage and production, though, also shifted in this era. Wampum lost some of its value among Europeans in this era, which increased economic pressure on Native groups. The Dutch United Colonies demanded that fines and trade be paid in wampum, even as wampum depreciated. The Narragansetts sold land to make up for this devaluation and to maintain access to European goods. Wampum's devaluation may have been connected with its increased production. New metal tools allowed Native people to drill holes in the shells faster, thus making it easier and more efficient to produce belts of wampum. This development may explain why wampum production started to involve women as well as men. In graves from 1600 to 1650, wampum-making implements accompanied only the corpses of men into the afterlife; from 1650 on, they also accompanied women. When Weetamoo produced wampum, then, she was doing something innovative, which her grandmother would not have done. The same was probably true of her position as a sachem. In both cases, these changes had to do partially with the loss of men, from wars in particular, but also with alterations in labor patterns.[46]

Weetamoo's incessant work on wampum, which seemed to Rowlandson mere vanity and self-indulgence, was in fact critical material labor for the war effort. What do people need in wars? They need political alliances and diplomatic support, and wampum would have helped to secure these necessities. However, they also need something more tangible: weapons, specifically here guns and ammunition. How do they obtain such items? In this case, they traded wampum. Weetamoo's labors here were probably connected to this imperative, a desire for smoothbore flintlocks in particular. Metacom and Weetamoo's refusal to hand over guns had helped to spark the war, and the importance of these weapons only increased when war started. Weetamoo's wampum would have allowed her and her representatives to obtain guns and powder from Dutch and French traders, whether directly or indirectly through other allies. Indeed, one historian contends that the blockage of arms trade routes by hostile Mohawks was a vital aspect in turning the tide of victory in the war to the English.[47] The work of wives and other women made war possible, if not always successful.

"She Snatched [the Bible] Hastily Out of My Hand"

As 1676 ground on, Weetamoo was probably becoming more and more concerned about the prospects for her and her people. Sometimes these frustrations flared up dramatically. Rowlandson recounted an incident in which Weetamoo came home to find her reading the Bible. Instead of leaving

Rowlandson to read, "she snatched it hastily out of my hand, and threw it out of doors." Rowlandson was horrified by this treatment of her beloved scriptures, but Weetamoo had her reasons. At a most basic level, Weetamoo may have been angry that her servant was sitting and idling, shirking her duties. This kind of behavior could not be tolerated, especially as it made Weetamoo seem a poor household manager, something both Indians and English derided. At the same time, there might have been a more general resentment of literacy. Weetamoo knew that the English gained much power from their own mastery of reading and writing, their treaties, their procla-mations. Hurling this book outside into the mud was a clear way to reject what one scholar notably termed the English "literall advantage."[48]

Weetamoo knew, too, about English veneration for the Bible, and the Christianity that represented a threatening new force in her world.[49] Mission-aries like John Cotton and Thomas Mayhew were controversial figures. Sachems in particular had reasons to object to their presence. First, mission-aries sought to alter loyalties and households, problematic for ideological and practical reasons. It meant that "praying Indians" did not put their own leaders first. More practically, missionaries also encouraged commoners to stop making tribute payments to sachems. Indeed, for some ordinary Indians facing the pressures of increasingly hierarchical societies, such might have formed some of the appeal of Christianity. This situation might have been the case for Hiacoomes, that early disciple on Martha's Vineyard. This was dangerous stuff for sachems like Weetamoo, Quinnapin, and Metacom. Many Native people were also dismayed by the perceived hypocrisy of Christians, as Weetamoo might have been by Mary Rowlandson. In one story from this war, when Native warriors attacked an English house, one man exhorted others: "That *God is with us, and fights for us, and will deliver us* out of the hands of these Heathen." His enemies then "*shouted and scoffed* saying: now see how *your God delivers you* . . . sending in many shots." Here again is that politically significant scorn fanning "the flame of their warres."[50]

Christian hypocrisy could seem insufferable. When Weetamoo cast that Bible out, she had just returned from a funeral. It was not just any funeral. It was for a beloved child, though we do not know whose. In the midst of war and suffering provoked by the English, this leader, agonizing over her family and people, was understandably enraged to come home to find one sitting there, reading a book that was the very symbol of the enemy. As the war dragged on, these losses became even more distressingly personal.

Weetamoo's own child, whom Rowlandson had not previously mentioned, also died soon thereafter. The child's age and sex are unknown. The careful mourning rituals suggest that the child was at least three years old, as Narragansetts, and many of their neighbors, gave full funerals only to children who were three or older. A baby with Quinnapin, who would have been very young indeed, would have been unlikely to receive this type of mourning, so it was probably an older child with a previous husband. Either way, the child was precious, and would have represented hope for the future in a dark time.[51]

Rowlandson recounted the child's illness and death briefly, with chilling indifference. The night after the child died, Rowlandson was given "a skin to lye upon, and a mess of Venison and Ground-nuts, which was a choice Dish among them." She also noted that after the funeral "both morning and evening, there came a company to mourn and howl with her; though I confess I could not much condole with them." These rituals and songs were supposed to ease the dead into the spirit world, and to ameliorate the anguish of the living. Williams reported that in these circumstances, the community consoled the family with the word "*Kutchímmoke, Kutchímmoke*, Be of good cheere" as they stroked their cheeks and heads. Archaeologists tell us that "children's graves were among the most lavish," indicators, probably, of inherited rank but also of the pained shock of the unexpected deaths of these beloved family members. Rowlandson refused to condole with another mother who had also lost a child to war. Her self-centeredness must have seemed intolerable. Indeed, she went on to recount how wretched *she* was in her own situation of captivity. Rowlandson, herself a mourning mother, showed such coldness about this child's death that even literary scholars have struggled to explain it. It may have been that Rowlandson was so devastated by the loss of her own child that she could not bring herself to empathize with another mother in a similar situation. Still, in the wake of this death, Rowlandson included not one single word of sympathy, only noting of the wigwam: "There was one benefit in it, that there was more room."[52]

Indeed, colonists were willing to sacrifice all kinds of people—children, women, and men—in order to gain "more room" for their "plantings." If that room was in households themselves, so be it. War reached deep into the hearts of families and crushed them. Some were more fortunate than others. Rowlandson was redeemed and restored to her household, though it was missing members now. She would never be the same: "I can remember the time, when I used to sleep quietly without workings in my thoughts, whole nights together, but now it is otherwise with me." Rowlandson and her editor, Increase Mather, took comfort in the Bible, Hebrews 12:6, "For whom the Lord loveth he chasteneth." The Lord must have loved Weetamoo, too. She lost her life, even before Metacom did, after she had lost so much already. According to Mather, she had earlier supplied canoes to Metacom, but had none herself by early August 1676. So she "ventur[ed] over the River upon a Raft," determined to support the alliance and to lead her people to victory. She was killed, possibly drowned, before she could do so.[53]

When the English found Weetamoo's body, they did not bury this "proud dame." Instead, they cut off her head and stuck it on a pole. Weetamoo was one of the few women in early America to be decapitated and displayed in a war in this manner, a final, twisted acknowledgment of her "potency" in life. She was a leader who had helped to raise a rebellion. While Metacom's body was mutilated more, putting her head on display was a grisly political statement. It was meant in part to be a warning to other Indians. It worked. When Indian prisoners of war saw it, they recognized her face, making "a most horrid and diabolical Lamentation, crying out that it was their Queens head." This "lamentation" echoed the mourning songs and rituals Weetamoo herself had led for children who had died, including her own.[54]

The war was technically over soon thereafter. Less than a week after Weetamoo's death, according to Mather, Metacom himself was shot by an Indian called Alderman, who "did formerly belong to . . . [the] Sachim of *Pocasset*," Weetamoo. The English did not bury Metacom's body either, drawing and quartering it. Even after its official end, the war lingered: in mourning, in continued skirmishes and struggles, in stories of resistance, and in households scattered, upended, and re-formed. Wives, now widows, gathered their children, and made their slow progress across the burned landscape, seeking shelter with those few Indian leaders who were left. Some of them became slaves in the households both of Indians and, more wretchedly, of the English. New households emerged from the crucible of war. Yet it is wise not to forget the old ones, and the authority and life of a plural wife.[55]

One of the most powerful people in Metacom and Weetamoo's War lived as a plural wife, as well as a sachem, and her plural marriage had its own significant politics. This wife flung the Bible outside onto the mud, where its pages fluttered in the breeze until an English wife went and scooped it up. Out of those pages floated many stories of ancient fathers and mothers, ones to confound New England settlers, who fretted over the blessed polygamists of old. The nature of marriage and authority caused controversies and excommunications for women who dared to suggest that they might, like Abraham's Sarah, have a husband who would "hearken" unto them. Wampanoags and others also wondered over these tales and why even Christians kept three wives. Marriages, singular and plural, provided a significant arena for bitter political contests. Leaders were expected to practice certain sorts of marriage, to control their own households, whether singular or plural. Failures to do so were a problem, for them and for their communities. Despite the fact that both English and Indian people puzzled over polygamy and power, there was still much, too much, that divided them. Cramped wartime households, and mournful uncertainties, did not create sympathies but only laid bare the differences. They also clarified that "There is not roome for so many. *Noonapúmmin autashéhettit.*"[56]

4. "Negroe Mens Wifes"

Like too many other early American tragedies, this one begins with a head on a pole. The head belonged to an enslaved man called Roger who hanged himself in 1712 at Ripon Hall, the plantation of Governor Edmund Jenings in Virginia. Such incidents expose the gruesome realities of early modern life and especially slavery. This plantation manager was warning other enslaved men and women that even death would not secure peace for a suicide. The manager's violence occurred not just in the dreadful display but in the tales he told about it. He generated an account exonerating himself and his behavior. He emphasized there was nothing wrong here, except romantic liaisons among enslaved people gone wrong: "not any reason [except] he being hindred from Keeping other Negroe Mens wifes besides his owne."[1]

The manager's notation is puzzling. One historian has contended that the episode with Roger was a situation in which the manager, "angered by Roger's display of power," prevented polygamy, with Roger killing himself because of his "African beliefs about honor." The evidence, however, also supports other readings. *Keeping* implies polygamy, not simply adultery, though even this point could be disputed. But then what does *keeping* mean? What also does the word *wifes* mean? In English colonies such as Virginia, marriages between enslaved people had no legal existence. Polygamy also had no legal existence. So there were no wives here in any legal sense, yet this manager used the word *wifes*, not *women*. Who was the manager's informant when he came to find Roger's body? What kind of narrative did that informant tell, and what purposes might it have served? How might it have been garbled or deliberately altered? Finally, who "hindred" Roger from accomplishing his designs? We don't know that it was the manager. It could equally have been those "other Negroe Men" or indeed the "wifes" themselves.[2]

Roger apparently hanged himself in the dusty quiet of "ye old . . . Toolhouse." Yet the manager probably displayed his head on a pole in the yard flanked by cabins of enslaved people in Ripon Hall. This gesture was to instill terror, so the manager ensured that people going about their daily lives would have had to see it—and smell it. The yard would have been where enslaved people gathered. But it also filled many other functions. It was a domestic space as well as a social one. In the normal run of life, it would have buzzed with the shouts of children, the clink of spoons against pots, the hum of conversations in the haze of pipe smoke. Silence probably attended that first dreadful confrontation, but eventually its horror became another part of the background. Roger was already dead when he was mutilated; the living suffered more. Still, the sickening reality of this world is that the severed head of a man would have overlooked women tending gardens and children scampering. Plants and people grew and bloomed insistently as a man's head decomposed above them. A discussion of family life in plantation slavery must therefore contend with that fundamental dynamic: the putrid monstrosity at its core and the fantastic vitality that sprang up around it.[3]

African-American slavery and the Atlantic slave trade reshaped marriage, both for those in bondage and for those who held them there. Ideas and practices of marriage also molded the lives of enslaved and free people. When slavery and marriage are put together, paradoxes abound. For the Civil War and Reconstruction period, these have received some attention. Yet too rarely have they been considered for the colonial period. Historians of slavery have done extraordinary work to uncover the grim yet hopeful realities of married life among enslaved people who could not legally marry. Most have acknowledged plural marriages, usually casting them as a means by which African customs continued in the Americas. In slavery, traditions such as polygamy could seem a subversion of European norms. But they were more than that; they were an indicator of the profound dynamics of Atlantic transformation.[4]

The argument in this chapter, as elsewhere, is that making use of older systems of household organization was a process, a strategy, and, sometimes, a contest. Recently scholars have begun to push harder at the meanings of plural unions, posing questions about how the institution might have differed in American settings. Plural marriages were not simply about holding onto traditions from the motherland, or even just resisting Euro-American norms. First, there was no singular tradition—or motherland. Marriage, plural or singular, did not mean the same thing to all West Africans or African Americans; there were considerable ethnic variations. Yet even for those from the same ethnic group or lineage or even the same household, the same situation could hold distinct meanings. Gender made a difference; so did rank and age. Conflicts could be intense, and they played out in family compounds. Polygamy was not merely a household arrangement; it was a political and economic structure of great importance and variety, responsive to changes. In West African settings, polygamous systems were already shifting due to the pressures of war and the Atlantic slave trade. In American settings, they receded because social and demographic conditions changed dramatically. Africans and African Americans drove these transformations.[5]

After all, the condition of "permanent exile," as one scholar has phrased what enslaved people experienced in the Middle Passage, altered the dynamics of domestic life. These transformative and painful processes underpin this chapter. Plural marriages had existed in West Africa for centuries as a way of life, and a source, as well as indicator, of elite status. However, they took on novel meanings in this era. In choosing them, enslaved people were making radically conservative choices: putting an old form to new uses. Ideas about tradition informed this process, even as neither masters and mistresses in their big houses nor enslaved women and men in their cabins simply did the same old thing. Ultimately, monogamy as the primary marital form in enslaved families mostly won out—in part because of what planters did, but more significantly because of what enslaved people did in the face of altered circumstances.[6]

Looking first to West African practices, then to a pivotal moment of transition in Virginia, allows us to see the continuities as well as the changes. Even institutions that looked the same on the surface, such as polygamy, changed shape. Marriages, monogamous and polygamous, came under considerable pressure in this time and place because household settings constituted the nexus for negotiations of power and authority for enslaved and free people. As one scholar has phrased it, "it was through community and kinship, not in its absence, that slaves and masters fought their battles." Too often the literature in the history of family has sidelined African-American families because they could not avail themselves of legal marriage, meaning that there is little by way of textual sources. However, this legal disability is important and worth interrogating. Marriage could be about two people loving each other. However, it was also a way to assert power, especially for men. Masters did not forbid legal marriage to enslaved people because they feared affections, kisses, and babies. They denied it because they knew its structural, legal, and economic advantages well themselves.[7] That power is the focus of this chapter.

"The Strong Attachment of the Blacks to Polygamy"

Polygamy among Africans and African Americans proved most worrisome to Euro-Americans in moments when Africans and African Americans seemed likeliest to exercise meaningful political power. So it appears when Europeans tread on African soil, navigating its complex realities and authoritative leaders. It reappeared in American settings most notably in the early republic, when slavery came under attack and the situation of free people in particular proved vexing. In moments of the direst slavery and political impotence, polygamy did not seem so problematic to Euro-Americans; they barely bothered to record it. This silence is telling. It supports the idea, fleshed out in the previous chapters, that polygamy provoked the most vigorous yelps when it accompanied substantive political claims. When it did not, Euro-Americans let it go, simply allowing it to confirm what they already believed: that people engaging in such practices were inferior in their persons and their households.

The paucity of sources on households among African Americans in and of itself also demonstrates who had most of the power in these settings. Part of the challenge of investigating plural unions is that it is difficult even to make it past the yard, into the cabins of enslaved people. These locations, controlled by African Americans, could be fiercely defended and minimally recorded spaces of intimacy. In one instance, an enslaved man threatened to "split the skull" of an interfering minister who dared to push past the yard, declaring that this busybody "had no right . . . for he might do what he liked in his own place, and have what company he pleased." The wall of silence put up to stop the record keepers still halts us. There are ways to proceed, though. One useful place to start is in the yards and houses of West Africa, to understand what the organization of such spaces meant to African families, some of whom were split up to cast more individuals into the fiery crucible of Atlantic slavery and death.[8]

Even if unrecognized by Anglo-American law, African plural unions were a reality. They were also a trope. Claims like those made about Roger justified brutality by people like the manager. Managers, overseers, and others would undoubtedly have preferred to imagine that family problems were what caused suspicious deaths among enslaved people. The manager used them here to emphasize that suicide did not stem from his mistreatment. He was covering himself, and what better way to do it than to point to the alleged depravity of Africans in their personal lives? Tales of African (-American) domestic disorder, such as the horrific one reported here, have served many purposes for the people who have told them—and told them and told them—ad infinitum, ad nauseum.[9]

Stories about problematic polygamy among Africans and African Americans were also powerful political statements about belonging and citizenship, rehearsed by non-Africans over and over. In numerous early modern accounts, polygamy served as a shorthand for societies lacking law and religion, in which a few brutal men exercised capricious power. Travel narratives about West Africa emphasized polygamy, hammering home the notion that Africans, especially their leaders, were "very prone to Whoredom, inchastity, etc" and "boisterous in their manner of making love." These kinds of exaggerated renditions of African domestic life cast it as deeply flawed, upending allegedly ideal gender roles. One writer claimed, "Each Man marries as many Wives as he pleases. . . . Whilst the Man only idly spends his time in impertinent Tattling (the Womens Business in our Country) and drinking of Palm-Wine, which the poor Wives are frequently obliged to raise Money to pay for, and by their hard Labour maintain and satisfie these lazy Wretches." Polygamy supposedly transformed husbands from manly providers into indolent drunkards, engaging merely in "Womens Business." Yet if polygamy made wives into dupes, it did the same to husbands. That same author noted that "the Women are of a Nature so much hotter than the Men, and that ten or twenty are frequently obliged to content themselves with one Man amongst them, who is frequently insufficient for one of them: Wherefore they are continually contriving how to gain a Lover and would rather suffer Death than forbear the delicious Sin." Indeed, supposedly, polygamy created rapists and liars out of desperate wives: "They are so very fiery, than [sic] if they can get a young Man alone they will tear the Cloaths off of his indecent Parts, and throw themselves upon him; swearing that if he will not yield to their Desires, they will accuse him to their Husband of Attempts to violate their Chasttity."[10]

Claims about African(-American) propensity to polygamy, just as with Native Americans, resonated in American settings, too. Asserting a people's "natural" tendency to polygamy helped to create modern American notions of race. "The strong attachment of the Blacks to *Polygamy*": such was the title of an article in the *Massachusetts Gazette* in 1788, in the wake of court cases that ended slavery in that state but left the status of African-American citizens unclear. "The besetting sin of the negroes" was what one magazine called polygamy in the 1840s as abolitionists and antiabolitionists took up sides. In debates about freedom for the wives of African-American soldiers during the Civil War itself, one senator sniffed: "You will find it very difficult to prove . . . how many wives [a soldier] has." Such assertions came out of moments of anxiety over black power. They implied that African-American inability to marry "properly"—that is, monogamously—rendered them unfit for freedom and full citizenship, despite the fact that for most enslaved people in Anglo-American colonies and states, legal monogamy was an impossibility.[11]

Such tales of polygamy reverberate through the centuries, making race by relentlessly rehearsing the wrong but robust idea that people of color have an intrinsic predisposition to this unchanging form of union. The implication was that such unconquerable tendencies therefore rendered them unsuited for freedom, citizenship, and full social and economic equality. This claim is as pernicious as it is potent. Polygamy in many African settings was not an indicator of disorder or dissipation. It was often the reverse: an indicator of carefully calibrated social orders as well as a sign of prosperity and kin connections. Polygamous systems also shifted under a range of circumstances. Roger's story and its context illuminate the significance of assertions about plural unions and domestic disorder, but they also reveal, however fleetingly, polygamy's lived realities, the ways it shifted in new environments, both in African and American settings.

"Polygamy Common"

Polygamy appears in nearly every travel account from West Africa, whether far to the north in Senegambia or much farther south and east near the Bight of Biafra. European men gazed in fascination, mouths agape, at what West Africans supposedly did at home, as well as how they looked. Sometimes the implied comparison discomfited observers. Admittedly, most authors were not so explicit as a Dutch one who declared, in a 1602 statement to launch a thousand stereotypes, that African men "are also blessed with a large Male member . . . surpassing our Dutch Nation . . . [and] they do not spare it, but make it work." Unnerved by their own possible inadequacies, European writers (male) worked hard to make clear that virility did not result in political or moral superiority. Indeed, the argument was that physical potency, more significant to early modern people than size, led to moral failings. So although this same observer conceded that "the men are all that a fine, upright Man should be" and that the women "have firm bodies and beautiful loins, outdoing the womenfolk of our Lands in strength and devotion," this situation nevertheless led to domestic and sexual excess.[12]

Nearly every account emphasized that polygamy was ubiquitous among Africans. The common phrase was that a man had as many wives as he could maintain or feed. Travelers also generally noted that elite political leaders, such as kings and magistrates, had more wives than anyone else. So Jean Barbot noted of the Senegalese: "Because these peoples have many Turkish and Arab customs, like the Turks and Arabs they can have as many wives as they can afford to keep." William Smith's account of his time in Guinea noted of one area that "most . . . have from Ten to Twenty Wives apiece; and those who have more account themselves the richer, being naturally of a lazy idle Disposition, insomuch that they seldom care to put their Hands to any Thing, but make their Wives do all Manner of Work for them, not only within Doors, but also in the Field." For such authors, polygamy traced out the drudgery of wives and the inherent laziness of husbands, as well as the general moral turpitude of natives, here as in so many other places.[13]

Entries for polygamy in the index of Willem Bosman's early-eighteenth-century Dutch travel narrative from Guinea, quickly (and poorly) translated into English, are typical: "Polygamy common among the Negroes. . . . They place their Glory in it. . . . They can't depart from it. . . . 'Tis the greatest Obstacle to their Conversion to Christianity." Polygamy springs repeatedly from Bosman's account of numerous rulers and traders. There was a grudging admiration for the fertility of Africans. In polygamy, "given that "the Men [are] Vigorous, it is not to be . . . wonder'd at, that their Issue [children] should be very numerous." Yet polygamy also functioned as a European trope for the capriciousness, violence, and untrustworthiness of African men. Bosman related the story of a vicious general so jealous of one of his wives that after she let a slave touch her necklace, he "caus'd both Wife and Slave to be put to Death, drinking their Blood." He claimed this general had had another wife's hands cut off, and that he reveled in mockingly making her try to perform household services with her stumps. Even African Christians should apparently not be trusted. Bosman recounted the presence of an "English Mulatto" who "pretends to be a Christian; . . . but . . . though he is Lawfully married in *England* he hath above eight Wives, and as many Mistresses." Bosman emphasized the drama and outlandishness of polygamy, in such exotic places as Fida, where men "have here forty or fifty, and their chief Captains there or four Hundred, some one Thousand, and the King betwixt four and five Thousand" wives, "warm Ladies."[14] Polygamy, and its power, appeared to be almost boundless.

"Separate Little Houses"

Bloodthirsty husbands and hot-blooded wives: such fantastical images of polygamy surely warmed many a European on a cold winter's night. Yet Bosman's account was no deviant outlier. Indeed, one scholar has called it "the authoritative account of black Africa for eighteenth-century Europe," a benchmark for accurate travel reporting. For all the monsters stalking their pages, there were still some genuine observations in these wild-eyed European portrayals of polygamy. Indeed, even the most flat-footed, tin-eared European observers recognized that there was considerable regional and national variation in how polygamy was practiced (something subsequent writers have not always appreciated). In some areas, they contended, a man took as many wives as he could; in others the practice was limited by Islam or related belief systems to four wives as a maximum.[15]

Africans offered their own, more sympathetic accounts. For instance, Olaudah Equiano's narrative recounted his experience of captivity among the Igbo in a more evenhanded way: "I got into the hands of a chieftain, in a very pleasant country. This man had two wives and some children, and they all used me extremely well, and did all they could do to comfort me; particularly the first wife, who was something like my mother." Venture Smith commenced his slave narrative with his own family history of plural marriage: "I was born at Dukandarra, in Guinea, about the year 1729. My father's name was Saungm Furro, Prince of the Tribe of Dukandarra. My father had three wives. Polygamy was not uncommon in that country, especially among the rich, as every man was allowed to keep as many wives as he could maintain."

Smith contended that he was the oldest child by the first wife. This plural marriage was not, however, a happy one. Smith contended that "the first thing worthy of notice which I remember was, a contention between my father and mother, on account of my father's marrying his third wife without the consent of his first and eldest, which was contrary to the custom generally observed among my countrymen. In consequence of this rupture, my mother left her husband and country, and travelled away with her three children to the eastward." So began Smith's journey, too. Such narratives acknowledged rules and customs governing these practices, as well as variations between regions. There was considerable mixing of peoples in all these areas. Yet by and large, polygyny, a system in which a man took multiple wives, was a known practice in all of them.[16]

Dahomey, the fabled city known for its female warriors, reveals the political stakes of polygamy in West African kingdoms in the eighteenth century. The palace complex, surrounded by a high wall ominously lined with a row of skulls, was simultaneously "the king's household, a city of women who carried out the king's orders, and . . . the policy-making apparatus of the state." The female soldiers leapt, armed, from polygyny itself, because the king's wives also served as his bodyguard. Other wives were advisers and administrators, traders and diplomats. In Dahomey, all the thousands of women, and even the few men (skilled artisans), were defined as wives to the king, regardless of gender or age. By the 1720s, the king already had more than two thousand wives (though he was intimate with few of them). Highborn and low-, they came from every possible background, the result of diplomatic negotiations, tribute from defeated nations, and captives from wars. The marriages were a metaphor for political power, as all the wives represented lineages. Their presence as subordinates to the king meant that all lineages in the kingdom were subordinate to the royal line. Polygamy was a central political metaphor as well as an institution.[17]

It is likely, then, that enslaved people like Roger carried with them from their own backgrounds a sense of how polygamy might function. His Anglicized name gives us no insight into his origins. However, enslaved people in that area of Virginia came from concentrations near the Bight of Biafra and Senegambia, with smaller numbers from Sierra Leone, the Gold Coast, and even Angola. Of course, slavers in these areas brought people from all over West Africa, and it is exceptionally challenging to pinpoint precisely the origins of individuals. Nonetheless, it is helpful to understand, even in a

[James Evans], *The King of Dahomy's Levée* (1793). This image shows at least some of the many wives arrayed around the king of Dahomey. Other wives, with baskets on their heads, labor in the background. From Archibald Dalzel, *The History of Dahomy, an inland Kingdom of Africa* (London: T. Spilsbury and Son, 1793). Courtesy of Beinecke Rare Book and Manuscript Library, Yale University.

limited way, how polygamy functioned in specific West African locales. To obtain some grounding, it helps to focus on the practices of marriage among what are called the Igbo people, who lived in and near the Bight of Biafra, in what is now Nigeria. Admittedly, even this more specific investigation is painted in broad brushstrokes. As with the "Algonquian" people we have seen, Igbo is a linguistic designation including a range of cultures and languages. It generalizes, but less than "African" does. It gives insight into the kinds of functions that polygamy held in specific West African settings. After all, "African" would not have been a description people there would have recognized or found particularly meaningful. Plural marriages were here part of a system, not simply an indicator of the capricious actions of a few tyrannical men. Europeans viewing Igbo and other households in the early modern era got one thing right: as in their own and other cultures, households both demonstrated and shaped power relations among West Africans.[18]

Among many Igbo peoples, lineage organized political and social structures. As one historian of the western Igbo has observed, "the real centers of political authority were located in the lineage heads," not in towns or even in chiefs. So lineage was the basis for political authority. Lineage, a unit smaller than a clan, was the major shaper of political and religious commitments. Power was measured in the ability to mobilize people and goods, but it could also include dominance over the land. Loyalties to the *umunna,* the *idumu,* the *ogbe* (all forms of lineage) determined war and peace, diplomacy and trade. Inheritance and providing a new generation for the ancestors were of paramount importance. Marriage allowed the orderly passing on of property and the ancestral line. On the whole, the Igbo were patrilineal, and indeed at least by a later period, property moved mainly from parents to sons.[19]

Marriage was important for many reasons, not least because it allowed for inheritance. It thus connected families vertically as well as horizontally, ensuring the all-important continuance of a lineage descending from particular ancestors. It was also an alliance between families and communities. It forged trade networks, and it passed on skills and customs from different places. It diversified knowledge, an especially significant feature in times of rapid change. Households, of a husband with a wife or wives, were the bricks of political authority. Wives could come from a variety of settings. Some were free and even elite; others could be captives. Obtaining the status of wives could help to ameliorate the inequalities that some women brought to marriage. Wives helped to generate wealth, through both productive and reproductive labor. Yam cultivation was especially important, and the labor of both women and men was critical to it. Wives also brought children, and thus ensured continuance of the lineage. Children were sources of labor, but also of important connections, and eventually of marital alliances themselves. Indeed, having a child marked status for wives, so that only mothers were entitled to wear items of value or elaborate headdresses. To be a childless, or even a son-less, wife could bring stigma.[20]

The range of kinds of marriage in precolonial Igbo society was wide, extending even to marriage between women. There was marriage by exchange, in which men swapped daughters; there was also marriage by "abduction" (in which parents of a bride agreed to have her taken by a man who could not pay bridewealth). Marriage could also be a form of pawning, as a man might marry off a daughter to settle a debt. There was also woman-woman marriage, in which a widow without sons contracted marriage to another woman, whose children (by a male lover) could then inherit from the deceased husband. This form of marriage was designed to solve the problem of inheritance patterns demanding sons. It is unclear how prominent this kind of marriage was in the seventeenth and eighteenth centuries, but it was in place by the nineteenth century. Both man-woman marriages and woman-woman marriages could be polygynous, involving many wives for whom the husband, whether female or male, paid a brideprice.[21]

Polygamy and monogamy had long rubbed together in these areas. Indeed, monogamy was a common institution, with polygyny reserved for the better-resourced and more powerful individuals in a community. Polygyny increased the productive and reproductive capacities of a given family, augmenting lineage possibilities as well as the number of laborers and thus also yielding a higher standard of living. It demonstrated and enhanced the power of high-ranking people; it indicated status as surely as gender. Such could affect internal household relations, as well as family rank. Having additional wives who had been enslaved could sometimes improve the condition of free wives, who gained their labor and also obtained an enhanced ability to spend time with their natal families because another wife could do their duties while they were away.[22]

"Each Wife lives in a separate little House," declared one observer on the Gold Coast. "Little House" was a way of designating a structure within a larger family compound, and might well have applied to Igbo households, too. Barbot contended that "each woman has in her husband's house a small hut." Women often lived in and ran their own homes within the general compound, and even the larger exterior spaces, containing several buildings, were often dominated by women. Still, the husband's authority marked the very architecture of compounds. The husband's house was at the central, often northern, position, distinguished sometimes by a different style of roof, indicating "public" space. He probably visited the wives in their own houses for intimacies, as his own house was more likely to be used for larger gatherings, debates, and war preparation.[23]

Gender, then, was a critical variable in household organization, but so were age and rank. Age-grades, or cohorts, structured life among Igbo peoples: younger people did menial tasks such as sweeping, older ones provided advice and leadership. The head of the lineage was often its oldest man, considered wiser and closer to the ancestors. Age could overlap with rank. A senior wife often controlled the whole compound. Smith claimed that "Rich Men . . . exempt two of their Wives from any Sort of Business. The first is generally his Eldest, or she who has born [*sic*] most Children to him; the other is always one of his youngest Favourites." In other areas, as among the Mina to the South, Barbot supposed that the first wife had "fully the care of the household" until she was "aged or infirm." European observers often claimed that all African wives were slaves, but such a contention, as in accounts of Native Americans, functioned in part to castigate indigenous men for their indolence. Even flawed European accounts demonstrate that differences between wives in terms of age and rank existed. Undoubtedly, wives did work hard, and many secondary ones, including some enslaved ones, did menial work for others, including the free wives. Still, even for enslaved wives, having many children could elevate status; even kings in some areas married captives as well as the daughters of chiefs. The household was the primary unit of labor and also a strong marker of rank in a larger community. A "person of property," or *ogaranya*, was "distinguished by his many wives, children, and slaves." Biafran lineage depended on these configurations and displays of property.[24]

Systems of Igbo household organization were not static, though. European observers saw polygamy, and, conditioned by their own stories, they presumed an enduring predisposition to lasciviousness. What they were probably witnessing, though, were recent and notable displays of centralizing masculine power. Polygamy had long existed and predated European inroads, but it probably intensified under new pressures of European presence and trading. The effects of the Atlantic slave trade, warfare to gain captives and to protect kin, had increased its importance in many areas, and possibly also made it more extreme. As one scholar has noted of the effects of the overseas slave trade in Africa generally, "more egalitarian ways of interacting may have given way to authoritarian systems predicated on military discipline."[25] They also intensified competition and drew lines more starkly between insiders and outsiders.

Dramatic political reorganizations reshaped this area in this period. In the sixteenth century, the Benin empire expanded in the west, prompting clashes and migrations. Ongoing wars in the seventeenth century between Igbo and Ibibio people ravaged the area to the east. Desire for access to trade with Europeans exacerbated these conflicts profoundly. Seeking guns and other goods, Igbo leaders captured more people for the slave trade, usually raiding old enemies. By the end of the century, the Igbo emerged victorious, thanks partly to help from new Akpa allies. The Akpa represented an impressive force predicated on masculine discipline and access to firearms. Despite the high value placed on young men in the Atlantic slave trade, and the profits to be made from them, Akpa warriors decapitated their enemies rather than selling them. Headless men conveyed messages of Akpa economic as well as martial prowess: the Akpa not only vanquished their enemies, but they were rich enough to afford the luxury of killing and mutilating them. In the face of this terrifying new alliance, the Ibibio became marginalized, either understandably fleeing or else being incorporated into Igbo lineages, in some cases as wives. This uptick in vulnerable refugees meant that wars provoked by the slave trade fed more victims into its maw, as raiders now preyed on those who had had to flee from Akpa warriors and their allies. Amid wars and migration, new lineages formed, and novel political alliances, forged out of blood and slave raiding, developed. Those left out suffered twice over.[26]

Here, as elsewhere, polygamy was a political response to changing landscapes. It structured differences between elite and commoner, between insiders and outsiders. Historians of a variety of African polygynous settings have pointed to this form of marriage as an elite strategy, one that contributed to rising inequalities between ranks and ethnicities, as well as to the formation of state institutions especially in the era in which the Atlantic slave trade was at its height. It was a form of marriage to establish and augment the authority of those at the top, at the expense of both women and lower-ranking men. Such may explain some of the more seemingly outlandish accounts by Bosman and others: the compounds with hundreds of wives and slaves, the elaborate ceremonials of many wives in attendance at the courts of rulers, the ambitious men at their center. In fact, some have argued that this kind of large-scale polygyny "was characteristic of the Slave Coast." The likelihood is that the pressures of the trade, especially in slaves and arms, contributed to a development of inegalitarian institutions, including polygamy.[27]

Igbo consolidation, like that of Dahomey, likely depended on polygamy, too, on a relatively few men concentrating power—and kin and wives and slaves—into ever fewer hands. Martial forces such as the Akpa, who joined the Igbo, tended to have more hierarchical organizations, with polygamy a fiercely protected prerogative. While there are few specific examples, a later example from another location, in which one of the wives of a local ruler was taken captive, can elucidate these processes. When this leader failed to obtain his wife's release by either negotiation or trade, he launched an attack, and a war, on her captors. Here, as in other locales in the early modern period, polygamy was a way for men to speak to other men of their privilege, their strong ties of lineage, and the many laborers—and warriors—they could mobilize. A new alliance of Igbo and Akpa, the Arochukwu confederacy, was headed by a council of men called the Three Fathers. Such a phrase demonstrates the importance of family in these political reconfigurations, as well as the sex and age of leaders. Who was excluded in these new alliances, though?[28]

Decapitated warriors held other meanings. Wars over captives and trade, and attendant political consolidations, also reshaped households, and again may have made polygamy more, not less, common. Women left more vulnerable may have joined larger compounds as a means of protection: nothing like a high wall festooned with skulls to make a mother and her children feel safe. It might have seemed preferable to be a secondary wife than simply a refugee outsider. Other women may have had little choice, entering households as captives. Kinship connections helped individuals to surmount chaos and uncertainty, growing in strength in this period and "assuming the role of state surrogate." Dependence on men who could mobilize people at the center of these networks may have also shifted domestic arrangements, enhancing the authority of already powerful men. In a parallel example from much farther afield, raiders captured a woman whose relatives then appealed to a local ruler, who managed to liberate her; no doubt this success gained him the gratitude and services of this woman's lineage. Revitalized networks formed by lineages enabled many individuals to endure devastating wars, slave raiding, and mass migration. Women's work and connections were critical to establishing these networks and to ensuring the continued functioning of lineages and even states. These systems, though, came to be transformed in the fierce furnace of the Atlantic slave trade itself. The most vulnerable—and least well protected by their kin—Africans found themselves carried across the ocean, where a brutal life of American slavery began.[29]

"All His Cry Was Poysned"

Roger's unsettled spirit, then, tugs us on the same journey, from West African compounds to Virginia plantations. The creeks and rivers that flowed out into the Chesapeake Bay and the Atlantic linked them to an old world. Yet that same set of waterways also cut them off. Lineage and kin had shaped the nature of unions among most West Africans; these powerful institutions no longer carried so much weight. While transformations had been occurring in their old worlds, dramatic alterations affected family formation and polygamy in American worlds. Roger and his "wifes" found themselves in another tumultuous period of transition, one that rocked the places they had known and those in which they found themselves. Domestic disorder was no more a timeless aspect of African-American life than it was for any other peoples, even amid the horrors of slavery. However, it accompanied the rapid reshaping of the institution in this time and place.[30]

Investigating the imposition of monogamy in detail in American settings shows how African people, women and men, reshaped institutions in new environments, and demonstrates that gender and sexuality were integral to the shape of plantation slavery in early America. "Did new sexual configurations [in which men dominated demographically] serve to empower African women?" one historian of West Africa has inquired. In general, one might wonder, do sexual configurations in which young men dominate demographically, such as prisons or ships, tend to empower women? Evidence from early-eighteenth-century Virginia, as well as material from elsewhere in the mainland and the Caribbean, suggests that the answer is *no*. Yet such an assumption has framed even recent work on slavery and marriage. These situations of male preponderance resulted in an increase in competition and did little to improve women's lives; indeed, they may have worsened them. Admittedly, there were moments of possibility for women in the "charter generations," times in which different kinds of family and gender patterns, including polygamy, might have emerged more strongly. Such possibilities became less likely in periods of entrenchment of new plantation regimes.[31]

Chattel slavery, present for many decades in Virginia when Roger died in 1712, expanded dramatically in the fifty years between 1680 and 1730. While estates were established farther west, plantations increased in size in old places, too, along those rivers and creeks. In the years around 1700, what had been prosperous farms, tended by a combination of enslaved and indentured laborers, started to become more recognizably plantations, increasingly higher-production operations dependent on the labor of enslaved Africans. The consolidation of land ownership supported this shift, as did a surge in the number of enslaved people imported. The Royal African Company brought many thousands; they continued to arrive after the RAC

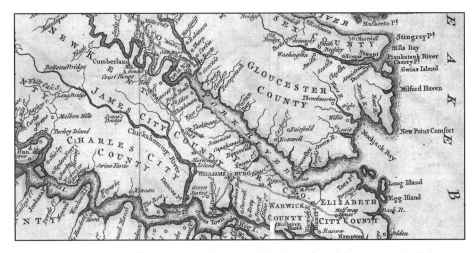

Joshua Fry and Peter Jefferson, *A map of the most inhabited part of Virginia containing the whole province of Maryland with part of Pensilvania, New Jersey and North Carolina* [London: Thomas Jefferys, 1755]. In this detail, it is possible to see "Rippenhall" (Ripon Hall) on the south bank of the York River, just north of Williamsburg. Courtesy of Library of Congress.

lost its monopoly. As has been well documented, this influx of Africans altered the nature of slavery in Virginia. Plantations developed and expanded quickly. Thousands of indigenous Africans from the Bight of Biafra, Senegambia, and other places joined creole Virginian-born enslaved people, reconfiguring social dynamics on those plantations.[32]

Ripon Hall, on the York River about twelve miles up from Yorktown, Virginia, was one such place of expansion. It was in an area of intersecting creeks, with gently sloping lands conducive to cultivation. Edmund Jenings purchased the land in 1687; he proceeded to direct the building of a large brick mansion, Ripon Hall, named after his ancestral Yorkshire home. Its name conjured an old world; its labor practices evoked a new one. By the time the inventory of goods was taken in 1713, there were thirty-seven enslaved people and four "Scotch" servants, probably Ulster Scots serving out indentures. There were two managers: William Jones, in charge of the big house and the tobacco houses, and John Hilliard, who ran the "Two Quarters" of enslaved people.[33]

These "Quarters" of enslaved people at Ripon Hall erupted with conflict, for Roger as for his "Countryman," George, in 1712. Hilliard looked on and reported. Apparently, George had "Complained of his being ill in his Stomach and Said his Country men had poisoned him for his wife." As he lay dying, "all his Cry was poysned." Despite the efforts of two doctors, George died, "a bad Loss," a managerial notation implying that he was a highly productive, highly valued man. So two impressive workers died in the same year over what appear to be domestic disputes, centered on jealousy over wives. Perhaps George was incorrect or even paranoid about being poisoned, but the account, taken together with that of Roger, suggests that these two men felt badly threatened or somehow thwarted in their domestic desires. In the end, these threats seemed sufficiently serious as to kill both of them. The reference to "Countrymen" and "Negro Men" implies that George was not born in Virginia but had been brought from West Africa. Such poisonings around domestic disputes took place in other times and places. At the estate of Henry Laurens in South Carolina in 1766, an enslaved woman named Chloe "died of poisin" delivered in the "potion from a jealous Sister . . . named Isabel. They were both the Wives of Mathias & it seems that Isabel droped some threatnings towards Chloe."[34]

Toxic domestic relations plagued Ripon Hall and other places, revealing moments in which individual enslaved people, both women and men, struggled to establish authority in households and communities. Such situations reveal the uncertainties of this period of transition. The population of the enslaved was beginning to reproduce itself, and there was an amelioration of the starkest sex ratio imbalances which had been a feature of earlier years. Such a setting meant that plural unions became more feasible in demographic terms. Yet it is not clear that they actually increased. Changes gripped Virginia in this period, and it is easiest to see them up close. If Ripon Hall experienced dramatic clashes rooted in masculine competition, neighboring plantations appear also to have been in domestic transition but with quite distinct results. A hard day's walk away, on the James River, there was another estate, Little-town/Utopia, owned by James Bray, with three cabins housing twenty-eight persons in 1726. This estate, which has been painstakingly excavated by archaeologists, reveals exceptional details about domestic transitions.[35]

"Debb's Quarter"

In the estate called Utopia, quite remarkably, an enslaved woman became the leader acknowledged even by managers and masters, probably because of her position as a senior wife. In Littletown, as in most Virginia plantations in this era, those recognized by masters as authorities among communities of enslaved people were usually men, as shown by the naming of housing clusters. However, in Utopia, the quarter was named Debb's. How and why did a woman come to control this space in such notable and unusual ways? Out of many possible reasons, the most plausible is that she was the senior wife in a polygamous household. Archaeological evidence suggests so. She must also have had a range of talents so notable as to have put this woman leader in the clear sightlines of even obtuse, indifferent managers. There must have been something rather exceptional about Debb herself. She may have had power based on a previous position (such as a trader) or lineage in West Africa, so widely acknowledged by other enslaved people that it registered even for the managers. She might have been a relatively rare Virginian-born creole at a period when many Africans arrived in that area, possibly in a relationship with a manager or master.[36] She might have had significant linguistic or diplomatic skills.

The suggestion that Debb's leadership stemmed from her position as senior wife comes from evidence about the architecture of Utopia; from the archaeological evidence there; and from Bray's other plantation. First, Bray and his manager seem to have been willing to recognize West African living patterns, as shown by buildings at Utopia. They may also have acknowledged Debb as the senior wife in a larger quarter. The architecture of the three slave cabins at Utopia closely and deliberately resembled West African housing compounds. For example, they flanked a yard and aligned to the cardinal points. The largest and most elaborate building, dubbed Structure 10 by archaeologists, was in the north, which in at least some African building traditions could represent "maleness and authority." Yet in the period in which Structure 10 was built, it was "Debb's quarter." Debb lived in Structure 10, and gave her name to it, yet it would have been strange to put a woman's quarter in this particular position. This house held a preponderance of women's things, and thus probably a lot of women. Yet archaeologists also think that men had a prominent role there. With the evidence taken together, polygamy was the most plausible situation there.[37]

The presence of an unusually high number of subfloor pits supports such a reading. Such pits, dug by enslaved people and a distinctive feature of life in the Chesapeake in the eighteenth century, "may be the purest archaeological form of self-determination." They had various functions: food and root storage, personal storage or "hidey holes," even religious shrines. There were pits at all of Utopia's buildings in this period, but the greatest number were at Structure 10, with only three of them likely used for food storage. Such pits might therefore have been a way to replicate the sovereignty of a wife in her "little House," a way to hold individual resources in a communal household. Indeed, one pit even held the remains of a wooden box with a lock on it. These pits may also show that ethnic or other rivalries may have been fierce in this period. While it may be impossible to state with certainty, the presence of so many pits suggests that there was here, as in Ripon, competition for resources and authority within a single household.[38]

Is it likely that Debb's position stemmed from her leadership as a senior wife? That would be unusual. Yet Bray's other plantation, Rockahock, shows a highly unusual gender pattern: a preponderance of women, not men, in contrast to nearly every other Virginia plantation in this era. Rockahock, twenty miles away on the Chickahominy River, had six slave quarters housing thirty women and sixteen men. At two quarters in particular, women substantially outnumbered men, by something like a 3:1 ratio. It is possible that these cabins were stations for seasoning, places where Africans adjusted to the grim reality of plantation existence. Yet they may also have been households of plural unions. The clatter of cooking pots and children, both of which are also listed in the inventories, suggests a modicum of stability, domestic labor, and sexual unions. So do some of the names of the enslaved people living there. The names that appear in inventories for newly arrived Africans were not those given at birth or early in life. Instead, they were given on the ship or on reaching Virginia. Three of the six men were called Jupiter, Cain, and Thunder. These names, rooted in classical, Old Testament, and natural worlds, may have been meant to evoke, even if sardonically, masculine prowess and even aggression. A few of the women's names also implied male recognition of desirability: Queen, Venus, and Beauty. One name, Parthenia, belonged to two adult females at Bridges, leading one archaeologist to argue that they might have been mother and daughter. If that is the case, it suggests enduring family life there.[39]

Bray recognized a female leader of a cabin, and he purchased more women than men. Why did he make such atypical decisions? It may have been because women cost less, but it also shows the uncertainties and possibilities of this period. Traders in the Bight of Biafra exported a higher proportion of women than did most others in West and West-Central Africa partly because of the political reconfigurations there in this period. At the same time, Virginians had never before experienced such an influx of newly arrived Africans. Those in charge may have followed different strategies for incorporating them into plantation life. A few like Bray may have given them wider berth and left them to build lives on their own terms. Enslaved individuals also did what they could to preserve resources, status, and lines of belonging: building housing compounds similar to those left behind; digging and making use of subfloor pits; and perhaps organizing themselves in houses dominated by wives. Women were a strong presence at Bray's plantation; they were elsewhere, too, though formal recognition of such powers was more elusive. Such women might well have preserved familiar ways of organizing space and labor where they possibly could. Bray seems to have been unusually receptive to such influences. Other planters and managers had different strategies, but family organization was central to them. The transition for enslaved families in these early years of expansion of slavery in Virginia was dramatic. There were changes among enslaved people on Bray's plantations, but the alterations were even more pronounced in most other Virginia plantations.[40]

"Brave Fellows"

Robert "King" Carter's considerable and well-inventoried holdings plainly show shifts in family organization. Reversing James Bray's atypical priorities, Carter, who chose first among those enslaved people who arrived in Virginia, purchased twice as many men as women. Nonetheless, Carter encouraged enslaved people to settle in domestic unions, even offering "securable and separate domestic environments" to those who were married or had children. The inventory at his death listed his 829 slaves in family groups within cabins: sometimes as married couples with children, sometimes women or men with children, sometimes groups of only men. So a typical group includes Harry, "Foreman"; Kate, "his Wife"; and their five children, from ages six months to nine years. Plural unions do not have a major presence, but they appear. In Forrest Quarter, there was a foreman, George, and "his Wifes," Betty and Bess. There were other listings of a single person, such as "Little Nanny" and her three children. There were also same-sex groupings of men, such as one with Prince, Mucca Jack, Robin, Dembo, and Echo. We should be careful of presuming that single-sex or single-parent households were somehow inadequate "families," an assumption that pervades earlier scholarly literature. Even households of unrelated men may have become families, with their own affections, hierarchies, conflicts, and intimacies. On the other hand, these kinds of configurations of men on their own also had potentially destabilizing effects, as they were likely to lead to competition over women and also over resources. In sum, if focused too much on monogamy and polygamy, we miss what was in fact another enormously significant transition: from household compounds that had largely been dominated by women to other kinds of households, sometimes monogamous but also occasionally all-male.[41]

The configuration of people on these plantations looks set in amber in these lists, static and unchanging. But it was a process, not a given, one that involved managers and planters as well as enslaved people. Enslaved people shaped their families, but they did so in highly specific contexts, ones influenced by the choices of those who controlled their labors. Carter was innovative in his plantation management strategies. Like most Virginian planters, he bought many more men than women. The ubiquity of homosocial male-dominated cabins was novel, the result of demographic imbalances stemming from the interests of planters and managers. They did not care if this situation resulted in aggrieved, unattached single men, as long as plantation productivity was at its peak. Carter's management strategies also affected enslaved leadership and domestic configurations. Carter pioneered Virginian use of enslaved foremen. West Indian planters had been using the system of specifically empowering one enslaved person to be a foreman in charge of others. In Virginia, traditionally, usually a leader was an entrusted enslaved person, informally authorized, as Debb was for Bray's Utopia. By contrast, Carter instigated a more formal system of leadership recognition, one in which women did not figure as formally recognized authority figures. Carter rewarded trusted foremen with houses of their own, for themselves and their families, as well as greater food rations.[42] The inventory of enslaved people recognized the push for men and "wives," even if the law did not.

In such circumstances, polygamy practiced by enslaved people was not simply a familiar "tradition," nor was it simply a way of flouting European authority (though it may have had this effect). It was also no longer a system embedded in protective lineage systems or household compounds largely run by women. Instead, it became a way of asserting masculine status at points in which few were available: not lineage, not property, not age. Masculinities therefore came under entirely new pressures. Plural marriages in West African settings did not empower women. Yet they were part of a larger system in which women could have official powers. This ceased to be the case in plantations of Virginia.

When we spy the occasional plural union, as on King Carter's plantations, its context was dramatically different from what it would have been in West Africa. African plural unions had a long history, shot through with the exploitation of women, both enslaved and free. Yet in American settings, the context for them in terms of gender was distinct: the sex ratio was strongly against polygyny, given the preponderance of men. Their practice had novel meanings, too. In early-eighteenth-century Virginia, the sex ratio was at its most even 3 men to 2 women. It even dropped at some points to 2 men to 1 woman. This fact alone begins to explain why plural unions were comparatively rare in these settings. Yet it also means that they took on even starker meanings. These kinds of numbers mean that it was difficult enough for many enslaved men to establish a union at all. Lower-ranking men, who remained in those same-sex groups, may well have resented the ability of a few leading men to have two wives, or even one wife and the extra food and housing space associated with that situation. Perhaps it was an incentive for them to advance, but there would also have been a lot of frustrated younger men, barred from the prerogatives of household authority and all its pleasures.[43] Treatments of polygamy have generally circled around resentments between women, but polygamous systems also generated considerable, sometimes murderous, tensions between men lacking the privileges of marriage.

Many of the people transported across the Atlantic were nonelites who had already endured slavery and poverty. Occasionally the powerful got mixed in, but on the whole, there were a lot of vulnerable people, already suffering fractured kinship and lineage. On arrival, weakened and traumatized by the voyage, they then stumbled out into the horror of the slave sale, further journeys, and bewildering new homes filled with menacing strangers. Once handed their meager allowance of food and clothing, they were sent to cabins, often filled, confoundingly, with a lot of men. Some men were sent to live only with other men, an arrangement which in their places of origin was unusual and temporary, for soldiers and others; women made homes. These new arrivals were then given their tasks, which for men often meant work they saw as women's: that is, agricultural labor. On American plantations, labor that had been a woman's job in West African settings became instead the relentless labor of enslaved people, both men and women. Such a situation probably prompted further aggression, as enslaved men worked to reestablish masculine status markers. There may also have been ethnic tensions in this process. In a few cultures, including, notably, those centered on the yam and kolanut, as the Igbo were, men had in fact long worked in fields. So in Igbo cultures, both women and men cultivated the land, albeit in distinct ways. Gender frontiers existed among Africans, too. The imposition of what might have seemed like Igbo forms of labor organization might also have prompted interethnic aggression.[44]

A system with a shortage of women and a lot of young men intent on proving their manhood in disorienting new households was not one likely to lead to a great deal of liberation or happiness for women, or indeed for men. It may have occasionally given women a greater choice of partners, but it also meant the omnipresent threat of violence, including sexual violence. Even when the manager of the plantation recognized a woman as a "wife," it did not mean that the marriage was respected, as Roger's thwarted attempt to "keep" such wives suggests. While such frustrations may have driven men like Roger to despair, other men almost certainly continued to use access to women as a marker of authority related to gender, age, and rank. Such women also had a lot more to fear than just other enslaved men. Free men, too, exploited and abused them, intent not just on showing their masculine prowess but also on intimidating enslaved women and men both. Rape of a wife, just as with the decapitation of a husband, was a sure way to instill terror.

The nature of communities of enslaved women and men in early-eighteenth-century Virginia shifted not only owing to changing sex ratios and gender patterns, but also because of alterations in patterns of age and seniority. Populations of enslaved people in early-eighteenth-century Virginia were predominantly male, and they were predominantly young. Age-grades had in part shaped life among many West African men and women. Among the Igbo, for instance, older women and men gained status, and the head of a lineage, its oldest man, held great power (and often multiple wives and a large housing compound). Young people did menial tasks for older ones. The system of American slavery, and its debilitating preference for young people, upended this structured way of organizing society. In first generations, age-grades came under enormous pressure, as the oldest and most distinguished people were left behind. After all, it was younger men, whose physical strength brought great wealth to men like Carter, who commanded the highest prices and were imported in high numbers. In other words, the disruption of traditional age-based markers of status by the

Atlantic slave trade may have caused an intergenerational set of disputes, as younger men came to win prerogatives which had been associated in West Africa with older men. Among such privileges would have been household authority and "wifes."[45]

In Anglo-American slave settings, the men likeliest to become husbands with more than one wife were younger or middle-aged men whose status came from productive labor or particular skills. The practice of plural marriages was not the same as it had been in West African settings, where it had been the purview of older heads of compounds and lineage. Age and senior status appear to have ceased to matter in the same ways. In Barbados in the seventeenth century, Richard Ligon recorded that masters allowed enslaved men who were "brave fellows" to have "two or three wives." The status of "brave fellows" is a bit unclear, but it implies physically strong, impressive men, the kind of productive laborers valued most by the slave system. Skilled workers and foremen enjoyed higher status, and some of them also had multiple wives. Henry Drax's roughly contemporaneous instructions on managing a Barbadian plantation asked that "[I] wold have you Continue Kind to Moncky Nocco who has bene ane Exelentt Slave . . . and head overseer. . . . [Give him a generous food allowance] . . . to dispose of as he shall think fitt to his mother *wifes* and family." "Excellence" and leadership qualities presumably placed Nocco in a position to take on multiple "wifes" as well to support his mother, a nod to lineage's power, as well as to Nocco's relative youth. This "worthiness" meant that he received more food and could maintain the women in his household. Such a recasting was typical in American settings. The kind of sage elder, the head of lineage, who would have had many wives in West African settings seems to have been supplanted by younger, or at the very least middle-aged, men who were considered to have "earned" this prerogative on American plantations. Of the five men who had two wives on Montpelier estate in Jamaica in a much later period, all were skilled workers, either in the first gang or carpenter, boiler, or head driver. None was old. The use of polygamy as a reward suggests the depth of masculine interest among enslaved people in showing power in this way; it also shows that masters and overseers not only allowed polygamy on plantations but even occasionally encouraged it.[46]

The meanings of polygamy in such plantation situations were distinct from those associated with it in West Africa. Still, plural unions as practiced on Virginia plantations in the eighteenth century did have continuities with

West African practices. Just as it had in West Africa, marital status, even if recognized only informally and outside the law in Virginia, brought more elite status. The evidence from Utopia, Ripon Hall, and a range of other plantations across the Americas strongly suggests that polygyny existed, and that it brought rewards to the men who could practice it: more resources, bigger houses, authority over men as well as women. In a system in which traditional variables of masculine status—whether rank, lineage, age, experience, caste, or labor patterns—were under considerable pressure, it is hardly surprising that a few men turned to domestic dominance over women as a way to regain status in uncertain situations. Careful examination of the world of early-eighteenth-century Virginia plantations (and as hinted at in other places) reveals that polygyny came out of negotiations between enslaved people and those who managed their labors and lives. So there was assertion of West African models, but this was not a simple story of agency and resistance. While earlier, more uncertain moments had included female leaders and polygamous households, increasingly planters dangled rewards associated with household authority in front of men who were in fact far from those who practiced "resistance": they were the men who had won the trust of overseers, managers, and masters. As in other settings, polygamy both demonstrated and enhanced masculine authority among enslaved communities for a few higher-ranking men.

Rank as well as gender mattered to these dynamics. The continuities were thus: plural unions marked status for men, and to a lesser degree wives in them, and women's work palpably supported and augmented men's status, in worlds old and new. Women labored incessantly in both worlds. For some women, slavery and marriage went together. Such women could have found in each role reason to lament what it meant to be a woman. Some few women, such as Debb perhaps, might have benefited from the higher status associated with a household of privilege, as well as the rank, both within and beyond the household, that would have attended being the senior wife. For many other women, though, subordination in both slavery and marriage would have extended to being ruled by other men and women, in dismal domestic settings.

Yet the context was distinct. In putting old forms to new uses, Roger and others were essentially advancing innovation rooted in traditional structures, not simply seeking to restore an old style of marriage. This reorientation spoke as loudly and eloquently to other enslaved people as it did to the Anglo-American managers and masters. Plural unions in American settings were much rarer, and thus arguably more notable indicators of status, for men who had lost critical ways of asserting their rank through lineage, caste, or age. Kin lines could not be followed or mobilized in the same ways, even as families remained vital to life. The pits under the ground demonstrate the sense of atomization—the way individual and smaller groups forged identities amid larger quarters—in these early generations. Men also competed with one another for women. Polygamy came out of fierce rivalries, ones that could also result in men being hanged or poisoned. Polygamy became a statement of power among those stuck in a system actively trying to render them powerless. Yet it also was a reward to "brave fellows." Women, too, paid a price in both West Africa and the Americas, for systems in which their labor supported men.

Roger's use of "tradition" was a complicated patchwork of defiance, assertion of older models, and power plays within communities of the enslaved, ones informed by rank, age, and gender. So too was the architecture of Utopia. "The restoration of some traditional domestic patterns among its African residents" is how one archaeologist describes Utopia's material culture. Yet it was not quite a restoration since "although the design of the sites is reminiscent of Central and West African living arrangements, the buildings themselves ... reflect an English vernacular ... tradition." Such a combination might well epitomize the ways in which radically conservative choices were made: old patterns, new materials. To build such a compound had one meaning in West Africa, where they were common; it had quite another on the other side of the Atlantic, where they were not. It must have come out of negotiation, if not actual conflict, between managers and masters, between managers and enslaved people, between overseers and those whom they oversaw, between women, between men, between women and men. Is it possible that Bray or his manager felt that allowing these styles would make for a more settled population of enslaved people? Or had enslaved people themselves, maybe the carpenter, asserted preferred designs? Maybe Debb and others had force enough to ensure that their views were incorporated into the buildings of Utopia. Even where women were not always accorded official authority, they left marks on the landscape of slavery: needles around a hearth, names on a list, family structures.[47]

After all, women were critical to these domestic reorganizations. There were continuities, but also distinct contexts. The texture of such plural unions, as well as their frequency, would have changed considerably. In the West African settings, these marriages would have been formally sanctioned and might well have involved kin who could offer protection. Such would not typically have been the case in North American settings. The transformation of marriage and childbearing was painfully profound for enslaved women and men. A woman who had many children in West Africa might formally have gained freedom or a higher rank: a possibility that did not extend to enslaved women in British colonies whose fruitfulness and unremitting, numbing reproductive labor was rewarded but rarely with freedom. Motherhood took on new, grimmer meanings. As one African historian observes, "among Igbo women, bearing children was a source of joy." Yet even in African settings, such was not true for all women; enslaved women and others may have hated bearing the children of their masters. Still, there could be positive meanings. For enslaved African-American mothers on plantations, the happiness brought by children was severely tempered by the bleak future of slavery they knew awaited those babies: endless labor, coercion, and violence. Some of these women were also bearing the children of masters and managers, which made such children, unwittingly, symbols of dominance and violence, palpable reminders of acts of violation. In places such as Virginia, an enslaved husband or father could not offer as much protection to a wife or daughter as he would have liked. Her chances of suffering sexual violence increased, and the range of possible violators was horrifically extended. If some few enslaved men used access to enslaved women to make claims about power and status to other men, so, alas, did an even greater number of free Anglo-American men. The rich irony is that such men could applaud themselves on avoiding the sin of polygamy, instead in some cases committing adultery by sexually exploiting enslaved women. The complicated nexus of sex and power in these relation-ships forms the subject of much historical research.[48] These white men could blame their own crimes on the heat and seductiveness of such "sable Venuses," deeply disrupting and disrespecting African-American households, the autonomy of wives and mothers, and the authority of husbands and fathers. Those tales have enduring, malignant power.

"The Endearing Ties of Husband and Wife"

In fact, despite all the breathless, condemnatory stories about African propensity to polygamy, Africans had frequently been monogamous. African Americans, even those from polygamous societies, became even more so. Some enslaved people in Virginia had already been enslaved or lower-caste people in West Africa, too, and in some cases, descendants of enslaved people. For them, monogamy was the most likely configuration. Monogamy for even greater numbers may have solved some problems in American settings. Still, the entire nexus for polygamy, the cushioning if constraining networks of kin and lineage in West Africa, had been stripped away. Life had revolved around lineages small and big. Instead, it came to focus on the model Anglo-American nuclear family unit. Female-dominated compounds receded in official terms. Enslaved people developed new strategies for building families. Systems with both polygamy and monogamy structured in terms of lineage and age-grades came to be replaced by ones in which monogamous households prevailed and in which age and lineage declined as key variables shaping life. Monogamous nuclear family structures may have served as a kind of lingua franca, in much the way that the English language replaced so many different African ones. Polygamy did not recede among African-American populations "naturally." Instead, it is helpful to consider that the move from a system in which polygamy and monogamy comfortably coexisted and were formally recognized to one centered on monogamy exclusively was a set of transitions for enslaved men and women, and that polygamy was merely one aspect of a much larger system of organizing families, communities, and polities.[49]

Enslaved women themselves may have rejected polygamy, its jealousies and rivalries. It may be that in part some limited protection for such women came from monogamous unions more recognized by masters and managers. That this system did not entirely protect them is of course plain from abundant evidence of sexual violence. But it may be that it was felt to offer the strongest protection in the face of ongoing predations from white men. In these situations, it seems unlikely that an uneven sex ratio, a heavy tilting toward younger men's demographic dominance, empowered African and African-American women. For some, it meant they were targets of sexual violence from men who competed with one another through access to women's bodies and labors. In the early eighteenth century, in Virginia, as in other places, there was a notable transformation in African-American family life and social structures, if a slow and submerged one. Monogamy as an exclusive institution came out of a series of fits and starts, out of contestations between women and men, between women, and between men.[50]

Were such households havens in a heartless world? Most historians of enslaved families have argued for, or even assumed, that this was how

African-American families functioned. They did sometimes, maybe even often, work this way, and without doubt, this world faced by enslaved families was heartless enough. Still, family life itself also included competition and conflict, cut across by vectors of gender, age, and status, among both African Americans and Anglo-Americans. Tracing the ancient and medieval European past of the family, one scholar has reminded us: *"Familia* long held this meaning of a band of slaves." Single-sex households of enslaved men could be *familia,* and family. So could polygamous and monogamous unions, and households headed by a single parent. Families performed many functions. Love and comfort were two vital aspects of families, but only two. Historians of colonial Anglo-American marriages, following historians of English ones, have spent a great deal of time on the debate about whether, and how, and when marriages ceased being dynastic and familial arrangements and became instead unions of affections. Rarely does this literature consider those marriages defined by communities, but undefined by law, such as those between enslaved people.[51]

Moving outward from African-American families, it is possible to get past tired and unanswerable debates about the increasingly affectionate nature, or not, of marital relations in the eighteenth century. Indeed, if slavery and its American rise brought new marital regimes for African Americans, they also did so for Anglo-Americans. Monogamy, like polygamy, is a complex and changing institution. Like polygamous marriage, monogamous marriage served the interests of men in particular. Colonialism and systems of slavery altered marriage patterns among Anglo-Americans, just as among African Americans; there was a dynamic interconnection. Virginia's elite married early, and they married often: far more so than in England. They intermarried incessantly, more than they would have done in England, and their women married young, younger than English counterparts. Whatever an increasingly sentimental culture might claim, marriage in the eighteenth century was not simply about two people loving each other. It was also a method by which to increase and demonstrate personal, family, economic, and political status. This fact depended on the legal and economic disadvantages of wives.

Fierce rivalries over women played out among Anglo-American men, too.[52] Such a point comes clear in the marital lives of Edmund Jenings, Robert Carter, and James Bray, three masters of estates where plural marriages of some kind seem to have existed. All of them were highly ambitious;

marriages, sometimes serial marriages, helped to secure their dynastic and personal goals. Edmund Jenings married Frances Corbin. Whatever her personal charms, the fact that she was sister-in-law to one political leader in Virginia, Richard Lee (the younger) and cousin to another, Ralph Wormeley, surely increased her attractions. The ambitious Jenings served for many years as Wormeley's deputy secretary of state before taking over the job himself in 1702. Marriage did not ensure his political and economic climb, but it surely did not hurt it.

Marriage also furthered the extraordinary ambitions of Robert "King" Carter. King Carter won his crown on the basis of family inheritances, as well as ruthless acquisition of land and enslaved people. His father, John Carter, married five women in succession: testament to the high mortality rates, and importance of marriage, in seventeenth-century Virginia. Robert was the son of the fourth wife, Sarah Ludlow Carter. When his elder half-brother died, he inherited the family fortune and "over the ensuing forty-two years, he accumulated the largest estate ever amassed in Virginia through a combination of agriculture, trade, and the fruits of officeholding." His estate was also enhanced by marriages. He married first in 1688, to Judith Armistead. She died in 1699, and he married again in 1701. His second wife, Elizabeth Landon Willis, was a rich widow. Again, while their marriage may have been a loving one (and it was an active one, as they had ten children before Elizabeth died in 1719), it was also one that supported his economic and social ambitions. His interests were familial: to build a dynasty, which he did. His children married well and increased family holdings. Marriage was the foundation for his economic and political ambitions: to accumulate massive amounts of property to ensure good livings for all his children. It also bolstered his economic position, when he took over the property of a well-heeled widow.[53]

James Bray also benefited considerably from his marriage to the oddly named Mourning Pettus, who apparently did not mourn her husband, Thomas Pettus, for too long when he died in 1690. She had married James Bray by the end of that year—if not before Pettus was cold in his grave, at least before his goods could be inventoried by his executors: a very short time indeed. When Pettus's executors arrived to take the inventory of household goods, they found that "we came to[o] late for [Bray] had Carried them away." The likelihood is that Bray had also taken most of the enslaved people working on Pettus's plantations. There were probably at least twenty such workers; only five appear in the inventory. We don't know whether James and Mourning loved each other. Was Mourning biding her time with a dying Thomas, until she could throw herself into James Bray's strong arms? Was she already fighting with the Pettus children and so an eager coconspirator in joining Bray in taking their property? Was she the hapless victim of a charming rogue who commandeered her inheritance and that of the Pettus children? Records do not tell us, but we do know that Mourning and James married with indecorous haste in a move that immediately enriched Bray. It also involved him in complicated wranglings with Thomas Pettus's heirs, but Bray emerged triumphant again, flashing the deed to Littletown/Utopia in 1700, when he rebuilt it (following fires in the 1690s that had destroyed the structures of the Pettus era). The whole complicated Anglo-African edifices of Utopia depended on the foundations of the union, as unseemly as it was, of Mourning Pettus and James Bray; families depended upon families. Marriage shaped lives in so many ways.[54]

Whether these men loved their wives or not, they exploited a marriage system in which, as one scholar has pointed out, "the new husband took control over all property the wife brought to the union." Indeed, there was an "almost desperate quality about the need to marry," as well as the young age at marriage (especially for women) and what might be termed the extreme endogamy of elite eighteenth-century Virginians, who married cousins and also married within a tiny cohort of some twenty families. It is true that the larger culture put pressure on marriage as simply a form of dynastic economic advancement, as an increasing critique of marrying for money came to dominate Anglo-American culture. Yet marrying with self- and family interest in mind remained the most dominant form of union among elite Virginians, a situation that might well have been connected with the sexual vulnerability of enslaved and servant women, as the diary of William Byrd indicates.[55]

Virginia's elite knew that, especially for men, marriage could bring power. Domestic choices cannot be severed from the larger political and socioeconomic context. Marriage—something masters and mistresses did— was not only about love. It was also powerfully about status and authority. Specific practices of marriage and sex, ones in which the law upheld the prerogatives of white men in both areas, supported their ambition and the accumulation of property and wealth. It did so in part out of a system that limited property for wives; forbade enslaved people any legal rights over their persons, families, or goods; and enhanced the holdings of husbands. Its denial to enslaved people, then, was also an act of power.

Enslaved men knew that, especially for men, marriage could bring power. "We have no Property. We have no Wives. No Children. We have no City. No Country." So began the central paragraph in a petition against slavery in Massachusetts in 1773 from an enslaved man, Felix, in a list of what one historian has termed "the perquisites necessary to exercise citizenship." The linkage here, of wives and children with property and civic and national identity, shows just what civil disabilities enslaved men endured. They knew all too well what they lost by being barred from marriage. Another petition noted: "The endearing ties of husband and wife we are strangers to for we are no longer man and wife then our masters or Mestreses thinkes proper." This petition continued: "How can a Slave perform the duties of a husband to a wife or parent to his child[?] How can a husband leave master and work and Cleave to his wife[?] How can the wife submit themselves to there Husbands in all things?" In such claims, the system of slavery made a sham of husbandly duties and wifely obedience; enslaved men used marriage and patriarchal privilege to call upon legislators to end slavery.[56]

Enslaved women, too, knew that marriage could bring power, though also uncertainties. "How could you be married and be a slave, monogamous and yet be subjected to forced separation and violation?" one historian has asked. One woman, "Fanny the property of Colonel Burwell," came before the Baptists in Virginia in the first decade of the nineteenth century for this very issue. The Baptists took discipline seriously, investigating members like Fanny, enslaved and free, for infractions, from "the many superfluous forms and Modes of Dressing . . . Cock't hatts [and] curl'd and powdered hair" to socializing with the "Carnal & Unbelieving," to "the Sin of Uncleanness." Another member accused Fanny "Of haveing two husbands living." In all likelihood, Fanny's marital crime stemmed not from the actual practice of polyandry. Rather, she had probably been sold away from her first spouse and thus remarried. Fanny wanted to live right, in fellowship with her Baptist community. She seems to have made a reasonably good case for herself, as records from March 1808 report that "Fanny gave information to the church of her situation and her relation being strengthened by some of the brethren they have come to a conclusion to leave the matter for consideration." However, by April 1808, "The matter being investigated[,] the church appears unanimous in her Excommunication and she is excommunicated." Fanny, trying to follow Baptist regulations, was condemned to excommunication because of her marriages. On the whole, disciplinary actions disproportionately targeted blacks. The Baptists did at some points condemn separating enslaved husbands and wives, with one 1797 decision that those who did so should be punished: "Is it agreeable to Scripture for any member to part Man & Wife. Ans[wer]. No. And any member who shall be guilty of such crimes shall be dealt with by the Church." Despite this ruling, few appear in the disciplinary records for this crime. By 1826, this church reversed the policy: "The committee appointed to take into consideration the expediency of framing a rule to prevent professors of religion from parting man & wife among their slaves reported they . . . were of opinion that they thought it best to have no rule on the subject." For enslaved couples, "no rule" meant no protection.[57]

To keep the attention on individuals and stories of disorder is to ignore larger structures of marriage as spaces of power and conflict. One historian has argued that "the invalidation of marriage" was part of a larger "system of white dominance over blacks." Emphasizing "besetting sins" made it seem as if domestic disorder was inevitable among certain populations. Consider the racist claims in a letter from even a committed abolitionist and minister in 1857: "The African has the largest organs of generation in the world, the most exotic heat; he is the most polygamous of men. The Negro girls of Boston are only *chaste* in the sense of being *run after*. After their first menstruation they invariably take a man—so say such who know." Such assertions suggest that Euro-Americans clung to these tired stereotypes in order to keep making race and difference, in a variety of novel contexts. To allege that individuals simply did not respect the institution of Christian monogamy was to ignore the ways that structures of law, state, and church made legal monogamy an impossibility for such individuals: women like Fanny and Debb, men like Felix and Roger. It was also a way to contend that polygamy indicated physical difference, showing itself in "unchaste" and "exotic" bodies.[58]

Slave traders and plantation managers and abolitionists alike recounted old and self-serving stories about alleged African propensities to polygamy. Those who made such claims severed African people from their countries and communities, in an attempt to render them timelessly and naturally prone to polygamy and disorder. Roger's head, then, might symbolize these dark processes. Still, it was much more than a symbol. It belonged to a human being, called Roger, who evidently had at least one wife. This woman, whose name is lost to us, might have loved Roger; she might have hated him. But we can assume safely that, whatever her story, in her life, she labored, she loved, she endured. This woman survived the horror of the Atlantic slave trade and the degradations attending the entrenchment of plantation slavery in Virginia. What did his widow(s) think and feel when staring at the rotting head of someone known, and possibly loved? Did he have children who had to look up to see their father's head dangling over them? Conjuring up these ancestors is haunting.

This man, termed Roger, was a son and a grandson, a husband, probably a brother and a nephew, and possibly a father. He had ancestors, who, in his view, protected and watched out for him. Men like Roger and the women in his life hardly possessed a uniquely "strong attachment" to polygamy. Rather, they had enduring ties connecting them powerfully to the living, the dead, and the unborn; polygamy was part of that world. Roger's act was one of both tragic submission to, and audacious defiance of, the grim realities of plantation slavery in the Americas. Roger probably did not attain the titles that mattered most in Igbo cultures, a process believed to transform a person into a respected and settled ancestor. To fail to achieve this status in life meant that, in death, a soul would wander the universe, causing pain for the living.[59] Indeed, even centuries on, the spirits of Roger and the women, men, and children of his community grieve us still.

PART TWO

Enlightened Encounters

5. "The Natural Violence of Our Passions"

Free women, like others in the eighteenth-century Atlantic world, knew that marriage could bring power. They further knew that, for them, marriage could also take it away. One such wife, writing to her husband in 1782, fretted that "Even in the freeest countrys our property is subject to the controul and disposal of our partners, to whom the Laws have given a soverign Authority." The "freeest countrys" still did not allow wives full liberty, as, by law, husbands held their property and thus "Authority." Even the most privileged women experienced subordination as a result. These personal problems were national ones. Indeed, she herself had been pondering the lessons of "all History and every age" about women's relationship to power and the state. She had been doing so through books, most especially a French treatise, Antoine Léonard Thomas's *An Essay on the Character, the Manners, and the Understanding of Women, in Different Ages.* From these readings, and from her own experience, she had decided that while men gave up much for the state, including their own lives and "blood," women gave up more, in sacrificing "those whom we Love most." With characteristic thoughtfulness and brio, she concluded therefore: "Patriotism in the female Sex is the most disinterested of all virtues" because women—denied property, "Authority," and full and direct political representation—personally gained nothing from their heroic sacrifices.[1]

The woman was Abigail Adams, and she was writing as a new nation struggled to spring forth from a devastating war and a startling political revolution. As her husband, John, worked to negotiate that settlement, in the wake of the American Revolution, the relationship of household and political orders took on new resonances and provoked questions. Some of the most marginalized people in the early modern world—illiterate African women on Virginia plantations whose traces remain mainly in needles on hearths and names on lists—pondered polygamy, despotism, and power. So did some of the most learned and vocal men and women at the center of what has been termed Enlightenment. The imagined dynamics of polygamy afforded an appealing way to mull over how men could and should exercise power, in households, societies, and nations. Throughout the Atlantic world, such concerns absorbed both women and men, as they read, wrote, chatted, debated, and even joined in revolutions. Abigail Adams read works by men like Thomas, but made up her own mind.

"If we take a survey of countries and ages, we shall every where see the women adored and oppressed." So opened Thomas's essay grappling with men's "violent fondness for the sex." Polygamy, with its unholy combination of adulation and brutality, epitomized men's fierce passions, so it captivated Thomas and many others. Marriage systems flagged complicated relationships between women and men, but they also defined relations between men. This essay circulated throughout the Francophone and Anglophone Atlantic, and it ended up in the hands of a number of interesting thinkers, including Abigail Adams and Thomas Paine. It first circulated in English in the 1773 edition Adams probably read. Thomas Paine reprinted part of it, with no attribution to the author, in Pennsylvania in 1775 after his own *Common Sense*. It also appeared in a British translation, unusually by a female author and translator, Jemima Kindersley, in 1781. This kind of tract shows the wide circulation of essays foregrounding issues of marriage and the proper exercise of masculine authority.

Ideas about polygamy in American, British, and French texts became critical to new ways of considering marriage and the state. These notions came to influence all kinds of contacts, including those in North America; they also came out of such encounters. Polygamy ceased to be cast as it had often been in the past: worrying behavior of infidels to offend a Christian God and his people. Instead polygamy became a problem because it corrupted domestic and political relations, unleashing the tyranny of husbands over wives. Polygamy was the supremely unenlightened form of marriage, demonstrating the necessity of imperialism. Polygamy showed that indigenous marriages were driven not by noble sentiments of affection but by lust, greed, and violence. The "logic of elimination," as one scholar has framed the ways in which colonialism displaced indigenous people, depended on household relations. Travel writers and social theorists were consummate storytellers, often spinning yarns about polygamy and its workings. They reached back to biblical and classical antecedents. They also looked about them, blinking at the wondrous, discomfiting diversity of the world. Few of them had firsthand experience of the systems of marriage they were describing—and denouncing. Their writings are shot through with their own darkest, most intimate longings, with a range of imperial anxieties. As one historian of eighteenth-century France has observed, in even the most "sober theoretical writings . . . erotic subtexts and agendas of domination were not far from the surface." Yet for all the muddle, such writers arguably instigated modern western understandings of polygamy.[2]

Marriage systems were vital for the proper functioning of the state because monogamy alone ensured fair and equitable relations in society as a whole. A polygamous husband wielded what one author called his "iron rod of a tyrant" over women, but also over other men. To marry the wrong way (or to allow others to do so) was to permit an aggressive male lust to run rampant. It was not that these theorists simply wanted to rescue women from the inequalities and violence of polygamy, though they did; they also wanted to rescue men from them. In condemning polygamous systems, authors lingered on its constraints on women: sequestered bodies, noseless faces, bound feet. However, though few have noticed, they also circled around the violation of men's bodies. These acts of male-on-male aggression included what early modern people called "sodomy," as well as castration and homicide.[3]

Civilization and progress, as well as social harmony, depended on getting marriage right. Americans—and others—started to position monogamy as essential for equality, virtue, and indeed republicanism itself. Polygamous men were threatening because they engulfed what should by rights belong to other men, including, in some cases, their very manhood. The eunuch—the man castrated to guard the wives of a harem—was the most formidable symbol of grotesque power differentials between men. In these accounts, instead of being united with other men in friendship and political bonhomie, a man in a polygamous society might get his testicles or his head cut off by another man out of jealousy. These kinds of notions formed the intellectual foundation for what became the United States; these same anxieties continued to well up in condemnations of Mormon polygamy. Many historians, working on nineteenth-century Mormon controversies over polygamy, have emphasized that particular context, with little attention to the long history of the establishment of ideas about polygamy that predated them. In this chapter I contend that Mormon controversies could not have taken the shape they did without the particular understandings of polygamy forged in global encounters and social theories of the seventeenth and eighteenth centuries, as women and men both struggled to figure out the best ways to soothe and manage men's "violent passions."[4]

"Poligamy Is Allow'd Amongst Them"

Surrounded by women's arms, Joseph Tournefort was at a loss. This French doctor and botanist had been called to diagnose the ailments of the wives of the Ottoman Empire's leading men, in their private apartments in Constantinople in the early eighteenth century. "At every door," Tournefort later recalled, "I found an Arm cover'd with Gause, thrust out thro' a small Loophole." At first he thought "they were Arms of Wood or Brass." They were in fact the arms of the women, otherwise hidden in the harem, whom he was expected to cure. He was not permitted to touch them, even to take a pulse. "It surpriz'd me when I was told, I must cure the Persons to whom those Arms belong'd," Tournefort confessed.

Tournefort's strange tableau of women's arms emerged from polygamy. It deformed marital relations, turning jealous husbands into prison guards. It also perverted other relations: between doctors and patients, but also between a visiting doctor like Tournefort and the husbands. Since the husbands saw other men only as potential rivals and adulterers, social relations between men were also ruined. Such travel writing—whether from the Levant, like Tournefort's, or from farther afield, such as the Americas or Africa—fed a growing appetite in Europe for exotic literature. Gender relations and the proper ordering of households weighed heavily on many individual male writers, and their texts were doing much work to establish certain claims about proper marriages. The cultural labor done by these travel accounts, especially in terms of household and marriage practices, was complex and highly conditioned by domestic circumstances: imperial anxieties but also marriages and gender relations themselves in periods of flux.[5]

For Tournefort, as for many others, the problem with Turkish polygamy was not that it was Muslim per se but that it corrupted relations leading to slavery for women and impotence for men. Tournefort observed that there were three kinds of female sexual partners for the leading men of the empire: wives, concubines, and slaves. All three lacked liberty. For Tournefort, all the women of the seraglio, or women's apartments, were "the least unfortunate Slaves in the World," regardless of their actual position there. In considering their lives, he concluded: "Liberty is always preferable to so slender and trifling a Happiness." Yet the effects of polygamy on relations between men were also worrisome. Tournefort noted that if he had touched a female patient, he would have been "stabb'd on the Spot." Male violence here, as elsewhere, accompanied polygamous systems. He concluded, "What can one say concerning a Place, where even the Prince's chief Physician is admitted to visit the Women who are sick, with the greatest difficulty?"[6] Adultery was the specter haunting this society: "Adultery is rigorously punish'd in *Turky;* and in that case the Husbands are Masters of the Life of their Wives." He contended that the most jealous husbands thus drowned their wives.[7] In one of the many cross-cultural references to fill such travel narratives, Tournefort explicitly compared this practice, unfavorably, to the more lenient behavior of Native American men: "The Savages of *Canada* are not so rigorous; for tho' they condemn the Adulteress, yet they agree that the Frailty being so natural to the two Sexes, they should mutually forgive one another."[8]

Depictions such as Tournefort's had little to do with realities of harem life for the sultan, but they conveyed to European readers the stark inequalities of polygamous systems. Both David Hume and Adam Smith, two notable theorists of eighteenth-century Scotland, used Tournefort's claims to bolster their own points about polygamy. Other representations also influenced Europeans who found the might of the Turkish sultan, in his household and in his empire, at once alarming and alluring. This clear linkage informs three drawings accompanying an early-seventeenth-century French account of the seraglio of the Turkish sultan. The images juxtapose the military magnificence of the sultan with his domestic control. Just as his large army follows him into battles, so his wives and concubines cater to his every whim, dancing for him and caressing him intimately. The last illustration made clear what pleasures and powers the sultan enjoyed. Hands trail on legs, arms, bottoms, and laps, as a fountain gushes tellingly in the background. The authority of the potentate over men and women stems from the fruitfulness and tyranny of his household. Such characterizations connect his martial and political ascendance with his sexual and reproductive domination. In this image, polygamy is dangerous, dissolute . . . and enticing.

Frontispiece, Michel Baudier, *General History of the Seraglio* (1631). The largest picture demonstrates the military might of the sultan, with his large army marching behind him. The second image depicts bare-breasted, plump-bellied wives and concubines dancing for him. The third illustration shows the women bathing the sultan. Michel Baudier, *Histoire Generalle du Serrail, et de la Cour du Grand Seigneur Empereur des Turcs,* 2nd ed. (Paris: Claude Craimosy, 1631). Courtesy of Department of Rare Books and Special Collections, Princeton University Library.

Tournefort's reference to Canadian "savages" shows the ways in which travel writers read each other, and echoed each other, though the exact source for Tournefort's claims remains elusive. "Savages" also practiced polygamy, in ways to underline their aggression and untrustworthiness. "They are very bloudy minded and full of Tracherie amongst themselves," declared an English observer, Christopher Levett, of early-seventeenth-century New England's indigenous people. He continued: "One will kill another for their wives, and he that hath the most wives is the bravest fellow: therefore I would wish no man to trust them, what ever they say or doe; but always to keepe a strickt hand over them." Levett also tied polygamy to the oppression and (near) slavery of women. He had apparently debated the issue with one of the Native American sagamores (or leaders) whom he had met: "On a time reasoning with one of their Sagamors about their having so many wives, I tould him it was no good fashion." Levett reported that the leader "then asked mee how many wives King *James* had, I told him he never had but one, and shee was dead, at which he wondred, and asked mee who then did all the Kings worke." Levett concluded the description of the encounter: "You may Imagin he thought their fashion was universal and that no King had any to worke for them but their wives." Whether such a conversation actually took place or represented local Native perspectives is perhaps less important than its overall message: in indigenous polygamy, men killed each other over wives, who were themselves servile and oppressed.[9]

"Savages" also appear in a text roughly contemporaneous to Tournefort's: Louis Hennepin's *Nouvelle Découverte d'un très grand Pays*, a text published in 1697, a few years before Tournefort started his 1700 trip to Turkey. Tournefort might have been referring to Hennepin's discussion of adultery—and polygamy. Louis Hennepin, a Récollet missionary who sojourned among Anishinaabe and others in North America in the late seventeenth century, declared: "Poligamy is allow'd amongst them. . . . They are exceedingly jealous, and cut the Noses of their Wives upon the least suspicion. Notwithstanding they have several Wives, they are so lascivious as to be guilty of Sodomy, and keep Boys whom they cloath with Womens apparel, because they make of them that abominable Use." Hennepin, like Tournefort, connected polygamy with male coercion and rampant sexuality. In the case of Turkey, some men became eunuchs; in North America, boys became sexual victims of such men's "lasciviousness." In both cases, the leaders who practiced polygamy reduced women to subjection, to mere arms or noseless faces. Yet such men also threatened other men in the most intimate ways, through castration or "sodomy."[10]

Belligerent husbands also populated narratives from West Africa, as we have seen. As elsewhere, polygamy connected with adultery and violence: "The men are . . . extraordinary jealous of their wives. If they surprise them in adultery, the husband will kill the adulterer if he can." Such brutality characterized polygamous marriages. So the king of Kayor had many wives: "So great is the king's authority over the people of the highest rank, that he will sometimes, for the least offence, order the offender's head to be immediately struck off, and his goods and chattels confiscated; nay, sometimes he will also order his wives and concubines to be put to death." Another eighteenth-century account of "the Inland Parts of Africa" emphasized that the women were "in great Subjection to their Husbands." In addition to the labor of childbearing and agriculture, such women suffered terrible punishments if caught in adultery: "If they are found lying with any other Men but their Husbands, they are liable to be sold for Slaves." The text aligned the tyrannical power of the king of "Barsally" with the Islamic practice of polygamy: "The King and all his Attendants profess the *Mahometan* Religion. . . . He is a tall Man, very passionate. . . . When any of his Men affront him, he does not scruple to shoot them. . . . He has got a great many Wives. . . . This King is potent, and very bold: His Dominions are large." His domestic potency paralleled and supported his "bold" political ambitions and extensive dominions, all of which rested on the capricious threat and exercise of coercion.[11]

Violence, eunuchs, and male self-indulgence also appear in accounts from the East Indies such as that by François Pyrard. Discussing Java, Pyrard described their weapons at some length, noting that all men of every class carried a blade. The flash of blades haunted other men, who had sacrificed their manhood to support those in command: "The women of quality are carefully guarded by the eunuchs, who are very numerous." Again, male laziness and female servility went hand in hand: "The men are exceeding idle; the slaves do the greater part of their business" while the masters "ordinarily busy themselves with nought, but sitting amid their wives—whereof each has a plurality." As female slaves played music, "the wives dance one after another, . . . doing each the best she can, and striving to please him; for she that pleases him the most then, sleeps the following night with him." Such a vision conjured up the exoticism and capriciousness of systems of polygamous power, as was also the case in an enormous travel compendium, by Melchisédech Thévenot, the first of its kind in French. In its massive jumble of global histories and contemporary practice, accounts of the pyramids jostled with portrayals of China and the Aztecs. Each chapter had a different focus and author, yet many of them had a section on marriage customs, including polygamy. These treatments—emerging from highly specific, and often deeply flawed, accounts—influenced imperial policy; they also informed social and political theory. One such imperial theorist was the intellectual omnivore John Locke, who had befriended Thévenot while in France. Locke owned his own copy of this book; he also meditated on polygamy as a system. In these texts of empire, as in the empires themselves, domestic chaos and polygamy lurked and tumbled, even as men dreamed of order and monogamy imposed.[12]

"The Violence of Our Desires"

Fragrant with dusky rose and orange blossom, Lady Polygamia, as one eighteenth-century author called it, poked a bejeweled slipper out from under her veiled form into European novels and social theories of all kinds. Her most famous appearance in eighteenth-century literature came in Montesquieu's *Lettres Persanes* (*Persian Letters*) of 1721. Such representations fed both an appetite for the allure of the exotic East and a smug sense of superiority in western monogamy. Opening ornate palace doors onto secret courtyards, novels, like travel literature, offered a hidden, intriguing world of polygamy and power. As scholars have noted, such eastern domesticity became "a grab bag of debauchery," a system of "sexy corruption" with a "polymorphously perverse yet powerful man" at its center. Montesquieu's *Persian Letters*, the best-known such representation, with its notable rendition of the harem, let readers linger imaginatively there, witnessing its delights and its horrors. Violence and desire saturated the harem, in this series of fictional letters exchanged between "Persians" visiting France and those back home.[13]

The sexual and romantic longings of unsatisfied wives and their castrated guards haunt the harem, thus providing an excellent means to meditate on power and its corruptions. "How unhappy is the woman who has such strong desires, when she is deprived of him who only can satisfy them," declared one wife in a typical letter to her husband. She bemoaned that she was trapped "in the fury of an irritated passion," enslaved "by the violence of her love." This denial of physical needs warped gender relations. Characters in the novel debated whether monogamy or polygamy promoted better gender relations. Polygamy led to a battle between the sexes, as men kept women confined while women trapped men with their physical charms. One character claimed that on being confronted with the idea that women held in harems would cause problems, Asians "reply that ten women in subjection are less troublesome than one who is refractory." Elsewhere, one "Persian" asserted that Mohammed had allowed plural wives in order to liberate men: "A plurality of wives saves us from their dominion; and moderates the violence of our appetites."[14]

The violence of men's sexual desires still afflicted even the eunuchs, seething with rage over their lost manhood. One wife in the novel confided to her husband, "I do not place in the order of men these hideous eunuchs" with their "deformity." In the words of one scholar, castration rendered a man a "non-man." The cruel First Eunuch described his own castration as a taking of his selfhood: "My first master . . . had induced me by promises, inforced by a thousand threats, to part with myself for ever." Eunuchs still suffered the sharp pains of physical desires as they went about their duties. The First Eunuch recounted the unconquerable longings suffered in the seraglio, "where every thing filled me with regret for what I had lost." He envied the master with his unfettered access to women's bodies: "I never led a woman to my master's bed, I never undress'd one, but I returned back enraged in my heart." His frustration resulted in his molesting one wife in the bath; she then leveraged the threat of reporting him to make him do her bidding. These experiences turned him tyrant to the women: "I always remember that I was born to govern them; and it seems to me as if I recovered my manhood, on every occasion I . . . command them." He summarized, "I am in the seraglio as in a little empire."[15] Big empires, as well as little ones, needed more harmonious relations . . . between men.

"What power was comparable to that of the caliphs! . . . A thousand eunuchs guarded the doors of their beautiful palaces, a thousand wives were destined for their pleasures. What vainglory!" So opened Jean-François Melon's 1730 novel, *Mahmoud le Gasnévide*, about a conquering leader whose dominance imprinted itself on neighboring countries as on his own domestic arrangements. Here were the extreme inequalities of polygamy, in which a single lordly man ruled over eunuchs as well as wives, concubines, and enslaved lovers. Such a system included an array of "domestic tensions," as Melon had it, inevitable costs of a structure that privileged "the liberty of desire" for the master over domestic harmony for all. It also symbolized imperial dominance: Mahmoud le Gasnévide was "master of so many different nations [and] looked for the best way to govern them all so as to make them happy." This form of polygamy was a rich metaphor for an age in which hierarchies and political power were being dramatically rethought. Jean-François Melon is better known as an economic theorist who defended slavery in his 1734 *Essai politique sur le commerce* (*Political Essay upon Trade*). Yet he also thought a lot about polygamy. So did Montesquieu, and not just in his *Persian Letters.*[16]

"The Genius of a Despotic Government"

The perversities of polygamy continued to occupy Montesquieu's *L'Esprit des lois* (*Spirit of the Laws*) of 1748, as well as many other texts circulating not only in France and Britain but also in the American colonies. Ideas about this form of marriage underpinned ideas about gender, citizenship, and virtue in the new United States. If fiery denunciations of non-Christian forms of marriage came themselves to seem relics of grimmer days, that logic of elimination still did not leave room for polygamy. That type of marriage served to prove that some people were backward and barbaric, not to be trusted. Harems and other polygynous arrangements came to be specters, haunting the better form of marriage—monogamy—practiced in American colonies and, later, states.

Domestic relations informed political ones, and violence and inequalities emerge as critical themes, pursued with a kind of careening logic, in *Spirit of the Laws*. Manly strength and feminine charms defined natural gender relations for Montesquieu, a great believer in the influence of climate. "Nature, which has distinguished men by their reason and bodily strength . . . has given charms to women." As Nature dictated sex and gender difference, so too had it also imposed a variety of environmentally determined marriage systems. Montesquieu argued that women, maturing faster in hotter climates, were at their marriageable peak at age eight: "Their reason, therefore, never accompanies their beauty. . . . These women ought, then, to be in a state of dependence." Given this early maturation, Montesquieu continued, "It is therefore extremely natural, that, in these places . . . polygamy should be introduced." By contrast, in temperate northern climates, "where the charms of women are best preserved" and where marriage occurs when girls have reached the age of reason, "it must *naturally* introduce a kind of equality between the two sexes, and, in consequence of this, the law of having only one wife." Nature and climate, not religious beliefs, were purportedly what made European and "Asiatic" marital regimes differ. "Thus the law, which permits only one wife, is *physically conformable* to the climate of Europe, and not to that of Asia." This distinction, Montesquieu continued, explains "why Mohometanism was so easily established in Asia, and with such difficulty extended in Europe." Montesquieu gestured to religion, but it was merely a gesture, in a discussion otherwise devoted to nature. For Montesquieu, climate made the physical difference in women's maturation. The only difference climate made for men was that they tended to drink more alcohol in colder ones, yet women did not. In northern climes, women "have therefore the advantage of reason over them." Some of this discussion would be humorous if it were not so disturbing. In hot climates, girls were sexually available at eight? This is Enlightenment? Denunciations of polygamy depended on some seriously twisted logic about gender and sexual relations.[17]

Once again, the squirming discomfort of imagined male-on-male violence concerned authors such as Montesquieu as much as or more than the oppression of women. Polygamy would inevitably bring adultery, in which men damaged other men's "property": that is, their wives. Wives left sexually frustrated by sharing a husband would naturally turn to other men. Yet even having a lot of wives would not satisfy insatiable husbands: "The possession of many wives does not always prevent their entertaining desires for those of others; it is with lust as with avarice, whose thirst increases by the acquisition of treasure." So men would damage other men through adultery. Then there were, inevitably, the eunuchs. As in *Persian Letters*, such men forfeited manhood through castration and were thus permanently politically diminished. Even if they were freed from service, "they can hardly be regarded as freed-men: for, as they are incapable of having a family of their own. . . . It is only by a kind of fiction that they are considered as citizens."[18] Polygamy therefore left a permanently disenfranchised and troubling class of men who could never properly head a household and thus were not full men.

In Montesquieu's rendering of polygamy, men also damaged other men through sexual violence. "May I not say, that a plurality of wives leads to that passion which nature disallows?" inquired Montesquieu, in a typical reference to men's desire for other men. As with adultery, one "depravity" led to another. He reported that "at Algiers, in the greatest part of their seraglios," there were no women present at all because men were interested only in other men. Montesquieu also noted that although "the emperor of Morocco has women of all colours, white, black, and tawny, in his seraglio," in fact "the wretch has scarcely need of a single colour," an allusion to his preference for men. So prominent was this theme that "the perfumes of Arabia" became code for sexual interest between men. At the same time, the heat of eastern climates also warmed men up so much that they became sexual predators of women. In the eighteenth century, rape was considered as much a violation of men by men, as of women by men since. "There are climates where the impulses of nature have such force that morality has almost none." Montesquieu contended that if a man was left with a woman, "the attack [was] certain, the resistance none. In these countries, instead of precepts, they have recourse to bolts and bars."[19]

Marriage form mattered to the state in part because it affected social and political relations among men. The "bolts and bars" that naturally attended polygamy deformed the political systems built upon it. In republics, where "the condition of citizens is moderate, equal, mild, and agreeable . . . an empire over the women cannot, amongst them, be so well exerted." In the climax of Montesquieu's discussion of polygamy and politics, he concluded: "The slavery of women is perfectly conformable to the genius of a despotic government, which delights in treating all with severity. Thus, at all times, have we seen, in Asia, domestic slavery and despotic government walk hand in hand with an equal pace." Montesquieu offered dark visions of the destruction that would be unleashed should European women, with their "levity of mind . . . their passions . . . their active fire," come to inhabit "eastern governments" in home and in state. In that case, men would be endlessly suspicious of one another, fathers fearing the rape of their daughters, husbands hankering for other men's wives. Republics could not stand on the basis on such imagined systems of violence and inequalities. Polygamy would mean that the "men would be . . . every where enemies; the state would be overturned, the kingdom overflowed with rivers of blood."[20]

"Barbarism . . . the Inseparable Attendant of Polygamy"

Rivers of blood, eunuchs, and passionate wives didn't dare run in the genteel, well-ordered streets of New Town in eighteenth-century Edinburgh, even in the imagination of one of its more famous residents, David Hume. Still, polygamy commanded attention. Hume considered it at length in "Of Polygamy and Divorces," an essay that appeared in 1742, some six years before Montesquieu's *Spirit of the Laws*. This bachelor directed his prodigious intellect at arguing against both practices in the title. He advised "drawing the Marriage-knot the closest possible." He tackled many similar themes as Montesquieu. Marriage, Hume acknowledged, varied over time and place. "Nature, having endowed man with reason, has not so exactly regulated every article of his marriage contract, but has left him to adjust them, by his own prudence, according to his particular circumstances and situation." This notion of the acceptable variability of marriages across cultures, which seems hardly surprising now, was in fact revolutionary then. After all, Christian churches, both Catholic and Protestant, had been defending one core version of marriage—monogamous, lifelong, between man and woman, set in motion by God with Adam & Eve—for centuries, even as radical reformers and ordinary people had flouted such teachings for an equally long time. Hume went farther than arguing for variety. He contended that it was "mere superstition to imagine, that marriage can be entirely uniform, and will admit only of one mode or form."[21]

Yet, although marriage naturally had a variety of forms, some versions were nevertheless superior to others. Hume's ideal—monogamous, heterosexual, and indissoluble—looked remarkably similar to the classic Catholic one, even as he notably rejected dogma in so many other areas. For such a forward-looking thinker, such a view was strikingly conservative, especially in the Scottish context, where more liberal divorce policies existed in this period. For Hume, divorce was a bad idea, and monogamy outranked polygamy, which corrupted both heterosocial and homosocial relations. Hume effectively replied to the fictional "Persian" who had asserted that "a plurality of wives saves us from their dominion; and moderates the violence of our appetites." Hume observed: "The advocates for polygamy may recommend it as the only effectual remedy for the disorders of love, and the only expedient for freeing men from that slavery to the females, which the natural violence of our passions has imposed upon us." Men's violence of sexual passions enthralled them to women, and thus perverted domestic relations. Hume continued: "By this means alone can we regain our right of sovereignty; and, sating our appetite, re-establish the authority of reason in our minds, and, of consequence, our own authority in our families." Men's household "sovereignty" depended on controlling their passions. "The natural violence of our passions" could bring men to their knees before women. Yet Hume rejected the claim that polygamy liberated men. For him, it ruined gender relations and destroyed the whole idea of consent. Polygamy transformed husbands into tyrants, and wives into cowering "cripples," as in China with its foot-binding. He used those extended arms of the Ottoman wives that had so disturbed Dr. Tournefort to demonstrate the political costs of the "frightful effects of jealousy."[22]

To give a man so much power over wives, even if it did release him from their thrall, was to subvert harmonious gender relations and indeed nature itself. "It may be urged with better reason, that this sovereignty of the male is a real usurpation, and destroys that nearness of rank, not to say equality, which nature has established between the sexes." While Hume did not quite endorse gender equality, he did allow that it might be possible. At the very least, the sexes were "near in rank." In a passage echoed across a lot of writings in the eighteenth century, Hume wrote that men would not naturally wish to exert such tyranny: "We are, by nature, their lovers, their friends, their patrons: Would we willingly exchange such endearing appellations, for the barbarous title of master and tyrant?"[23] Polygamy, then, was a subversion of good order as well as nature.

Hume's Scottish version of polygamy was gentler, more pastel, than Montesquieu's stark and vivid vision. He did not linger on eunuchs, but he, too, considered polygamy injurious to male friendship: "Jealousy excludes men from all intimacies and familiarities with each other. No one dares bring his friend to his house or table." Hume used the biblical example of King Solomon to argue that Solomon would have been much happier had he sensibly exchanged his hundreds of wives and concubines for "one wife or mistress, a few friends, and a great many companions." Friendship between men was more worthwhile than thousands of willing female lovers. Hume privileged "love and friendship" over sensual indulgence, thus concluding "Barbarism, therefore, appears, from reason as well as experience, to be the inseparable attendant of polygamy." He thus celebrated "our present EUROPEAN practice with regard to marriage."[24]

Other contemporaries also argued for monogamy as the best way to organize society and to increase population. In one French tract of 1751, *La Monogamie*, the theorist and mathematician André-Pierre le Guy de Prémontval declared "that every man has an essential right to claim marriage" and that such a right was "one of the most sacred human rights." Men needed to defend this right because Prémontval, like many men of his era, knew how many benefits marriage brought men. "Polygamy," he contended, "injures this right in the most direct way possible." This thoughtful scholar fretted over calculations of polygamy and population growth; for him, the numbers did not add up. He conceded that if a man had twenty wives, then of course he could have many more children than if he had one. Such was good for him and the growth of his family. However, Prémontval demanded, what about the nineteen men whom he was depriving of wives and children? The polygamous husband was denying other men the ability to marry. Systems of exclusive monogamy were essential to permit every man to claim his sacred human right to marriage.[25]

"Despotism Is Always Favourable to Polygamy"

Adam Smith, also writing in the late eighteenth century, circled around similar themes of polygamy and power in his lectures. Like Hume and others, Smith allowed for variety in marriage and its forms over time and place. For Smith, marriages improved with the progress of civilization. He actually cast sexual jealousy as a positive good, a mark of increased civility: "In those countries where the manners of the people are rude and uncultivated, there is no such thing as jealousy" nor was there true love. He contended that "the foundation of jealousy is that delicacy which attends the sentiment of love." Such delicacy and love could attend marriages only in civilized cultures. Yet such jealousies could grow too extreme: "When manners became more refined, jealousy began, and rose at length to such a height that wives were shut up, as they are among the Turks at this day." Civilized could collapse into tyrannical.[26]

Still the question remained for Smith: did "the principle of justice" demand lifelong monogamy? Somewhat surprisingly, the answer was no. He contended that neither divorce nor polygamy was "altogether contrary to the principle of justice." In part, his definition hinged on female consent. "If a woman consents to be one of five, or twenty, or more wives, and the law allows it, there is no injury done her, she meets with the treatment which she might naturally expect." There was an ominous quality to this claim, about what treatment she might expect. Still, consent made the difference. However, although Smith contended that divorce and polygamy were not contrary to justice, he, like Hume, also did not think they were wise: "It must always be a very bad policy where they are established or allowed." Polygamy thus resulted in the destruction of "tranquility," a central domestic virtue for Smith. By contrast, "polygamy excites the most violent jealousy, by which domestic peace is destroyed." Wives became "rivals and enemies," and their children competed for favor. He conceded that "in the seraglios of the Eastern monarchs there is the greatest peace." However, the cost of this peace was "the most imperious discipline." In Africa, where "discipline" was not "severe enough," "we find the most horrid disorders." Inevitably, polygamy also brought eunuchs, whom wives "detest." The man who ruled the seraglio "is by no means happy, though apparently so." The sensual pleasures of polygamy for husbands were only illusory and passing. In fact, this husband became a prisoner of his own jealousy.[27]

"Polygamy takes place under despotic governments," declared Smith bluntly. A polygamous husband could not entertain male friends, or even a male physician, "as Tournefort tells us." Polygamy also brought gross inequalities between men: "The greater part of men can get no wives, and many of them are castrated." That some men lost so much to serve other men, as well as the impossibility of friendship between men, marred the social and political system. Polygamy also had a "bad effect upon the manners of the country." Virtuous male citizens could not unite into political parties: "As the men have no trust nor dependence upon each other, they cannot form into parties, and therefore the government must always be arbitrary." As the domestic government was arbitrary, absolute, and corrupt, so the political system would be, too. Moreover, "In every country freedom puts out polygamy; there is nothing that free men will less submit to than a monopoly of this kind, but despotism is always favourable to polygamy." Trust between men was essential for the clean functioning of the home, society, and government. The correct form of marriage underpinned the political project of the state.[28]

"Which We Moderns Denominate Love"

In the revolutionary era, such theories about tyranny found considerable purchase. Ever-growing audiences of women as well as men on both sides of the Atlantic devoured histories, theories, and novels centering on domestic tyranny, as well as on its relation to social and political order. One bookseller's newspaper advertisement in 1779 specifically noted that the collection of Hume's *Essays* he was selling included "Of Polygamy and Divorces." Despotism, so utterly bound up in systems of polygamy, became a central preoccupation, as in the treatise by Antoine Thomas with which this chapter opened. "Man," Thomas averred, "has never missed an opportunity of abusing his power . . . has been at once [women's] tyrant and their slave." He continued: "Upon three quarters of the globe, Nature has placed [women] between contempt and unhappiness."[29] Thomas contrasted European systems with American and Asian ones: "More than half the globe is covered with savages, amongst all which people the women are extremely miserable.— Man, in his savage state, is at the same time fierce and indolent." Thomas claimed that among the American Indians, women were "a conquered people, obliged to labour for their conquerors," the men. Asia was different, but no better: "If we look amongst the Orientals, we shall find another species of despotism. . . . Confinement, and the domestic servitude of women, is. . . . consecrated by the laws." "All Asia," Thomas assured his readers, "is covered with domestic prisons."[30]

The hallowed eighteenth-century virtue of civility meant that relations between women and men, as well as between men, could be improved over this "savage state." After all, improvement was another key ideal of the era. Yet despite the emphasis on women, eunuchs appear again as symbols of the deforming tendencies of polygamy: "The most humiliating despotism subjects [wives] to the authority of monsters, who, being of neither sex, are a dishonour to both." This kind of language emphasized that gender fluidity, stemming from polygamous systems, could only ever be "monstrous." This man who was not a man was here, as elsewhere, both evidence of the violence of polygamy and one of its sources. Again, polygamy meant that men could not trust one another: "A Mohamedan places his supreme delight in his seraglio. . . . This violent fondness for the sex . . . informs him that other men have the same violent passions: the beauties of his seraglio which delight him, he knows, could delight other men." An anxious jealousy permeated the atmosphere.[31] Again, the poisoning of masculine relations informs the portrayal of polygamy.

Grappling with Thomas's tract, women focused less on eunuchs than on women and their relationship to civic virtue and the state, as Abigail Adams did. In 1781, a woman, Jemima Kindersley, published a new English translation of Thomas's *Essay* and also wrote two introductory essays to it. While women did occasionally write such historical and theoretical texts, it was unusual. Her introduction furnished arguments for the need for better education for women "in these present times." Kindersley contended: "Should I teach one woman to believe what great and good things she is capable of, and to raise herself above the follies with which she is surrounded; my labours will be amply repaid." Jemima Kindersley and Abigail Adams both engaged directly with Thomas, but moved beyond or even took issue with some of his claims. However, they probably agreed, or at least left no record of disagreement, with his assessments of global gender relations and polygamy. Kindersley claimed that she had planned to write her own essay but was so enchanted with Thomas's own that she settled simply for translating it from French.[32]

"Polygamy Is Condemned by Nature"

Marriage, tyranny, and savagery also underpinned William Alexander's *History of Women,* first published in London in 1779 and reprinted several times, including in Philadelphia in 1796. He denounced women's oppression around the globe, in order to celebrate modern European systems of monogamy. Alexander's two-volume history of women was a dizzying journey around the world, across thousands of years. In keeping with Scottish stadial theory, which saw civilization as a march from barbarism to civilization, Alexander emphasized women's "progress from slavery to freedom." Alexander compressed times and places into an unwieldy mass, but with a clear objective: to establish that the treatment of women demonstrated nothing less than the course of civilization. Building on earlier stadial theories, Alexander tracked marriage systems as useful ways to measure the progress of civility more broadly. Among "savage people," men used their superior physical (and possibly intellectual) strength to "enslave" women as "the whole history of every savage period and people is a proof." Yet among civilized people, Alexander declared, men had been "taught by culture, and softened by politeness" not to exert that power over women. Such language was typical of Scottish stadial theory, and Alexander built on earlier treatises such as that by Adam Ferguson. However, Alexander continued, in no era of human history had men "sufficiently attended to the happiness and interests" of women. Male "adoration" for women had only rarely resulted in their "good usage."[33]

"It would be an endless talk to enumerate all the nations which practiced polygamy." Alexander's righteous resentment over the mistreatment of women throughout history propelled his analysis of this phenomenon. Alexander contrasted polygamy, spurred only by "that animal appetite," with monogamy, a system sustained by "that composed sentimental feeling which we moderns denominate love." He commenced with Cain's descendant Lamech, who "took two wives" so that "all the inhabitants of the East followed his example." However, Alexander conceded that polygamy was not solely about male sexual indulgence but also about "grandeur and state," which he felt explained why Solomon had had so many wives. Polygamy also transformed husbands into despots, while reducing wives into slaves. A polygamous husband "finds it necessary to rule [his wives] more with the iron rod of a tyrant, than the love and affection of an husband." Yet Alexander thought it would be difficult to eradicate this system as "wives are confined by all the tyrants of the East [and] enslaved by all the savages of America and elsewhere."[34]

Legal regimes, designed by men, had stacked the decks against women, in terms of both polygamy and the double standard in adultery laws. Alexander observed that men had allowed themselves many wives but only very rarely the reverse. He summarized "savage" systems by pointing to native Americans: "The Brazilians take as many wives as they think proper, dismiss them when they find it convenient, and punish their incontinence with death." He noted that European law was not much kinder to women; indeed, "the power of a husband is considerably extended by the laws of the gospel, and of the constitution, both over the person and property of his wife." Nevertheless, he claimed, as did so many others of his generation, that European husbands had learned to mitigate the rigors of the law. Alexander argued that European dowry structures in which wives carried property with them "obliterate the slavery of a wife to her husband [and] put a stop to polygamy." Despite Alexander's concern for women, though, he still contended that polygamy's central problem was its destruction of relations among men. Like Prémontval, he proclaimed "that all men are by nature equal, and have consequently an equal right to a wife." So if "one man marries a variety of women, there can be none left for several others." This injustice also resulted in the need for eunuchs. For Alexander and many others, household order underpinned political order. "Let us remember," Alexander reminded his readers, "that wherever the women are the slaves of the men, the men themselves are slaves of a despot."[35]

Similar themes animated other work, such as that by William Paley. A clergyman whose writings formed a mainstay of education in both Great Britain and the United States, he too worried that polygamous wives were "degraded into mere instruments of physical pleasure." Children were neglected, and adults fell into "voluptuousness . . . which dissolves the vigour."

Yet polygamy also damaged relations between women because of the "contests and jealousies amongst the wives." Then there was the problem of men left without wives, who, in Paley's reckoning, would turn to sex with other men. Paley decried "the manifold, and sometimes unnatural mischiefs, which arise from a scarcity of women."[36] The inequalities of polygamy, and its ruination of the proper platonic relations between men, engaged Paley, as so many others.

The perils of polygamy also appeared in American periodicals. Indeed, some of Paley's works were reprinted in American newspapers in 1796. Polygamy, "promiscuous love," and "savages" also formed points of focus. A 1793 essay, "Thoughts on the State of American Indians," argued that establishing "marriage between a single pair" was an "important step . . . in bringing the aborigines of this country to civilized manners." Without this shift, the essayist contended, Native Americans could not fully enter civilization because "the institution of marriage, is one of the foundation principles of civil society." After all, "it is in the narrow circle of domestic society that good members of the community are formed." Marriage did a great deal: raising "the female sex from that state of degradation in which savage nations have confined them," as well as laying "the most solid foundation for domestic happiness and the increase of population." It also gave women the chance "to temper the fierce passions, and humanize the coarser feelings of the men." In providing legitimate children and their care, marriage also contributed "to the wealth and strength of the community." By contrast, "polygamy is condemned by nature" because the sexes were roughly equal in number, and so monogamy was fairer and more likely "to promote population." Polygamy also sowed "jealousy, distrust, and inhumanity," and therefore was "incompatible with the interests of society or morals."[37]

The "inhumanity" of polygamous systems also preoccupied the author of another essay, "On Love," in New York Magazine in 1791. This writer singled out the seraglio as a space lacking human affection. "Behold in the seraglios human nature at the lowest point of abasement." Yet again, eunuchs appear as the terrifying symbol of despotism who took out their unhappiness on the wives for whom they were supposed to care: "Wretches there, maimed in body and mind, know only to be cruel. . . . To crush a feeling heart under the despotism which has proved fatal to themselves, is their only joy." Such a claim could have come straight from Montesquieu's Persian Letters. By contrast, "love cannot harden hearts, nor extinguish social virtue. The lover becomes a husband, a parent, a citizen." Citizenship in the new republic depended on true love, on virtue, and on householder status. The harem thwarted the possibility of love between citizens by making some men eunuchs: nonmen because they lacked full manhood and noncitizens because they could never represent their own households as husbands and masters.[38]

"Carnal Delights of the Spiritual-Wife System"

These eighteenth-century arguments reemerged over the course of the nineteenth century, in rather less lofty texts than those associated with the Enlightenment and Revolution. The figure of the powerful Turk continued to appear in cheap print and even pornography, as in the 1828 British publication *The Lustful Turk*. This erotic epistolary novel recounted the sexual awakening of European virgins taken captive by the Turks and made the unwilling/willing playthings of the "Dey," or ruler. One of the protagonists informed her friend back home: "You have no doubt heard of the cruel treatment experienced by females who are unfortunate to fall into the power of those barbarous Turks." The Dey's cruel treatment included—but was not limited to—deflowering her and several others, often with the help of his minions, the eunuchs. Eunuchs did everything from delivering the Dey's mail to stripping and holding down the women, whom the Dey then whipped, caressed, and penetrated. After one especially sordid encounter involving anal sex, one such woman sighed: "I sensibly felt the debasement of being the slave of a luxurious Turk."[39]

Such lurid ruthlessness also characterized what one scholar has termed "the sexual magnetism of the Mormon male," provoking "the hypnotized passivity of his innocent victim." A disaffected former wife of the noted polygamist and early Mormon leader Brigham Young became a vocal critic of polygamy, recalling Young's smoldering, "pitiless" stare, "that steady, unflinching gaze." His power was seductive and mesmerizing. She admitted that on meeting him, "I felt his power then as I never had felt it before, and I began to understand a little how it was that he compelled so many people to do his will, against their own inclinations." She concluded, in a chapter headed "The Prophet Rejoices at my Yielding," "I learned the lesson better still subsequently" when she became his unwilling/willing wife. Cartoons and other texts highlighted the Mormon husband as the keeper of a harem. One such illustration offered a more decorous update of that early-seventeenth-century image of the seraglio.[40]

Joseph Ferdinand Keppler, "A Desperate Attempt to Solve the Mormon Question," *Puck* [New York: Keppler and Schwarzmann, February 13, 1884]. The panel on the lower left shows the Mormon polygamous husband as a Turkish despot, smoking a hookah, with wives offering Mumm's champagne, coffee, and fruit, as other wives fan him, play music, and dance for him. Courtesy of Library of Congress.

Beyond the seductive charms of Latter-day Saint men, the secret and exclusive nature of LDS Temple rituals also fired wild imaginings. Many a denunciation of the Mormons gave a detailed, graphic, and utterly spurious account of marriage ceremonies in the inner sanctum of the Temple. After a reference to Islam, and "the voluptuous paradise . . . of the imperial harems of the modern Sultan," the authors of one 1854 account fretted that women were "forced to become the abject and willing slaves of the Sultan Brigham, and find their highest enjoyments in the sickening pleasures and carnal delights of the Spiritual-Wife system." The authors proceeded to detail "the Endowment" ceremony as a hotbed of sexual activities: between women and men, between men, and between women in "licentiousness and unbridled libertinism." They denounced "these series of degrading and unnatural doctrines and ceremonies, in which men and women promiscuously enact many . . . disgusting scenes. . . . Each man is allowed as many wives as he may desire." They condemned Brigham Young as the "chief actor in the debauching scenes of the Spiritual-Wife system." In their account, the male participant was stripped and bathed, with the officiant rubbing oil over "every part of his naked person," with, as the text coyly added, "nothing excepted." Each woman was also stripped to "a perfect state of nudity." She was then bathed by other women, who focused specifically on her breasts and "loins." The authors concluded by demanding "what intelligent, educated, and virtuous female" would "barter her rich inheritance of honor and female purity for the ambiguous and unsatisfactory position assigned to the frail Sapphos and Lesbias of a Mormon harem," thus implying that wives turned to each other for decidedly impure intimacies.[41]

Other accounts emphasized equally impure male-on-male aggression in such Temple ceremonies: "You . . . have to undress—the presiding elder examines you to see whether every part of your body is sound: if a male, even to see whether 'he be wounded in the testes'; if not, he is allowed to pass and receive his endowment." Supposedly, "if he is not sound, they make a eunuch of him—whether he like it or not. Many a man, who had taken a good-looking wife with him, and would not give her up to any other man when required (by the High Priest), was also made a eunuch of." Jealous resentments, along with tyrannical leadership resulting in castration, once again symbolized the gross inequalities of this system.

"Unnatural" longings and profound power differentials between men: here was the continued image of polygamy stemming both from travel

THE KEY TO THE MYSTERIES OF MORMONISM.

Detail, *The Key to the Mysteries of Mormonism*, from fold-out illustrated panel in Increase Van
Deusen and Maria Van Deusen, *Spiritual Delusions: Being a Key to the Mysteries of Mormonism,
exposing the Particulators of that Astounding Heresy, The Spiritual-Wife System, as Practiced by
Brigham Young, of Utah* (New York: Tuttle and Moulton, 1854). Here the polygamous husband
has one wife gazing at him while the other looks irritated, and other wives hold babies in the
background. There are other polygamists in this chaotic scene. On the left side, a devil floats,
symbolizing lust and libertinism. Courtesy of DeGolyer Library, Southern Methodist University.

accounts and theorizing of the eighteenth century. "Savages" and "tyrants"
could never marry, or rule, properly. The horror evinced by these writers
was as much for the men left castrated and disenfranchised as for the women
trapped in domestic prisons, with "intelligent, educated, and virtuous
females" reduced to the trifling playthings of despots. The proper political
order could not depend on such deformed household relations. Liberty had
better not to shade into libertinism, with its attendant debauchery. Republicanism depended on virtue and monogamy. Without those, both intimate
and political relations were perverted, and social links irreparably damaged.[42]

A republic of virtuous men could not survive the unmanning that
attended polygamy and "promiscuous love." Some of these themes animated
controversies over polygamy in the 1780s, the subject of the next chapter.
Yet these concerns about the virtue of republican men hardly ended in the
early national period. "Search out the cause of decay of every perished
Republic, and you will find it was licentiousness," advised one opponent of
the Mormons. In words echoing eighteenth-century claims about rights to

marriage for men, this nineteenth-century critic announced, "Polygamy leads to the concentration of power and privilege in the hands of the few, and is thus the cause and instrument of tyranny. If one man be permitted to have four wives, three other men in the world are deprived of their natural rights to one wife each." The example of four wives, that allowed by Muslim law, linked Islam and Mormonism. It also showed the gross inequalities of polygamy in both. Indeed, "The man with four wives must have means of supporting them; he must monopolize power, property, and privilege; while the man not permitted to marry one wife is deprived of other rights and reduced to an inferior position." Polygamous husbands denied an innocent man of his "natural rights" as well as his manhood and property mastery. Such a marginalized man, debarred from marriage and thus lacking household authority, "is not a *man; he is only a soldier, sailor, servant, eunuch!*"[43]

6. "Such a Revolution as This"

In 1782, when most Anglo-American people lamented "our present unhappy Difficulties," they meant the American Revolution. After all, the conflict between Great Britain and thirteen of its colonies had ripped apart the fabric of empire, affecting the lives of millions in unexpected and often horrific ways. When church members in Norfolk, Connecticut, fretted over these "Difficulties," however, they meant a more local affair. True, many of the congregation had served in the fighting, and they had suffered enduring losses and privations. Still, what had so rattled the town was a controversy, increasingly rancorous and lasting for months, over "Poligamy." A church member, Dr. John Miner, had publicly spoken in favor of allowing polygamy; his talk provoked an outcry and a trial. In these debates of the 1780s, the problem of polygamy took on strange force. Ordinary people, religious folk, grappled with the issues that had transfixed theorists mulling over global encounters, civilization, and marriage and which would continue to inform confrontations with the Church of Jesus Christ of Latter-day Saints. These polygamy controversies of the 1780s, centered in churches as well as libraries, launched a range of issues, as well as voices, on both sides of the Atlantic. A few dissenting Protestants had long argued in favor of polygamy; some would notably do so in the nineteenth century. They thought that reorganizing marriage was a theologically sound way of reorganizing society and strengthening the nation.[1]

In the 1780s, on both sides of the Atlantic, people were talking about polygamy. Indeed, in December 1780, as Britain struggled to win ascendance in North America, a noted London society announced a debate on whether an increase in population "would compensate for the confusion, Polygamy would create in society?" They noted that there would be a second debate that evening on "the present aspect of American affairs" only "if time permits." In other words, the American Revolution took second billing to a debate on polygamy. Such priorities are unexpected, given the emphasis historians on both sides of the Atlantic have placed on the role of the American Revolution in altering not just geopolitics but society. It seems curious that in such a charged political moment, people became preoccupied with polygamy. What explains this interest? What was the connection, if any, between these disputes over marriage and the American Revolution?[2]

Could a man espouse polygamy and still be a good Christian? Two polygamy apologists, one in Connecticut and the other in London, did not differ on any of the doctrines constituting the usual flashpoints for Protestants: the nature of Christ, baptism, or the Eucharist. Still, to endorse polygamy publicly was to provoke scandal and censure on both sides of the Atlantic. Church and secular courts had long regulated morality, but more frequently its practice than mere thoughts. As we have seen, evangelical churches of various kinds, including Methodist churches in Virginia, patrolled the domestic behavior of their members. But they did not so frequently prosecute congregants for thinking wrong about what might seem a less than central issue; Miner's church did. Arguments over polygamy triggered public outcry in the midst of what would seem a much more pressing conflict.[3]

It is helpful first to understand the basic lines of argument both men brought to bear. John Miner, the American defender of polygamy, offered two major justifications for polygamy: religious and social. It had existed since "the days of Adam." He gave what he imagined would be the counterargument: "But may we not argue that as the old testament times were dark and shadowy, that therefore the fathers might be ignorant, and the practice of Polygamy might be wrong in reality." As we have seen, this line of analysis had a long history in New England. Still, Miner contended that although those times were obscure, there was no darkness about the law of God. God could have spoken against it yet never did, nor had Jesus himself. Miner also argued for the social advantages of polygamy. He denied what his church claimed, that polygamy was "repugnant to the divine will, and hurtful and dangerous to the happiness of society, and especially destructive of family government." By contrast, he stressed that it could support well-ordered families. Moreover,

"Polygamy is in no way subversive of any of the good ends for which marriage was designed; either in family religion, family government, or the conveyance of property; but in some cases may and always would be, a benefit to some particular men." He thought it especially useful in times and places with a preponderance of females, as in times of war, arguing that then "Polygamy would be reasonable, lawful and right in the sight of God." He saw no reason that having a plurality of wives should signal a man's "unbridled lust" any more "than a man's having a plurality of farms, houses, and riches . . . is a demonstration that he is a worldling, covetous, and wicked." While he conceded that plural unions might lead to quarrels between wives, such was no reason to forbid the practice. By the same logic, he reasoned, "a man should have no more children than one, because they may quarrel." While surely some families would have problems, such was an unavoidable aspect of family life, hardly unique to polygamy.[4]

Martin Madan, the English defender of the same year, also pointed to social and theological justifications for polygamy. Madan's goal was the prevention of "female ruin." He contended, "As our laws are at present framed, women are exposed to *seduction, prostitution,* and *ruin.*" His unusual remedy was to require that a man consider himself married to any (unmarried) woman with whom he had sex. Madan thus defined marriage as the carnal union of man and (unmarried) woman, and claimed that were such intercourse recognized as the divine form of marriage, all manner of social ills would cease: "No *brothels* would teem with harlots—no streets swarm with *prostitutes. . . . Adultery* and *whoredom* would no longer dare to face the light." Madan assumed that men would find it difficult to remain faithful to one woman. He highlighted situations in which wives were either infertile or else had "incurable disease of mind or body, unconquerable violence of temper, perpetual refractoriness of disposition, [or] levity of behaviour . . . such as may destroy the whole comfort of a man's life." Madan argued that in such cases men (and men only—on this point, he was unequivocal) should be allowed more than one spouse. Madan pursued these points with relentless biblical interpretation, relying on his knowledge of Hebrew, Latin, and Greek: "So a man who has two wives is no more a sinner now, than he would have been in the days of the Patriarchs." He also repeatedly emphasized Jesus' statement that he came to fulfill the law, not to abolish it. Madan used Reformation arguments about the need to return to original texts to know the meaning of God's word. He maintained that this allowance of polygyny would make Christian missionaries more successful, and would help spread Christianity around the globe.[5]

Both Miner and Madan were in a long Protestant tradition, yet the conflicts that arose around them reveal a great deal about their particular contexts. It may be that those in Connecticut who argued over Miner knew nothing about the massive scandal occurring at the same time in England over Madan. It may be that some did, or that Madan's controversies helped to spur Miner's. No one involved in the American debates ever mentioned Madan, and there was a breakdown of communication across the Atlantic occasioned by the American Revolutionary War. Yet whether their works emerged spontaneously and separately, or whether there were links between them impossible to recover now, both authors were responding to changes in society and nations. For Miner, Madan, and many others, polygamy was a useful way to discuss a range of pressing concerns swirling around households, authority, sexuality, religion, and order.[6]

No one has ever linked these scandals in any detail, though they broke at the same time among literate Anglo-Americans in a period of considerable connection. The two polygamy controversies of 1780–81 allow an exploration of the specifics of each setting and the revolutionary alterations uniting them. The argument here is that for marriage and gender roles, the American Revolution was a symptom, not a cause, of dramatic cultural transformation, though it then also accelerated other kinds of change. Christians who championed polygamy, veterans who questioned authority, women who scandalized contemporaries, even a doctor who promised patients hourlong orgasms: they are all here, in the strange and little-known story of polygamy controversies of the 1780s. This tumultuous history allows us to see the American Revolution in novel ways. Troubling speech, chattering, hissing, vibrations, and "large Debate" sounded throughout an Anglo-American world beset by revolution. We cock our ears first, improbably, in a small town in western Connecticut in 1776.[7]

"Discoursing . . . in Favor of Polygamy"

The sudden, indignant cries of babies splashed with baptismal water rang out in the meetinghouse in Norfolk, Connecticut, in 1776. So did the intoning of the minister, the Reverend Ammi Robbins, who announced their Christian names to the congregation. Such names included Freelove, Thanks (twice), and a pair of sisters, Desire and Mercy. If mere mention of that monumental year connects these children with new orders, the names themselves linked them with older ones. Even in the late eighteenth century, parents in Connecticut gave their newborns the kinds of Puritan-with-a-capital-P monikers that seem more consonant with the English Revolution than with the American one. Such names, like those of parents Mindwell and Hopestil, reflected continuities. Indeed, Desire's mother was also Desire. Names belonging to ancestors publicly transformed tiny new bodies into members of communities of faith, sweeping newborns into the long, vertical embrace of family. Entering the public record in that year of independence, little Freelove Barber and her cohort straddled two different kinds of worlds.[8] So did another child baptized in Norfolk that year, Amos Miner, son of one Dr. John Miner.

The Reverend Robbins, who baptized these children, had taken up his position in 1761, three years after the town itself had been founded. He held it for decades. "The town and ecclesiastical society were one and the same body at that early day, and continued to be so for more than fifty years," declared one early town historian. Yet the church building itself was not completed until 1770. The first meetinghouse was a relatively simple one: "fifty feet by forty, and of suitable height for galleries, without a steeple." It had no bell, and, more crucial in winter, no heating. Nevertheless, law and custom dictated that everyone in town attend Sabbath meetings, year-round. Chilly parishioners built little Sabbath huts nearby, with stoves in them, to huddle over in winter. But still they came. Frigid or not, the church provided a spiritual foundation in Norfolk by the 1770s.[9]

Norfolk itself had been founded in 1758, a move by various settlers from other parts of New England. It was nestled in Connecticut's western edge, not far from the foothills of the Berkshires. It is not an urban area now; it certainly was not then. A later town historian declared of these first settlers: "They were alone in the wilderness. Their communication with other places was slow, difficult and infrequent. . . . The early inhabitants of these interior towns were in a great measure cut off from the rest of the world." Still, despite pride in brave pioneer forebears, Norfolk was hardly "cut off" from the rest of the world. The town voted to join the Revolution, unsurprising for such a Congregationalist New England town. Men from the town served for the entire duration of the Revolutionary War, from Jared Abernethy and the aptly named Freedom Wright, who "marched from the Connecticut towns for the relief of Boston in the Lexington alarm, April 1775," to John Miner, who served five months in Swift's Regiment in 1780 and beyond. The tides of the American Revolution affected many, if not most, of the families in Norfolk, as men went to war, and—at least most of the time—came home to tell the tales.[10]

Other tides, of changing social orders, also affected this town. In 1780–81, little "Desires" still cropped up in the baptismal records. So did an Oliver-Cromwell Phelps (a proud Puritan past indeed, though also one with revolutionary republican overtones suited to the 1770s). Yet other names, such as Amy, Clarissa, and Charlotte, start to pepper the records, becoming ascendant. Such fashionable names invoked new sentimental literature, not old religious injunctions (Mindwell!). Invoking the names of sighing, lovely heroines showed that parents were progressive and cosmopolitan. Clarissa was the eponymous heroine of Samuel Richardson's 1748 epistolary novel. The wicked Lovelace seduced and abandoned her; she died brokenhearted. Charlotte was the tragic heroine of Johann Wolfgang von Goethe's *Sorrows of Young Werther,* as well as of an early American novel in which the protagonist was a victim of masculine designs on her virtue, with predictably tragic results. If the names, like the literature itself, implied the vulnerability of women navigating the world, they surely were meant more to signal the sensibility of the parents. Once ideals for daughters were about Thanks and Mercy in the face of a demanding God. Now parents privileged softer sentiments: tender affections, the pursuit of happiness, and the virtuous conquest of man's base desires. By 1780, even in small and sleepy Norfolk, old orders were changing. Still, for some, like Dr. John Miner, they were not changing quickly enough.[11]

John Miner was apparently a doctor, an uncommon title usually indicating advanced training or a medical apprenticeship. There is no record of his study at Yale College, the obvious place for a Connecticut boy with professional aspirations. Other records do not mark him out. There are many John Miners in Connecticut records; most were local farmers, not learned men. It seems most likely that he was born in 1752, and was around twenty-eight at the time of the fracas. Such an age was also consonant with military service in 1780 in the 7th Connecticut (or Swift's) Regiment, evidently just before this controversy broke out. He served for only a few months, posted in the Hudson Highlands. He was discharged by early October 1780. John Miner was married, though the name of his wife seems to have disappeared. Unusually, Ammi Robbins, who kept careful records of babies baptized in Norfolk, did not record the name of Mrs. Miner, on more than one occasion. What we do know is that she was mother to two children with John: Elizabeth, baptized in April 1773, and Amos, baptized in December 1776.[12]

Whatever his married life, John Miner came to believe that there were theological and social justifications for polygamy, and he shared these opinions. He called these conversations "talk sake," implying a semiformal debate: "I have all along freely and frequently conversed on the subject, chiefly for talk sake, and sometimes for, and sometimes against it." Winter evenings in rural Connecticut in the eighteenth century were long. Debating various issues, including polygamy, would have filled them nicely. Miner contended that such "talk" was not especially consequential: "I well remember to have heard church members give their opinions in favour of Polygamy, years ago; but never heard of any body being offended at it." At some point in 1779, "I happened, while I was discoursing chiefly for talk sake, at sundry times and places, to give my opinion in favor of Polygamy, in plain words, not once thinking of an offence." Somehow, the situation began to reek of scandal: did Miner advocate polygamy? One founder of Norfolk, Asahel Case, thought he did, and that such beliefs were dangerous.[13]

"A Charge of Heresy, & Scandalous Conduct"

"A Charge of Heresy, & Scandalous Conduct": so started with a bang church proceedings against Miner in October 1780.[14] The charges must have been brought shortly after Miner's return from military service, suggesting that they had been brewing for a while. Perhaps on his return he had pushed Asahel Case into public proceedings, or maybe they had been awaiting his return to move ahead. While Miner had probably not seen much action in the Hudson Highlands in the summer of 1780 (as the Continental Army had established itself with considerable force), what a homecoming! If Case had imagined he would silence Miner with the charges, he was wrong. The novelty of the proceedings, as well as Miner's refusal to concede, only exacerbated the scandal. That the whole episode paralyzed the church council can be seen in the nervous notations in the remaining records. After the initial accusation, "since the Matter then in debate was new & not attended to heretofore," the Council decided to adjourn. "After long Conversation, it was determined yt. [that] It was expedient to have a larger Council, on an Affair so new & uncommon." Ultimately, the council determined that it needed to appoint a special committee to decide the matter. Miner argued that the committee should consist of clergy and laity, and that the church should choose one half, Miner the other. "Whereupon a Large Debate ensued." The church refused Miner's proposal; he then rejected theirs. In the end, the church appointed a committee of clergy from neighboring towns to decide the matter. The case was sufficiently unusual as to prove exceptionally controversial. Should Miner be forced to recant his endorsement of polygamy? If he did not, what was the church to do?[15]

Debates turned on two central points. The first was "whether it is consistant with ye Word of Go[d] for a Man to have a Plurality of Wives at ye same time." The second was "whether it be censurable for a B[rothe]r. To hold & adhere to ye Dn [Doctrine] of Poligamy, altho' he does not put it in practice." Miner had plenty to say about both. The records do not include much of the substance of Miner's arguments, but they do make clear his increasing challenge to church authority. Miner initially admitted that he believed in polygamy, but he denied that it was heretical. He had help from two "advocates," Giles Pettibone, an officer in the Revolutionary War, and Asahel Humphrey. Both Pettibone and Humphrey were stalwarts of the Norfolk community. Apparently, they agreed with Miner up to a point that there were biblical justifications for polygamy. "The matter was largely debated." By December 1780, the church determined that Miner's views were heretical. Yet they adjourned until January 1781, when Miner "read his plea . . . when there appeared so many bitter Invectives & Harsh treatment of his Br[other]s. That he was stoped."[16] Some kinds of talk were more acceptable than others. By the end of that dramatic meeting, the church decided finally to "cast off s[ai]d. John Miner from their Comm[union] . . . no longer to treat him as a Christian Bro[ther]." Yet even following his excommunication, the scandal continued. Four men, "ye four delinquent Bro[ther]s," continued to support Miner: Samuel Turner, Henry Akins, Jared Abernethy, and Jesse Tobey. Although Miner was expelled in January, another meeting in May 1781 returned to the fracas. The cases of Miner's supporters dragged on into 1782. The church again called for reinforcement from other churches, to help in what its representatives termed "our present unhappy Difficulties." In March 1782, Abernethy "confessed his Sins in opposing ye Ch[urc]h. in censuring Dr Miner." By September, Henry Akins and Jesse Tobey had confessed "for giving ye Ch[urc]h justification to enquire into Their Conduct respecting Polygamy." They were restored "to Charity & Communion." Turner would not recant, so he, like Miner, was excommunicated.[17]

Miner argued that he did not deserve excommunication simply for believing, not practicing, such alternative beliefs. For him, marriage was not a religious matter but a state one: "The marriage institution is however a civil institution of vast importance to the well being of community in this apostate world." To disagree about its specifics was not a matter of heresy. Miner stressed that belief in polygamy was at worst a circumstantial error, not an essential error. He meant that good Christians might reasonably disagree on it: as for instance, whether the Sabbath should be kept on a Saturday or a Sunday. He could not believe what had happened to him. "It is really astonishing, that . . . such a revolution as this should took place; that I should be cut off, as I am this day, from the privileges of communion." He looked forward to the time in heaven, when all would be right. In the meantime, he averred: "I shall content myself with publishing the whole of this strange process to the world, that better geniuses may undertake to right this matter."[18]

"This Strange Process"

How had this situation begun, and why did it continue for so long? There were at least five developments of particular importance. First, Miner contended, "others" became "more than common inquisitive about it." Were more people asking him about it personally? Was it a more general topic of conversation? If there was greater interest in polygamy in Connecticut in 1780, it was hardly the only place, as we shall see. That general upsurge of concern over polygamy may also have prompted the second development cited by Miner. It was a sermon given by a visiting minister: "Rev. Mr. Searles preached a very good sermon on family education and government, about this time . . . cited Mal. ii. 14,15. which he explained to prove against Polygamy." As we have already seen, numerous Protestants found no justification to condemn polygamy in either Old Testament or New. Malachi 2:14–15 seems more about divorce than polygamy: "the LORD hath been witness between thee and the wife of thy youth, against whom thou hast dealt treacherously: yet *is* she thy companion, and the wife of thy covenant. . . . Let none deal treacherously against the wife of his youth." However, divorce is not something that makes any appearance here. That John Miner was somehow dissatisfied with "the wife of his youth" may well be part of the story, a third point. However, it is difficult to know. Some of the more notable proponents of divorce and polygamy, such as John Milton, had been unhappily married themselves. The church records include a whispered accusation that Miner had been "lying in Bed with ye Wife of David Hawkins."[19] Still, even the church council, eager to punish him, "*Voted in ye Negative*" to the "particular" of adultery. Miner never even bothered to refute this point in his own defense.

A fourth point involves small-town politics and masculine tussles for authority. Miner felt he was hounded to keep discussing the increasingly vexed issue of polygamy. He complained that "those with whom I had lately been discoursing, began to pelt me about it, as if they had thereby gained a notable advantage over me." Miner continued, "This brought on the talk briskly again, and increased in me a fresh zeal for dispute; that I had indeed by this time got to be very apt to talk about it." However, there seems to have been some positioning of men against each other, using this debate to score points. One contemporary minister rued that church discipline was too often "made a means to revenge little private quarrels." Although the records do not divulge the nature of these issues, it seems likely that the trial boiled down to local animosities, brought into the church. As one historian of eighteenth-century Connecticut has phrased it, "The meeting house became the battleground for all the issues dividing the town."[20]

That Miner went to the trouble of publishing his own defense suggests that he was determined to fight. He was shocked and furious at his excommunication. Case was a founder of the town, and Robbins the respected minister. Miner directed a lot of ire at Robbins, with whom there were tensions even before the trial. Miner styled himself "doctor." Robbins was a Yale graduate. Was there some way in which these men were proving their intellectual prowess through these controversies? If so, the trials only exacerbated these strains. For a man to be publicly brought to trial was humiliating enough. For him to be excommunicated was a major blow. Such a man would not be chosen for public offices, and others might even shun him. Yet if masculine conflict partly explains how this controversy played out, so does masculine solidarity. Miner had loyal supporters, who themselves were eventually accused of heresy. Like Miner, both Tobey and Abernathy had served in the Revolutionary War. So had plenty of men in Norfolk. This shared military service may have given them a sense of confidence and brotherhood. It may also indicate a generational shift; Miner and his supporters were younger men, raising families. They may have pitted themselves against the older generation. Tobey, Abernethy, and Miner did not fight in the same regiments, but they did all share time in military service. The timing of their services might also indicate that they were from less advantaged backgrounds, unlike Case, who served early and briefly. To serve for longer periods, and after 1777, implied they were less well heeled than those who served earlier and for shorter times. This shared background may have given them some confidence. Another humble soldier who served in this war found his sense of self transformed by what one historian terms "a memory, above all, of respect from his betters."[21]

The American Revolution might have altered some men's willingness to defend their views, however powerful and well respected their enemies were. Still, other longer-term transformations were also at work. Miner's lengthy defense was meant to go some way in reestablishing his reputation. Unwilling to take his excommunication quietly, Miner brought the "great debate" to a wider audience, publishing the tract with the major printers in Connecticut, Hudson and Goodwin (who also published the *Connecticut Courant*). As one historian has pointed out, "college-educated men"—in other words, perhaps men like Miner—"helped to transform public speaking and writing" in this century. Even in the 1740s, many thought it was unacceptable for men other than preachers to speak or write publicly on theological matters. Yet there were always some who disagreed. There was a fine tradition of religious radicalism in Connecticut, from the very founding of the Old Testament–oriented colony of New Haven to relatively recent renewed conflict with a group called the Rogerenes.[22]

The Rogerenes, named after their late-seventeenth-century founder John Rogers, were dissenters who shared features with Quakers. They had run into conflict with authorities in New London and elsewhere since the late seventeenth century over issues such as whether to mark the Sabbath on Saturday or Sunday. There was especially tense conflict in New London in the 1760s. Like John Miner, John Rogers, grandson of the founder, went to print to condemn the cruelties of the orthodox. The right to speak was a central issue, as Rogers defended the right of women to prophesy and teach in church. He denounced a minister who was fearful "lest these women should speak to him of the things of God." He also complained of one selectman who apparently "beat our women with his hands, and rub[bed] dirt and dung in their faces, and force[d] it into their mouths." Their enemies even "offered shameful abuse to our women in the dark," with one husband of such a woman crying out "that the Sodomites had got his wife." There were political overtones to these bodily violations, which included tarring women and men, as a newspaper reported that "the Sons of Liberty at New-London have taken such methods with the sect called Rogerenes, that they are prevented from disturbing the worshipping assemblies."[23]

The intermingling of politics and religions probably influenced the Miner case too. He kept insisting that he had no wish to practice polygamy, but he hotly defended his right to pronounce it acceptable. This was, after all, the decade in which the First Amendment, giving people the right to free speech, was established. Miner's supporters endured months of separation from the church, and, in one case, full excommunication. Even those who recanted may have remained outside full church acceptance. As late as 1785, records note that Jesse Tobey "had for a long time withdrawn from the Ch[urc]h & Claimed it as his right to worship acc[ording to] His Conscience." Here is rights talk, though not the sort usually associated with the American Revolution. Tobey's rebellion, and Miner's revolution, were of a different sort from the political upheavals, but connected and equally important. Such dramatic, if long-term, transformations, and larger questions about who had a right to express publicly views about polygamy and other matters, under-pinned what might have been a fifth reason for the Norfolk discussions in 1780 about polygamy: a major public controversy about it in England the same year. Neither Miner's own account nor the church records ever mention the British fracas. It is possible that they were unconnected. In that case, it is an intriguing coincidence that polygamy became a point of major contro-versy independently in the same year in two locations an ocean apart and at war with each other.[24]

"The General Topic of Conversation"

Unexpected as it may seem, in 1780, polygamy became a preoccupation in England. It is difficult to comprehend fully the American controversy without understanding this English one. In London in June 1780, the Reverend Martin Madan, a Methodist-leaning minister, published *Thelyph-thora; or, a Treatise on Female Ruin*, a two-volume (later expanded to three) treatise calling for the reform of marriage law in England. It called in partic-ular for the legalization of polygyny. This publication provoked a wave of reviews and countertreatises, newspaper notices, poems, plays, and prints. By the end of the year, the topic formed a staple of London debating societies. As one critic observed: "Witness the infinite letters, epigrams, and lampoons, in almost every news-paper, on this subject; witness the public disputations in places of amusement. . . . Witness also the ridiculous and contemptible figure exhibited . . . in . . . many of our print-shops." Even beyond the metropolis, Madan's doctrines were purported to be the subject of intense discussion. According to a Cheshire preacher, *Thelyphthora* was, despite its weightiness, "much read, and more talked of," indeed "the general topic of conversation, in almost every company where I go."[25]

In his marital remedy for disorder, Madan rejected the power of clergy to make marriage. For him, agreement between the parties—in fact, mere sexual union—was sufficient. As he wrote memorably, "I cannot suppose, that the *matrimonial*-service . . . can make the parties more *one flesh* in the sight of God . . . than the *burial*-service can make the corpse . . . more dead." Somewhat surprisingly, given his evangelical background, Madan did not suggest that men should be encouraged to reform themselves. He claimed that for men, sexual desire, "that natural, but violent passion," was akin to hunger or thirst: implanted by God to preserve life, leading to problems only if overindulged. He presumed that men required sexual outlets, best provided by wives. Madan essentially advocated marriage as a form of control, and not necessarily an especially pleasant one, for male sexual yearnings. He made reference to "the painful oeconomy of a family-life" and the "incumbrance of a wife and family." Such is not the language of cheerful domesticity we might expect of an evangelical husband of the era, despite, as we shall see, an ongoing Methodist criticism of prioritizing family over faith.[26]

In passing, Madan condemned utterly the possibility of polyandry, assuming that men, and only men, should have the advantage of polygamy. He did so on three grounds. First, he pointed to women's inferiority, asserting that woman was rightly placed "under the absolute power of her husband . . . not at liberty to make any contract whatsoever, without her husband's consent." Before he became a minister, Madan had been a barrister. His legal background perhaps partially explains his claims of women's inability to form "contracts" (with another husband) as a major reason for their continued subordination, but this is rather circular logic. Second, in an argument from nature, he claimed that women produced fewer children if they had more partners, so this purported lack of fertility proved that "polyandry

. . . is contrary to nature." Finally, he pointed to the fact that women carried with them the family line by giving birth, so the allowance of polyandry would lead to social confusion. Here is a classic statement of patriarchy; the father had to be sure of which child was his, for purposes of inheritance. There were, then, aspects of Madan's theories that were in fact profoundly socially conservative.[27]

"One of the Most Dangerous [Works] . . . Which This Age Hath Produced"

Despite this lack of radicalism in some points, Madan's proposals still much disturbed contemporaries. Madan's prestigious family and unblemished reputation added to their distress. One anti-Madan author conceded: "That he was born of a family well-connected . . . several members of which have been conspicuous by their talents, is most readily admitted." His father, Colonel Martin Madan, the son of a wealthy Nevis planter, was a commander and a member of Parliament; his mother, Judith Cowper Madan, was a poet who corresponded with Alexander Pope. His brother Stephen later became a bishop; another brother, Frederick, served (and died) in North America, as a colonel of the Foot Guards. His cousin, William Cowper, was a well-known poet. One critic expressed his dismay that Madan's views should be published by "a man of your education, character, and connections." Although he had trained as a barrister, Madan had experienced a conversion on hearing a Methodist preacher, and was ordained in the Church of England. Madan became one of the coterie of the major Methodist patron the countess of Huntingdon.[28]

Madan occupied a prominent position as chaplain of the Lock Hospital in London, one of the first hospitals in the world dedicated to the treatment of those suffering sexually transmitted diseases and also a site of evangelicalism. It was a major public role, a celebrity pulpit for a well-connected cleric; he was no meek handholder at bedsides. Whatever his Christian beliefs and duties there, Madan was not the kind of man to kneel before the dirty feet of a penitent Mary Magdalene. Indeed, he apparently found the physical symptoms of the hospital's ravaged patients so revolting that he refused even to walk in the wards. Still, this position helped propel Madan into considerations of the problem of sexual and social turmoil. So popular was Madan's preaching there that a new chapel, well known for its music, was built. His mother, Judith (not, obviously, an unbiased source), claimed that his gifts were "a fine voice and something gracefull and pathetick in his manner." She also noted that he "is very much admir'd in Town, and has overcome much prejudice [against Methodism] in many." Before the scandal, he was one of the select ministers chosen to preach in a royal chapel in March 1780. He also wrote and revised many hymns (including some of "Hark! The Herald Angels Sing") for which he is still remembered.[29]

In other words, Madan, for all his Methodist leanings, was solidly Establishment. Quietly, if perhaps unhappily, married to one woman, Jane (Hale) Madan, and the father of five children, he had the kind of character that might be expected of an evangelical minister. His previous publications included the 1763 *Scriptural Account of the Doctrine of Perfection;* he later translated Juvenal. Methodist critics contended: "Had this Treatise been wrote by a professed libertine and abandoned debauchee, it would not have been a matter of surprise . . . or had it been the production of a priest of the church of Rome, *the mother of harlots and of the abominations of the earth,* it might be easily accounted for." Since Madan was a prominent Protestant clergyman, however, it was vital to refute it. Another critic claimed dramatically that "considering the author . . . the present [work] is one of the most dangerous . . . which this age hath produced." *Thelyphthora* appeared with a major publisher, James Dodsley, whose publishing concern also printed Samuel Richardson's *Sir Charles Grandison,* Lord Chesterfield's *Letters,* and writings by Samuel Johnson, Laurence Sterne, and Edmund Burke.[30] So his platform was large.

Mechanisms for short-lived panics and obsessions were in place in England and especially London by 1780. Something like one-third of Londoners read a newspaper, and the more salacious the news, the more likely it was to be published, read, and discussed. Newspaper printers also published pamphlets, such as some of those criticizing *Thelyphthora.* By 1775, in London alone, there were around 120 printers and 110 publishers, and it was a cutthroat business. There was much to titillate and condemn in Madan's theories, though *Thelyphthora* itself, with its thousand-plus pages of biblical and philological interpretation, was heavy going. *Thelyphthora* was assuredly more talked about than read, since debating polygamy was a more engaging pastime than slogging through a minister's scholarly parsing of New Testament Greek.[31]

In fact, *Thelyphthora*'s scandalous ideas were already circulating before its publication in June 1780. Early that year, debates were held in London on such topics as "Would it not be a just and equitable law, that every man who had seduced a woman should be obliged to marry her?" and "Would a repeal of the Marriage Act be consistent with the principles of sound policy?" While these might be assumed to reflect long-standing concerns, the topic of a March debate in the Lycée Français, whether the advantages of polygamy outweighed its abuses, was incontrovertibly connected to the brewing Madan scandal. Letters indicate that individuals were discussing the work before it appeared, especially since the countess of Huntingdon, Madan's former patron, allegedly offered to gather a petition with three thousand signatures to try to stop him from publishing. Once the book was published, a torrent of reviews, pamphlets, and poems appeared by the autumn of 1780, just the same period the Miner controversy was exploding in North America. Although there were unique aspects of Madan's scandal, there were nevertheless many links to Miner's predicament. Arguments about polygamy were also debates about 1780's shifting gender, sexual, social, and political order.[32]

"Multiplicity of Wives . . . the Favourite Tenet of Most Fanatical Sects"

First, both these controversies were religious ones, involving infighting among dissenters. How far could and should the Protestant Reformation go in terms of reforming marriage? In some senses, the English Reformation and subsequent laws had left marriage reform incomplete. There had long been attempts to control and regulate marriage, to deal with perceived problems of secret marriages and bigamy. Yet these had not worked very well. The culmination of these campaigns had come only recently, in the controversial 1753 Marriage Act, which sought to end clandestine and irregular marriages. Still, there were several attempts in Parliament—in 1754, 1765, 1772, and 1781—to repeal it. It was also a source of general debate, as we have seen. Marriage law in England was an uneasy accommodation of Reformation, reform, continuity, and complexities. This same patchwork also characterized British colonies, where there was considerable variation in marriage policies (such as age of consent for marriage or justifications for its dissolution).[33]

The infamy attending Madan's treatise threatened to disgrace the Methodist cause, so many of its leaders rushed to publish rabid refutations. Before publication, Madan's heterodox notions were an open secret among Methodists. A fellow evangelist, Richard Hill, had apparently implored

Madan: "If you have any love for your christian friends . . . any concern for the glory of God, the peace of his church . . . you will not publish the *Treatise*." For all their willingness to flout religious conventions, evangelicals were highly sensitive to charges of marital and gender subversion. As one historian of eighteenth-century Methodism has contended, "contemporaries certainly understood this much: that Methodism somehow represented an undercutting of family life as conventionally ordered." Indeed, both satirical and serious pieces imagined Methodists involved in sexual excess, well before Madan's treatise. In 1754, one anti-Methodist tract, invoking Münster, highlighted dissenters' sexual profligacy: "Many *Authors* have shewn a *natural* Connection between *Enthusiasm and Impurity*. And 'tis observable in *Fact*, that a *Multiplicity of Wives*, and promiscuous Use of Women, has been the *Favourite Tenet* of most *Fanatical Sects*." The founder of Methodism, John Wesley, had publicly argued that Christians should focus on religious, not secular, concerns and therefore should ideally refrain from marrying (also: masturbating). Although Wesley eventually married, he claimed he did so partly to avoid charges of libertinism. Both English and American Methodists largely abandoned the early commitment to celibacy, "quickly [making] efforts to accommodate their married preachers." Women, notably the countess of Huntingdon, also achieved importance in Methodist circles. Yet the prominence of such women may have meant that Methodists were even less eager to be connected with domestic radicalism, as it would have given their critics, who already viewed Methodists as a lunatic fringe, further leverage against them. Huntingdon's sister had already scandalized contemporaries by cohabiting with her fiancé before they had married. When Madan forged ahead despite the countess's offer to gather a petition to stop him, many evangelicals, including his former assistant, fell over themselves to publish rebuttals.[34]

Both controversies also show the continued vibrancy of anti-Catholicism in eighteenth-century Anglo-American culture, especially in dissenting circles. *Thelyphthora*'s vivid anti-Catholicism was considered one of its more alluring aspects. After all, the war begun against American colonies in 1775 had become a more traditional war against Catholic France by 1780. The Gordon Riots, in which the mere possibility of Catholic emancipation, the right of Catholics to vote in elections, brought violence to London in June 1780, reflected in part the vicious flareup of long-standing competing impulses. Madan saw himself as the spiritual heir to Martin Luther (who had defended bigamy, as we have seen) and other reformers who returned to the original biblical languages to make audacious propositions to change the world: "As *Rome* was not *built* in a day, so neither could it be *demolished* in a day.—The Protestant *Reformers* did *much* towards its demolition, but they could not do *all*." Moreover, Madan vehemently attacked "papist superstition" on the topic of clerical celibacy in particular. Madan argued that polygamy, like clerical marriage, had been outlawed only because of faulty Catholic impositions. Madan published a third volume of *Thelyphthora* in 1781, and it offered a (nearly five hundred–page) history of how contemporary marriage law descended from erroneous Catholic teachings, not from God himself.[35]

Madan's alluring anti-Catholicism, his facility with ancient Hebrew, Greek, and Latin, and his barrister's abilities to argue a point with verve rankled many critics worried about the spread of his heretical ideas. One conceded: "You have sent your lady Polygamia abroad in a vesture of wrought gold." Another lamented: "Some eminent and faithful ministers of the gospel have imbibed your sentiments, and are even earnest in the propagation of them." The first fretted that "there are many judicious men . . . so far corrupted by this book, as to embrace the sentiments and scheme of this friend to Polygamy." One of these complained, "I am acquainted with a worthy good man, who . . . seriously mediated a design of abridging the book *to give away among the poor*." Miner himself might well have been one such supporter. Certainly, he shared Madan's vehement anti-Catholicism, denouncing the "superstitious spirit" of "the bishops of Rome" as they "went on from one degree of grandeur to another, and from one cruelty to another."[36]

"The Arts and Wiles of Seducers"

A second reason why many critics feared the enthralling gleam of "Lady Polygamia" was the discomfiting acknowledgment of the problems of sexual disorder and, in particular, the vulnerability of young women. Madan's proposals touched on the ongoing unease about the exploitations of women, especially poor ones, in contemporary English society. Madan argued that "GOD's laws are laid aside, for that system of baseness and barbarity, which permits men, with impunity . . . to betray . . . thousands . . . of unhappy women, who . . . instead of becoming nuisances . . . might have been the comforts of their families . . . the ornaments of civil society." He contended that in his system, "millions of women (especially of the lower sort) would be saved from ruin." As Lock Hospital chaplain, Madan was familiar with the misery of "ruined" women, even if he could not stomach their bodily sufferings in person. In a 1763 pamphlet, Madan told the sad story of one woman, "F.S.," seduced, impregnated, abandoned, and thus forced into prostitution. F.S. repented her previous life—"I abhor my polluted body, and my more polluted soul"—and died singing God's praises. But the problem of pollution, both physical and moral, did not die with her. It spread out of the wards into the streets, pleasure gardens, taverns, and houses of the land. Madan's sermon preached at the Lock Hospital in 1764 begged for sympathy not just for the wives and children of men who had infected them with sexually transmitted diseases but also for those "who have been led away by the arts and wiles of seducers."[37]

Madan's campaigns against "female ruin" resonated in a society saturated with seduction stories, illegitimacy, bridal pregnancy, and prostitution. Seduction had long formed a chief trope of many tales, most notably Richardson's *Pamela* and *Clarissa* (in which the heroine spent time in a brothel). By the late eighteenth century, such narratives highlighted the plight of young women. At the same time, there was evidently a rise in both bridal pregnancy and illegitimacy rates. Prostitution seemingly flourished in London. These social ills generated many possible solutions, but all agreed they were a problem. Since many concurred with Madan's analysis of the problem, it was difficult to dismiss his points out of hand. Social disorder stemming from sexual indulgence was a key theme of one of the satirical prints produced by these controversies, *Polygamy Display'd* (1780).[38]

Such themes also animated the Miner controversy, though less dramatically. Illegitimacy and bridal pregnancy both increased substantially in late colonial New England. Masculine sexual indulgence had also become a popular theme for humor in print culture. As one historian has observed, by the middle of the eighteenth century, "male sexual license was becoming a casual, even a joking matter in New England." In Philadelphia, according to another historian, "the pursuit of sexual conquest, especially for men, had become commonplace and comical." That seduction had become a more prominent theme in the minds of the good citizens of Norfolk, Connecticut, can be seen in those names for daughters, those Clarissas. Miner, too, fretted over unfettered sexuality and argued that marriage itself, even plural marriage, was "a natural and lawful remedy against the unbridled rein of lust, that is against fornication." Marriage had long been a perennial topic of

[Unknown], *Polygamy Display'd, or Doctor Madman restored to his senses* (London, 1780). Madan is shown at the center of two pummeling wives, as a third shadowy wife on the left picks his pocket. Two wives on the left resort to fisticuffs. A crying child and that classic trope of household mayhem, the fighting dog and cat, contribute to the chaos. Behind a screen at right, a couple—another wife and another man—canoodle. The screen depicts several images of the consequences of such household bedlam: a figure in jail, others dueling, two figures on the gallows. Here was a representation of the ways in which polygamy radiated outward into social disorder. Courtesy of Lewis Walpole Library, Yale University.

popular culture, a source of playful discussion. Consider an item from the *London Magazine* in 1740, reprinted in the *Boston Evening-Post* about an implausible law in Prussia that men who seduced women would be "obliged to marry them." The joke was that Prussian women would then become the seducers. Yet increasingly, from London to Boston to Philadelphia, newspapers, almanacs, and magazines all offered "humorous" accounts of marriage and its manifold discontents.[39]

"The Happiness of the Marriage State"

There was a transformation in ideals of marriage in the late eighteenth century, on both sides of the Atlantic, a third reason for this sudden interest in polygamy. One historian of English sexuality has posited that the main shift in marriage was an increased criticism of marrying for money, but the constellation of concerns about marriage goes far beyond that single point.

In the eighteenth century arose the then-radical notion—now taken for granted—that marriages should be happy: not simply fruitful or blessed by God or economically helpful or advantageous. The ideal of happiness in marriage (and the idea that discontent might be cause for divorce) went from the margins to the center in this era. This critical shift prompted a lot of discussion, some of it in the formal debating clubs that proliferated especially in urban centers in this era. These debating societies in London and elsewhere increasingly put marriage front and center in their topics; whether it was acceptable to marry for money was only one of the topics considered. A classic debate, which seemed perennially to draw crowds, was "Whether the married or single life was more happy?" There were also issues about the way men behaved in worlds both domestic and social: "Is it true," posed one society in 1777, "that man acts as the tyrant as well as the lord of creation?" In 1776, one society considered cohabitation: "Is not the cohabitation of an unmarried man and woman, though attended with harmony and fidelity till death, an immoral connection?" A few years later the same society debated "Whether any degree of ill-treatment from a husband to a wife, can justify the latter in defiling the marriage-bed?" Apparently, the issue of such justifiable adultery "was debated for some time, with the speakers being undetermined." That a late-eighteenth-century audience did not roundly condemn cuckoldry under any circumstances seems surprising.[40]

Interest in harmonious marriages reverberated beyond the metropolis. The Pantheon Society of Edinburgh, that great capital of Enlightenment, serves as a useful and well-documented microcosm of the kinds of changes occurring in this period (though no records exist after 1779). The society began in 1774 as an occasion for men to leave their houses of an evening and join together in debates, from "Would it be proper to prohibit Emigrations?" (a major issue in Scotland in the 1770s) to "Has Great Britain a right to Tax her Colonies?" ("a great Majority" of members agreed it did). In 1774, the society asked, as many London societies did, "Is a Married or a single State most Conducive to Private Happiness?" Of the 132 "gentlemen" in attendance, eighty-seven voted for marriage. Later that year the society inquired "Whether ought Love or money to have the greatest influence in promoting Marriage?" The clerk for the society reported, "The House this night was extremely Crowded, & the debate upon the Whole afforded great entertainment to the Visitors. It was carried by a great Majority that Love ought to have the greatest influence in promoting Marriage."[41]

Marriage and love in fact helped to alter gender relations in the Pantheon Society. Initially for men, by the start of 1775—after that popular debate on marriage—the society had "unanimously agreed to admit Ladies to hear the debate." Some members worried about this move, wondering whether debates would become too crowded. So they also "unanimously agreed . . . that the tickets (including Ladies tickets) should never exceed 200." At that first mixed meeting, "Ten Ladies were present who appeared to listen with unusual attention to the debates" on "Whether is a Nation in a State of Barbarity or a nation in a State of Luxury and refined manners the happiest?" Again, the emphasis on happiness is striking. The "Ladies" declared unanimously for "refinement." A 1776 debate on slavery included 15 women and 91 men, a bare majority of whom agreed that "the African Slave Trade ought not to be tolerated in the Colonies of a Free State." In early February 1776, 51 women and 179 men listened to a debate on whether it was "good policy to have Ladies for Soveraigns." The "great Majority" agreed that "females ought not to be troubled with Soveraignity and that their Empire over the Men was sufficiently powerful." All but two of the women present "were of ye same opinion." Over the 1770s, proportions of women kept rising.[42]

Marriage was a popular topic among both women and men at the Pantheon Society. In 1775, in addition to arguing over whether "lenient or coercive measures [were] more likely to terminate the differences betwixt Brittain and her Colonies," the Society also considered whether divorce should be allowed. In 1776, the society wondered how best to make marriages happy: "Whether does the Happiness of the Marriage State depend most on the Husband or Wife?" Most agreed on the wife, a contention that demonstrates the critical nature of gender relations to marriage's proper functioning, as well as the notion that both wives and husbands had a right to be happy in marriage. One evening in early 1778 centered on whether it was "proper to enter into the matrimonial state without parental authority," the majority conceding that parental consent was "not necessary."[43] Marriage, they agreed, should be based on personal interest, attraction, and consent, not family advantage.

When marriage was on the evening's agenda, the popularity of the debates grew with women as well as men. One woman even made her views heard. In December 1778, the society debated that classic, "Whether should Love, or Money, have the greatest influence in forming the Matrimonial Connection?" The society clerk used punctuation to evince his surprise at the "348!" people there, noting that "the house this Evening was fuller than perhaps at any former Debate." Indeed, the room got so hot and the debates grew so heated that the society decided to adjourn and to continue a week later. At this point, "406!" attended, of whom 180, nearly half, were women. The member keeping records also noted that "a more ingenious and interesting debate has scarcely occupied any former meeting of the Society," with most members declaring for love over money. While the society still did not accept a woman speaking, it did let one publicly share her opinion: "The anonymous Sentiments of a Lady were read by Mr Anderson . . . they were received by the Audience with every mark of respect and applause."[44]

The Pantheon Society records demonstrate both the increasing presence of women in public debates and the fascination both women and men had in what made for happiness: in marriage and in life. It also shows the increase of women's voices in the public arena. Such developments were interconnected. We find similar interest in marriage and its workings, as well as the possibility of female voices, in other, less likely sources: political writings on the American Revolution. British and American writings about the Revolution not only appealed directly to women but also used analogies that celebrated wives who refused to accept servile obedience. One article in colonial newspapers recast the generic form of ads for runaway wives (in which husbands disavowed their absconding wives' debts) as mirrors of political rebellion. "Loyalty" advertised that "Liberty's" debts should not be honored, and American Liberty, the put-upon wife, replied, "My reason for leaving him was because he behaved in an arbitrary and cruel manner." Cruel behavior justified separation on the part of a wife, an argument also made by wives in newspaper ads. Two 1775 English pamphlets deployed the marital analogy in order to argue against British tyranny toward its colonies. In a pro-American British one, written specifically to women, the author imagined an altercation between a tyrannical Britain and an indignant America, who resents the use of her pin money to pay her husband's debts. Their conversation escalates to a fierce match, in which America claims: "I can be *obedient* but not *base*. A *wife* but not a *slave*," to which the husband replies: "This is the language of rebellion, Madam!" He doesn't actually threaten to spank her in the pamphlet, but he might as well. When the wife persists—"This is the tone of tyranny, Sir"—the husband declares: "Whips and chains shall inforce obedience." The wife then appeals to the law, and says she would rather separate than demonstrate a *"base and servile sub-*

mission." The author concluded: "This Ladies is exactly the case between England and America, except that a wife would be certain of relief from *the law*, whereas America must trust to . . . *arms.*" Whips and chains, obedience and submission: such indeed was the provocative "language of rebellion," underpinning the American Revolution as surely as any about rights of free-born Englishmen. Novel understandings of marriage gave women and men new ways to make sense of, and to talk about, political discontent.[45]

Analogies between marriage and revolution also figured in John Cartwright's *A Letter to Edmund Burke*. Its radical author explicitly rejected the far more prevalent parent-child analogy, instead imagining Britain and America as a courting couple. He demanded: "But shall he, like an Eastern despot, doom her to a splendid wretchedness in his seraglio . . . knowing too well she is no better than the slave of his lustful appetites?" Or was Britain to descend even further in civility, from Eastern despot to savage: "Like a still worse Barbarian . . . unmoved at her tears . . . shall he brutishly . . . become her impious ravisher?" Coercion and wretchedness lay in the harem or in rape: no happy marriages here. He warned Britain that he might be surprised to find that the woman thus stabbed him in retaliation, rather than allow her honor to be violated. He hoped that the tyrant Britain would lose his "inebriation" before this scenario came to pass, "recollecting their mutual tenderness . . . and the inseparable nature of their interests." The result then would be "an union agreeable to nature, to justice, and to freedom." Such comparisons linked domestic relations to imperial ones: Britain should act like a tender husband. By late 1780, of course, Britain was in no position to act the despot. Still, such appeals suggest the sense that women had a stake in the revolutionary outcome, and that women—and men—would respond to analogies based on marriage, happiness, and consent.[46]

"To Restore That Manly Firmness and Vigour"

Marriage's internal dynamics concerned contemporaries both in terms of consent and contentment, as here, and in terms of fertility and population growth. Population worries haunted the British in the eighteenth century. Although the 1750s might have been the zenith of such concerns, they had not dissipated by the 1780s. They took on urgent force in the context of a war that depended on military impressment and the use of foreign mercenaries. One of Madan's arguments against the 1753 Marriage Act, which he condemned, was that, by making marriage more difficult to achieve legally, it had limited population growth, a danger in wartime. Madan also lamented economic want that prevented many marrying: "We should see the true reason why our *fleets* want sailors, our *armies* men . . . why we complain of scarcity of people, . . . and why we are forced to have recourse to *foreign auxiliaries* in our days of common danger. The reason of all this is, we have not *people enough*." With complicated feats of mathematics typical of would-be reformers, Madan offered calculations, based on the popular notion that prostitution rendered women barren and that thousands currently did not marry, designed to prove that polygyny would augment the population. His critics, claiming that women would cease to marry or bear children because of their hatred of polygyny, asserted the opposite.[47]

Marital sexuality also preoccupied many, including another notable of 1780, Dr. James Graham, whose Temple of Health and Hymen in Pall Mall in London attracted both fascination and mockery that year, just as Madan's theories did. Historians have generally dismissed Graham, like Madan, as one of the era's eccentrics. Contemporaries also paralleled these two theorists, both of whom proposed reinvigorated marital sexuality as a panacea for England's ills. Graham suggested that improved fertility would be "sufficient to man our fleets, and increase our armies, as would bid defiance to our most inveterate foes." Far more than Madan, Graham emphasized the need for cheerful domesticity. Graham "saw household bliss as a kind of perpetual foreplay" for the fertile married sex to follow. Also like Madan, Graham argued for the need to end prostitution and to promote marriage, suggesting that a tax be levied on the unmarried, and rewards given to married couples for each child born.[48]

Like Madan and others, Dr. Graham fretted over the leaky British spermatic economy, with its wasteful prostitution and masturbation: "Every succeeding generation becomes more and more weakly. . . . The degeneracy and imbecility of body and mind . . . destroys the state." Such themes resonated in the public lectures he gave (and printed). Graham also aimed to help others put his theories into practice. In his Temple, he rented out to infertile couples a night in his "celestial bed," stuffed with stallions' hair, which coursed with electric currents. He bragged that his miraculous vibrating bed, which promised to transform the critical moment of orgasm into a "critical HOUR," could make the barren fecund. According to Graham, this bed and the resulting enjoyable and fruitful sex to be had in it would promote

Britain's national interests, by increasing population as well as personal happiness. Individual and national happiness depended on British men's potency, sexual and otherwise. As one historian of English erotica in this period has argued, "vigour" had sexual connotations, associated with men and, more specifically, with male genitalia (where it was considered more important than size in attracting women). Vigor also had political overtones. Graham exhorted his readers: "It is therefore incumbent on us to restore that manly firmness and vigour, which, from the depravity of human nature, by means of luxury and dissipation, has for more than a century been lost."[49]

"We Look to Manhood"

Such concerns surround the American Revolution, a fourth reason for these polygamy controversies. First, the American colonies seemed to enjoy population growth far surpassing Britain's, a troubling comparison for commentators in Parliament and elsewhere. Benjamin Franklin's well-known 1751 essay on population, which specifically argued that America was exceeding Europe in population growth, circulated widely in Britain. The population comparison filtered into other discussions, as when, in a debate on a possible repeal of the 1753 Marriage Act, one speaker contended that the North American colonies had greater population growth because the Marriage Act did not apply to them. This same anxiety prompted the careful registering of emigrants leaving North Britain in the 1770s. One satirical poem closed with the jesting claim that putting Madan's theories put into practice would allow the conquest of America, since Britain would then no longer need German mercenaries or "Hesse supplies." The poet noted that if prominent leaders such as the prime minister, the secretary for the colonies, and the first lord of the Admiralty would take "twenty spouses" each, then Britain would "bring fresh heroes forth," allowing them to emerge victorious.[50]

Links between vigor, gender, and military success appeared in less satirical contexts, too. Those sympathetic with the American cause endlessly exploited the child-parent analogy to conclude that while America was a hearty young man, Britain had become a useless old woman. These analogies rejected the notion, pressed by those loyal to Britain, that Americans owed gratitude and obedience to their British mother country. They went much farther, painting Britain as old and decayed in contrast to a hale, hearty America. One patriot bragged: "We look to manhood—our muscles swell out with youthful vigor; our sinews spring with elastic force." Another boasted in a convoluted metaphor that if America was a child, "she is certainly a sturdy, large-boned one . . . in the bloom of vigour and health," who would soon "ripen into manhood." This blooming America thus had the right "to renounce an old, stern, encroaching step-dame . . . greatly impaired with the refinements of luxury, and the arts of debauchery." One even went so far as to call Britain not a stately matron but "an old abandoned prostitute."[51]

Calling the mother country an old prostitute was a dramatic way to make a political point. Yet this kind of analogy, playing on gender and age, circulated on the British side too. Even pro-British authors acknowledged the force of these metaphors, while rejecting their implications. In a treatise printed in New York and London, Samuel Seabury inquired: "Do you think . . . that Great-Britain is like an old, wrinkled, withered, worn-out hag . . . You will find her a vigorous matron." Another denounced the Americans, who had entered "a vigorous state of adolescence, or rather manhood," yet refused to help alleviate "the distresses of your exhausted parent." A 1768 British pamphleteer warned that America might "ris[e] upon [Britain's] ruins . . . to spurn and reject her in her state of desolation . . . springing fresh, young, and vigorous." One 1778 British author observed pointedly: "States are subject to all the vicissitudes of the human body. . . . Shall an old palsied man wrestle with the young and vigorous? . . . Absurd and fanciful indeed!" As one scholar has noted, such an emphasis suggested an "acute sense of Britain's place in the world and serious concerns over the nature of the population."[52]

Debauched prostitutes, decayed parents, effeminate fops: was this the new domestic order of Britain? Similar concerns resonated powerfully in the Madan controversies. Some few criticisms of Madan's marital system focused on the possibility that husbands would become tyrants, as critics inevitably trotted out the stock figure of the "eastern despot." A few critics derided Madan's system as one that would transform peaceful English households into disgraceful Eastern seraglios, in which a petty tyrant lorded over his cowering brood. One satirical poem, whose author was identified as "Mohammed the Prophet," claimed that through Madan, Muslim ideas would infiltrate England: "M—d—n, inspir'd by thee, shall teach our law, / And give new *Korans* in *Thelyphthora*." Such references to Muslim marriage practice worked as a shorthand for the kind of tyranny that was to be rejected in English households. One critic warned: "If Polygamy were ever to have the sanction of the law . . . the wives of Christians must . . . be imprisoned like many among the Turks." One newspaper humorously reported a group of five hundred women rioting against Madan, burning him in effigy after denouncing his attempts to keep them in "a Turkish seraglio" and "Mahomet's paradise." Yet such stereotypical denunciations were not in fact as prevalent as might be expected.[53]

However, the majority of polygamy's critics contended not, as we might expect, that polygyny would make men too powerful. Instead, they argued that it would render them powerless. For instance, images of women taking on masculine authority make an appearance in anti-Madan cartoons. Overall, concerns prevailed about women overstepping their roles, and two other familiar themes resurfaced: violence (especially between women) and sexual frustration. Even Madan admitted that he could imagine "the distractions which most probably *must* be the effect of jealousy between the women." Female fury is the presumed reaction even to the idea of polygamy, as one satirical poet imagined women's replies: "Your giddy girls, gay widows, maids, and wives / . . . Enrag'd, to meet contempt where praise is due, / They burn his book, and fain would burn him too." Some critics coupled polygamous wives' animosities and their sexual frustration, or, as one had it, "revenge and prostitution." Richard Hill emphasized that "every habitation where peace at present dwells, is liable to be turned into a temple of discord, if not into an human slaughter house, by wives cutting their own, each others, or their husband's throat . . . in fits of frantic jealousy." He contended that few women would submissively accept polygamy: "There might be here and there . . . a meek, passive female . . . yet . . . they are not very numerous. . . . Multitudes . . . could neither maintain their chastity, nor with-hold their rage; so that revenge and prostitution seem to be natural twin children of every polygamous intercourse." Hill claimed that only "some bold, boxing Amazonians" would be able to manage polygamy, as they would simply kick other wives out of the house. Another opponent claimed that Madan "would . . . confound all houshold peace and love, by making every house a Magdalene [hospital for prostitutes]." Concerns about unmanly men also had political valence. These anxieties swirl around the popular caricature of the 1770s, the macaroni, or fop. As one periodical inquired, "Whither are the manly vigour and athletic appearance of our forefathers shown? . . . [Not in] a race of effeminate, self-admiring, emaciated fribbles." Audacious women, too, sparked concern in newspaper scandals of the 1770s.[54]

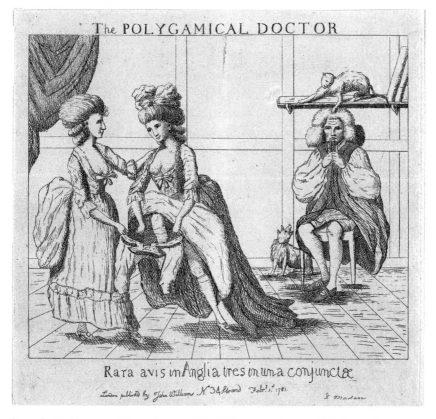

The POLYGAMICAL DOCTOR

Rara avis in Anglia tres in una conjunctæ

London published by John Williams N. 34 Strand   Febr. 1, 1781.

[Anon.], *The Polygamical Doctor* (London: John Williams, 1781). One wife helps another put on the breeches that the cornered Madan, clutching his volumes, has apparently given up. Here again are the cat and dog of domestic chaos, with the cat pawing Madan's barrister's wig itself. The caption reads: "A rare bird in England, three joined in one." This Latin motto evokes Juvenal's claim that a faithful wife was a "rare bird," the black swan virtually impossible to find. Courtesy of Library of Congress.

"Bold, Boxing Amazonians"

If men lacked "manly firmness," then, at least some contemporaries laid the blame with assertive women, those "bold, boxing Amazonians" draining them of vigor. Shifting public roles of women was the fifth and final reason for these controversies. It is hard to believe that such claims still had so much traction in the era of the American Revolution. Based on recent work on eighteenth-century England, we are told that "by 1800 . . . women had come to be seen as comparatively delicate, defensive, and sexually passive. . . . This shift was already well advanced by the middle of the eighteenth century." Another British historian contends that in roughly 1780, "gender play," and the possibility of celebrating or even condoning "bold, boxing Amazonians," gave way to "gender panic," as women were expected to be passive and feminine. Yet by contrast, historians of the American side of the story have emphasized the years immediately after the Revolution as ones of sexual experimentation. One historian of Philadelphia declares: "Following the American Revolution, sexual expression in the city blossomed." Transformations on both sides were perhaps more halting and piecemeal than such overarching contentions allow.[55]

It is also critical here, as elsewhere, to push past the idea that claims about women and sex were only about sex. Such assertions about women's desires were a long-established way of discounting their public participation. So, while these critics derided sex-mad women in order to undermine Madan and his theories, they were also using them to score points about the discomfiting presence of *all* women in public life. After all, that debating club of Scottish ladies and gentlemen did not accept that females should be rulers, though there had been such in Britain before. Novel public appearances by women help to explain the use of this old stereotype of sexually frustrated women. These images appear in another anti-Madan cartoon. This print on women petitioning falls in a clear tradition of using allegations about women's lusts to discredit the moral worthiness of their political involvement.

Women's insatiability was a familiar trope from classical times, one that notably appeared during another moment of revolution: the 1640s, in the guise of a polygamy narrative. In 1646, the anonymous *Parliament of Women* ridiculed women's political organizing, telling the story of how a matron of ancient Rome, on hearing that the Senate had made marriage with two wives legal, organized a Parliament of Women, which petitioned for the right of every woman to have two husbands, "one for delight, the other for her drudgery." Unsatisfied wives in seventeenth-century England, complaining about husbands who failed to give them "a good stirre-up," noted: "In our own cases we will be our own Lawyers, and plead our own rights. For wee have Tongues to tell our own Tales." One such tale, told by Mistris Tattlewell, was that "every woman should have two husbands . . . [as] every deepe Well ought to have two Buckets, while one is comming up, the other going down." Aligning women's biting appetites and their tattling tongues, this pamphlet scorned women's ability to organize politically, with their Parliament becoming chaotic, full of gossip, and "tumultuously breaking out into

THE LADIES PETITION FOR TWO HUSBANDS.

The humble Petition of M.rs MARY MOUTHWATER, KITTY COLEBLACK, BRIDGET BITESHEETS, FANNY FRIZZLERUMP, SUKEY SCRATCHIT and LUCY LONGFORT, to the Rev.d D.r Thelypthorn, praying to reverse the doctrine of Polygamy &c to prove from deep Antiquity that every Woman ought of right to have two Husbands, instead of permitting each man to take two Wives.

[Anon.], *The Ladies Petition for Two Husbands* (London: J. Sharpe, 1784). A brigade of women, with names like Bridget Bitesheets and Fanny Frizzlerump, offer a cheeky petition to Madan for the right to have two husbands. One declares saucily: "I'll undertake to make the feeble stand." The next adds: "My slender Waist will not else expand," connecting fertility with desire. They conclude: "For One alone cannot our wants supply." Courtesy of Library of Congress.

clamour."[56] Its appearance coincided with a moment, in the midst of a Levelling revolution, which prompted worries about the "common sort," including women, entering public debates in new ways.

"We do and shall disclaim that Tyrannical Government, which men have over us." So declared the women in the 1656 *Now or Never: or A New Parliament of Women*. Domestic complaints then give way to inevitable ones about women's sexual frustration. Another such satirical petition appeared in 1710 during Queen Anne's reign, yet another moment in which women (especially the queen's female advisers) were considered overinvolved in politics. Reveling in double entendre, the title gives a flavor of the whole: *The London Ladies Petition, to Have the Chusing of Able and Sufficient Members, Instead of Their Husbands, That May Stand Stiffly by the Church.* This long strand of mockery of female political involvement continued into

[Philip Dawe(?)], *A Society of Patriotic Ladies, at Edenton in North Carolina* (London: R. Sayer and J. Bennett, 1775). Here is a representation of what happens with women entering politics and petitioning at the outbreak of the American Revolution. Another dog, this one licking the neglected child on the floor, underscores the chaos and tumult, as well as the ways in which women, paying attention to men who are not their husbands, ignore their rightful domestic duties. Courtesy of Library of Congress.

the era of the American Revolution, not only with the Madan petition cartoon but also with the well-known British satire of the women of Edenton, North Carolina, petitioning for redress. In such representations, the political point was clear: women's involvement in politics could stem only from "levity" and desire and would only ever end in domestic and social chaos.[57]

Female activism made people nervous, on both sides of the Atlantic. Women organized politicized spinning bees; more controversially, they also joined in petition campaigns and food riots. In these riots, women protested the high price of products available during the Revolutionary War. Such actions could provoke negative reactions; the *Connecticut Courant* sarcastically condemned female food rioters for "such unexampled a Spirit of Heroism." In other areas, locals were equally scathing about the female "Spirit of Heroism." Many in Philadelphia were ashamed of the involvement of young women in the 1778 Meschianza organized by the British military during its occupation of Philadelphia. Women from prominent local families dressed up as Turkish maidens in this masque. Apparently, this situation led to a debate in Philadelphia in which some espoused what a local newspaper termed "fallacious and dangerous sentiments so frequently avowed in this city, that female opinions are of no consequence in public matters." When a Pennsylvania matron, Esther Reed, organized a campaign to raise money for patriot soldiers by sewing shirts, she declared that patriotic women needed to erase the shame of their "female fellow citizens" being too familiar with the British. Outlining an innovative plan in which Pennsylvania women would forgo luxuries and contribute to the army, Reed, in her 1780 *Sentiments of an American Woman,* declared that women "aspire to render themselves more really useful." She continued: "If the weakness of our Constitution, if opinion and manners did not forbid us to march to glory by the same paths as the Men, we should at least equal, and sometimes surpass them in our love for the public good." She noted that women were "born for liberty, disdaining to bear the irons of a tyrannic Government."[58]

Yet it was not only American women entering public life in novel ways. Female debating societies including the Pantheon Society in Britain similarly encouraged women themselves to enter public discussion of them. One of Madan's critics noted that while an assembly of gentlemen had rejected Madan's polygamy in debate, an assembly of women "seemed to favour Mr. M.'s scheme." La Belle Assemblée, a London debating society specifically for women, proposed: "The women of Great Britain [ought] to have a voice in the election of Representatives, and be eligible to sit in Parliament as well as the men." In 1780, the Oratorical Society requested that people not applaud in the middle of speeches because of the "confusion" it caused for women speakers from "the natural timidity of those who have but lately assumed their rights and privileges, by bursting those chains, with which through custom and illiberality, they have hitherto been fettered."[59] For women, such "rights and privileges" included public speaking. Some speakers and writers thus argued that women should "have a voice," perhaps even in Parliament.

Others were horrified by the idea of women's public speaking: "What Women of the slightest Pretensions to Modesty, or common Decency could stand up in an Assembly of a thousand Persons, and hazard their Thoughts and Language on Subjects which they are supposed never to have studied? . . . Would not such Assurance and Effrontery render them absolutely disgustful?" queried one letter writer to a newspaper, castigating female debaters at La Belle Assemblée. This author argued that women were merely reciting speeches by men, since it was implausible that women could possess such eloquence. Such harrumphing about "common Decency" generally indicates that someone feels he is losing a culture war. Yet many agreed. Those careful debaters in Edinburgh let a woman voice opinions only when a man read her anonymous words.[60]

Two women, at least, recorded their thoughts about Madan in their letters. One of them, Mary Cawthorne, found that her "mind has been much harassed respecting Mr: Madan's Book." She felt that God's law must be immutable, but that Moses' laws were evidently not, so polygamy was no longer allowed. She invited her male correspondent to share his opinion. Another was the well-known intellectual, Elizabeth Carter. In May 1780, she wrote to her friend Elizabeth Robinson Montagu. Carter first mentioned the efforts of the countess of Huntingdon to persuade Madan not to publish *Thelyphthora* by offering to obtain three thousand signatures, yet another example of women's involvement in politics and religion. Carter continued: "A young friend of mine, to whom Mr. Madan gave an account of his extraordinary system, told me that it is founded on the principle that every man shall be obliged to marry any woman whom he has seduced. But the book will soon speak for itself." It is difficult to interpret "extraordinary" here, but it implies that there was something curiously compelling, if also horrifying, about Madan's proposals. In the same letter, as it happens, Carter also recounted with distaste a public debate, attended by five hundred, on the topic of predestination. In the course of the debate, a "gentlewoman" who hissed at one of the speakers was admonished by the moderator "and told it was only for serpents to hiss," another notable, if again hardly untroubled, example of women's public role in such discussions. Despite her own intellectual ambitions, Carter was herself unimpressed with such unladylike public behavior.[61]

For a woman to speak up in such a setting—let alone to hiss—was still provocative in 1780, on both sides of the Atlantic. Women's public role may have received a further nudge on the American side given the front lines on which women found themselves, but it was also highly significant on the British side. Debates over polygamy allowed women to find and sound their voices in unprecedented, powerful ways. Polygamy was a good way to talk about the American Revolution and other things too: authority, subjugation, unions, happiness, and how women and men should behave with each other. Polygamy debates reveal both continuities and changes. Continuities underlay the continued importance of religion, anti-Catholicism, and concerns about dissent (religious and otherwise). Yet new anxieties swirled around gender, sexuality, marriage, fertility, and national strength. These long-standing changes came to a head in debates on polygamy. The war itself—from its solidarity among veterans to its chaos and loss of life—as well as the novel force of female participation, accelerated other changes.

Yet the American Revolution might be seen less as the major instigator of transformation (which is often how American historians have cast it) than as a manifestation of a wider set of changes, more ongoing and submerged. For what was the Revolution if not about the sense that new kinds of people—in rural Connecticut, in urban Scotland, and in a lot of other places, too—could weigh in to what had been the world of kings and ministers in the metropolis? If silversmiths and upstart lawyers criticized the policies and structures of the government, it was because they now felt they had the "rights and privileges" to express themselves publicly. So did men like John Miner and women like Esther Reed. However, it was not the American Revolution itself that loosened these tattling tongues; such public participation had already crept into view on both sides of the Atlantic well before that.

In 1776, one declaration announced to the world that Americans were now independent of Britain. In 1778, another declaration announced one woman's views on the necessity of love in marriage. The Declaration of Independence spoke to "a decent respect to the opinions of mankind." The anonymous lady's declaration spoke to a crowd of 406[!] Edinburgh ladies and gentlemen. Is there a connection between such declarations? There are certainly parallels. Both required that those who crafted them pluck up their courage, to face the hostile reactions they assumed would be provoked. Both spoke to unions and their discontents, the ways in which relations might flourish or sour in particular circumstances. Both confirmed their right to speak on such matters. Most important, both assumed that a new and better world was swinging into view, and that novel kinds of relations based on "the pursuit of happiness" underlay it. While there is no easy line of causality in such complex matters, the first declaration did not cause the second one. If anything, one might argue, this new willingness to air views in public was a fundamental precondition to the American Revolution, as was an increasing sense that individuals in unions had a right to be happy in them. This process began before the crisis that would lead to the American Revolution; it continued during that event, on both sides of the Atlantic.[62] Revolutionary notions—argued, debated, printed—had the capacity to recast structures of households, nations, and empires. Polygamy seemed to some no more radical than some other ideas which seemed equally bizarre and dangerous at the time: that Americans should have independence; that Catholics should have equal rights with Protestants; that women might vote or serve in Parliament; that Anglo-Americans should not involve themselves in the Atlantic slave trade. With hindsight, it is easy to see how naturalized certain of them have become. Yet all put into play fundamental subversions of old orders and seemed to some, at least, useful ways to solve enduring problems and inequalities.

If denizens in rural New England were debating polygamy fiercely in the 1780s, it becomes a touch less surprising that another freethinking Protestant dissenter from upstate New York also considered it some fifty years later. We don't know whether young Joseph Smith ever heard or read about the views of Miner and Madan, though he might have. *Thelyphthora* continued to circulate in the new American states. One newspaper advertised a copy for rent in 1784, "as there are very few copies of this excellent work in the country," yet many wished to read it. Early Mormons were recruited most heavily among former Methodists. In any case, long after the dust had settled on the late unhappy difficulties of the revolutionary era, some Americans (and others) would pursue happiness not in celestial beds, but in celestial marriages.[63]

7. "The Repugnance Inherent in Having Multiple Wives"

In 1780, half a world away, the problem of polygamy smacked other men in the face, too. Sitting in the San Carlos mission at Monterey in Alta, or Upper, California, Father Junípero Serra warned of "the direst consequences" following "scandals which go unstopped and unpunished." Polygamy, sexual disorder, and insubordination here, as elsewhere, seemed to well up together. He was requesting military assistance from the Spanish governor of the Californias, Felipe de Neve, to quell a rebellion brewing on his doorstep. Baltasar, the Indian head, or *alcalde,* at the mission, had turned traitor. The alcalde was supposed to be the most obedient convert in the mission, but Baltasar refused to comply. Fed up with Spanish control of every aspect of his life, including his domestic arrangements, Baltasar had begun "to do just as he pleased," including practicing sororal polygamy. He also ordered the flogging of another Indian, a privilege normally reserved for the friars themselves. Serra had been itching to "correct" him. However, since Neve had ordered that such alcaldes also be given "exemption from correction by the Fathers," Baltasar went unpunished. He had then fled the mission with a "group of malcontents . . . inciting the people here." These miscreants included men practicing polygamy, and women too. The rebels who joined Baltasar "have, each, a gentile woman [*su muger gentil,* a woman unconverted to Christianity] with them, and have left their Christian spouses [*sus esposas christianas*] here at the mission." Serra lamented that Spanish marriage policy was "one of the most serious obstacles to winning over the gentiles—whether they be men or women [*de uno, y otro sexo*]—to the Christian faith."[1]

Plural marriages continued to vex authorities in large swaths of North America in the period during and after the American Revolution. Polygamy was supposed to wither away; it did not. Strong men like Baltasar still used it to demonstrate and augment their privilege—and to subvert authorities. Women, too, entered into it, apparently of their own choosing. The governor of Alta California had assured Serra that "the natives of these parts will, in the course of time, develop into useful vassals for our religion and our State." Empires, states, and religions depended on cultivating "useful" and subordinate indigenous people, even in novel situations of republicanism and reform. The infrastructure of monogamy was as embedded in new republican nations like the United States as in older monarchical ones like the Spanish Empire. Yet many, many people continued to deny the power of empires, states, and religions to make or recognize their marriages. Such episodes of subversion, and the bids for power they included, peppered the landscape, sometimes prompting desertion and hand-wringing, as for Baltasar and Serra here, and sometimes provoking more violent reactions.

There was both continuity and change in confrontations over polygamy. There was continuity because polygamy was still cast as an obstacle to civilization, a practice to be eradicated. Polygamy should disappear in the face of progress, Christianity, and "enlightenment." Colonizing powers in the contact zones of North America still viewed domestic regulation as central to a larger policy of "reducing" troublesome people. Attending to polygamy here shows us that, even amid what appears to be perennial denunciations, though, much was changing. Polygamy was now recast less as an anti-Christian practice than as a backward one, in ways more aligned to the intellectual developments we have seen in the two previous chapters. Some Indians themselves started to announce publicly how willing they were to leave polygamy behind, but even these claims did not erase the ominous, deepening sense that some people were naturally inclined to practice it. This idea of "inherent" inclination meant that it became more indelible, somehow in the blood, rather than a practice of irreligion to be converted away. Here was a critical moment of making race. This is true even in three quite different settings that form the focus here: Alta California, the Great Basin of Utah, and the Cherokee Nation. In many respects, these settings could not be more different, yet all of them show that polygamy itself took on new meanings in just this key era.[2]

For many embattled indigenous men, the defense of household sovereignty was also a means to defend broader autonomy in the face of American and other encroachments. While scholars working on these distinct areas have seen coercion and alterations in household dynamics, rarely have they explored fully the connections between the two, or how there was a parallel shift across various settings. The ubiquity of these conflicts over sovereignty emerges from such disparate locations, as do complicated connections forged by linkages of polygamy and slavery. Polygamy had long been practiced in all three areas. Its continuance in this early national period was, again, not simply Native people clinging to tradition in the face of change. Colonial and missionary presence, as well as rising American national power in the wake of the American Revolution and its attendant unleashing of the violent energies of settlers, changed older systems of polygamy into newer, meaner systems, ones to be aggressively defended from outside interference.[3]

"Answering the crises created by American imperialism, Indians responded by reimagining their nations," observes one scholar of the early republic.[4] Some Indians also responded by reimagining their households. Imperial contacts perverted household relations and made men defend household prerogatives fiercely, centering mastery in novel and sometimes disturbing ways. This shift was not necessarily salutary for household subordinates, including wives and enslaved people, who navigated such systems. The continuance of polygamy in new contexts took on starker, sharper meaning in this era. Older systems of polygamy, which had often involved more egalitarian gender and social relations, toughened into more hierarchical, patriarchal forms, connected in unexpected ways with coercion and slavery. In the face of encroachments of all kinds, indigenous men insisted on their right to do as they wished, including practicing new kinds of polygamy, in their domestic lives: a personal claim to household sovereignty with larger political resonances. Whether in showy red garments, staged fistfights over wives, or the ejection of missionaries from the house, polygamous husbands, across a remarkable range of settings, continued to raise hell.

"One of the Most Serious Obstacles to Winning Over the Gentiles"

Why would California Indian women and men choose polygamy and rebellion over the safer choice of Spanish Christian life? Clearly, not all of them did, as some wives—and husbands—stayed in the mission. Yet a number of "gentile women" and men took to the hills, refusing to be "won over" to the program of the Franciscans. They had their own trajectories. Indigenous Californians tended to live in small communities, under the leadership of what the Spanish called "captains." Trade, diplomacy, and kinship unified them. However, California Indians were diverse; indeed, they spoke more than eighty languages. Even European observers passing by, such as the soldier Pedro Fages, acknowledged differences in government, religion, customs, housing, and clothing. "Marriage was an extremely important institution" in knitting together these communities. Some were monogamous and others, including several in southern California, had captains who were "not only privileged to have two wives (the other Indians having only one) but he may put them away at his own caprice, and take from the same village any other two he may desire, provided they are maidens."[5]

Polygamy was a privilege of rank across many of these communities. Even as late as the 1850s, there were accounts of a "chief," Canoa, in Los Angeles who only reluctantly gave up two of his three wives. Canoa apparently found it "highly ridiculous" to have the priest join him in "the holy bonds of matrimony" when he had already been married to this woman for years. The use of polygyny by some leaders suggests that it was here, as elsewhere, a status symbol and that rank differentials through household practices were common. There were conflict and rivalries, as well as peace and trade, between distinct Indian communities. Some competition involved women: "There frequently are [wars] among the various villages as the result of disputes concerning the fruits of the earth and women." Sometimes these wars resulted in "bringing away some of the women, either married or single." So polygamous California was hardly an entirely harmonious world before Spanish settlement, and some of the conflicts centered on marriage and women. There was continuity here into the colonial period, even as Spanish presence changed a great deal.[6]

In the 1770s, in Alta California, the Spanish established missions, supported by secular *presidios* staffed by soldiers. The leader of the missions was Father Junípero Serra, a Franciscan of dreams and schemes. In his mind's eye, he saw the natives of both halves of California, Baja and Alta, worshiping Jesus in neat and tidy rows in mission churches. He imagined a people transformed from gentiles and seasonal sojourners into settled farmers and homemakers, united in the sacrament of Christian monogamous marriage, with their babies presented for baptism. Far from his home island of Mallorca, he had chosen the challenges of missionary life to bring his

A Californian Woman habited in the Skin of a Deer

[Unknown], *A Californian Woman habited in the Skin of a Deer*, ca. 1780s. There is no indication of this woman's background, but the drawing makes clear that she faced the Spanish presence in California. Courtesy of John Carter Brown Library, Brown University.

vision to fruition. However, so many people rattled and halted the progress of his gospel at every turn in California. Indians as well as Spaniards frustrated his designs, pursuing instead their own idea of the good life.

Serra's Alta California missions were, comparatively, late Spanish American missions, founded after the Jesuits had been expelled from places like Baja California in 1767. Franciscans remained zealous, though. The first of the missions of Alta California was San Diego, founded in 1769. A chain of other missions soon followed in the 1770s and early 1780s, under Serra's energetic command. It was the culmination of his life's work. He himself was based at the mission of San Carlos, in Monterey, founded, along with a presidio there, in 1770. By 1784, these nine missions stretched over five hundred miles, from San Diego in the south to San Francisco in the north. They had the backing of imperial officials in Mexico City and elsewhere as the Spanish sought to end the threat of Russians moving south into California. However, these officials, intent on implementing the reforms of the Bourbon monarchy, were sometimes at odds with what missionaries themselves desired. Such secular officials included the feisty and energetic Felipe de Neve, the governor to whom Serra was writing in frustration in 1780. With chilly politesse, Serra and Neve fought in the letters they exchanged. The missions also had to include soldiers, sometimes stationed at nearby presidios, but sometimes in the missions themselves. To the friars, these troops, under secular rather than Franciscan command, were a necessary evil. The soldiers were the guns and machismo protecting the missions and their resources; they were not well behaved.[7]

For Baltasar and other California Indians, the Spanish presence was catastrophic. They faced disease, including sexually transmitted ones, and depopulation in new and debilitating ways. They also confronted a range of other challenges: sanctimonious and discipline-minded Franciscans; unruly and swaggering soldiers; an imperial authority keen to "reduce" them into order, slavery, and quietude. Imposing European-style households on these Indians was part of that plan for reduction. At one mission, San Luis Obispo, the priest tried to enforce a scheme by which "all the adult women" would marry men of his choosing, whether they wanted to or not. For one man, who did not want his lover married off to another man, this unwarranted interference prompted "so much distress that I cannot sleep at night." Of course, there was no univocal Spanish side any more than there was a single Indian view. There were fights for authority between those vigorously on the side of Catholicism and those less committed to it, both Native and Spanish. There were some who accepted imperial and church authorities, and there were others who did not.[8]

So what happened to drive Baltasar and his followers far beyond the reach of the missionaries at San Carlos? Serra's stories about Baltasar's polygamy and rebellion reveal much about masculine conflicts over authority. Serra was upset by the polygamy and subversion of Baltasar and others, but he was also concerned about Baltasar's popular mandate and the restructuring programs of the empire. In other words, his fight was as much with the new governor, Neve, as it was with Baltasar. In a program of Bourbon reform, Neve had decreed that alcaldes should be elected, not chosen by Franciscans. Neve had also included the provision that such alcaldes should be exempt from punishments. These were reforms put in place to placate the natives, but Serra and his fellow California missionaries did not welcome them. They were used to handpicking their most trusted Native converts as alcaldes, treating the Indians as the wayward "children" that Serra believed them to be. He wanted to ensure that Indians "not be given a less exalted opinion of the Fathers than they have had until now." He was particularly aggrieved that Neve appeared to support Baltasar over Serra: "The alcalde from here went to complain to His Lordship against the Fathers; he was well received; and the Fathers were referred to as being wrong." Serra emphasized that these newfangled policies, and the election by other Indians, had let power go to Baltasar's head. Neve had only encouraged these rebellions by failing to show solidarity with Serra.[9]

That Baltasar had been elected in the first place suggests that he was recognized as a leader by at least a substantial portion of his mission community. Did he have this rank by birth or connection, or had he in part earned it through his behavior, including, perhaps, his domestic life? Elsewhere, Serra complained that these new elected alcaldes were "so puffed up" with their own authority "that they really thought they were gentlemen." Serra complained that one alcalde, probably Baltasar, even donned special red clothing, presenting himself to the governor with panache. These privileges of rank were important to men like Baltasar. Probably coming from an indigenous community in which leaders had more than one wife, he would have assumed plural marriage as a basic privilege of leadership as well as a way to bolster it. When Serra first reported the rebellion of Baltasar, he noted that the alcalde had a large following "among whom are those we most need, such as the blacksmith, a number of carpenters and day workmen." This statement implies that the rebellion was supported by an elite indigenous leadership, well-trained men who thumbed their noses at the authority of the friars and who expected to rule their own communities. For Serra, Baltasar's rebellion demonstrated that democratic and humane reform was not only unnecessary but dangerous. Polygamy disputes played not just Spaniard against Indian but Spaniard against Spaniard, with "elections and the establishment of a New Commonwealth." For Serra, such reforms, based on elections by the people instead of imposition by the friars, only allowed disorder to flourish.[10]

Serra emphasized that indigenous rebels were also sexual deviants. From his perspective, how could such men govern communities when they could not control themselves? In Serra's view, the election of alcaldes by Indians themselves, as well as the lack of corporal punishment for leaders, would only lead to chaos. Therefore Serra emphasized that Baltasar was a polygamist, as were his followers. Naturally, in Serra's view, Baltasar became a "deserter, concubine-keeper [or "whore-master," as one eighteenth-century translator put it], inciting the people here." Yet it was not only the mission in San Carlos suffering these problems. The alcalde at San Gabriel, Nicolás, "was supplying women to as many soldiers as asked for them." At San Luis, "the alcalde kidnapped another man's wife and took off with her." At San Diego, "they have had to put up with a great deal from their alcaldes," though Serra refrained from going into detail. For Serra, democratic reform and elections only unleashed beasts.[11]

Sexual misconduct was in fact at the heart of these insurrections, but not in the way Serra imagined. In fact, there were very good reasons for men like Baltasar to assert themselves through polygamy—and for women to join them. Indigenous people emphasized their domestic autonomy in the face of two grave threats: slavery and sexual violence. Friars like Serra always seemed so surprised when Indians resisted, but non-Spanish sources start to suggest what mission life was like for Indians: backbreaking at best, atrocious at worst. Russian observers winced at the behavior of friars toward indigenous Californians. One 1806 Russian report condemned "the missionaries of California" who "have completely enslaved their neophytes." This observer sympathized with the plight of the Indians, whose "hearts are consumed with melancholy," so that many of them fled the missions "but they are returned." Another offered the cynical view that the real purpose of the missions was only "to have free workers." Indeed, "the savage Californians never come voluntarily; mounted Spanish soldiers catch them with lassos and bring them to the missionaries." Another lamented that both women and men were "compelled to work hard," in European labor configurations, with men cultivating fields and women spinning wool for trade. One cosmopolitan Russian compared the slavery of the Natives to better-known forms: "The lot of these Indians, so called Christian Indians, merits all kinds of pity. Even the situation of Negro slaves cannot be worse. The Indians are subject totally to the unlimited arbitrariness and tyranny of the friars." He continued that the Indians could never be free: "Those who dare to quit this 'paradise' in order to try to return to their former life among their free fellow tribesmen are caught and put into irons for punishment."[12]

There was much to denounce in missionary life. Admittedly, the Russians were not especially positive about the Spanish, their colonial rivals. However, an even more sickening catalogue of abuses fills the letters of the Franciscans themselves. One newly arrived Franciscan was horrified by "the terrible suffering they [the Natives] experienced from punishments and work." Serra himself lamented: "It breaks one's heart to hear the stories of how docile and responsive the gentiles are. . . . But what are we to do, when our own sins stand in the way of our accomplishing miracles?" As ever, the likelihood is that reported incidents of abuse are only a small percentage of those that actually took place. Along with slavery and physical coercion, there was a widespread campaign of sexual violence waged by soldiers against indigenous people. The mission of San Luis Obispo, founded in 1772, looked shaky from the start, since many of the soldiers there included "the most notorious molesters of gentile women." One such "rascally soldier was caught in sin with an Indian woman," which "upset the poor Father considerably." In 1772, at Mission San Gabriel, "the secular arm down there was guilty of the most heinous crimes, killing the men to take their wives." In 1773, the soldiers, trained to herd cows and mules, "would catch an Indian woman with their lassos to become prey for their unbridled lust. At times some Indian men would try to defend their wives, only to be shot down with bullets." One little boy there had to watch as soldiers entered the mission where he was living, holding aloft the head of his father, the "principal chief." The soldier who carried it had left the mission, probably "to get himself a woman." When the leader tried to stop him, the soldier and his companions shot and beheaded him. Other children and adults also suffered in this mission. One friar, an "old father," lamented "such disorder" when he saw a soldier "actually committing deeds of shame with an Indian [man] who had come to the mission." Whether this situation was forced or not is hard to know, but coercion attended other assaults: "Even the children who came to the mission were not safe from their baseness." This same father was so "sick at heart" at these molestations that "he took to his bed, and . . . retired to San Diego."[13]

San Diego, though, was no better, beset with "a thousand evils, particularly those of a sexual nature," as the head of that mission, Father Luís Jayme, put it in 1772. From the perspective of many Indians, what the Spanish described as "our religion and our State," their "civilization," was horrifying:

"There is not a single mission where all the gentiles have not been scandal-ized." Jayme limited himself to detailing cases from San Diego, but there was still plenty to report. There was the partially blind woman, who tried to run but could not do so fast enough. She was raped by two soldiers. The case became public when she became pregnant. According to Jayme, she was so "ashamed" that she killed her baby. He recounted another case in which two soldiers seized a woman and raped her in the corral. They then released her and found another woman, whom they also took into the corral. The first soldier "sinned with her there. He came out, and the soldier Bravo entered and sinned with her. He came out and the soldier Juan María Ruiz entered and did the same. He came out and the soldier Castelo entered and did the same." Jayme did not report another case in which three soldiers chased two women who had gone out to dig for plants in a canyon. They caught one, whom two of the soldiers raped. The third soldier grabbed the other one, assaulting her so violently that she subsequently died. Her death meant the case went to secular authorities despite Jayme's silence. Although two of the soldiers were eventually imprisoned (the third went to Baja and disappeared), they were in a few years released and sent to the settlement at Monterey, free again. The Franciscans condemned the behavior of these soldiers and lamented it, but they did not do much else. In 1773, Serra advised the authorities that the officers should "remove the soldier or soldiers who give a bad example, espe-cially in the matter of [sexual] incontinence," replacing them with others "not known as immoral or scandalous." The officers did not do so. Some years later, Serra was still fretting about "their unconcern in the matter of shameful conduct between the soldiers and Indian women."[14]

These appalling violations naturally prompted insurrections by the Natives who endured them. The first major one was at San Diego in 1775. Only months after Jayme's dreadful account of abuses, eight hundred Indians crept into the mission in the middle of the night. They set fire to several houses and targeted the friars. Even faced with angry, armed rebels, Father Luís Jayme greeted them in his customary way: "Love God, my sons!" Whether the rebels loved God, they seem to have hated Jayme. They "stripped him of everything, even the coverings of modesty, and began to fire innumerable arrows into his naked body and to rain blows upon it." Authorities reckoned that one of the leaders was a baptized Indian, Diego, whom they imprisoned. Although he was later released, there was lingering suspicion about him. Supposedly, when he saw the friar, he had shouted: "So long . . . there'll be no more whippings." This phrase implies slavery and the corporal punishment that would go along with it, even for a baptized Christian like Diego. Diego was not only the first adult to be baptized at San Diego. Although no one seems to have noticed, he had also been the translator for the Native women who had brought rape charges against the soldiers. He knew what had happened to his countrywomen in excruciating detail. He also knew that most of the soldiers had gone unpunished, and that the friars had done little.[15]

This context of slavery and sexual violence helps to explain why men like Diego and other "malcontents," both women and men, refused the imposition of Spanish mores, as did rebels in other, smaller uprisings. They refused to be what one scholar has termed "spoils of conquest." One of those incidents, at the mission of San Luis Obispo in 1776, was sparked, one Spanish observer thought, by the rape of the wife of a chief. In 1785, some local Indians attacked the mission at San Gabriel, but the soldiers had been tipped off. So this insurrection, and the attempt to "kill the priests and the soldiers," did not succeed. Its leaders, a gentile woman, Toypurina, and the baptized alcalde, Nicolás José, were then questioned by authorities. Nicolás had probably already been punished by the friars for sexual and religious misconduct, and may have been retaliating. Toypurina testified that she had led this rebellion because "she was angry with the priests and all the others at the mission, because we were living on their land." In denouncing "all the others at the mission," she implied the treachery of other Indians, against whom she was also waging this battle. She therefore "encouraged them [her people] to be brave and fight." The women and men who joined leaders like Toypurina and Baltasar also rejected mission life. Women may well have preferred polygamous relations outside the missions, with other indigenous men, to being left vulnerable to the Spanish. If the Spanish instigated a campaign of reduction on the very bodies of indigenous people, such individuals refused to accept it: some by burning missions, others by fleeing to communities beyond the missions which included plural marriages "as in their heathenism."[16]

Polygamy may also have been a way for Baltasar and others to increase their own authority in relation to other Indians. There were complicated dynamics among indigenous people as well as with Spaniards, though the former are much harder to access. There were rivalries over women as well as over policies. One friar claimed that San Luis Obispo mission was destroyed by fire "set without any other reason than to take vengeance upon other heathen who were their enemies and our friends." Men like Baltasar were departing the mission and rallying other men and women under their own leadership. Indeed, it is possible that some of these dynamics—disputes between Indians—may have underpinned similar violence at San Diego. That domestic power merged with other forms of political dominance, in communities dealing with the shocks and horrors of colonialism, seems clear in California, as in so many other places we have seen. For men like Baltasar, polygamy, like scarlet clothing, sent a clear signal: he was a man of status who asserted his power against other men, Native and Spanish.[17]

"The Depravity of the Heathen in Their Natural State"

Such masculine dynamics, and the shoring up of power in stark ways among indigenous men, characterized other parts of the West, including the area around the Great Salt Lake in what would become Utah. Polygamy had probably long existed in this area, but it changed under the pressure of colonizing powers. One of the first Spanish accounts, by two Franciscans in 1776, recorded polygamy's incidence. The friars had gone out from the missions in New Mexico, snaking north through what would become Colorado, Utah, and Arizona to explore possible new places for missions. One of the "Sabuaganas" whom the friars encountered told them that the high-ranking young man whom they met had two wives. The Franciscans reported, with some wishful thinking, that the man was embarrassed by this fact. They rejoiced that "these barbarians are aware or cognizant of the repugnance inherent in having multiple wives at one and the same time." Friars wanted to believe the best of these Natives and this youthful leader in particular. In other words, there was hope for them yet. However, this language of barbarism and repugnance, from Franciscans, shows how novel vocabularies of polygamy affected even these dusty and difficult encounters, far from Europe. Friars condemned polygamy, as they always had. However, they did so in novel ways, presuming that it was barbarism, a source of "repugnance," not simply heathenism, as in seventeenth-century encounters. Such an incident prompted the friars "to exhort them not to have more than one" wife. Perhaps unsurprisingly, they did not report on the wives or their sense of the matter.[18]

That a high-ranking leader with multiple wives was young may in fact reflect new orders. New sorts of men were increasingly becoming dominant in these areas: younger, more aggressive men who had mastered skills with horses and guns. It seems doubtful they were the easily embarrassed sort.

Even before the arrival of Euro-American settlement in this area, Ute cultures and politics shifted in the wake of the arrival of the Spanish, largely due to animals, not people. Like nearby Comanches, Ute life came to center around the horse, for both riding and raiding. This situation meant Utes could range wider, and it also meant that leadership became more central-ized, under strong men. Such men won their position in part on their excep-tional abilities in hunting, raiding, and war; leadership was less about kin connections and more about personal achievements. The whole area of La Comanchería to the east of the Utes was beset by raids and counterraids.[19]

In the face of new pressures, then, Indians reimagined their house-holds here, as in other areas; for women and children, this reorientation was not salutary. Households became places of greater hierarchy and coercion. Political consolidation among Indians such as the Utes—in response to novel people, animals, and practices—carried with it a tougher regime of marriage for at least some women. Although polygamy had been a practice of the Utes, its nature, with the rise of horse culture, shifted—and worsened. Scholars of this area have noted the increase in the work of hide processing as well as polygamy, with wives less companions than laborers. Most captives were women and children, often from enemy groups, and the likelihood is that many women, including those from the Paiute groups that often were targets of Ute violence, entered into households as secondary wives. House-hold labor took on more commercial import, and households here, as in other areas, became a way to consolidate and show both economic and polit-ical power.[20]

These martial cultures, in which domestic choices were clear markers of fiercely protected masculine authority, come through even in rituals governing marriage and divorce. Blood spilled even onto courtship and wedding rituals. In one account from a visitor, Jacob Hamblin, there was what seems to have been a staged brawl over a wife. One man, determined to marry the wife of another man, had stolen her. Her husband came to retrieve her. The interloper did not let her go without a fight—literally: the two men "stripped them-selves, except about the loins, and tied their hair back. The husbands commenced the fight, bruising each other's faces, and causing the blood to flow, like the more civilized (?) duellists and prize fighters." As each man fell down, other men, friends, replaced them, as the women, including the wife at the center of the dispute, looked on. She was eventually brought into the proceedings and was dragged through the water as women and children joined in a general melee. Although she then fainted, the fighting continued for the rest of the day and into the next. The following morning brought another staged contest over another woman, who was also dragged until the observer "could see no signs of life in her." The day after, the wrangling continued over the first one. The interloper won, but she refused to go with him. Although crowds again dragged her, she still "would not live with the man who had won her." She ended all of this violence still married to her original husband, but with both aching and bruised for the effort.[21]

Such treatment of women appalled Hamblin. He marched over to the chief and threatened to leave if they did not "stop such conduct." The chief "replied 'that was the way they get their women.' " Hamblin advised him that "there was a better way, that if an Indian wanted a wife . . . that he should marry them, and they should love their women."[22] The chief took counsel, and returned the next day to ask that Hamblin not report the incident "for they were ashamed of it." The chief promised that if Hamblin would "throw away all you have seen," then "we shall stop such fights." Since Hamblin obviously did report the incident, it is unlikely that such contests ceased. In fact, though Hamblin patronizingly advised love, there is no indication that there was not love here. The woman at the center of the ceremony, probably not a captive, may have loved her first husband and, despite the pugilistic talents of the would-be interloper, she declined to join the latter. She was not forced to do so. For all the bruises, there was still female agency here. Nevertheless, the entire ritual suggests the glorification of masculine vigor and violence, and the linkage of these attributes with access to women.

This culture of domestic aggression radiated outward, in ever more horrific ways. Success in this area depended not only on the raiding and trading of horses but also on the raiding and trading of people, most notably women and children. Such captives usually came from other conquered groups, such as the Paiutes, and these women suffered sexual violence, as captives and as wives. One visitor to the area reported that in the 1850s, Native children were sold, "boys fetching on average $100, girls from $150 to $200." He attributed this difference to the fact that "the girls were in demand to bring up for house servants." There are other, darker explanations for the value placed on young women in this trade. The whole system of slave trading unbalanced life. Slave raiders, whether Ute or Spanish, brought terror to the inhabitants, especially among less dominant Native groups. When one old man was interviewed about the situation decades later, he recalled that "they were scared to death. When a Spanish party was in the country, the women tried to take their children and run away and hide." Apparently, while the women feared immediate violence from the Spanish, they were also anxious about being sold, or having their children sold, by their own husbands: "They were as much afraid of their husbands as of the Spaniards." Ute and Spanish raiders bought children, and they also kidnapped them. Some mothers resisted: "Some of them followed the caravans for days seeking an opportunity to steal their children back. When one succeeded she was hunted ruthlessly and if caught was taken into slavery with her child." Despite the personal risk, "this danger did not deter them from making the attempt."[23] They were not usually successful, however.

These loving, haunted mothers and their children paid the price for the violence unleashed by a volatile political situation and the entrenchment of a more brutal system of slavery. It was a world of kaleidoscopic, jostling authorities: Indians from different groups including Comanches and Apaches as well as Utes; Mexican officials struggling to maintain control over their northern borders; Americans, including Mormons, trapping, trading, and settling. One of the most famous Ute leaders, Wakara (or Walker or Walkara) took advantage of these uncertainties to become a thorn in the side of both Mexican and American officials. Wakara was a raider, a trader in humans and horses, and a notorious polygamist. His domestic arrangements supported his broader authority. In 1840, Wakara engineered "the biggest robbery of livestock that California ever experienced." At the mission of San Luis Obispo, Wakara and his men rode off with more than twelve hundred animals. On a smaller scale, such activities continued throughout the 1840s. Sometimes accompanied by wives "in the guise of a peaceful trader," Wakara and his men launched raid after raid, all the way to southern California. By September 1849, the American prefect of Los Angeles begged the governor for more guns because "the District is particular exposed to the depredations of Indian horse thieves and other evil disposed persons." Mormons settling in the Great Salt Lake area recounted that Wakara and other Utes showed up with "men, women, and children" and "several hundred head of horses for sale," raided from the western end of the old Spanish trail in California. When Mormons chided Wakara for thievery against Spanish-speaking authorities, he dismissed them: "My men hate the Spaniards, they will steal from them and I cannot help it." By 1853, though, Wakara started raiding in Utah as well, leading to repeated battles with the Mormons and what has been called "Walker's War."[24]

"This slave trade gave rise of the cruel wars between the native tribes of this country, from Salt Lake down to the tribes in southern Utah. Wakara and his band raided on the weak tribes, taking their children prisoners and selling them." So observed one American in Utah, who failed to see that their settlement there had opened a Pandora's box of the most vicious forces. Mormons were appalled by this trade in children, but their presence, along with other Americans and Mexicans, had exacerbated the horror of this system of slavery. Wakara's brother Sanpitch arrived at the Mormon Indian Mission among the Paiutes in 1855: "Their business was to trade for children." Sanpitch proceeded to buy "three girls, giving one horse and two guns for them, and many beads." One girl's starving parents "cried much on seeing their daughter go." The sympathetic Latter-day Saint who recorded these sales continued: "From the oldest girl, aged about 12, as she was carried off, I beheld the tears falling fast and silently, and my heart pained to think that she might become a slave to the Mexicans."[25]

Slavery and polygamy both underpinned this western world; visitors could find them unsettling. One such sojourner was Solomon Carvalho, an artist and writer from South Carolina, who found this world to be both like his United States of America and yet not like it. Slavery hardly shocked a South Carolinian, but polygamy and Native authority did. Authoritative men intent on showing and securing their powers did so through baffling, awe-inspiring domestic displays. At one Mormon wedding, Carvalho found it "a most unusual sight to see a man dancing at a cotillion with *three wives,*" as "they all enjoyed themselves with the greatest good humour." Carvalho was also amazed by Wakara, whom he met and painted, as he accompanied Brigham Young and others intent on ending Walker's War. In Carvalho's account, Young asked Wakara to come to him, but Wakara refused, demanding instead that Young come to him. The Americans, firmly put in their place, entered Wakara's camp and its "guard of honor" to ask for peace. In another diplomatic play, Wakara let "intense silence" prevail before other chiefs stood up to state their grievances, which circled around the violation of sovereignties in households and polities, the killing of women as well as warriors. One complained that "Americats [Americans] have no truth—Americats kill Indian plenty—Americats see Indian woman, he shoot her like deer." Another recounted that his own son, who had gone hunting, and wife, who had gone to look for him, had been killed by an American. Throughout these statements, "Wakara remained perfectly silent." When pressed, he replied, "I got no heart

Solomon Nunes Carvalho (1815–ca. 1894), *Portrait of Wakara,
1854.* This portrait was probably painted during Carvalho's visit
to Wakara's settlement with Brigham Young and others.
Carvalho portrayed Wakara in paint, as in words, as a dignified
leader. Courtesy of Gilcrease Museum, Tulsa, Oklahoma.

to speak," making clear that that was the end of diplomacy for the day. As
Carvalho put it, Wakara was "a great chief. He stood upon the dignity of his
position [as] the representative of an aggrieved and much injured people."
When Wakara finally did deign to speak the next day, he lamented that when
he went away with his men to sell horses, "the Amerecats come and kill his
wife and children," centering the murder of his family as a violation of his
larger sovereignty. Household and national autonomy were thus explicitly
linked. In the end, Wakara agreed to peace, but on his own terms.[26]

Wakara's silences and speeches dismayed the "Amerecats." Ute life,
seemingly unsettled and unsettling, both undermined and paralleled Anglo-
American values. Ute mobility, violence, disregard for the law, and polygamy
disturbed many Americans, such as Carvalho. Yet equally alarming was how
impressive Utes were at the things many Americans valued: conquest,

orientation to markets, negotiations, complicated economies trading in horses and people. Visitors saw a world in motion, but they did not realize it, refusing to acknowledge how colonialism was reshaping American households. Instead they cast it as what one visitor to the West termed "the depravity of the heathen in their natural state."[27]

"Polygamy Is Abolished"

There was political capital from claims of "heathen depravity" in settled areas to the east just as in what seemed more unsettled ones in the West. These assertions went hand in hand with the forces of American imperialism; for many authorities, polygamous people were uncivilized and hence unworthy of political and economic control. Yet such claims failed to distinguish between quite diverse systems of plural marriage. Polygamy as practiced by nineteenth-century Utes was a tough system disadvantaging many women. By contrast, polygamy as practiced by Cherokees in the East had long been part of a system of marriage and gender in which women had considerable powers. Yet even for Cherokees, forced to reimagine households in the face of American imperial pressures, plural marriages and slavery changed and worsened in the early national period in the face of new economic and political pressures.

Although the Cherokees have been called matriarchal, there were strong men here, too, using polygamy in innovative ways. Plural marriages had long been part of Cherokee life. Older mourning rituals demonstrated how established plural marriage was: "The surviving wife unites with [the husband] in mourning for the deceased [wife], and both continue in that state two months. During this time they observe all the rules of mourning, and have no intercourse with each other, as husband and wife." Polygamy was accepted, though limited to elites, and often sororal (involving one man marrying sisters). In this case, as in most Cherokee marriages, the husband moved into the house of the wife/wives, in matrilocal patterns. Polygamy was part of a package of marital practices favorable to women. For Cherokees, divided into seven clans, the clan was a central source of identity, and it followed the mother's side in these matrilineal cultures. The children in a marriage belonged to the wife's clan, not the father's. Polygamy could strengthen clan and family lines, as sisters lived together and raised one another's children. The fact that wives continued to live in their own families and communities meant that they had resources if they chose to end a marriage; the children, belonging to their clan, stayed with their mothers in cases of separation. Whether sisters or not, and whether in plural or monogamous arrangements, married Cherokee women had rights to their own property and to their own children.[28]

Cherokee marriage practices violated American laws and customs, and there were considerable efforts to make them conform—at least in theory. Ending polygamy was one clear—and limited—way to do so. The Cherokee Nation began making changes to marriages between white men and Cherokee women. In 1819, the nation passed a law against polygamy for white men, though only advised against it for Cherokee men going forward: "It shall not be lawful for any white man to have more than one wife, and it is also recommended that all others should also have but one wife hereafter." An 1825 regulation clarified and reinforced this policy: "It shall be unlawful for a white man (citizen of the United States) living in the Nation, to have more than one wife; neither shall he make use of the woman's (his wife) property without her consent." This policy still emphasized the Cherokee right of a wife to her property, something not recognized in this era by U.S. laws. Still, by 1825, the focus had shifted to marriages between Cherokees, with the law moving beyond "making it unlawful for whitemen to have more than one wife" to legislating that "it shall not be lawful hereafter, for any person or persons whatsoever, to have more than one wife."[29] So technically polygamy even between Cherokees became illegal.

This legislation was part of a larger project by many leading Cherokees to align more closely with American laws and mores. Faced with unrelenting encroachment on their lands and working to retain autonomy in the face of an aggressive new set of states in the United States, many Cherokees made heroic efforts to demonstrate their civility. If Americans looked to condemn all Indians for their inherent "depravity," some Cherokees were increasingly determined to give them no basis for such claims. As one letter writer phrased it in 1835, "The spectacle of a civilized and christianized community of Cherokees will be exhibited before the world, that will bear a comparison with any other community." Cherokees keen to publicize these efforts made much of this legal change governing polygamy. Elias Boudinot (or Buck Watie) emphasized the progress Cherokees had made, and were continuing to make in his "Address to the Whites" in 1826. Boudinot acknowledged that many "even in this enlightened assembly . . . would throw back their imaginations to ancient times." Still, he pointed out, if Indians had a past existence as "heathen savages," "eighteen centuries ago what were the inhabitants of Great Britain?" He assured his listeners, "I am not as my fathers were—broader means and nobler influences have fallen upon me." Proof lay in legal changes undertaken by the Cherokee Nation: "Many of the laws display some degree of civilization, and establish the respectability of the nation. Polygamy is abolished." So for Boudinot, polygamy literally topped the list of laws undertaken to show the "respectability" of the Cherokee Nation, also demonstrating that "female chastity and honor are protected by law."[30]

Cherokee girls in the Brainerd missionary school, run under the American Board of Commissioners for Foreign Missions from New England, also stressed the ways in which Christian Cherokees with names like Lucy and Sally were entering the full stream of enlightened civilization. Many of them noted in letters, some of which were sent to New Englanders who supported the missions, that while old customs remained, improvements were occurring, led by women and girls themselves. While one student, Elizabeth Taylor, acknowledged that "the unenlightened parts of this nation assemble for dances around a fire," she also pointed out that "the white people were once as degraded as this people and that encourages me to think that this nation will soon become enlightned." Lucy McPherson worried that "the Cherokees in our Country are sometimes cruel to their families." Still, she took consolation from the fact that "some of them are more civilized. . . . They feel more anxious that their families should have an education." Sally M. Reece conceded that many Cherokees "have yet a great many bad customs but I hope . . . this nation will soon become civilized and enlightened." While these repeated claims to enlightenment suggest the palpable presence of missionaries peering over the shoulders of girls dutifully writing letters, they also imply that such language of civilization, not, for instance, of Christian suffering, had become the central vocabulary even for missionaries. The ubiquity of these contentions suggests, again, that enlightenment and barbarism came to replace, or at least stand beside, older vocabularies of Christian and heathen. Families were the arena in which to show progress. Emphasis on how refined Cherokees were, by these young women as well as by men like Boudinot, was in part a way of demonstrating their elite status to other Cherokees.[31]

Yet despite these assertions, many older "customs" including polygamy continued. Here, as elsewhere, missionaries struggled to end it. Its continuance exposes the divisions of opinions within Cherokee communities about it. Cherokee sororal polygamy could be a peculiarly vexing practice to end, especially when the wives were not necessarily displeased with the arrangement. As one perplexed missionary inquired, "Shall a converted heathen who has, & lives with two wives, be required to put away either?" He elaborated: "Probably it is not uncommon for a Cherokee when he takes two wives to take two sisters & contract with them both at the same time; and as this contract is considered the marriage . . . we should not know which to have him put away." This concern may have been prompted by the situation of Charles Reese, or Reece, who "had three sisters for his wives at the same time." Yet he wanted to become a Christian. In the end, a combination of death and divorce solved his problems—at least to some degree. One wife died. He left the other two sisters, with his house, property, and children, while he moved in with another woman: monogamy (of a sort) at last. To the missionaries, this situation was not ideal, but it did seem to signal the end of polygamy. Presumably, the sisters and their children remained in the house together, with their own property. These women probably saw a system allowing polygamy but also divorce as perfectly compatible with their own desires; they were not rushing to adopt lifelong indissoluble monogamy. To this missionary, though, what seemed Reese's terminal lack of respect for indissoluble monogamy and Anglo-American laws "illustrates a striking trait in the Indian character." Here is one of the many leaps of this era from one particular person's marital situation to inherent "Indian character," even from a reasonably sympathetic observer.[32]

In fact, among Cherokees, there was only a single case ever brought under antipolygamy laws, and it was an 1829 case resting on the 1819 legislation against white men engaging in it. Even literate and well-heeled Cherokee plural wives did not go to court to end polygamy. The objection of the Cherokee wife who brought the suit, Elizabeth Hildebrand Pettit, was not polygamy per se but an unhappy marriage and a complicated property dispute against a white husband, James Pettit, who was apparently neither loving nor honest. Elizabeth had left James because of "the abuse and repeated ill treatment" she had apparently endured. She asked the court to award damages under the 1819 law, which they did, to the tune of five hundred dollars and his farm in the Cherokee Nation. They also revoked his Cherokee citizenship. James did not accept this verdict but instead asked for a stay and apparently "endeavoured to disperse of his goods & Chattels in such a way as to be beyond the reach of law." Elizabeth's uncle sent to Missouri for information on the first marriage to bolster the legal case. It turned out that his first marriage may not have been legally contracted, so the polygamy charge was unsustainable. In the meantime, Elizabeth had taken him back, and the case collapsed. Altogether, there was no successful suit brought by any Cherokee under the antipolygamy legislation. Cherokees, women and men, were hardly clamoring to end polygamy. However, considering wider changes to Cherokee dynamics demonstrates that continuation of polygamy was not simply holding onto tradition. There were changes afoot, related to gender and age and rank, and focusing on polygamy here, as elsewhere, makes this shift clear.[33]

"In respect to marriage, we have no law regulating it & polygamy is stilled allowed to Native Cherokees," conceded one leader, John Ridge in 1826, even after the tougher 1825 antipolygamy law. He admitted that fuller legal reform of marriage had failed because "nearly all the Members of our Legislature . . . had been married under the old existing ceremony [and] . . . were afraid it would reflect dishonor on them."[34] This is a telling statement, with a problem here for Cherokee leaders. The Cherokee Nation, led by the kind of elite men who had long practiced polygamy, now had to show reform of marriage practices that looked suspect to American eyes. This complicated relationship with "old existing ceremony" underpinned what happened with polygamy in the Cherokee Nation. The usual sense, even among some scholars of Cherokee history, is that polygamy started to look problematic to "enlightened" Cherokees like Ridge and Boudinot, even as others, more set in traditional ways, continued to practice it. One scholar has contended: "The monogamous standard of whites had become the law of the Cherokee nation. Those in the rising generation might now feel embarrassed if a parent or grandparent did not conform to the new standard."[35] Yet it was not so simple.

The willingness of the council to abolish polygamy on paper was, ironically, a mark of the loss of women's status. Polygamy was part of a constellation of gender and family organization that came under notable new pressures in the early nineteenth century. This whole range of practices had been considerably more favorable to women, involving as it did matrilineal powers, women's councils with political authority, access by wives to divorce, their children, and their own property. None of these advantages was available in Anglo-American traditions. Removed from its larger package of greater gender equalities and formal recognition of women's powers, polygamy in

JOHN RIDGE,
A CHEROKEE.

F. W. Greenough, *John Ridge, a Cherokee* (Philadelphia: I. T. Bowen, 1838). Ridge is shown here in a blue gentleman's suit, writing what appears to be a letter in English. Like many Cherokees, Ridge was keen to demonstrate his "civilized" status. Courtesy of Library of Congress.

Cherokee worlds of the early nineteenth century became a way for at least a few men to shore up their status in innovative, if sometimes disturbing, ways.

Cherokees faced relentless encroachment on their land, loss of hunting grounds, and towns increasingly surrounded by hostile settlers. They also endured the endless efforts of missionaries and agents to bring them into the "civilized" ways of patriarchal households. Men struggled to hunt successfully in increasingly constricted and depleted areas and turned to other sources of economic and social status. Cherokees also started to cultivate cotton in greater numbers, and missionaries encouraged Cherokee women to take up weaving and cloth production, leaving fieldwork to others. Often those who picked up this burden—or, rather, had it thrust upon them—were enslaved African-American men and women.[36] At the same time, Americans evinced contempt at seeing Cherokee women farming, and encouraged a reconfiguration of labor along Euro-American lines so that Cherokee men—and African-American women and men—were in the fields and Cherokee women were at the hearth. For many Anglo-Americans in the South, enlightenment and civilization excluded polygamy but included slavery.

There were a range of changes—to political structures, to settlement patterns, and to labor organization and economics—all of which combined to alter Cherokee patterns of gender and domestic life and the contexts for polygamy. First, there were significant political changes. Even into the late eighteenth century, the clans, on matrilineal lines, dominated community life.

They enacted justice and vengeance; they organized politics; they decided on war and peace. They also had social and familial roles, such as selection of marriage partners. There had also been councils of men and of women contributing to these political decisions. Even into the eighteenth century, "war women" such as Nancy Ward had formal powers. By the early nineteenth century, in the face of aggressive American encroachment, the Cherokees turned to a more centralized formal political structure controlled not by women and men in clan configurations but by men in "a constitutional republic, complete with a bicameral legislature, district and superior court system, executive branch, and bureaucracy." The power of the clans, and of women, diminished. The abolition of polygamy has been seen by one scholar as a further "blow to matrilineality," since sororal polygamy had strengthened relations between women of the same clan.[37] Polygamy was a complicated issue for the chiefs who led this consolidation, as they were the elite men most likely to practice it. Therefore, the Cherokee Nation was slow to outlaw it for such individuals, and there were no successful cases actually brought against it.

Even when Cherokee women in this era did enter formal politics, as with women's petitions presented to the National Council to prevent removal, they appealed again to "enlightenment" and "civilization." In one of these petitions, women argued that if they were removed across the Mississippi, they would be "brought to a savage state again, for we have . . . become too much enlightened to throw aside the privileges of a civilized life." Part of what such women meant was that removal would imperil missionary work and schools. Yet these were only part of a larger shift into different kinds of houses and settlements. "Civilized life" was a double-edged sword for Cherokee women. It meant the erosion of domestic and clan powers. For many, "civilized" meant monogamous, scattered, and isolated. Cherokees in this era moved increasingly from traditional wattle-and-daub homes to houses made of wood and bricks. They also moved out of the towns where they had so long been clustered and into the river valleys, in dispersed farms and plantations. There were gains and losses for women in these changes, as housekeeping took on new importance, and dispersal—and loss of clan connections—could bring a sense of atomization.[38]

Traditional structures of labor, in which men hunted and women farmed, also came under new pressures. This long process had been ongoing since at least the eighteenth century: "Formerly the women got their own wood for cooking. . . . They also carried all the water for family use. It was considered disgraceful for men or boys to be seen carrying water. The women pounded all the corn, and prepared food." However, in the new order, according to one leader, "there is not to my knowledge a solitary Cherokee to be found that depends upon the chase for subsistence—and every head of a family has his house & farm." This leader assured Anglo-Americans, "The hardest portion of manual labor is performed by the men & the women occasionally lend a hand in the field, more by choice, and necessity than anything else." On the whole, claimed one Cherokee leader, women "very contentedly perform the duties of the kitchen. . . . They sew—they weave—they spin, they cook our meals, and act well the duties assigned them by Nature as mothers." The story began to circulate of a Cherokee chief who scoffed at attempts by missionaries to replace hunting with farming. The chief supposedly told the Indian agent, "They may suit white-people, but will [not] do well for the Indians," as he departed for a lengthy hunt. While he was gone, his wife and daughter started to spin and weave. On his return, he was astonished to find that they had made "more cloth in value, than the Chiefs Hunt of six months amounted to." A smiling, concili-atory chief then conceded to the agent that "his wife & daughter [were there-fore] better hunters than he." With that admission, the chief then "requested to be furnished a plough & went to work on his farm."[39]

Many Cherokee men, such as this chief, were reluctant to take on farming because it had traditionally been women's work. This tale, which may well have been fictional, smoothed the troubled transitions in gender and sexuality that accompanied a larger Cherokee transformation. It domes-ticated the complex labor shifts, and lightened the heavy burdens of coercive patriarchy. It also helped to ameliorate the "disgraceful" humiliation endured by Cherokee men who were now expected to do what had been women's work. Finally, it ignored the complex, painful realities of a system of increas-ingly racially exclusive slavery, in which Cherokees, like the "whitemen" around them, were trading and directing the labor of enslaved African Americans. This was another major change, as older traditions gave way to a system of plantation slavery in the nineteenth century.[40]

Yet the truth in this tale of the chief and the economic prowess of his spinning women—that there was profit to be made in the labor of women, both free and enslaved, and that women's work in cloth production may have increased in importance—suggests why polygamy was not in fact disap-pearing. It became increasingly economically advantageous to have wives who could run households, produce cloth, and oversee the work of enslaved African Americans on plantations. Indeed, women in their petitions to the National Council emphasized that Cherokee men should "Cultivate and raise corn & cotton and your mothers and sisters will make clothing for you which our father the president [of the United States] has recommended to us all."[41] The weaving and spinning of Cherokee women, as well as their enslaved African-American counterparts, took on particular importance, in a new order of slavery and racial exclusion.

Here, as elsewhere, complex change provoked by colonialism transformed systems of plural marriage. Ambitious Cherokee men combined aspects of older Cherokee forms such as polygamy and new ones such as plantation slavery to consolidate their power and to further their goals. These themes unite in the story of one of the most successful, if controversial, Cherokee leaders of the early nineteenth century, James Vann. Moravian missionaries described him as a man "feared by many but loved by a few." Subsequent scholars have described him as "perhaps the wealthiest man in the Cherokee Nation" as well as "a critically important figure at this turning point in the Cherokee renascence." James Vann is not easily categorized as either a traditionalist or as a progressive. He was a great Cherokee nationalist for whom "whitemen" were dangerous and not to be trusted. Yet his own father was one of them, though his mother was Cherokee. He had nothing but contempt for those who argued that Cherokee security lay in taking on "civilized" ways. He probably agreed with a visitor to his house, The Flea, who denounced "the constant attempts of the white people to get *more* land from the Indians," as well as the fact that "some Indians allow themselves to be taken in by the white people." However, some key Anglo-American practices, including patrilineal inheritance, patriarchy, and plantation slavery, aided him a very great deal. Vann's father followed Anglo-American inheritance practices, not matrilineal Cherokee ones, and so left his fortune to his son. James Vann built it up, trading as well as building a plantation, Diamond Hill, in what is now Georgia. He became a leader in Upper Town, an increasingly important political player who fought against American settlers.[42]

Vann was an ambitious man. His aspirations took the form of securing ever greater wealth for himself and his family (which was not a traditional Cherokee priority) and fighting for Cherokee autonomy (which was). He ran his household like the most patriarchal of patriarchs, exploiting the labor of enslaved people. He could also be an extremely brutal master—and husband. Yet there were Cherokee traditions in evidence as well. James Vann was a polygamist, and he used this form in ways both old and new. He married sisters: notably several sisters, Anne (Nannie or Nancy) Brown as well as her half-sisters, Elizabeth (Betsey), Mary (Polly), and Margaret (Peggy), whose maternal uncle, Charles Hicks, was a political leader himself. This was old-school: sororal polygamy capitalizing on matrilineal connections (a maternal uncle). Yet much was also Anglo-American: he inherited from a father and so did his wives, including the best-known of them, Peggy Scott. This bequest helped him to buy and build Diamond Hill. It was also in keeping with Anglo-American practices, not Cherokee ones, that Peggy and the other wives moved to his house, rather than his coming to theirs.[43]

James Vann's household was a troubled one, "an epicenter of domestic violence," as one scholar has characterized it. There was fluidity in Vann's marriages, as there were separations and divorces, often instigated by the wives, as well as other women to whom he was evidently not married. The Moravian missionaries, whom he supported and who lived nearby, flinched at "the cruelty and tyranny that is practiced in the house," praying that he be freed "from Satan's chains which bind him so tightly." They recorded more than one episode of a drunk Vann "acting as if he had lost his mind . . . in the house shooting, burning, and ravaging." There was also domestic, possibly sexual, abuse, including one night in which "he mistreated his wife so badly that it cannot be repeated." In one especially dreadful incident, when four enslaved people stole all his money while he was away, he burned one of them, Isaac, to death in front of all the enslaved people at Diamond Hill. The endemic violence and drunkenness at Diamond Hill stemmed from Vann's personal problems, but they occurred in a larger context of complicated shifts in gender, status, and race and the painful situation of the Cherokees in the early nineteenth century.[44] An established Cherokee world was fast becoming unmoored by American invasions, and it created anxieties and "tyranny."

There were many ways to deal with this challenging new world. Some Cherokees used monogamy and Anglo-American gender organization to show their enlightened status. They "abolished polygamy," demonstrating their progress and enlightenment. James Vann's wife Peggy, though she had lived in a complicated polygamous marriage, was one such woman. She and her sisters had kept family together in part through polygamy with Vann. Following James Vann's death in 1809, however, she grew even closer to

Moravian missionaries. When he died, there was loud lamentation; the Moravian missionaries complained they could hardly comfort her "because of the loud crying" of the "heathen mourning." Still, she increasingly added Christian practices, including monogamy, to her life. She was baptized in 1810, a great victory for the Moravians, who had not been terribly successful in their mission thus far. She also acted as a translator. She continued to run the Vann household. In 1812, she married Joseph Crutchfield. She preached to other Indians, as after the 1811 earthquake, when she "took advantage of this opportunity to extol to them the love and seriousness of God." In 1818, she even joined "many of the most respected Indian women in their nation" in that petition to the National Council arguing against removal because it would imperil their ability to be "enlightened" Christians. Altogether, her monogamy, like replacing the din of "heathen" mourning rituals with quiet acceptance of the Lord's will, showed her accommodation of civilized and Christian ways. Her continued willingness to speak to the council, as Cherokee women and especially "war women" had long done in political crisis, showed that she kept some of the old ways even in a revitalized form. She gave up polygamy, ultimately, but she maintained relations with her sisters and seems hardly to have lamented her past life as a plural wife.[45]

Yet other Cherokees chose different paths. James Vann had hardly been the only polygamist in the neighborhood. There was also an enslaved man, Gander; a local Cherokee whose wives sold baskets, named No Fire; and one more elite, "Mr. George Fields," a name to indicate status (and brother of Richard Fields, who became a chief). Yet in a situation of encroachment and loss of hunting lands, the economic basis for polygamy shifted. Some of these men, like Vann, melded new and old forms in innovative ways, including polygamy, which augmented personal and political power. There was a cost, to their wives and certainly also to enslaved people. Such men used the labor of both to bolster their status in these shifting, uncertain terrains. Vann showed Cherokees, as well as American officials and Moravian missionaries, that he was not a man to accept limitations on his autonomy: as a man, a husband, a master, and a Cherokee. Polygamy here, as in other settings, was a way for this powerful leader to show his status and to consolidate his position. When one missionary went to talk to him about his troubled domestic life, Vann "jumped out of bed, took the bottle, and drank as in a rage." He declared that "it was his house, and he could drink, dance, fornicate, and do whatever he wanted in it: it was not anyone's business."[46]

This huffy insistence on domestic autonomy reflected Vann's sense that, as besieged as he and his people felt, it was his right as the master to do as he liked in his own house. Such a claim of patriarchal sovereignty was hardly in keeping with the clan-dominated world of the Cherokees and shows how much it had eroded, even for a Cherokee nationalist like Vann. For Cherokees in the past, what a man did in his house, with their kin, was everybody's business. To proclaim the right to rule one's own household was to assert privilege and freedom like a white man and exemplar of the Anglo-American order. It was also a claim of sovereignty over a household in a new political order in which Cherokee autonomy in their homelands, their right to "do whatever they wanted in it," was under grave threat.[47]

"Polygamy, with All [Its] Corruptions and Evils"

The trajectory of the most powerful polygamist at Diamond Hill revealed new orders of gender, rank, and race; so did the trajectory of its least powerful polygamist, an enslaved woman named Patience. While it is difficult to access the meanings of polygamy amid these enslaved populations, it is worth lingering on even the limited view available, from the records of diligent Moravian missionaries, to underline the limits of household sovereignty for some in this era. Enslaved people, Native and African American, lacked the ability to shoo interfering outsiders out of their homes; wives were also limited in such powers. Not only were masters like Vann given license to do what they wanted in their own houses, but in fact they sometimes interfered violently with others in them. Native men's claims to household autonomy had their limits, but enslaved African Americans, it is worth recalling, lacked such sovereignty at all. As a 1767 legal decision in Maryland declared: "Slaves are incapable of marriage by the civil law, because incapable of the *civil rights annexed to it*." In more sympathetic terms, one abolitionist subsequently lamented, "The poor negro is considered as having no right in his wife and children." Therefore, even in monogamous unions marked by formal ceremonies, involving masters and clergy, "slave weddings were bittersweet moments suffused with irony" because they had no legal standing, and the same master who presided over such ceremonies could turn around and separate the couple by sale or inheritance. For if "God made marriage," as one former slave observed, "the white man made the law." Masters like Vann had no compunction about interfering in the households of enslaved people. Some did so in the vilest ways, subjecting those in them to the worst abuses, sexual and otherwise. They also separated families to serve their own economic interests. And a few even considered it their responsibility to control the domestic lives of the enslaved people who labored for them. "Marriage is to be encouraged," one plantation manual advised, as otherwise, in the words of another, "bigamy and polygamy, with all their corruptions and evils, will prevail."[48]

Still, occasionally, polygamy did prevail. Gander, an enslaved man who lived and died at Diamond Hill, evidently had two wives, Jene and Patience. We do not know a great deal, but he was a "new Negro" at Diamond Hill. As we have seen, some masters allowed polygamy for "brave fellows," and Gander was James Vann's favorite. He occasionally attended Moravian church services and did some work for the church. It was therefore a great shock to everyone at Diamond Hill, including the Moravians and James Vann, when Gander's body was found in the creek there in 1806. Vann suspected the enslaved miller "Negro Ned" of violence, and in characteristic fashion, Vann was all too eager to mete out punishment to the person(s) who had done this. It turned out, however, that the cause of Gander's demise may have been Gander himself, and his distress at relations between his two wives.[49]

Gander's two wives, Jene and Patience, seem to have had quite distinct temperaments. Jene was described as "mean spirited." She may be "the Big Jenny" belonging to Vann's estate who later "cursed, swore, and repeatedly wishe[d] her soul to eternal damnation." Jene may have made Patience's life worse, but it was already grim. Even Moravian missionaries were aghast at the cruelties endured by the aptly named Patience—though not from Gander. Having been transported from "Guinea" to Charleston, South Carolina, where James Vann had purchased her, she had been forced to walk barefoot in winter the nearly four hundred miles to Diamond Hill. As a result, her feet had rotted from frostbite, and she had to "scoot" on her hands and knees to get around and to do the work of "pulling cotton." Apparently, when Gander had "fetched" Patience to his house for a visit, Jene was so "annoyed" that "she nagged him endlessly until finally Gander went away from her indignantly . . . and afterward jumped into the water." Whether Gander meant to end his own life or it happened accidentally, he died there. When Moravians related the tale to Vann, apparently "the news . . . relaxed him somewhat. . . . They hurried home, happy and thankful that the investigation was satisfactory to Mr. Vann." As with Roger's suicide in Virginia in

1712, managers and masters found bleak tales of domestic unhappiness among enslaved people more "satisfactory" than other sorts of explanations for sudden death on plantations.[50]

Whatever had happened to Gander, in a few years, Patience had apparently remarried "an African" whose name was not recorded. Was this a countryman? Even several years after Gander's death, the Moravians complained that "her language is still very unintelligible." Patience had this husband also snatched from her in 1810, though for different reasons. The husband's owner, Mr. McNair, also owned the mill and many of those who worked in it, and he had decided to sell several of them down the river to Natchez. One of them, the Negro Ned whom Vann had earlier suspected of foul play against Gander, was so distraught that he and his family were to be sold that Ned "cut his [own] throat," though he survived. His three oldest sons ran away. Ned's throat was stitched, but thereafter "he could not speak a word." Perhaps because Patience had heard this news about Natchez, she made her agonizingly slow way to McNair and asked "for permission to be allowed to move in with her husband." McNair "was shocked because he had decided to sell this Negro only because he believed that he did not have a wife yet." This is an interesting claim. However, it was now too late; the husband was heading for Natchez. McNair was supposedly so "deeply moved" by Patience's "woeful crying and tears" that "he had to leave silently."[51]

Patience's sufferings were not at an end. She turned up at the Moravian mission the following year, "crawling on her knees . . . with her two little friendly children at her side." She was in "dire distress," with her and her two children hungry. She complained "that the other Negroes treat her very badly; they give her little to eat." The Moravians fed her and the children, while also assuring her of God's love for "the poor, the wretched, and crippled on earth." Patience "cried with joy and gratitude." She returned a week or so later to attend services. She was there again a year later. Having "crawled here on her knees," Patience "listened very attentively" to the sermon on Matthew 11:27–30. Patience's rapt attention seems unsurprising for a sermon centered on Jesus' invitation: "Come unto me, all ye that labour and are heavy laden, and I will give you rest." Patience's last appearance in the records occurred after one of the worst episodes yet: when she, close to giving birth, was "horribly beaten" by a notably cruel overseer. We do not know what happened to her, her "little friendly children," or the baby she was expecting. Here were the desperate realities of life in slavery at Diamond Hill.[52]

For Patience, domestic life—even a polygamous marriage—may have brought some joys, including a husband and children. But it also brought a lot of misery, including challenging relations with other enslaved people. The key variable here was less about polygamy than about the other relations and the treatment of masters and overseers. This instability and violence, from masters who sold husbands away and overseers who beat pregnant women, were the sources of Patience's misery, in this new Cherokee order of southern plantation slavery. Patience and Gander, and thousands like them, enduring the most dismal circumstances, also had to suffer claims that they had no respect for marriage, monogamy, and decent family life. Even those more willing to concede that problems stemmed from slavery, not "inherent depravity," stressed problematic tendencies. One minister—and master—hoped that "very great reforms can be made among the Negroes, in the sacredness and perpetuity of their marriage relations." Still, he contended that among enslaved populations, "Polygamy is practiced [and] . . . carries, in its perpetration, vast inconveniences and endless divisions and trouble," linking it with a fundamental "insensibility of heart."[53]

African Americans knew better. Gander was so palpably distressed at the fighting in his home that it was thought to be a cause of his death. Patience wept bitterly when her husband was sold away; she crawled on hands and knees to get bread and milk for her children. She and other African Americans ignored or flouted the fictions of ministers, lawmakers, and masters. Instead they joined in unions of their own accord and definition, from being sweethearts to "taking up" together to cohabitation to partnerships recognized by churches and even, at some level, masters. None of these forms of unions included legal recognition or rights. Yet some of them, including Patience's own, may have ameliorated the worst horrors. Patience's marriages and family life and James Vann's own were quite distinct, stemming from different impulses and with diverse outcomes.[54] Yet for many white Americans, they seemed to indicate the inferiority of both Indians and African Americans.

"Whitemen" and "Amerecats" were busy in the early nineteenth century. So many of their voices converged to condemn the "inherent" depravities of other, polygamous Americans. Households were where that true "character" was revealed, and polygamy proved their inferiority and inherent barbarism. For centuries, as we have seen, many sojourners had witnessed polygamy in many settings and shaken their heads at the problematic nature of those who practiced it. There is persistence in such denunciations that continued into the nineteenth century. Yet in the past, there had been a much more explicit connection with Christianity, or lack thereof. What is notable is that, even for sympathetic observers and in fact Christian missionaries—from Franciscans in the West to New England missionaries in the Cherokee Nation—the problem was less explicitly about religion or heathenism than about "inherent traits." Here was Enlightenment in action in American settings: polygamy was inherently backward and barbaric, and so were the people who practiced it. This way of casting polygamy laid critical groundwork for what happened next.

In the midst of multiple, contending jurisdictions and imperial aggressions, men defended their households, and their polygamy, with force, in complicated and sometimes contradictory ways. They asserted their mastery over a setting they felt they controlled—their households—in the midst of many they did not. According to Serra, Baltasar did "just as he pleased," which meant enacting polygamy and inflicting corporal punishment on another Indian. In other words, doing as he pleased meant treating his subordinates with the same violence the friars used against mission Indians. It also meant taking for himself that which the friars had attempted to usurp: domestic decisions. Wakara refused to leave his camp to meet with Mormon leaders; they had to come to him. He did "not intend to leave it to see anybody." James Vann reeled on Moravians to remind them that he could do as he wished in his house: "It was not anyone's business." All of these moments show indigenous men asserting sovereignty as "representative[s] of an aggrieved and much injured people." Again, "traditional" practices had very different contexts and thus novel meanings. The sense of grievance pulsated in their household decisions and their political and social ones; it is impossible to disentangle those imperatives.

Women did not necessarily gain much from these embattled assertions of sovereignty. Many situations worsened and became less egalitarian, whether polygamous or monogamous. Polygamy was not in many cases the key variable in determining oppression; such a point comes clearest in the situations like those at Diamond Hill. Violence, wars, slavery, and reorientations made familiar systems worse. Still, such women endured and did what they could. There was Toypurina and other women like her, who were "brave and fought." There was the woman at the center of staged fisticuffs for her favor, dragged through the river, but still she "would not live with the man who had won her." There was Peggy Scott Vann, who turned to Christianity and monogamy even while organizing politically with other women in time-honored ways. And there were the second wives like Patience, whose hobbled lives were painful witness to the horrors of slavery much more than of polygamy. Women could not often make their voices heard in public spaces and in the records, but silences mattered too: "I got no heart to speak."

Polygamy remained a source of unease for many, many Americans by the middle of the nineteenth century. Increasingly coded as inherent barbarism practiced by racially inferior groups, it existed all over the land, from the Pacific and the high Rocky Mountains of the West to the Atlantic and the green Appalachians of the East. It continued to be a way for ambitious men to prove their leadership and to shore up authority in novel and complex situations across a lot of places. It was both part of the new United States order and outside of it, gnawing at people worried over the dangers of democracy and the unleashing, even elevating, of new voices. What if reform and democratic impulses led to rebellion and rethinking of accepted marriage traditions; the world would be rocked. At the same time, the defense of household authority could also be a complex defense of sovereignty imperiled by competing, aggressive forces of imperialism. Amid "enlightned" reform, polygamy was abolished. Yet polygamy continued. Indeed, in contests over sovereignty, both within and beyond the household, it would soon become the cause of national crisis.

8. "Defence of Polygamy by a Lady"

Belinda Hilton was a wife determined to pursue happiness by escaping her husband. Heart pounding and petticoats hitched, she fled. Her husband took her to the train, where she was supposed to head north to visit family. Instead, she got off at the first station and ordered her trunk. She waited all day at a hotel depot for the next train heading west. Although she had been a dutiful wife, she later recalled, "I had not the least compunction of conscience or one thought I was doing wrong in leaving my husband. My heart was filled with joy and thanksgiving for I never doubted for one moment but what I should get along alright." Belinda did get along all right, but it wasn't easy. Counting her limited cash, she bought a second-class ticket and hoped for a quick journey. However, "a drunken man" accosted her and would not leave her alone, "insulting" her until she gave up and bought a full-price ticket in the first-class carriage. She got off the train at its termination, staying at a hotel in a strange city that night: scandalous, risky behavior for a young woman on her own. The next morning, she headed on another train to a trusted stranger's house, where she "never told them I had been married neither my right name for I feared I might get into trouble if I did."[1]

From the tales told about wives in the early Church of Jesus Christ of Latter-day Saints, we might imagine that Hilton was fleeing a polygamous tyrant, the kind of despotic villain who stalks novels, cartoons, and other texts of the nineteenth century. In fact, it was the reverse. She was running away from her legal husband, Benjamin Hilton, traveling from Boston to Latter-day Saints (LDS) circles in Utica, New York, in July 1844. She was hurtling toward, not from, plural marriage. After earning money for two

Belinda Marden Pratt. This undated
photo came from her later years.
Courtesy of LDS Church History
Library, Church of Jesus Christ of
Latter-day Saints.

months in Utica as a seamstress, she headed with a friend for the promised
land of Nauvoo, Illinois, a Mississippi River town then the center of the
growing LDS movement. She later recalled: "I need not say we had many
adventures traveling as we were alone without a protector and some not very
pleasant ones but the Great Father protected us and we accomplished our
journey in safety." At midnight on September 30, 1844, when the women's
boat landed at Nauvoo, "many kind friends" greeted them. Brigham Young
himself, whom Belinda had met briefly in Boston, "welcomed me and blessed
me."[2] By the end of 1844, Belinda had become a plural wife in the LDS
Church, gaining not just a husband but also four fellow wives.

This tale is not what we expect. Indeed, all is not quite how it seems in
the dramatic story of early Mormon polygamy. How did a woman who by all
accounts seemed a conventional New England wife of the early nineteenth
century, a woman who moved with her husband from her family in New
Hampshire to the booming city of Boston in the early 1840s, become a plural
wife in a domestic arrangement in Utah that would shock Americans? How
did she become not just a plural wife but such an ardent defender of this system
that she would become the first American woman to defend polygamy in print?
This chapter focuses on her tract, its context, and the events that led up to it. In

the past, only men, like Martin Madan and John Miner, had entered into such public printed debates over polygamy. But this was a different time and place.

In the period from the 1830s to the 1850s, women were publicly sharing their views on polygamy in novel ways. Adopting the long view allows us to appreciate anew the radicalism of early Mormon women, connecting them with broader American cultures. Many people, both women and men, agreed that marriage law and practices needed reforming. A *Defence of Polygamy by a Lady,* published by Belinda Marden Hilton Pratt in 1854, shows that women unleashed their voices in powerful new ways. Earlier voices of women on marriage were so secondhand, too often filtered through men's writings, and not often given in public settings. Here, at last, is a woman writing publicly about polygamy. Her words ring out clear and strong: in her memoirs, her letters, and in print. One scholar of early Mormon polygamy has noted, "Belinda was herself a bit of a revolutionary. She had left a legal husband in Massachusetts in 1844 in order to join the saints in Nauvoo." What was revolutionary about Belinda Marden Hilton Pratt was not just that she defied her first husband, ran away, and became a plural wife, though all these actions had revolutionary implications. Equally if not more significant was that she wrote and published about it. Much of the power of early Mormonism lies in its tracts, its hymns, its writings. Even its critics were astonished, finding it a "remarkable fact, that a sect so ignorant should in so short a time have produced such a multitude of printed works." (Also important, of course, were the tales told about the Mormons.)[3]

Still, Belinda's tract has never received a great deal of analysis, drawing limited attention even in Mormon history and none at all in any general intellectual histories of polygamy. Such scant consideration is unfortunate, as this treatise provides a unique opportunity to add an intellectual history of women and Mormon polygamy to the rich social histories of those topics already existing. It also shows how women reshaped debates about plural marriage in the nineteenth century, even offering robust woman-centered defenses of the practice. For centuries, writers had lauded polygamy as a system which accommodated male desire. Belinda cast it as a system designed to accommodate female desire, as well as one that protected, rather than oppressed, women and children. She centered her ideas in wider American cultures of reform and feminism, not just those of Mormon theology.[4]

Belinda's defense of polygamy is eloquent, earthy, and passionate. It still has the power to discomfit. It's strange to find if not a feminist at least a woman-centered vision of polygamy in a publication by the sixth wife of a nineteenth-century LDS elder; such women have been treated as dupes or at best patient martyrs to polygamy, participants in the "liberty of self-degradation." Belinda's writings help to answer that enthralling question: why were some women willing to adopt polygamy? Belinda's tale drops us not into the Great Salt Lake Basin (at least not yet) but instead smack onto the bustling streets of Boston and wider national cultures of debate about marriage.

"We Are Now in a Transition State"

Belinda Hilton was hardly the only American woman to identify problems with her era's system of monogamous marriage and gender relations. Since the 1780s, there were continuities: women still lost legal rights to property at marriage, and divorce options remained quite limited. Yet much had also changed since the 1780s. Criticisms of traditional marriage grew fiercer, more sustained in print and public by women themselves. In the 1780s, Anglo-American Protestant cultures emphasized happiness and love as ideals as the basis for marriage. By the 1830s, love was not enough, and happiness was less a fond hope than a minimal expectation. Women and men debated the nature of marriage, the rights of women and men in marriage, even marital sexuality. There were also women and men putting into practice new ways of being married—and unmarried. In short, many people from all kinds of backgrounds agreed that there was something wrong with modern American marriage, though they offered wildly disparate solutions to the perceived problem.

At this time, in law and sometimes in practice, marriage in the United States was monogamous and usually for life. A double standard in terms of sexual appetite had become entrenched in late-eighteenth-century life: that men wanted, indeed required "sexual outlets," but that women—at least elite white women—were less prone to such passions. Such went along with what has been called the rise of separate spheres: the notion that women's highest, indeed sole purpose, was in creating and maintaining domestic havens for husbands and children. Yet in the 1830s and 1840s, a growing number of feminists started to allege that modern marriage did not provide enough intellectual or physical stimulation for wives. They argued for change. Increasingly, ordinary Americans, as well as radical visionaries, came to the conclusion which at least some Native Americans had reached by the early seventeenth century: that marriage might be viewed essentially as a private contract between individuals and families, severed with the simple consent of both parties, property shared out, with no intervention from religious or secular authorities—a way of organizing marriage that indeed seems radical still.

Women's desires and opinions, publicly declared by women themselves, were central to a transformation that brought the United States substantially more progressive laws on marriage and divorce than many other nations, and resulted in events such as the 1848 Seneca Falls women's rights convention. Many individuals pushed back against American state regulation in their daily lives, testing out everything from celibacy to complex marriage to polygamy. Few of the proposed subversive alternatives to traditional Christian monogamy have prevailed, but people in the 1830s and 1840s could not have foreseen that outcome. New ideas about gender and marriage were not theoretical for Belinda and thousands of others; instead, women like her put them into practice, though not always in ways we assume. Belinda's story allows us to view these profound changes from the perspective of an ordinary woman, a daughter of New England farm folk who found herself not just caught up in waves of revolution but also leaping into those bracing waters feet first.[5]

In part, the period of wondering aloud about marriage coincided with a period in which the government became more involved in the making and unmaking of marriage. State laws especially on divorce and married women's property were shifting, often under pressure from women themselves. Partnerships unrecognized by the state had long existed, and continued to do so long into the nineteenth century. Laws allowing divorce for an ever greater variety of reasons proliferated in just this period, drawing more people into the embrace of state systems. More women than men were seeking divorce, so women were major agents of this change. By 1839, Massachusetts allowed full divorce for "three years' wilful desertion or refusal to cohabit by either person." In 1842, it even permitted divorce "when the other [spouse] joins and remains three years with a religious sect or society professing to believe the relation of husband and wife unlawful." Such a law recognized the presence of new Utopian religious organizations. At the most liberal end, the neighboring state of Connecticut allowed divorce in 1843 for intemperance and cruelty, expanded by 1849 to "any such misconduct . . . as permanently destroys the happiness of the petitioner, and defeats the purpose of the marriage relation." This was a major innovation. People had always left unhappy marriages, of course, but they had not been able to do so legally. Breach of happiness was now sufficient to obtain the legal end to a marriage. These changes also increased the power of states, as more people sought formal ends to marriage.[6]

Yet in abolitionist-inclined northern circles (of the sort Belinda would have encountered in 1830s Boston), law and government power seemed to be problems themselves, as many states supported slavery in the South. Criticisms of both slavery and marriage emphasized the desperate problems of cruel tyranny in the home. A few thinkers even conflated the two, seeing women's condition in marriage as a form of slavery itself. The abolitionist writer Lydia Maria Child emphasized the condition of many wives as slaves in global historical contexts. One elite southern woman, frustrated by her husband's frequent absences, complained to him: "I belong to that degraded race called woman—who whether her lot be cast among Jew, or Turk, heathen, or Christian is yet a *slave*." Another woman ushered in the new year of 1846 with a toast: "Woman—the slave of man—may the day soon come when she knows the sweets of Liberty."[7]

Some women and men sought those "sweets of Liberty" in Utopian communities, with reimagined households at their core. One of the best known was Shakerism, founded by "Mother" Ann Lee, a late-eighteenth-century English visionary. This group eschewed marriage and espoused celibacy. One Shaker pamphlet celebrated "A life of *innocence* and *purity*, according to the example of Jesus Christ . . . [with] Love, Peace, Justice, Holiness, Goodness, Truth." Its communities, many of which flourished in the United States, were organized into "family order," composed of relations tied not by blood or marriage but by spiritual connections. Some married individuals left spouses to join the Shakers, a worrisome trend for many; indeed, Shaker authorities assured critics, "No believing husband or wife is . . . to separate from an unbelieving partner, except by mutual agreement; unless the conduct of the unbeliever be such as to warrant a separation by the laws of God and man." Each Shaker "family" was headed by both a female and a male elder who shared authority equally. Since women did not have children once they joined the Shakers, and since other children (those of converts or adoptees) were cared for communally, women could work and lead just as men did, though in sex-segregated ways.[8]

An equally radical but distinct (and less popular) system characterized the communities founded by John Humphrey Noyes, first in Vermont and later at Oneida, New York. He fretted over salvation and what he called "the carnal mind," which he termed "enmity against God." Eventually he decided, "If men love God with *all* their heart, they cannot sin." At Oneida, Noyes instituted a system of "complex-marriage" in which individuals moved between sexual partners, forbidden to pursue monogamy, which Noyes saw as a selfish "special love." All were to live in harmony, without the infrastructure of monogamy or private property. To limit procreation, Noyes urged the practice of what he called "male continence," in which men somehow had fulfilling sexual intercourse without ever ejaculating. He advised his male followers that "the sweetest and noblest period of intercourse with woman" was not orgasm but rather entry, "that first moment of simple presence and spiritual effusion before the muscular exercise begins." If a few men at Oneida did not entirely agree and failed to avoid ejaculation, any resulting children were to be raised by the community. While neither Shakers nor the Oneida community was vast, they survived with hundreds of followers for decades. They deliberately recast marriage and sexuality, rejecting the authority of church and state to regulate them. They also notably limited procreation, thus freeing up women from the drudgery of repeated pregnancies and child rearing. Stories about all these Utopian groups reverberated across a wider American landscape, as periodicals publicized their activities.[9]

In this rich ferment of schemes for improvement of self and society, feminist visions emerged. Such was part of a broader movement of women explicitly debating and writing on all matters. Some women agonized over the burdens of wives around the world; they saw their struggles as connected ones. American women began to do in histories of their own what William Alexander and others had done in eighteenth-century Europe, placing women's subordination in marriage in a broad historical and anthropological context. Yet they did so with greater punch and brio. A more extreme Enlightenment entered American homes through women's publications.[10]

Women were intent on rescuing other women. They did not emphasize the barbarity of polygamy, with its iron rods and its eunuchs, against the gallantry of monogamy, as writers from Montesquieu to Alexander had done. It was not that these women were in favor of polygamy; they saw it as inegalitarian and problematic. But so, they averred, was monogamy. Minimizing the contrast between these two systems highlighted that both had historically benefited men and constrained women, "in all ages and countries, not even excepting enlightened republican America," as Sarah Grimké put it. Their grievances circled around marriage, polygamous and monogamous, as an institution and a practice. Lydia Maria Child, Sarah Grimké, Margaret Fuller, and other women and men agreed that marriage needed reform, as did gender relations. As Elizabeth Cady Stanton confided to Susan B. Anthony in 1853, "I feel as never before that this whole question of woman's rights turns on the pivot of the marriage relation."[11] There seemed to be an array of possible solutions, from legal change to acknowledgment of female desires to baked potato suppers. Enlightenment came in many forms.

In the United States in the 1830s, such intellectual work became possible but hardly easy for women like Lydia Maria Child, the abolitionist feminist writing in Boston. While researching and drafting her extensive global history of women and marriage, for instance, Child faced a variety of challenges. First, there were financial problems stemming from her husband's failed business ventures. Then, not unrelated, there was what her biographer describes as a "sexually unfulfilling marriage" beset by ever more tensions. Finally, just as Child reached a critical stage of research at a major library, the Boston Athenaeum, the trustees there suddenly revoked her library privileges in the fallout from her earlier incendiary abolitionist work. Her *Appeal on Behalf of That Class of Americans Called Africans,* one of the earliest American abolitionist books, not only had condemned southern slavery, a claim largely acceptable to New England audiences, but also had denounced northern racism and laws against intermarriage, less tolerable causes for New England's elite.[12] It's difficult to write a deeply researched book without access to a good library, as Child learned. Nevertheless, she persisted.

"I am a slave, a favored slave." This quotation from Lord Byron appeared on the frontispiece of Child's 1835 *The History of the Condition of Women,* setting up the vision of wives, "adored and oppressed," as drudges the world over. Child guided readers through the exploitation of women from Afghanistan to Van Diemen's Land (Tasmania), from ancient to modern times. Child's outrage at slavery colored the entire work, as did a sense of the exploitation of women over time and place. She identified ancient Jewish polygamy as "calculated to stifle the best emotions of the female heart." However, she noted, "even under the most barbarous and tyrannical forms of society, the salutary influence of good and sensible women is . . . acknowledged." Indeed, in Child's *History,* polygamy rarely comes in for the fist-shaking treatment it did in eighteenth-century histories by men. Eunuchs make only the most fleeting appearance, since Child was

most concerned with the effects on women, not men. Although she acknowledged, as most did, the tyranny of the Turkish sultan's harem, she also
emphasized how exceptional this setting was. In fact, she observed, "Women
of the middling classes in Turkey appear to enjoy a very considerable degree
of freedom and consideration."[13]

Child offered an evenhanded account of polygamy. She emphasized
women's perspectives in a way that few (no?) previous authors had done. In
Greenland, for instance, she claimed that "The first wife, if she have children, is considered the head of the family. When she dies, the junior wife
takes her place, and is generally very kind to the motherless little ones." This
insistence on the positive relations between mothers and children in polygamy
is notable, as is the point that a polygamous wife could be "head of the
family." Child also allowed that love could exist in polygamous systems, an
unusual contention. She offered examples of male exploitation in monogamy,
too. Child derided ancient Roman monogamy, as "husbands were intrusted
with a degree of power, which modern nations would consider dangerous."
Christianity did not entirely alleviate such problems: "Throughout Christendom, the law allows but one wife. Licentiousness abounds in all cities; it is
not confined to a class of women avowedly depraved, but sometimes lurks
beneath the garb of decency." This linkage, of "one wife" and "licentiousness," thus undermined the notion that monogamy was a pinnacle of protection for women. Altogether, Child summarized that "that true and perfect
companionship, which gives both man and woman complete freedom . . . is
as yet imperfectly understood." True companionship occurred only when
women's situation equaled men's.[14]

"The page of history teems with woman's wrongs, and it is wet with
woman's tears." So announced Sarah Grimké in her *Letters on the Equality of
the Sexes,* written as a series of epistles to her sister Angelina. Grimké noted
her debt to Child's account. An emphasis on equality, reformed marriages, and
the need to improve women's situation also underpinned Grimké's analysis:
"All history attests that man has subjected woman to his will, used her as a
means to promote his selfish gratification, to minister to his sensual pleasures,
to be instrumental in promoting his comfort." She rejected marriage as unstable
at best and violent at worst: "Ah! how many of my sex feel in the dominion . . .
that what they have leaned upon has proved a broken reed at best, and oft a
spear." For Grimké, herself unmarried, marriage was central to the subjugation of women; she never bothered to single out polygamy as a peculiarly

odious form. Indeed, she contended, "man has exercised the most unlimited and brutal power over woman, in the peculiar character of husband—a word in most countries synonymous with tyrant." In marriage, even modern enlightened ones, women lost their individuality, their independence, even their "moral being." She concluded: "We are much in the situation of the slave." Yet too many women still saw marriage as "the sine qua non of human happiness and human existence." Marriage needed fundamental reform. Grimké wanted wives to stop spending all their time in tasks like cooking elaborate dinners, arguing instead that husbands should "encourage their wives to devote . . . their time to mental cultivation, even at the expense of having to dine sometimes on baked potatoes, or bread and butter."[15]

A desire for greater "mental cultivation" for women, and a domestic situation of equality, also motivated another noted author, Margaret Fuller. She addressed her 1845 treatise "to you, women, American women," her presumed female audience. Marriage should be "intellectual companionship," not just a practical arrangement. Fuller cast Euro-American marriage systems as an improvement, but a limited one, over systems in "the Oriental clime" or among "natives of this continent." In both, Fuller noted, polygamy flourished. In the East, she argued, men exploited women sexually, thereby destroying "the chastity and equality of genuine marriage." Among Native American "chiefs," Fuller contended, wives "were but servants." Yet like Child, Fuller pointed out that such systems had some advantages. Women in these systems were "not polluted," and men were punished for adultery. In her view, polygamy was far from ideal, but it was at least an honest system in which women could work and live without shame or prostitution.[16]

"We are now in a transition state," Fuller declared, "and but few steps have yet been taken. From polygamy, Europe passed to the marriage *de convenance*. This was scarcely an improvement." In other words, monogamy for family interest was not much better than polygamy. Even modern American monogamy was problematic, as unmarried women, who served as lovers and prostitutes for philandering husbands, were "polluted" and "lost." Men could have affairs without scandal, Fuller noted, but women dared not do the same. According to Fuller, part of the problem was the common belief "that men have not only stronger passions . . . but of a sort that it should be shameful for [women] to share or even to understand." As Fuller phrased it, this claim meant "that the least appearance of coldness or withdrawal, from whatever cause, in the wife is wicked, because liable to turn her husband's thoughts to illicit indulgence; for a man is so constituted that he must indulge his passions or die!"[17] In other words, most agreed that if a husband cheated, it was probably the wife's fault.

Fuller denounced this sexual double standard, acknowledging that women might indeed "share" such "shameful" passions. No wonder the book outraged so many. Edgar Allan Poe sneered that it was a book "few women in the country could have written, and no woman in the country would have published, with the exception of Miss Fuller." Even Fuller's friends were discomfited by her frankness about female sexuality. One woman complained, "Margaret speaks of many things that should not be spoken of." Lydia Maria Child, who knew firsthand the sharp sting of unfavorable publicity, was more sympathetic, though no less astonished: "It is a *bold* book. . . . I should not have dared to have written some things in it, though it would have been safer for me, being married. But they need to have been said and she is brave to do it."[18] Child's statement, when she herself had lost reputation and sales for her own *bold* antislavery writings, demonstrates how dangerous Fuller's views seemed at the time.

For Fuller, marriage swallowed women up, whether they wanted it to or not. "That is the very fault of marriage, and of the present relation between the sexes, that the woman does belong to the man, instead of forming a whole with him." Fuller concluded that women should have options: marriage and motherhood only if they chose them. They might instead decide to pursue intellectual and professional ambitions. Fuller conceded that many women would still choose marriage and motherhood, but they should not be compelled to do so: "Mothers will delight to make the nest soft and warm. . . . No need to clip the wings of any bird that wants to soar and sing, or finds in itself the strength of pinion for a migratory flight unusual to its kind." In other words, if a woman wished to "sing" or even, exceptionally, to fly far on strong wings, no one should stop her. A few women indeed flew far.[19]

"The Consequences of Venereal Excesses"

After all, these were seeking times, and Belinda herself was a seeker. She was born in New Hampshire, the youngest child of Rachel and John Marden. Her parents, born in the 1770s, were of that generation in which New England's Mercies and Desires became its Clarissas and Amys. These were new names for a new nation, an exciting moment of change, but not equally for all. For if, as scholars have contended, there was a revolution in fertility limitation in these new United States, nobody seems to have alerted Rachel and John, though they were exactly the sort of literate New England folk supposed to have led this transformation. In ye olde colonial way, Rachel Marden was big-bellied and fruitful for more than twenty-five years. Every one of her fourteen babies survived, an unusual record in an era when child mortality haunted families. Her world was one of relentless childbearing and rearing, a heavy body and leaky breasts, as she spent virtually every other year pregnant. Belinda, born on Christmas Eve in 1820, was the last of these fourteen children. It must have been a crowded house, though she also had siblings to take care of her. If her mother was weary and a little hollowed out from the unremitting blessings of motherhood, it would not be much of a surprise. John died when Belinda was in her teens. Early widowhood probably exacerbated Rachel's sheer exhaustion, even if it did leave her with a widow's third, all the bedding, one cow, and three sheep.[20]

Still, for all their modest means, all the Marden daughters married. In fine New England tradition, Rachel and John were "strictly moral and members of the Congregational Church." Belinda married a local young man, Benjamin Hilton, in New Hampshire in May 1840. She recalled that a Baptist minister performed the ceremony, which might indicate Benjamin's background or her own religious searching by this period. After all, the period of Belinda's youth was an era of great religious and cultural ferment. The movement known as the Second Great Awakening brought intense preaching, theological debates, and revival meetings to all parts of the United States, including New England. Preachers visited, offering a rich array of religious possibilities. Belinda noted subsequently, "I was continually ambitious to find the right kind of religion, never feeling assured that those I was acquainted with were right." Restless in religion and in other realms, Belinda and Benjamin moved from one New Hampshire town to another, before settling in Boston, probably in 1842.[21] Looking for something new, against the bleak Calvinism of their parents, young people like Belinda and Benjamin went to hear visiting speakers.

To note that Boston in the 1830s and 1840s had a lively culture of public speaking is to understate the matter. The city was a hive of novel ideas, scandal, and violence. Rioters broke up lectures from visiting abolitionists and even halted dietary reformer Sylvester Graham, for whom the graham cracker is named, when he came to lecture in 1837. Boston afforded a dizzying array of local talent as well as visiting speakers. On the streets of the city, Belinda could have brushed past Ralph Waldo Emerson and his children's tutor, Henry David Thoreau, deep in conversation. She could have bumped into William Lloyd Garrison, the notorious abolitionist whom rioters had dragged in 1835 and who continued to publish his highly influential abolitionist newspaper *The Liberator*. Possibly she spoke with members of the Boston Female Moral Reform Society and the Ladies' Physiological Society of Boston, led by Mary Gove; she may even have attended their meetings. She might have heard lectures about marriage and morals of people from all over the globe, at the Lyceum and in other venues. Belinda might have literally crossed paths with teacher Margaret Fuller, then editing *The Dial*, a Transcendentalist journal, and soon to publish her groundbreaking book.[22] Belinda Hilton might have read or heard about those feminist critiques of marriage, especially as both Fuller and Child were local.

Belinda herself may have attended talks by Sylvester Graham as well as Mary Gove and the Ladies' Physiological Society. Such reformers linked social ills to physical overstimulation and, more specifically, overindulgence in the "solitary vice," or masturbation. One historian has described this practice as "America's dominant sexual obsession" in the middle of the nineteenth century. Graham lectured across the Northeast, on what he called the "laws of life and health." He warned listeners to avoid alcohol, meat, and other stimulations. He declared that women and men were subject to the same laws of life and health, including sexual ones. The most incendiary aspect of his theory was that ladies, too, should avoid the "solitary vice": outrageous public recognition of women's masturbation in a mixed-gender space. Making such a public statement offended many, which is why his seemingly anodyne 1837 "Lecture to Mothers" nearly got him beaten up in Boston.[23]

For Graham and others such as Mary Gove, marriage did not solve the endemic problem of the "solitary vice." In 1842, Mary Gove (herself an admirer of Fuller's) tutted that marriage could "not save people from the consequences of venereal excesses." To Gove, the world was a menacing place of possible overstimulation in every direction, for young women as for sedate matrons. Even seemingly innocent treats like fiction and candy ensnared the unsuspecting. Gove enumerated peril after peril on that road to hell and masturbation: warm baths, lack of exercise, corsets, novels ("the early reading of love tales, amatory poetry, romances &c."), alcoholic drinks (which "even in small quantities, degrade and sensualize"), animal meat ("flesh is . . . more stimulating than vegetables"), even sweets which "excite unholy passions" such that "the young . . . are often . . . led to licentiousness by confectionary!" Against this wave of ills, there were a few safe havens. Gove recommended that young people be encouraged to "read history," which she thought would counteract the alarming stimulation of other kinds of books.[24]

Still, of all the many perils, "no form of nervous excitement is so injurious as the solitary vice" which was "exceedingly common" among both women and men. Indeed, Gove thought masturbation flourished especially at "houses of ill fame" and "female boarding schools." The consequences were grave: "Impaired eye-sight, palpitation of the heart, pain in the side, and bleeding at the lungs, spasms of the heart and lungs, and sometimes sudden death are caused by indulgence in this practice." Gove was a woman lecturing and writing for women. Here, then, was clear recognition of female physical desires, as well as what seemed to be discontent and ill health affecting even seemingly happily married women. Gove quoted a married female patient of Graham's who recounted her fall: "My parents were very luxurious in their mode of living, using much animal food and large quantities of the different condiments." If even confectionary led to licentiousness, what could ham with mustard do?! Given this carnal childhood, it is little wonder that the woman "became addicted to solitary vice." Naturally, this behavior led to heart palpitations, dizziness, headaches, and other assorted ills. Still, unaware of the dangers, she continued to practice the solitary vice "to a great extent" leading to "wretched health" until the miraculous clean-living regimen of Dr. Graham saved her. This case study demonstrates the ways in which women imbibed these theories. So do notes from women attending his talks. One woman in Maine grumbled that when Graham's presentation emphasized that blood from eating meat was "stimulating, exciting, irritating," "he might have here made remarks on the effect of such blood on the genital organs."[25]

Belinda might have heard such lectures herself. For the price of a newspaper, she could also have opened up a world of novel communities. One 1842 Boston newspaper printed a story about Robert Owen and Fanny Wright, two notable social reformers: "It is said that [Fanny Wright] and the Owens are opposed to the marriage covenant, and hold to the promiscuous intercourse of the sexes, notwithstanding they are all married and no one has ever accused them of immorality." The paper then quoted Robert Owen's notions of radical restructuring of marriage in his community, in which the couple had to declare their intentions, wait to get to know each other, and then participate in a communal ceremony to register their marriage. If they were unhappy, they registered their desire to separate, waited to test it, and then separated formally. The paper noted "the substance of the proposed plan takes the celebration of marriage from the clergy and places it in the assembled community; and it gives the parties the right of separation when mutually agreed." The article continued that such was the standard form of practice among some Quaker communities, thus normalizing this unusual practice.[26] Communities already informally patrolled marriage and cohabitation, so it was not such a great leap to imagine a formalized system of community oversight and approval.

A month or so before her westward journey, Belinda might have picked up another local newspaper aimed at working-class people, the *Boston Investigator*. It included an account of a "Social Reform Convention" recently held on Tremont Street, by a member "of the Skaneateles Community, (N.Y.)." This group was a small and short-lived Utopian community, one of those founded in 1843 by the Society for Universal Inquiry and Reform. The group eventually set up several communities in Indiana, Ohio, and New York State. The newspaper noted that marriage reform was part of their platform. As many did, the group declared marriage "a true and natural relation ... admirably adapted to promote love and virtue." Its leaders denounced "bigamy, polygamy, adultery, concubinage, and licentiousness." So far, there was little to distinguish them from any of the usual claims about marriage filling contemporary periodicals. However, this "Social Reform Convention" suggested a new way of ending marriage: "When such parties have outlived their affections and can no longer contribute to the happiness of each other, the sooner they shall separate the better." They argued "that the power of divorce which now rests in the arms of the State, belongs to the individual parties interested, and that the forms and ceremonies growing out of the Church and State impart no authority or power." Stemming from a Quaker rejection of formal authority, such notions pointed to a growing sense that unhappiness in marriage, not just adultery or cruelty, might be grounds for a divorce, that happiness was requisite in marriage, and that the relationship between state and individuals in marriage should be recast.[27]

Just as Belinda was contemplating her own troubled marriage in April 1844, she might have seen stories of marital subversion in the *Boston Courier*.

This issue (the only one surviving from that year) includes several tales of women and men practicing sex and marriage in ways outside the legal system. One article borrowed from a Portland, Maine, newspaper, under the ironic headline "Morals of the East," reported on indictments against both one Philip Hodgkins for "bigamy" and his female partner, "the woman who had been living with Hodgkins, as his wife." The article noted, "There is no name given in the statute for the offence for which she stands charged." States sought to punish women who chose to cohabit with men not legally their husbands, who might even be married to other women. Yet states struggled even to define the nature of this crime. Female collusion in bigamy was a complicated issue, as Belinda herself would find. Yet multiple wives represented the "morals of the east," with the reader primed to associate polygamy with Asian despotism. Such an article, along with its wider circulation, suggests that people increasingly saw in print as well as in their own communities such flouting of marital law. The same issue also reprinted an account from a New York periodical on the case of a woman and man accused of contributing to the death of Eliza Ann Munson "by injuries arising from an abortion." While such articles were hardly new, they foreground women's decisions to pursue practices at odds with law. These critiques and reforms of theories and practices of marriage, rejecting the authority of the state, furnished a rich soil in which new ways of handling personal marital unhappiness might thrive.[28]

"Continually Ambitious"

Did someone thrust a handbill directly into the calloused hand of Benjamin Hilton, or did he or Belinda spy the notice near their house, whether the first one in South Boston or the one to which they moved in 1843, on Kneeland near Washington? Perhaps it was posted to catch the eye of people heading to or from the nearby Worcester railroad depot. Belinda later recalled: "In the winter of 1843 we were attracted by a handbill stating that a Mormon Preacher would hold three meetings in the Boylston Hall. Not having any particular thing to hinder we thought we would go in and hear him." The Hiltons were a young married couple, with a decent income and no children, reasonably well educated and well meaning, exactly the sort of people who could partake of Boston's cultural and religious ferment. At the Mormon meeting, Belinda claimed that she was instantly transfixed: "I had an overwhelming testimony that what he preached was true and was so rejoiced that I seemed to myself light as air, as though my feet scarcely touched the ground." In her memoir, Belinda's revelation continued to guide her, those floating feet ultimately taking her away from her husband, her sisters (still in New Hampshire), and the life that she had known.[29]

Belinda's powerful experience echoed many that had taken place over the previous decade or so. Joseph Smith and others had gathered many converts to his Church of Jesus Christ of Latter-day Saints, founded in upstate New York in 1830. Smith had also had a restless search for his own true religion. He had found it, in what he described as a series of angelic visions in the 1820s. The Book of Mormon, which resulted from these prophecies, was the lodestone for a new Christianity, one centered on the Americas. Others joined the prophet Smith, founding the church. Thanks to a strong missionary impulse, these early converts quickly found other followers in meetings of all kinds. One such gathering was a large meeting in Philadelphia in 1840, led by Smith himself. According to one such early convert and leader, Parley P. Pratt, "brother Joseph arose like a lion about to roar; and being full of the Holy Ghost, spoke in great power, bearing testimony of the visions he had seen." The audience was "astounded; electrified . . . overwhelmed with the sense of the truth and power by which he spoke." Many converted. The kind of speeches that Belinda and Benjamin witnessed in Boston would have explained these new revelations and emphasized a new American narrative of redemption. In other meetings, men like Parley himself preached, in private houses and in larger spaces, such as Tammany Hall in New York. He and others also offered healing miracles, as when he "laid [his] hands" on a child with "brain fever," who was cured, inspiring further conversions.[30]

From the first, at least according to Belinda, her husband was never as transported. "Mr. Hilton felt different . . . said I was too enthusiastic." The church's teachings, as well as its startling American vision and the role of the larger-than-life Joseph Smith, were contentious, well before polygamy became a public issue. In any case, a few months later, Benjamin came to believe, too, coming home in the middle of the day to confide that "he was so wrought upon that he could not work or sleep." Accordingly, both were baptized in waters so cold that "the ice had to be broken and held back with poles." Yet, as Belinda before, Benjamin still doubted, "never feeling assured." He started to prefer the meetings of a Masonic-like group, the Odd

Fellows, to those of the Saints. Still anxious to please, Belinda noted later that she "did not mingle much with the Saints for fear of displeasing my husband." Belinda's experience was similar to that of a much more well-heeled Boston woman, Augusta Cobb, who also left her husband, as well as several children, to join the Saints. Cobb became the second plural wife of Brigham Young. Yet something happened between the Hiltons' joint baptism in 1843 and the summer of 1844, when Belinda fled. Her memoir recounts only that she felt closer to the Saints, while her husband became increasingly "bitter" about them, even forbidding Belinda from "going to meeting." She came to meet with Brigham Young, Parley Pratt, and others. She would have gone to her family in New Hampshire, but they "were as bitter" as Benjamin was, dead set against this new religion.[31]

Belinda portrayed the decision to leave her family of marriage and birth as partially inspired by the encouragement of male LDS leaders, as well as by her own sense of being caught between an increasingly hostile family and a miserable marriage. It was challenging, not to mention scandalous, for a woman to travel on her own, supporting herself financially. Yet Belinda did. Later, Belinda portrayed her decision as inevitable, the only option that made any sense. Just as Fuller, Child, and others did, she used her writings to make points not only about her faith but also about her right to happiness in marriage. In other words, her memoir reveals what Belinda wanted to reveal: how revelation could transform a life and release a woman from unhappiness. In her memoirs, Belinda acknowledged that she had not given her real name, had crafted a story to serve a greater good. So, too, did she shape her personal memoirs. The complex interplay of revelation and secrecy defined early Mormonism. Belinda's unpublished writings similarly omitted details so personal and painful they still seemed impossible to reveal to those closest, even decades later.[32]

There is a critical aspect of Belinda's story unmentioned in her own writings and so by any subsequent family or scholars. For the better part of 1843, Belinda was pregnant. She must have been carrying their daughter when she and Benjamin plunged into those icy baptismal waters. Their child, also named Belinda, was born sometime around the end of October 1843. She seems to have been the couple's first. It was perhaps the impending birth that prompted their move from South Boston to a more central neighborhood, a commercial one where Benjamin could more easily find work as a cabinet and pattern maker. It was the start of their new family, and perhaps slightly overdue for a couple in their twenties who had been married since the spring of 1840 (had she miscarried earlier pregnancies?). Yet as for so many other families in this period, that great joy was too quickly followed by great sorrow, when Belinda the daughter contracted "canker" (or scarlet fever) over that winter, dying at just three months old. Her little body was interred in the South Burial Ground in late January 1844.[33]

Shared grief sometimes brings couples closer. It did not have this effect on the Hiltons. Instead, Belinda apparently found solace in her faith. Perhaps Belinda saw her child's death as punishment for her husband's "apostasy," or maybe she blamed herself. She may have longed for reunion with her little Belinda. Her family in New Hampshire must have known about this loss, as the Hiltons would have written them to share the news. Yet given the absence of any remaining letters between them, we simply do not know. What we do know is that by late July 1844, fewer than six months after her daughter's death in Boston and a month after Joseph Smith had been killed by an angry mob in Carthage, Illinois, Belinda turned her back on that little house in Boston and the prospect of a life with Benjamin. Rural isolation was a problem for wives in this era, but urban isolation could be painful, too. Belinda had grown up with the din of a busy, noisy farmhouse crammed with sisters and brothers. By contrast, this house was so quiet, especially after her daughter died. Taking care of the house and preparing meals, perhaps with part-time help but possibly not even with that, Belinda was lonely and longing. Benjamin did not seem sympathetic. Her misery, and her desire for something better, prompted her flight. Even if she had to lie her way across the continent, working her fingers to the bone as a dressmaker to pay her own way, nothing would stop her from joining the Saints. So Belinda found herself in Nauvoo on September 30, 1844. Fewer than two months later, she would be married in the church to that charismatic leader of early Mormonism, Parley P. Pratt.

"The Highest Form of Marriage, Meriting the Greatest Glory"

Parley Pratt was an exceptionally energetic and charming man, and he poured those gifts into building up Mormonism. When asked for an autobiographical account at age forty-six, he replied that it would seem "far more strange . . . than the thousand volumes of modern fiction." An early convert to Mormonism in 1830, he became "an indefatigable missionary," traveling not just all over the East Coast and to Indians in the Missouri area but also to

Undated photo, Belinda and Parley Pratt. In the early years, it was most common for polygamous husbands to appear in photos only with one wife at a time, as in this photo. Courtesy of
LDS Church History Library, Church of Jesus Christ of Latter-day Saints.

Canada, Great Britain, California, and even Chile. He was also a leading
pamphleteer of this American faith. Indeed, Parley's works remain among
the most widely read of any in Mormonism. His brother, Orson, also a
prolific author, declared, "The press, if rightly used, can be made a mighty
engine of truth." Orson and Parley Pratt made that engine hum and thrum
for decades, with LDS-themed newspapers, pamphlets, treatises, and books
rolling from their presses and out into the world. Parley was also a member
of the Quorum of Twelve Apostles who governed the early Mormon church,
especially after Joseph Smith's lynching in 1844.[34]

Parley was apparently among the first to whom Joseph Smith confided
his developing radicalism about marriage. Parley later recounted that in
conversation with the leader in 1840, he learned about "the first idea of eternal
family organization, and the eternal union of the sexes in those inexpressibly
endearing relationships." Moreover, "I learned that the wife of my bosom

might be secured to me for time and all eternity." There was comfort here, as Parley's first wife, like Brigham Young's, died young; reunion with the lost love of youth was much anticipated. Altogether, plural marriage was merely one part of a profound recasting of marriage and family in LDS theology. Three aspects, beyond polygamy, were especially significant. First, marriage was transformed from a civil ceremony to a religious one, in what one scholar has termed the "resacralization" of marriage. Even divorces could be decreed by church authorities. Mormons, like other Protestant dissenters, developed their own marriage ceremony, with groom and bride agreeing mutually to be permanent "companions" with the presence of an officiant, a member of the priesthood (always male but not a special clergyman). These ceremonies could take place in a house as well as in a sacred space such as the Temple (which eventually became the preferred location).[35]

Second, as Parley's statement about "time and all eternity" indicates, marriage became everlasting if done as a sealing by an authorized officiant. There could be marriages simply on earth ("for time"), but there could also be ones to those already gone or unconnected on earth ("for eternity"). Then there were marriages recognized both on earth and in heaven, for this life and thereafter ("for time and eternity"). Third, marriage became necessary for salvation, and indeed, as one scholar has framed it, the marriage rite itself "gave men and women rights to access heavenly powers." In his later years, Joseph Smith saw marriage as increasingly central to salvation and the spatial and rank organization of the celestial worlds. Marriage made both brides and grooms into "holy progenitors" and sanctified their offspring. Eternal, or celestial, marriage was a critical way of ensuring that a person achieved the highest level of "exaltation" in the afterlife. In this era, plural marriages were "the highest form of marriage, meriting the greatest glory among those exalted." In a rare written blessing from Joseph Smith on his sealing to Sarah Whitney in 1843, he promised that she should be crowned "with a diadem of glory in the Eternal worlds." Moreover, she and "also all her Fathers House Shall be Saved in the Same Eternal glory."[36]

Marriage then became a powerful marker of holiness, a way of gaining status in both this life and the next. This general recasting of marriage included plural marriage for men, who were exalted by marriages and children. Joseph Smith had been developing these ideas for years and became increasingly emboldened about sharing them with his inner circle in the early 1840s. However, the practice of polygamy remained secret (at least to the outside world) until 1852, when "the doctrine of a plurality of wives" was announced before "this enlightened assembly," a special conference of church elders in Utah. This doctrine was then published in a special edition of the church newspaper, the *Deseret News*. Following quarrels with his wife, Emma, Joseph received an important revelation. In chapter 132 of *Doctrine and Covenants*, the doctrine of celestial marriage took shape. According to this text, if men made marriage according to God's law, "then shall they be gods." This passage also upheld the examples of Old Testament polygamists: Abraham, Solomon, and David. Plural marriage's blessedness, and the necessity for wives to accept it, was not confined to ancient times, though. The revelation boomed: "I command mine handmaid, Emma Smith, to abide. . . . If she will not abide this commandment she shall be destroyed."[37]

Even before the public pronouncement of polygamy, the Saints had already faced much animosity. Driven out of Missouri, the Saints fled to Illinois, founding the town of Nauvoo in 1840. In Nauvoo, they built their Temple and their communities. In 1844, Joseph Smith was killed by a mob following his imprisonment in nearby Carthage, and Nauvoo, too, ceased to be a haven for them. By 1847–48, many headed to the Great Salt Lake Basin under Brigham Young's leadership. Rumors of polygamy and "the spiritual wife business" exacerbated the hostilities the Saints faced. Once in Utah, they built a new kind of society with communitarian principles and plural marriage. Although only one of the flashpoints for anti-Mormon sentiments, polygamy became an increasingly significant one, for two reasons. Externally, as we have seen, polygamy had for so long been connected with depravity, lawlessness, and despotism. Internally, it mattered more, as it helped to define rank among the Saints.

Joseph Smith's early death reinforced the importance of plural marriage. In addition to its theological centrality, polygamy also took on political and social significance. For men like Parley Pratt and others in the Quorum, plural marriage became a way to establish themselves as Smith's rightful heirs. Polygamy was here again largely the prerogative of high-ranking men. It was also how ambitious men proved their leadership credentials. There had been relatively few plural marriages beyond Smith before his death. Yet in the autumn of 1844, Parley, among others, went on a marriage spree, taking Mary Wood, Hannahette Snively, and Belinda Marden as wives in quick succession. Belinda and Parley first met in Boston, by 1844 if not before. The handbill she remembered might have been produced by him; he was on a mission in Boston in 1843. Belinda may have learned about polygamy even in Boston, as a few beyond Smith were practicing it by then.[38]

Belinda, along with Parley and his other wives, left Nebraska (near Winter Quarters) for Utah territory in June 1847, in the wagon company of Daniel Spencer and Peregrine Sessions Company. The nearly two hundred people, in seventy-five wagons, arrived in September 1847. Like most of these trips, it was not without its accidents and tragedies, with one child run over by a wagon and killed. Still, it was one of the less eventful ones, as the Sioux "Indians [were] numerous but friendly" along the way, with some of them "the moost genteel Indians I ever saw," according to one traveler. Parley Pratt led services. For Parley Jr., a boy at the time, the journey was challenging but fascinating, with "the novelty and bustle of camp life." When his father's wagon driving was dissipated between wives on the way, two of them, Belinda and Agatha, took up the reins and drove themselves and their children across the country.[39]

It's reasonably easy to understand why Parley might have wanted to adopt plural marriage; it's less easy to explain why Belinda was willing to do so. She was already legally married. From the perspective of Belinda and the LDS Church, however, she was very married to Parley, sealed for time and eternity, destined to be a mother of children and of the early church. She became one of the many Mrs. Pratts. From the perspective of the state, though, she became over the next few years an adulteress, the cuckolding Mrs. Hilton, cohabiting with an adulterer, and, eventually, the mother of bastards. Enemies of Mormons would have seen (indeed did see) her new husband as a wicked seducer, turning her head (and body) away from her rightful wifely duties. Why did this nice young New England woman choose such outrageous behavior? Her own words, published in 1854 after ten years of plural marriage, contain her answer.

"Polygamy Leads Directly to the Chastity of Women"

By January 1854, Belinda Pratt had been settled in Utah Territory for several years. She apparently wrote a letter to her sister in New Hampshire that year, published as a *Defence of Polygamy, by a Lady of Utah*. In 1854, Belinda was the sixth wife (and fifth living one) of Parley, mother of four children. The foremost expert on early Mormon pamphlets has noted: "It is curious that the most earthly defense of Mormon plural marriage was written by a woman."

Indeed it is, as sex and reproduction form key aspects of its analysis. "Mormon theology was never overburdened with otherworldliness. There was a fine robustness about it that smelled of the frontier." So observed one author some decades ago. Another, more recently, has framed early LDS attitudes more poetically: "They were much like other Americans who had their boots in prairie mud and their heads in the stars."[40] Belinda's treatise exemplifies these points.

Belinda's treatise was one of the most widely read defenses of Mormon polygamy. Parts were reprinted not just in the United States but in England, India, and Australia. It was even translated into French. One magazine, a critical "gentile"—non-Mormon—one, conceded that "Mrs. Belinda Pratt's 'Defence of Polygamy' is certainly an extraordinary ethical treatise, both in the subtilty of the argument, and the vigor of the diction." Belinda had received a disapproving letter from her sister Lydia on January 11, 1854, the story goes, and had sent her response by January 12, a timeline that seems unlikely for a lengthy, organized argument for plural marriage from a busy mother of four. Many female authors of this era couched their politics in the form of novels or firsthand accounts or letters. Even Sarah Grimké published her audacious tract as a series of letters to her sister. Choosing the epistolary form was a deliberate act. That Belinda presented herself carefully in writing is clear. Even her own autobiography admits as much. Her husband was one of the most prominent expositors of Mormonism in print in the nineteenth century. Both husband and wife knew how to publish a defense of polygamy by a lady in its most palatable form, designed to offer a woman's perspective without provoking offense. A letter between sisters was the obvious way to do so.[41]

It was shocking for an American to advocate publicly for polygamy. It was audacious for a woman to publish on sex and reproduction. For Belinda Pratt to do both meant that her printed text had to be framed very carefully indeed. The fretfulness of Margaret Fuller's friends demonstrates that most women shied away from such boldness. Making her treatise simply a letter to her sister allowed Pratt to include a range of provocative ideas, invoking a presumed female audience, as Fuller had done. In the pages of the *Boston Medical and Surgical Journal*, Mary Gove contended that there was "nothing objectionable or indelicate for one woman to tell another these important facts." Such "fictive privacy" in same-sex spaces allowed even elite women to discuss freely and frankly their bodies and their desires. In adopting the conceit of a letter to her sister, Belinda capitalized on the acceptability of women discussing such matters in spaces ostensibly limited to women.[42]

Pratt focused on four major justifications for polygamy: theological, natural, social, and familial. In each area, she stressed the experiences of women and to a lesser degree children in novel ways. She made standard Protestant arguments for polygamy, in a long line of thinking we have seen with John Miner and Martin Madan. She began with the example of Old Testament patriarchs such as Abraham and Jacob. She also included a standard Protestant denunciation of the clerical celibacy and enforced monogamy of the Catholic Church, which she termed "the result of 'Mystery Babylon,' the great whore of all the earth." So the "law of Rome . . . leaves females exposed to a life of single 'blessedness,' without husband, child, or friend . . . or to a life of poverty or loneliness." She contended that such laws "give rise to murder, infanticide, suicide, disease, remorse, despair, wretchedness, poverty, untimely death, with all the attendant train of jealousies, heartrending miseries, want of confidence in families, contaminating disease, etc."[43]

Yet there was a twist in Belinda Pratt's theology of polygamy: an emphasis on what became known as the "law of Sarah" and women's involvement. Every writer in the Protestant polygamous tradition pointed to the example of Old Testament patriarchs such as Abraham and Solomon, and Smith was no exception. *Doctrine and Covenants* 132 lays out the "law of Sarah," according to which the first wife was supposed to give permission for subsequent wives. This revelation was directed at the resistant Emma Smith, who did not approve polygamy. There was a loophole, in that a husband could take additional wives without adhering to this law if necessary: "Because she did not believe and administer unto him according to my word; and she then becomes the transgressor; and he is exempt from the law of Sarah." Nevertheless, the ideal was that existing wives would join in such decisions. Belinda Pratt emphasized Sarah's agency in instigating polygamy, noting that it had been Sarah's idea for Abraham to take her handmaid, Hagar, as his second wife. Pratt twice called the "honorable and virtuous" Sarah "a pattern for Christian ladies to imitate" because "the wife of a polygamist . . . encouraged her husband in the practice of the same, and even urged him into it, and officiated in giving him another wife." Sarah's importance in Old Testament polygamy, so that Abraham "hearkened" unto her, is innovative, as previous pro-polygamy writers had emphasized only the agency of the patriarchs.[44]

Belinda Pratt also focused on arguments from nature. For centuries, male writers such as Hume emphasized procreation in marriage and the propagation of the species. Such views find repetition in Belinda's tract: "Let us come to nature's law. What then appears to be the great object of the marriage relations? I answer: the multiplying of our species—the rearing and training of children." Increasing the population of the Saints was theologically significant. Promises of fruitfulness echo in *Doctrine and Covenants* 132: "Abraham received promises concerning his seed, and of the fruit of his loins . . . out of the world they should continue . . . as innumerable as the stars." One twentieth-century author contended controversially that early LDS Temple endowment ceremonies were "essentially fertility worship." Fruitfulness, exuberantly glorified even in family quilts, has been an enduring Mormon theme. Parley Pratt's own 1844 writings emphasized the benevolence of natural heterosexual affections, which became problematic only when twisted into vice: "From this union of affection [between man and woman], springs all the other relationships, social joys and affections. . . . Were it not for this, earth would be a desert wild, an uncultivated wilderness." The inhabitants of Sodom, he went on, were "not destroyed for their natural affection; but for the want of it. They had perverted all their affections, and had given place to that which was unnatural." He warned that the same was true "in the present age." Leaders in particular needed to direct their affections for positive good.[45]

Where earlier authors focused on men's sexual needs in polygamy, Belinda Pratt stressed instead those of women. She posited that "natural law would dictate, that a husband should remain apart from his wife at certain seasons." She continued that a mother knew that when she was pregnant, "her heart should be pure, her thoughts and affections chaste, her mind calm, her passions without excitement." She claimed that a "kind husband" would therefore not "subject [her] to anything calculated to disturb, irritate, weary, or exhaust" her, so "refrain[ing] from all those untimely associations which are forbidden in the great constitutional laws of female nature." In short, it was not right for a pregnant wife to have sex. "Polygamy," she averred, "leads directly to the chastity of women, and to sound health and morals in the constitution of their offspring."[46]

At one level, such arguments might seem simply an assertion that a pregnant wife not be wearied by a husband's sexual attentions. Yet the language implies that such intercourse would provoke a pregnant woman to become, in Belinda's terms, impure, unchaste, even excited. Even most radical men of her time referred to orgasms in starkly negative terms. Sylvester Graham fretted: "SEXUAL DESIRE . . . when it kindles into a passion . . . disturbs and disorders all the functions of the system." As for orgasm, Graham was equally suspicious of "this violent paroxysm" with "the tremendous violence of a tornado." He described it thus: "The powerfully excited and convulsed heart drives the blood, in fearful congestion, to the principal viscera,—producing oppression, irritation, debility, rupture, inflammation, and sometimes disorganization . . . generally succeeded by great exhaustion, relaxation, lassitude, and even prostration." John Humphrey Noyes was no less damning, recommending that men avoid orgasm altogether (he never seems to have considered that women might have them). "It cannot be injurious to refrain from furious excitement." He argued for the wisdom of avoiding that "reflex nervous action or ejaculatory crisis which expels the seed." In other words, both Graham and Noyes, men pilloried in their times as sex radicals, agreed that an orgasm was a disruptive crisis, certain to disturb, irritate, and exhaust. So did Belinda Pratt. Graham and especially Noyes, however, meant men's orgasms; she meant women's.[47]

Belinda Pratt's line of argument closely resembled that of the radical reformers Mary Gove and Thomas Nichols in their *Esoteric Anthropology*, which appeared in 1853, one year before Belinda's *Defence*. Mary Gove Nichols, whom we met earlier in her campaign against the "solitary vice," became an infamous proponent of free love, along with Thomas, whom she had married in 1848. Yet both of them worried over the effects of sexual excitement during pregnancy. The first part of their book, by Thomas, acknowledged women's sexual desires, as, for instance, during ovulation: "She is full of ardour, has a great capacity for enjoyment, and is seldom satisfied with a single sexual act." Yet he contended that sex, and especially "enjoyment," during pregnancy were deeply problematic for women and children: "It is the law of all nature . . . never to be violated *even among savages,* out of Christendom, that there should be no sexual union during gestation." He continued: "Sexual intercourse during pregnancy is a disturbance of that function and an injury to mother and child, especially if the female partakes of its enjoyment." His wife, Mary Gove Nichols, repeated these injunctions, in language similar to Belinda's: "Violent exercise of the body, or violent passions of the mind, tend to abortion and miscarriage." She contended that during pregnancy, the mother's "person should be sacred, her passions calm, her mind serene and full of peace and hope and happiness. No work should weary her, no anxiety disturb her, no lust excite or torment her."[48]

Like Mary and Thomas Nichols, Belinda Pratt recognized the power of female sexual desire, even while agreeing that sex during pregnancy—or at least women's enjoyment of it—should be limited, if not entirely eliminated. She thus argued, albeit in a muted way, for the right to bodily autonomy, for women's right to refuse sex at certain times. This impetus was not unconnected to new cultures of family planning, or to nineteenth-century ideas about how sexual indulgence, if too frequent, could mar the development of a fetus. Yet folded into this concern over fertility is also a surprising emphasis on female sexual satisfaction. When Pratt pointed to the laws of Rome, she similarly emphasized that single women would be "exposed to temptation; to perverted affections; to unlawful means to gratify them." These statements suggest that women indeed experienced temptations and sexual affections outside marriage, possibly even same-sex ones. Here is exceptional acknowledgment that women experienced sexual enjoyment: not what we would expect in a public tract from a nineteenth-century Mormon plural wife.[49]

Such arguments about "perverted affections" indicate a third line of analysis, polygamy's social benefits, a standard argument in pro-polygamy tracts. Earlier writers had declared: "Polygamy is in no way subversive of any of the good ends for which marriage was designed; either in family religion, family government, or the conveyance of property; but in some cases may and always would be, a benefit to some particular men." These writers had emphasized that polygamy would prevent "female ruin," seduction, and prostitution. Yet again Pratt emphasized the role of women. She celebrated what she termed "the Patriarchal order of family government." She asserted that "a nation" organized on such principles "would have no institutions tending to licentiousness; no adulteries, fornications." In such a nation, "wealthy men would have no inducement to keep a mistress in secret, or unlawfully. Females would have no grounds for temptation in any such lawless life." Instead, women would enjoy roles as wives and mothers "in some virtuous family, where love, and peace, and plenty, would crown her days."[50]

There is one final innovative turn here: a positive portrayal of relations between wives in ways that virtually never appear in earlier defenses of polygamy. Critics of Madan and others had argued that polygamy "would . . . confound all houshold peace and love." Even pro-polygamy writers imagined "the distractions which most probably *must* be the effect of jealousy between the women." In male-centered visions of polygamy, even positive ones, the assumption had long been that wives would inevitably suffer from jealousy and resentment. Belinda Pratt emphasized instead warm relations between wives based on shared mothering. She acknowledged that at this point, her loving husband had "seven other living wives, and one who has departed," as well as "upwards of twenty-five children." She noted that "all these mothers and children are endeared to me by kindred ties,—by mutual affection,—by acquaintance and association." She underscored the positive relations she had with the other wives as mothers: "the mothers in particular by mutual and long continued exercises of toil, patience, long-suffering sisterly kindness." Their shared labors as mothers made them sister-wives. She allowed that "we all have our imperfections in this life; but I know that these are good and worthy women."[51] Conceding that tensions existed, as she well knew from her own experience, she still focused on the affections in novel ways.

Belinda Pratt concentrated on what she termed the "family circle," as well as "kindred," phrases she used to describe both her family in New Hampshire and the Pratt household. She declared that she would not visit New Hampshire again until its laws against polygamy were "modified by enlightened legislation" and "the customs and consciences of its inhabitants, and of my kindred" were altered. (They never were.) Belinda Pratt signed her letter "with sentiments of the deepest affection and kindred feeling." In some sense, this conceit of a family letter allowed Mormons to connect themselves with the larger family of Americans, with whom they were linked by "kindred feeling." Mormon women such as Pratt wanted to win acceptance, or at least tolerance, from American authorities and in some cases, their own families. Yet were they willing to proceed without the blessings of "dear kindred" or the American nation, with its currently not very "enlightened legislation"? Of course they were. When had Belinda ever been stopped by convention or family?

"It Was a Divine Principle"

Why were women like Belinda willing to live in polygamy? She herself noted that on arrival in Nauvoo, she immediately "accepted all the revelations of God, Polygamy included." After hearing criticisms from other Saints, Belinda came to doubt the rightness of this system, but intervention from "a good sister" and President Young himself helped her recognize that "it was a divine principle." She concluded in her memoir: "Never from that time . . . has there been a doubt in my mind concerning it." Belinda's claims of initial horror giving away to sudden acceptance were common to many such memoirs.[52]

Belinda was convinced by many factors, including religious imperatives. LDS theology dictated that polygamy was a higher good: hard in this life but rewarding in the next, especially for husband-priests. Celestial marriage allowed a man to ascend to the highest echelons of heaven. Family life could continue after death. Belinda had lost at least one child. She had now found family for life and eternity, an abiding consolation. There were practical reasons, too, for her decision. Mobility was a major factor. Belinda had already sunk a lot into the decision to leave her family and flee to the Mormons. Even if she did not know of polygamy before her reckless flight, she learned of it in Nauvoo. By then, though, Mrs. Hilton had behaved scandalously, deserting her legal husband. Even just her trip, the train rides and the hotel nights, had tarnished her name in Boston. Was Mr. Hilton likely to forgive and forget? The answer, judging by later events, was negative. Her family of birth had declared her crazy for her beliefs; was she going to slink back and seek refuge with them, as they tutted "I told you so"? She was physically separated from her old life, a pariah in her former community.

Her new Mormon community was more welcoming, and less self-righteous, than her own family had been. In her new life, no one dismissed her as "too enthusiastic." She would have met other women, indeed Parley's other wives, who had also left their families of birth and joined this new family. There was a warm embrace for lost lambs like Belinda in Nauvoo, as the Saints worked to establish themselves, while mourning their slain leader. Parley and others were familiar and encouraging; the Saints bonded together in the face of attacks, from irate former husbands and other Americans. This solidarity unnerved non-Mormons. They blamed men like Parley for "sundering of family ties and connexions," seducing wives, daughters, and sisters away from their families of birth.[53] This contemporaneous criticism privileged male agency, but women like Belinda had their own reasons for converting to this new faith.

Belinda's trajectory raises the possibility that new systems of marriage might have appealed because current ones did not. After all, in monogamy, a bad husband could "tyrannize" all the more. That house in Boston had been an unhappy one. We lack Benjamin's perspective. He might have been an otherwise pleasant husband chagrined by his wife's religious commitments, or he might have been a terror. Much later, when Parley married another woman with a violent husband, he wrote to Belinda, "She is the very counter part of your self. . . . She is groaning under a bondage tenfold more terrible, & hard to break than yours once was. . . . She has sworn the peace against a tyrant who rules with a rod of Iron." Such a claim, neatly reversing the idea that polygamous husbands were the tyrants, suggests that while Benjamin was not murderously abusive, he nevertheless kept his wife in "bondage." There is no record that Benjamin and Belinda ever officially divorced. Belinda asserted later, "My husband Mr. Hilton obtained a divorce from me by the false swearing of apostates." This assertion is a strange one; by November 1844, she was cohabiting with the already married Parley. In this case, Benjamin could have obtained a divorce on the basis of her adultery. There would be no need for "false swearing." Parley's allusion to "bondage," along with scandals stemming from a subsequent trip Belinda and Parley made together to New York in late 1845, suggest that Benjamin did not let her go without a fight.[54]

Belinda's experience of monogamy had not been especially positive, which may have made polygamy seem more tolerable. For her, monogamy had brought tyranny. Having a good husband part-time might have seemed preferable to having a bad one full-time. Belinda's particular choice was also a form of birth control for her. Her husband had thirty children. Her mother had fourteen. She had five. Of course others had different trajectories, but still these numbers mattered. In the early nineteenth century, many American women sought, more successfully than had previously been the case, to space out births; polygamy was one way to do this. Perhaps some polygamous wives were not dupes or victims but pragmatists.[55]

Yet Belinda, and many women like her, were willing to accept polygamy in part because marriage remained so vital. Like most Americans in this period, marriage seemed the bedrock of both individual and social happiness, the best way to order life, family, and society, the "sine qua non" of women's existence, as Grimké had phrased it. Belinda was no exception. LDS celestial marriage was a system in which marriage was abidingly transcendent. Belinda's desire for marriage here, shared with many, found fulfillment in a theology of marriage: as a means of rising through the ranks and shaping family and community, in both this life and the next. Polygamous marriage privileged households and sociability.

Plural marriage was also a form of domestic organization that went hand in hand with more liberal policies in keeping with a reformist impulse. Mormons instituted generous divorce policies, and wives frequently instigated these divorces. If Mormons had not practiced polygamy but had initiated their own marriage ceremonies beyond the state, liberalized divorce laws, published tracts by women acknowledging female health and desires, and enacted female suffrage remarkably early—all of which they did in fact do—early Mormonism would have a very different reputation. That early Mormons are not generally so remembered is testament to how powerful antipolygamy was, and is. Polygamy remained a male privilege, central to men's patriarchal prerogatives in both this life and the afterlife. This was a very different solution to the perceived limitations of marital monogamy. Nevertheless, it stemmed from at least some shared impulses. Even the sex radical Noyes had worried over the "carnal mind" and eternal salvation.[56]

In her treatise, Belinda acknowledged both sides of what has become an enduring debate about the relationship of LDS women and polygamy. Was it a source of oppression or liberation for women? It was both; in other words, it was marriage. Polygamous marriage, like monogamy, constrained, yet it also afforded spaces for pursuits of happiness. The plural marriage system became more conservative once the Saints settled in Utah; adopting polygamy in that first generation was a different and more controversial decision than inheriting polygamy from mothers and fathers, which entrenched its more patriarchal aspects. For women in this first raw generation, polygamy with easier access to divorce against monogamy for life with limited possibility for divorce might have looked like the safer bet, and a reasonable way to limit childbearing. Yet it was also a system of patriarchal control and "male supremacy," not conducive to anything like full equality, even as there were lines that connected Belinda Pratt with reformers like Margaret Fuller.[57]

Marriage to Parley could be challenging, of course, but often in ways that monogamous marriages also were. His wives had to rely on a husband who did not always make sound financial decisions, who did not always prioritize family over other endeavors, and who was away a lot. Lydia Maria Child knew such problems firsthand; so did Belinda Pratt. The diffusion of Parley's finances and time across so many wives and children exacerbated those challenges, and there was the problem of jealousy. Still, Parley's letters "fizz" with romantic ardor. On his many missions, he sent letters home—some to individual wives, some with a paragraph for each wife—in which he flirted and cajoled and joked and longed. Writing to Belinda on a transatlantic voyage in 1846, he concluded: "What would I not give for one glance at my family Circle, one Sweet word—one kiss—or even a Single line to Say that you live. . . . —O Cruel fate. But Hush this Repining—you *live*, and you will live eternally—you *love*—and you will always *Love* . . . well I am happy." At the end of the voyage, he declared: "O My *Dear*—*Dear* Belinda! Shall I ever See you again?—Will the Light of those eyes, and the Smiles of that joyous Countinance again Smile upon me? Will that Sweet voice ever again Greet me and those arms—that swelling Bosom and beating heart again welcome me to my home? O the joy would be so Great."[58]

Parley's letters to his "lambs" envisioned wives pulled into laps, eyes lit up with delight, and an awful lot of "good sweet kiss[es]." Visitors noted that Parley had no hangdog shame about polygamy, one remarking on his ease at introducing five of his wives, including a "Boston divorcée." The visitor concluded: "What a spectacle, and that, too, in our own country!" Parley's epistles also show no compunction about wooing each wife in front of the others. There was so much of Parley's energetic love to go around! John Humphrey Noyes would have understood: "Men and women find universally, (however the fact may be concealed,) that their susceptibility to love is not burnt out by one honey-moon, or satisfied by one lover. On the contrary, the secret history of the human heart will bear out the assertion that it is capable of loving any number of times and any number of persons, and that the more it loves the more it can love. This is the law of nature, thrust out of sight, and condemned by common consent, and yet secretly known to all."[59]

Parley's wives did not enjoy anything like the liberties he did, and there were hard feelings, often as much about finances and labor as about anything else. Plenty of plural wives had worse experiences, with husbands and other wives. Still, the practice of polygamy could take many forms. If each wife lost some of Parley's attention, she gained relations with other wives and children. Some of these kinds of relations were familiar to nineteenth-century blended marriages following the death of a spouse; indeed, Belinda became a devoted mother to Nephi, Parley's oldest son with his deceased first wife, Thankful. The exigencies of childcare, borrowing, and sharing of goods and services meant that while each wife had some autonomy, she was also part of a broader network. There were positive as well as negative aspects to this system.[60]

"What a Spectacle, and That, Too, in Our Own Country!"

Most Americans were not ready to accept polygamy. Indeed, it cost Parley his life in a national scandal, one of the most dramatic polygamy-related crimes of the century. Like Belinda, his last wife, Eleanor McComb McLean, endured an unhappy marriage to a man who rejected the Saints. Parley had met Eleanor while on a mission in San Francisco. Her husband, Hector, apparently an alcoholic whom she had already taken to court for domestic assault, was less forgiving than Benjamin Hilton, a situation worsened by the presence of children whom Hector did not wish to lose—or at least did not wish Eleanor to have. Hector was determined to end what he saw as his wife's adultery with a wicked seducer. Hector chased Eleanor around the country, charged her with kidnapping his children when she fled with them in terror, and finally took the law into his own hands. In 1857, Hector killed Parley, shooting him, stabbing him, and shooting him again. Hector was acquitted of murder by a local court in Arkansas, who thought his actions justified by adultery. The case made headlines nationally, and this news probably reached Benjamin Hilton, who had lost his own wife to Parley Pratt. He might have agreed grimly with an earlier assessment of an antipolygamy newspaper: "The poison of thine own corruptions which destroyed so many is now upon thee." Many Americans agreed, seeing such violence as the natural outcome of polygamy. The Saints saw the event as proof of yet more virulent anti-Mormonism.

For all its national resonance, Parley's death was also a domestic crisis. Parley left nine widows ranging in age from twenty-seven to forty-five. He had struggled financially for years, and many of the wives already contributed to the family economy. His death made this situation only more challenging; thirty children were left. Yet only three widows, one of them Belinda, married again, and all three marriages ended unhappily. Belinda married Thomas Box as his second wife in 1858, but had ended the marriage by 1870. Nevertheless, Parley's widows in Utah remained committed Mormons there. Parley's presence remained indelible. Belinda remembered Parley fondly; on May 13, 1881, she noted in her diary that it was "the 24th Anniversary" of his death.[61]

There were two former wives, though, who did not remain part of the larger household even in this life. Polygamy in Utah featured wives who stayed as well as ones who left. By the time of Parley's death, two wives had already departed. His second wife, Mary Anne, the one who had to move from monogamy to polygamy in 1844, never embraced that transition. It took many years of increasing unhappiness, but she divorced him in 1853. That shift to polygamy was a particularly awkward one for many, including notably Emma Smith, for understandable reasons.[62] In 1849, another wife, Martha, also departed the Pratt household—and Utah and Mormonism altogether.

The flight of this unhappy wife prompted a series of conflicting stories; we do not, alas, have her own account. We do know that in January 1849, Martha had a son, who died a month later. Other wives had given birth in 1848, so it may have been especially painful to suffer this loss in a larger household full of thriving infants. Parley blamed her flight on another man. He recorded in family papers that she had been "seduced" by a lapsed Mormon, who had lured her into "prostitution and elopement to the gold mines with unprincipled men." Other tales, by enemies of Mormonism, linked Martha's disappearance with the polygamy of Wakara and the Utes, who also reportedly traded in "the slavery and merchandise of women . . . the usual attendant of polygamy." One visitor to Utah contended that "some of the [LDS] elders, who have been best supplied with wives, have disposed of the superfluous to Indian chiefs, or half-breeds . . . for a valuable consideration in horses, furs, or other articles of ready merchandise." The same author asserted that Parley had traded "one or two" wives for "a fine stud of horses," on which he had "made a handsome speculation." Another visitor went into further details: Parley's "house was somewhat over-stocked with wives, and as they are a species of property here, having a marketable value, it occurred to him that he might drive a good bargain with Walker, the Indian chief." In this narrative, Parley offered to trade one wife for ten horses, a proposal readily accepted. However, supposedly, in the time it took for this bargain to be concluded, Martha, "the inmate of his harem chosen for this exchange," was hideously and quickly transformed by her own agony at having been so traded away. So when Martha, drawn and red-eyed, was brought to Wakara, he rejected her with disgust, supposedly remarking, in offensive pidgin: "Me no want old white s—w."[63]

The supposed sale of a rosy-cheeked English wife to an unruly, ill-spoken "savage" was proof of how problematic Mormonism was. Historians have emphasized how polygamy made Mormons seem racially other to white Americans in the nineteenth century. Yet as we have seen, antipolygamy was already a powerful racial shorthand, neatly to be imposed on the Mormons. This continuous loop linked Turks, Indians, Africans, and Mormons in stories such as the ones about Martha Pratt: she lived in a harem and was traded by a Mormon elder to an Indian chief. This conflation emphasized male power run amok. Mormons and savages treated wives as property, with "marketable value," thus exploiting women out of an unholy combination of lust and greed.[64]

Polygamy "belongs now to the indolent and opium-eating Turks and Asiatics, the miserable Africans, the North American savages, and the Latter-Day Saints," declared one of its fiercest critics, Benjamin Ferris. He described polygamy as "the offspring of lust" leading to "the rapid degeneracy of races." There could never be true affection or respect in polygamy: love was only lust. As one historian has observed, "Mormons and Indians disrupted Anglo-American assumptions about how settlement should occur and who should benefit from it. Unlike Native societies, however, Mormonism developed out of the heart of Anglo-American cultures and religion and operated as a sort of shadow critique, which is why it upset people so much."[65]

How was it that people like Parley and his wives could embrace a form of marriage associated with Turks, Africans, and "savages"? Explanations for this seemingly inexplicable choice had to circle around the husband's lust, greed, and moral turpitude, and the exploitation and victimization of women. To link Mormon polygamy with the slavery of women in Ute cultures was to make these connections crystal clear. Yet Parley Pratt did not trade his wife for horses; Wakara probably had a wife or wives who ran a household with authority, though he also had suffering chore wives from different nations. As we have seen, Ute polygamy was itself hardly the timeless phenomenon it seemed to nineteenth-century American authors. These forms of plural marriage were distinct. So too were Turkish, Asian, and African versions. Conflating them was a facile but powerful way to dismiss them all.

A few decades earlier, feminists had argued that all wives were like slaves; by the 1850s, polygamy became a useful tool for the reinterpretation of monogamy. Now plural wives, not monogamous ones, were the slaves. These wife-slaves were Mormon, Indian, Asian, and African. To transform a gender-based critique into one which emphasized instead racial and religious difference was, implicitly, to valorize Christian monogamy as the only acceptable form of marriage, one that preserved whiteness and civility. Women authors' antipolygamy can seem progressive, but in fact there were conservative and regressive aspects. In loudly denouncing polygamy, they were quietly celebrating monogamy as it currently existed, which included the loss of property and even identity for women in many, if not most, states.[66] Antipolygamy, while feminist in some respects, also separated some women from others.

Antipolygamy was also pro-government. Images of greedy, lustful husbands and duped wives did a lot of powerful political work. In exposing the infrastructure of monogamy, these tropes did more than make Mormons into a racial "other," though they certainly did this. They showed why Mormons, like Indians, Africans, and Asians, needed to be forced into monogamy. They also celebrated the rightness of monogamous marriage and the power of the government to enforce it. The government forced adherents of a religion to renounce its theological principles, articulated, espoused, and practiced by its founder and great prophet. Radicalism in marriage matters would not be tolerated. Many Americans preferred to reject polygamists altogether as somehow controlled only by lust and greed, or else duped and forced, unable to give fair consent. For many Americans, polygamists deserved everything they got. Their flaws in marriage practices required the strong arm, even the iron fist, of government power, whether from federal, state, or territorial authorities. Even many Southerners and Northerners, for all their bitter discord, could agree on the need for intervention to stop polygamists.[67]

The federal state, in ridding the land of what many saw as "barbarism," colonized a lot in fifty years from 1840 to 1890; marriage had a significant role in these alterations. One 1850s critic of the Mormons imagined future changes: "We may confidently expect that the Mormons of a hundred years hence will be very different from those of to-day, and that future generations will redeem, in some *degree* the errors of the past and present." The church did come to renounce what most saw as its greatest error: plural marriage. It did so after a series of powerful government initiatives. These campaigns, while horrifying to Mormons and others, were nothing like so violent and vicious as those against Native Americans in the same period. Mormons were not massacred as Indians were.[68]

Still, in a campaign waged in press, courts, and prisons, the United States showed just how far it was willing to go to end polygamy in Utah Territory. Throughout the 1850s and beyond, books, newspapers, magazines, and speeches cast Mormon polygamy as irredeemably problematic and backward. Political theorists laid claim to the foundational nature of monogamy for the nation and even the race. The theorist Francis Lieber argued against admitting Utah into the Union in 1855. He noted that the Mormons, practicing polygamy, went far beyond the "book speculation" of pro-polygamy men like Martin Madan. For Lieber, as for many others, monogamy extended from religion into race. As Lieber phrased it, "It is one of the elementary distinctions . . . between European and Asiatic humanity . . . one of the pre-existing conditions of our existence as civilized white men. . . . Strike it out, and you destroy our very being, and when we say *our*, we mean our race." A civilized republic ruled by honorable white men could not allow polygamy.[69]

Soon political action followed. Four major acts of Congress—the Morrill Act of 1862, the Poland Act of 1874, the Edmunds Act of 1882, and the Edmunds-Tucker Act of 1887—kept escalating penalties in order to deprive LDS polygamists of rights and property, to force a shift in church policy, and to demonstrate the power of the federal government. Court cases did the same, most notably the 1879 decision in *Reynolds v. the United States*, which declared that polygamy, threatening to civilization itself, was so incompatible with the American republic that they could not coexist. This decision emphasized the vital importance of marriage to social and political stability: "Upon it society may be said to be built, and out of its fruits spring social relations and social obligations and duties with which government is necessarily required to deal." Polygamy existed only in systems of "despotism." Building on the theories of Lieber and others, the Court declared that "Polygamy has always been odious among the northern and western nations of Europe, and, until the establishment of the Mormon Church, was almost exclusively a feature of the life of Asiatic and of African people."[70] Polygamy's "odiousness" was fundamental, incontrovertible, in the blood.

According to many, then, polygamists were inherently barbaric and despotic, unassimilable in the republic of white men voters. If they would not give up polygamy voluntarily, then the federal government would force them to do so. In the 1880s many Mormon leaders were locked up in federal prisons as "cohabs," guilty of cohabiting with other women (which is how polygamy could be prosecuted by law). Wives and children were left without heads of household, and many families faced deprivation due to heavy fines. Two further court decisions in 1890 made the church's position even more untenable. One Idaho ruling disenfranchised not just actual polygamists but anyone who advocated its acceptability. Even believing in the rightness of polygamy could spell trouble: shades of John Miner and his disputes in Connecticut! Another decision, *Late Corporation of the Church of Jesus Christ of Latter-day Saints v. United States*, also added fuel to the flames.

It upheld the seizure of church (as well as personal) property of those who practiced polygamy and thus "return[ed] to barbarism." In desperation, LDS president Wilford Woodruff issued a "manifesto," placed in *Doctrine and Covenants*, formally agreeing to follow federal law. He conceded: "My advice to the Latter-day Saints is to refrain from contracting any marriage forbidden by the law of the land."[71] Many did refrain, but plenty did not, as far from all Saints agreed with this decision.

"The Government of the United States is great and powerful." So conceded Belinda in a speech from early 1879 at the beginning of the concerted national campaign to end polygamy in the territory. Federal power followed a culture war over polygamy, as well as one of who should rule in the West. Ideas and practices of marriage were deeply woven into these contests over authority in the West—and elsewhere. Marriage was *the* central problem for Utah Territory. Belinda continued, defiantly, "But He who rules above is greater . . . though all Nations should Legislate against it yet he will . . . bring to naught all their plans and schemes." Belinda was an organizer and a campaigner to the end of her days. She became president of the Millard Stake Relief Society, the women's organization of the LDS Church, and she publicly denounced the "Antipolygamy crusade." She derided as "enemies" those who would "deprive us of our rights as Citizens Wives Mothers and children," looking to the Constitution to protect those rights. She thus claimed her citizenship, as a plural wife and supporter of plural marriage. She revisited these themes in a Pioneer Day Speech in 1885. Like many other Mormon women, she worked to preserve plural marriage. A series of extraordinary alterations over nearly fifty years, from her 1844 flight to the 1890 renunciation of polygamy, had transformed her world profoundly. Throughout most of this time, and right up to her death, she supported the principle of plural marriage.[72]

For Belinda, it had not always been easy, but she had managed to "get along alright." She had found a new religion and with it, a new family circle. She became a grandmother, a stalwart member of her ward and her relief society. Still, Belinda did not forget that once she had been an unhappy young woman in flight, who had left her marriage without "one thought I was doing wrong." She defied convention, law, and her own husband, seeking something better out west. She even took up the reins to drive herself and her family to Utah. Settling there in a domestic configuration that shocked the world, some young women like Belinda evidently found contentment or at least a system they defended. Others, like the unnamed young Paiute woman whom we met in the previous chapter, shed silent tears as they embarked on their journeys in the West. Leaving no direct testimony themselves, their own painful domestic trajectories were recorded only in passing by uneasy witnesses. Yet both kinds of stories are relevant to the history of polygamy, that "relic of barbarism," as well as to the history of the United States. In celebrating her defiance in her memoirs in the 1880s, the fifth Mrs. Pratt preserved them and so defended her choices and her claims to citizenship. She had already emphasized her autonomy and choices in 1854, boldly and unexpectedly centering women and their desires in her defense of polygamy. There is indeed power in language.

Conclusion

Nestled between the snowy Wasatch Front and the placid waters of Utah Lake, Provo seems one of the most peaceful landscapes in the United States. The "disorders of love" hardly appear to ripple the serenity of this tidy city, Utah's second largest. Provo is the site of the largest LDS Missionary Training Center in the world, as well as Brigham Young University. Mitt Romney, former U.S. presidential candidate and great-great-grandson of Parley P. Pratt and his fourth wife, Mary Wood, is one of its better-known graduates. The Honor Code at BYU "emphasizes being honest, living a chaste and virtuous life, abstaining from alcohol and tobacco, using clean language, and following other values in line with the doctrines of the Church of Jesus Christ of Latter-day Saints." Many of Provo's wholesome residents agree with such principles. Of those who identified their religion in the most recent census, 98 percent were Latter-day Saints. The BYU code does not mention same-sex physical relations, but they, too, are forbidden. Indeed, a flier for a 2018 campus event, the first of its kind publicly to discuss "same-sex attraction," was apparently altered from rainbow to blue at the behest of administrators.[1] At BYU, rainbows might be considered a little outrageous.

Still, Provo's current gleaming conformity does not tell the whole story. In its shadows lurks a disorderly history of domesticity. One of its former residents and graduates of the Brigham Young Academy High School there, Annie Tanner Clark, had lived polygamy herself: as a child of plural marriage and as a plural wife. She and her already-married husband had lived partly in hiding in the 1880s, during the federal crackdown on plural marriages. Writing her twentieth-century autobiography long after the Latter-day Saints had officially renounced polygamy, she pondered how it was that the church could give up polygamy, which had so shaped her own life. She agreed that it was better for the church to "work with the government of our country than against it," noting her "relief" at the 1890 Manifesto. She also conceded that "volumes could be written about the struggles of polygamy," and women's "great sacrifice" in it. Nevertheless, she had herself remained a plural wife even after 1890: "It did not occur to me, for one minute, to give [it] up. . . . I was happily married." Even in her autobiography, she did not entirely condemn the system. She claimed, "I developed an independence that women in monogamy would never know." Moreover, "No one could make the women of Utah feel that they had an inferior position." This thoughtful Mormon mother, who worked hard to support her children after the end of her marriage and the death of her husband, pondered how it was that Christians could account for such dramatic change. Like many a Protestant considering the vexing example of saintly polygamous ancestors, she could not help but wonder: "Is God 'the same yesterday, today, and forever?'" Still, she took comfort in rainbows: "With so much joy and gratitude I admired the rainbow as it extended across the eastern mountains . . . remembering, as I did, the covenant that the Lord had made to ancient Israel that the rainbow is a sign the Lord will not destroy the earth again with a flood."[2]

Rainbows look especially striking across the high mountains near Provo, a city that was of course founded by polygamous Latter-day Saints. In 1875, Brigham Young, America's most famous polygamist of his day, announced that the Provo branch of the University of Deseret would become the Brigham Young Academy. Such marks the official founding of BYU. One of its first students was Reed Smoot, the son of a Mormon leader and his fifth wife, and later a senator. Brigham Young's divorce to Ann Eliza Young was confirmed in the same year; in 1876, she published a scandalous six hundred–page exposé of polygamy in Young's household, *Wife Number 19*. Her account linked polygamy, violence, and tyranny in ways now familiar. She dismissed Utah Territory: "Between Blood-Atonement, Massacres of the Gentiles, and the worst phases of Polygamous Marriage, there was nothing good in the Territory." She condemned Provo in particular as "one of the most powerful of all the Mormon strongholds in Utah," riven by "many deeds of violence."[3]

Violence had indeed long marked the area. Provo's name comes from Étienne Provost, a French-Canadian who became a notable fur trapper of the

West. Ambition drove men like Provost to travel and trap and trade in these western mountains; these men, celebrated in later histories as "wild mountain men" and "beaver men," were the vanguard of colonialism. Their presence transformed the people and the ecologies of the very mountains themselves before settlers had arrived. These *coureurs de bois,* as the French called them, were "wild," too, in their domestic lives. Provost came out of a milieu in which such traders often married more than one Native woman, *à la façon du pays.* Such marriages carried considerable political and economic weight, as they gave these traders vital access to networks of trade among Native American communities. The fur trade in North America depended on these networks, and on the marriages and métissage forged from them. Women and men were central to this fur trade activity, as they had been for centuries.[4]

Yet the naming of this space for this French-Canadian trapper was an exclusionary act itself. It deliberately obscured the presence of the people who had lived there longest: Native Americans. Provo began as Fort Utah, an outpost in what then nominally belonged to Mexico (and earlier Spain), a small perch on a landscape actually dominated by indigenous people. Plural marriages underpinned the Indian communities on the shores of Utah Lake itself. Utes in the area practiced polygamy, as did many others, such as Paiutes. Captive women were often incorporated into households as wives, and leaders, including the notorious Walker, were noted polygamists. Yet the forms of polygamy they practiced themselves had shifted under colonial pressures and violence. Many forms of plural marriages, then, have existed in what is now Provo. The Franciscan friars who traveled there in the 1770s found men with multiple wives, and they preached against it. Carrying with them the reformist impulses of the Catholic Reformation, such missionaries saw plural marriage as an embarrassment as well as a grave sin against a Christian God. Monogamy was a necessity for a Christian people, one of the many ways in which heathen could, indeed must, become godly.

Monogamous heterosexual marriage as the only form of allowable marriage was one of the legacies of colonial conquest. Still, marriage palimpsests glimmer throughout what is now the United States: in Florida as in Utah, in New Mexico as in Illinois. Other cities and landscapes with a history of polygamy, including those in Canada and Mexico, echo in this tumultuous past. Many North Americans, more than is usually recognized— including even the two major U.S. presidential candidates of 2012—are descended from polygamists, though few wish to celebrate or even admit it.[5]

Like it or not, plural marriages are part of American history, its colonial past as well as its extraordinary diversity. Multihued layers of marital regimes cram North American history, welling up from the choices, both intimate and public, of women and men of all sorts. Gender and domestic decisions have underpinned the history of these confrontations in profound and abiding ways. Ideas about what women and men should do, and how they should marry and procreate, have also been central to that history, as have their practices, even if textbooks and timelines have not always made that centrality clear. The complicated, conflicted histories of even seemingly harmonious places like Provo demonstrate that the imposition of one kind of marital regime on all kinds of people was, and is, the product of many centuries, and many battles, in colonial and imperial settings. Such is a story of shifting powers of nations and empires as much as individuals. This trajectory reveals the most intimate dynamics in households as well as the most world-transforming confrontations between them. Those who argued for lifelong heterosexual monogamy have denounced, punished, and expelled those who disagreed with their vision.

Perversions abounded in early America. One of the most fundamental of them was the way in which the violence of colonialism altered the most intimate of human relations. Such is why consideration of "love in settler colonies" elucidates the very nature of hegemony and the processes of colonialism more broadly. The political significance of marriage comes clear in the complicated intersections of cultures and their gender and domestic regimes. I have offered arguments about the ways in which the stories about polygamy have functioned to secure state power, to make race and religion, to justify brutal treatment of deviance, to ensure that "they" and "us" appeared always distinct. Even when, indeed especially when, polygamy has been sidelined, its marginalization, connected with race and religion and rank, has been significant. Casting polygamy into a prehistory, a lower level of civilization, has done a great deal of vital political work; it still does.

What if we, like that Taos woman who argued for marriage "as in their heathenism," started to notice that infrastructure of monogamy, even to question its power? Would we all go up in a puff of smoke? Would civilization as we know it come to a screeching halt? It seems unlikely. Although polygamy, like other forms of marriage, has historically oppressed women, should we continue to assume that any configuration of marriage beyond one plus one would, too? Feminist and other scholars have suggested it might not, that polygamy is not, as even John Cotton might have allowed, intrinsically defiling. This book is not a polemic for polygamy, and the forms of it that exist today are on the whole deeply troubling. Still, many of the staunchest defenders of exclusive monogamy in the past seem rather strange and not very pleasant bedfellows these days.[6]

Tales about monogamy, its progressive qualities, and polygamy, its regressive ones, have become part of modern understandings, but it may be time to push past them. Native Americans and West Africans were no more always clinging to tradition than Euro-Americans were always creative innovators. Polygamy has often taken the form of innovative traditionalism, as people have invoked its ancient qualities even as they pursued novel kinds of social and political orders. Polygamists could be modern, with newfangled visions of the necessity of happiness and love in marriage, satisfying mutuality in sexual relations, affections to children paramount. They could also prioritize the wishes of the spouses and communities themselves, rejecting the authority of "our religion and our State" to decree what counted as a real marriage. Monogamists could cling to tradition, invoking ancient pasts, marriage's time-out-of-mind quality. To accept a limited vision of what marriage looks like is also to let the state decide on the most intimate choices.[7]

In colonial and postcolonial contexts, to love, to marry, and to divorce have sometimes been revolutionary acts. Many individuals and families have lived marriage outside the state, or questioned the way the state regulated marriage, or ignored legal niceties about their relationships, or even suggested that the authority of state and church in regulating marriage be overturned. This is an alternative tale of marriage. Such acts preceded the nation, and they also shaped the nation. The nation-state grew stronger, but there was always pushback against it. In a great variety of circumstances, women and men subverted the imposition of a single view of what constituted an acceptable household. Gender, as well as race and rank, informed these colonial encounters. Relations between women, and between men, have been as critical to the history of polygamy as those between women and men. Women suffered exploitation in both polygamy and monogamy. Yet they also found benefits in both, at least sometimes. They also had agency in shaping marriage regimes and choices, even if sometimes in painfully constrained ways. They read and thought and wrote about polygamy; they also lived it. Both kinds of activities made a difference to the nature of these American confrontations and to ideas and practices of marriage.

That American marriage palimpsests remain obscure, in our understandings and also too often in our histories, is testament to the power of those who sought to impose, for reasons both noble and ignoble, a single marriage regime. It shows the embedded power of the infrastructure of monogamy. These inherited and too often unquestioned structures of marriage, gender, and sexuality remain with us. It is challenging but important to think harder about them, to move beyond the binaries and pairings. The unexpected lightning zigzags of this tale also undermine notions of simple progress from barbarity to civility, from oppression to liberation, from colonies to nation.[8] Our jagged, colorful history, made by all kinds of women and men in a variety of configurations, cannot be contained in such straight black-and-white lines. To examine contests over marriage is to appreciate the glittering richness of our pasts—and, perhaps, our futures.

Notes

Introduction

1. Alonso de Benavides, *Memorial que Fray Ivan de Santander de la Orden de san Francisco, Comissario General de Indias, presenta a la Magestad Catolica del rey don Felipe Quarto nuestro Señor* (Madrid: Imprenta Real con Licencia, 1630), 32–33. There are three English translations: Alonso de Benavides, *The Memorial of Fray Alonso de Benavides, 1630,* trans. Mrs. Edward E. Ayer, annotated by Frederick Webb Hodge and Charles Fletcher Lummis (Chicago: privately printed, 1916); Fray Alonso de Benavides, *Benavides' Memorial of 1630,* trans. Peter P. Forrestal, C.S.C., with introduction and notes by Cyprian J. Lynch (Washington, DC: Academy of American Franciscan History, 1954), 28; and Alonso de Benavides, *A Harvest of Reluctant Souls: The Memorial of Fray Alonso de Benavides,* trans. and ed. Baker H. Morrow (Niwot: University Press of Colorado, 1996), 31–32. This episode is briefly discussed in Ramón A. Gutiérrez, *When Jesus Came, the Corn Mothers Went Away: Marriage, Sexuality, and Power in New Mexico, 1500–1846* (Stanford, CA: Stanford University Press, 1991), 73–74.

2. Benavides, *Memorial que Fray Ivan de Santander,* 32–33. On conflicting interpretations, Elsie Clews Parsons notes: "Inferences from miracles are rarely identical." Pueblo Indians of a later period, especially those in Taos, evidently regarded lightning deaths as a sign of righteousness, and thought "upright" leaders would become lightning themselves. Parsons, *Pueblo Indian Religion,* two vols. (Chicago: University of Chicago Press, 1939), I: 43, 170–71.

3. "RUMOR," *Voree Herald,* May 1846, vol. 1, no. 5.

4. Polygamy is a system of marriage in which one person, whether man or woman, has more than one spouse. Polygyny means one husband has multiple wives. These terms are used interchangeably here, as most early American polygamy was polygyny. There were occasional instances of a woman having multiple husbands—polyandry—but very few.

5. I use the full term, Church of Jesus Christ of Latter-day Saints, where feasible. In keeping with many church institutions, including, for instance, the *Journal of Mormon History*, I also use Mormon and LDS. I do not mean to show disrespect, but the full title is unwieldy and also confusing to some outsiders.

6. "Republican Party Platform of 1856," June 18, 1856, *The American Presidency Project*, University of California, Santa Barbara, online at http://www .presidency.ucsb.edu/ws/index.php?pid=29619.

7. Both Daniel T. Reff and Baker Morrow emphasize Benavides' personal and Franciscan ambitions. Reff, "Contextualizing Missionary Discourse: The Benavides *Memorials* of 1630 and 1634," *Journal of Anthropological Research* 50, no. 1 (1994): 51–67, 53, 59, 61, and Morrow, "Introduction," in Benavides, *A Harvest of Reluctant Souls*, xi.

8. On Münster, see R. Po-Chia Hsia, "Münster and the Anabaptists," in *The German People and the Reformation*, ed. R. Po-Chia Hsia, 50–69 (Ithaca, NY: Cornell University Press, 1988), and Lyndal Roper, *Oedipus and the Devil: Witchcraft, Sexuality, and Religion in Early Modern Europe* (London: Routledge, 1994), ch. 4.

9. Herman von Kerssenbrock, *Narrative of the Anabaptist Madness: The Overthrow of Münster, the Famous Metropolis of Westphalia*, trans. Christopher S. Mackay, 2 vols. (Leiden: Brill, 2007), 2: 597, 580.

10. Ibid., 2: 493, 494.

11. Leo Miller, *John Milton among the Polygamophiles* (New York: Loewenthal, 1974), 50.

12. Both Jewish and Muslim law attempted to ensure equal treatment for wives and children in plural marriages, and such marriages were usually a minority. Muslim law allowed up to four wives; only elites could afford such arrangements. Some Jewish plural marriages stemmed from an injunction for levirate marriage, in which a brother assumed responsibilities for his brother's widow by marrying her. There was not complete accord; Ashkenazi Jews ended polygamy around 1000, while Sephardic Jews continued the practice. Initially, for Christians in the early common era, exclusive monogamy was less about Christianity per se than about ancient Greco-Roman preferences. In the first centuries of the common era, civil Roman law and Christian teachings merged, but the Western Church did not prohibit polygamy (as a breach of canon law) until the thirteenth century. John Witte, Jr., *The Western Case for Monogamy over Polygamy* (Cambridge: Cambridge University Press, 2015), 65–195, 141. "In 1563, the outrage of polygamy merited it a

higher position on the list of anathematic errors than divorce, rules governing consanguinity, and even the mandate of clerical celibacy"; Leslie Tuttle, *Conceiving the Old Regime: Pronatalism and the Politics of Reproduction in Early Modern France* (Oxford: Oxford University Press, 2010), 37. On missionary issues, see Dana L. Robert, *Christian Mission: How Christianity Became a World Religion* (Chichester: Wiley-Blackwell, 2009). In terms of broader accounts of early modern polygamy, all three center on European intellectual developments, with Witte the only author who spends much time on the American setting. Even his treatment is limited. See John Cairncross, *After Polygamy Was Made a Sin: The Social History of Christian Polygamy* (London: Routledge and Kegan Paul, 1974); Miller, *Milton among the Polygamophiles;* and Witte, *The Western Case for Monogamy.*

13. Such works include, though are not limited to, Martha Hodes, *White Women, Black Men: Illicit Sex in the Nineteenth-Century South* (New Haven: Yale University Press, 1999); Martha Hodes, ed., *Sex, Love, Race: Crossing Boundaries in North American History* (New York: New York University Press, 1999); Kathleen DuVal, "Indian Intermarriage and Métissage in Colonial Louisiana," *William and Mary Quarterly* 65, no. 2 (2008): 267–304; Peggy Pascoe, *What Comes Naturally: Miscegenation Law and the Making of Race in America* (Oxford: Oxford University Press, 2009); Anne F. Hyde, *Empires, Nations, and Families: A New History of the North American West, 1800–1860* (Lincoln: University of Nebraska Press, 2011); Andrew R. Graybill, *The Red and the White: A Family Saga of the American West* (New York: Norton, 2013); Ann McGrath, *Illicit Love: Interracial Sex and Marriage in the United States and Australia* (Lincoln: University of Nebraska, 2015); and Nicholas Guyatt, *Bind Us Apart: How Enlightened Americans Invented Racial Segregation* (New York: Basic, 2016).

14. Daniel Lord Smail and Andrew Shryock, "History and the 'Pre,'" *American Historical Review* 118, no. 3 (2013): 709–37, 712. Put another way, "Infrastructure demarcates developed from undeveloped places"; Ara Wilson, "The Infrastructure of Intimacy," *Signs: Journal of Women in Culture and Society* 41, no. 2 (2016): 247–80, 271. There have been helpful studies of "gender frontiers," "sexual middle grounds," and intermarriage. Kathleen M. Brown, *Good Wives, Nasty Wenches, and Anxious Patriarchs: Gender, Race, and Power in Colonial Virginia* (Chapel Hill: University of North Carolina Press, 1996); Richard Godbeer, *Sexual Revolution in Early America* (Baltimore: Johns Hopkins University Press, 2002); Juliana Barr, *Peace Came in the Form of a Woman: Indians and Spaniards in the Texas Borderlands* (Chapel Hill:

University of North Carolina Press, 2007); and Jennifer M. Spear, *Race, Sex, and Social Order in Early New Orleans* (Baltimore: Johns Hopkins University Press, 2009). Yet few studies focus on marriage as a structuring set of principles and practices in early encounters. The most significant exceptions are Gutiérrez, *When Jesus Came,* and Ann Marie Plane, *Colonial Intimacies: Indian Marriage in Early New England* (Ithaca, NY: Cornell University Press, 2000). This drama has also been addressed to some degree in work on other parts of the former British Empire. The classic treatment is Sarah Carter, *The Importance of Being Monogamous: Marriage and Nation Building in Western Canada to 1915* (Alberta: University of Alberta Press, 2008). Also see Bettina Bradbury, "Colonial Comparisons: Rethinking Marriage, Civilization, and Nation in Nineteenth-Century White-Settler Societies," in *Rediscovering the British World,* ed. Phillip Buckner and G. Frances, 135–58 (Calgary: University of Calgary Press, 2005); Rebecca Gill, "The Imperial Anxieties of a Nineteenth-Century Bigamy Case," *History Workshop Journal* 57 (2004): 58–78; Shino Konishi, " 'Wanton with Plenty': Questioning Ethno-historical Constructions of Sexual Savagery in Aboriginal Societies, 1788–1803," *Australian Historical Studies* 39, no. 3 (2008): 356–72; Laura Rademaker, "The Importance of Marrying Straight: Aboriginal Marriage and Mission Monogamy in Twentieth-Century North Australia," *Gender and History* 29, no. 3 (2017): 641–57; and Nafisa Essop Shiek, "Customs in Common: Marriage, Law, and the Making of Difference in Colonial Natal," *Gender and History* 29, no. 3 (2017): 589–604. On intersectionality, see Sumi Cho, Kimberlé Williams Crenshaw, and Leslie McCall, "Toward a Field of Intersectionality Studies: Theory, Applications, Praxis," *Signs: Journal of Women in Culture and Society* 13, no. 4 (2013): 785–810. Most theoretical treatments of polygamy start only in the nineteenth century, but this history long predates the Mormons. Angela Willey, " 'Christian Nations,' 'Polygamic Races,' and Women's Rights: Toward a Genealogy of Non/Monogamy and Whiteness," *Sexualities* 9, no. 5 (2006): 530–46; Margaret Denike, "The Racialization of White Man's Polygamy," *Hypatia* 25 (2010): 852–74; and Marta Ertman, "Race Treason: The Untold Story of America's Ban on Polygamy," *Columbia Journal of Gender and Law* 19 (2010): 287–366. On race, intimacies, and empire, see, among others, Ann Laura Stoler, *Carnal Knowledge and Imperial Power: Race and the Intimate in Colonial Rule* (2002; Berkeley: University of California Press, 2010); Anne McClintock, *Imperial Leather: Race, Gender, and Sexuality in the Colonial Contest* (London: Routledge, 1995); Elizabeth Povinelli, *The Empire of Love:*

Toward a Theory of Intimacy, Genealogy, and Carnality (Durham, NC: Duke University Press, 2006); and Durba Ghosh, *Sex and the Family in Colonial India: The Making of Empire* (Cambridge: Cambridge University Press, 2006).

15. This argument appears in Sarah Barringer Gordon, *The Mormon Question: Polygamy and Constitutional Conflict in Nineteenth-Century America* (Chapel Hill: University of North Carolina Press, 2002); and Nancy F. Cott, *Public Vows: A History of Marriage and the Nation* (Cambridge: Harvard University Press, 2000).

16. "In Latin American history then, persistence is itself a historical problem"; Jeremy Adelman, "Introduction: The Problem of Persistence in Latin American History," in *Colonial Legacies: The Problem of Persistence in Latin American History,* ed. Jeremy Adelman, 1–14 (New York: Routledge, 1999), 9, 12. The "need to confront the continuity at the heart of patriarchy" has also preoccupied historians of women and gender; Judith M. Bennett, *History Matters: Patriarchy and the Challenge of Feminism* (Philadelphia: University of Pennsylvania Press, 2006), 54. On infrastructure: "When infrastructure works as it should, we often stop seeing it"; Wilson, "Infrastructure of Intimacy," 248. Susan Leigh Star also emphasizes infrastructure's "*embeddedness.* Infrastructure is sunk into and inside of other structures, social arrangements, and technologies"; Susan Leigh Star, "The Ethnography of Infrastructure," *American Behavioral Scientist* 43, no. 3 (1999): 377–91, 381. Infrastructures also "emerge out of and store within them forms of desire and fantasy"; Brian Larkin, "The Politics and Poetics of Infrastructure," *Annual Review of Anthropology* 42 (2013): 327–43, 329. As one recent feminist exploration of Canadian legal rulings against contends, "The polygamy case was also a victory for carceral politics. . . . The justice relied on both conservative moral and biological evolutionary perspectives to justify the need to criminalize polygamy. Both of these lines of reasoning are antithetical to the theoretical commitments of most feminisms"; Melanie Heath, Jessica Braimoh, and Julie Gouweloos, "Judging Women's Sexual Agency: Contemporary Sex Wars in the Legal Terrain of Prostitution and Polygamy," *Signs: Journal of Women in Culture and Society* 42, no. 1 (2016): 199–225, 220. See also Ann Laura Stoler, "Tense and Tender Ties: The Politics of Comparison in North American History and (Post)Colonial Studies," *Journal of American History* 88, no. 3 (2001): 829–65, 863.

17. Dissent of Justice Antonin Scalia, no. 02–102, *John Geddes Lawrence and Tyron Garner, Petitioners, v. Texas,* [June 26, 2003], https://www.law

.cornell.edu/supct/html/02-102.ZD.html, section I; Montesquieu, *The Complete Works of M. de Montesquieu*, 4 vols. (London: T. Evans and W. Davis, 1777), 1: 336; Anon., *Martin's Hobby Houghed and Pounded, or Letters on Thelyphthora* (London: J. Buckland, 1781), 86. See, for instance, Margaret Denicke, "What's Queer about Polygamy?" in *Queer Theory: Law, Culture, Empire,* ed. Robert Leckey and Kim Brooks, 137–53 (Abingdon: Routledge, 2010).

18. Povinelli, *The Empire of Love,* 17.

19. Most modern American polygamy, practiced by branches of what are called "Mormon fundamentalists" (not affiliated with the Church of Jesus Christ of Latter-day Saints), are extremely problematic, sometimes combining polygyny with the abuse of minors, incest, coercion, and violence. They often center around a charismatic man. The most notorious example concerned the Fundamentalist Church of Jesus Christ of Latter-day Saints, its now imprisoned leader Warren Jeffs, and the Yearning for Zion Ranch compound in Texas (raided by U.S. authorities in 2008). These horrible situations have prompted numerous memoirs, such as Carolyn Jessop, *Escape* (New York: Penguin, 2008), as well as fictional representations such as David Eberschoff, *The 19th Wife* (New York: Random House, 2001) and HBO's *Big Love.* On early modern divorce, English people, as well as those in France and Spain, had very limited access. There was more possibility in Scotland and in colonies such as Massachusetts, though it was still limited. See Leah Leneman, *Alienated Affections: The Scottish Experience of Divorce and Separation, 1684–1830* (Edinburgh: Edinburgh University Press, 1998). Massachusetts allowed a slightly higher number of divorces than England in the eighteenth century, even though its population was about 3.5 percent of the size of England's. Nancy Cott, "Divorce and the Changing Status of Women in Eighteenth-Century Massachusetts," *William and Mary Quarterly* 33, no. 4 (1976): 586–614, 593. See also Dirk Hartog, *Man and Wife in America: A History* (Cambridge: Harvard University Press, 2000); Norma Basch, *Framing American Divorce: From the Revolutionary Generation to the Victorians* (Berkeley: University of California Press, 2001); Merril D. Smith, *Breaking the Bonds: Marital Discord in Pennsylvania, 1730–1830* (New York: New York University Press, 1992); Mary Beth Sievens, *Stray Wives: Marital Conflict in Early National New England* (New York: New York University Press, 2005); Clare Lyons, *Sex among the Rabble: An Intimate History of Gender and Power in the Age of Revolution, Philadelphia, 1730–1830* (Chapel Hill: University of North Carolina Press for the Omohundro Institute of Early American

History and Culture, 2006); and Kirsten Denise Sword, "Wayward Wives, Runaway Slaves, and the Limits of Patriarchal Authority in Early America," Ph.D. diss., Harvard University, 2002. Elizabeth Cady Stanton, "The Man Marriage," *The Revolution,* April 8, 1869, 217–18. On Stanton and Anthony, Laurel Thatcher Ulrich, *A House Full of Females: Plural Marriage and Women's Rights in Early Mormonism, 1835–1870* (New York: Knopf, 2017), xiii. On "nasty wenches," see especially Brown, *Good Wives;* Carol F. Karlsen, *The Devil in the Shape of a Woman: Witchcraft in Colonial New England* (New York: Norton, 1987); and Sharon Block, *Rape and Sexual Power in Early America* (Chapel Hill: University of North Carolina Press for the Omohundro Institute of Early American History and Culture, 2006).

20. Lydia Maria Child, *The History of the Condition of Women, in Various Ages and Nations,* 2 vols. (Boston: John Allen, 1835), 2: 284–85.

21. Annette Gordon-Reed, *The Hemingses of Monticello: An American Family* (New York: Norton, 2008), 129–30, quotation 147. See also Thomas Foster, *Sex and the Founding Fathers: The American Quest for a Relatable Past* (Philadelphia: Temple University Press, 2014). On polygyny and fertility: Steven C. Josephson, "Does Polygyny Reduce Fertility?" *American Journal of Human Biology* 14 (2002): 222–32, 226. On motherhood, Emma Griffin, "The Emotions of Motherhood: Love, Culture, and Poverty in Victorian Britain," *American Historical Review* 123, no. 1 (2018): 60–85.

22. Blackstone's *Commentaries,* that great eighteenth-century legal handbook, offered the classic formulation: polygamy was "condemned both by the law of the new testament, and the policy of all prudent states, especially in these northern climates." William Blackstone, *Commentaries on the Laws of England,* 4 vols., ed. John Frederick Archbold (London: William Reed, 1811), vol. 1, book I, ch. 15 ("Of Husband and Wife"): 436. One English law, Lord Hardwicke's Marriage Act of 1753, aimed (controversially) at standardizing marriages, but it applied only in England. See Rebecca Probert, *Marriage Law and Practice in the Long Eighteenth Century: A Reassessment* (Cambridge: Cambridge University Press, 2009), and her "Control over Marriage in England and Wales, 1753–1823: The Clandestine Marriages Act of 1753 in Context," *Law and History Review* 27 (2009): 413–50. Other edges of empire, including Scotland and the American colonies, had more liberal policies on marriage and divorce. On the rise of state involvement in these processes, see Isabel V. Hull, *Sexuality, State, and Civil Society in Germany, 1700–1815* (Ithaca, NY: Cornell University Press, 1997); Eric Josef Carlson, *Marriage and the English Reformation* (London: Wiley-Blackwell, 1994); Sara

McDougall and Sarah M. S. Pearsall, "Introduction," Special Issue: Marriage's Global Past, *Gender and History* 29, no. 3 (2017): 505–28. On Anglo-American settings, see especially Mary Beth Norton, *Founding Mothers and Fathers: Gendered Power and the Forming of American Society* (New York: Knopf, 1996), and Cott, *Public Vows*. On the issue of bigamy in particular, see Alexandra Parma Cook and Noble David Cook, *Good Faith and Truthful Ignorance: A Case of Transatlantic Bigamy* (Durham, NC: Duke University Press, 1991); Richard Boyer, *Lives of the Bigamists: Marriage, Family, and Community in Colonial Mexico* (Albuquerque: University of New Mexico Press, 1995); Bernard Capp, "Bigamous Marriage in Early Modern England," *Historical Journal* 52, no. 3 (2009): 537–56; and Sara McDougall, *Bigamy and Christian Identity in Late Medieval Champagne* (Philadelphia: University of Pennsylvania Press, 2012). The book is not about secret bigamy, cases in which a deceitful man kept a wife in every port. It is also not about adultery, long-term concubinage, or relationships such as that between Thomas Jefferson and Sally Hemings, as significant as they have been. Polygamy was a form of marriage, so it also does not mean one person having sexual relations with many people or polyamory or ethical nonmonogamy (in which one person openly has multiple sexual partners, sometimes in a settled long-term way).

23. See Cairncross, *After Polygamy Was Made a Sin;* Miller, *Milton among the Polygamophiles;* and Witte, *The Western Case for Monogamy.*

24. "kissabamigouta" or "femme separee d'avec son mary qui ne veut plus le voir quoyq[ue] dans le mesme village," Jacques Largillier [and Jacques Gravier], *Dictionnaire Illinois-Français,* ca. 1690s, Watkinson Library, Trinity College, Hartford, Connecticut, 221. Since the original document has no page numbers, I have given the page numbers listed in the most accessible version, the online database of the Miami-Illinois Digital Archive at https://ilaatawaakani.org/index.php.

25. My linguistic abilities—stretching to French and Spanish and a bit of Latin but no farther—and a desire to work in the original languages also determined this shape. There are fascinating debates among German-speaking Americans, but I did not feel I could do justice to them. See A. G. Roeber, *Hopes for Better Spouses: Protestant Marriage and Church Renewal in Early Modern Europe, India, and North America* (Grand Rapids, MI: William B. Eerdmans, 2013). E. De Jongh, *Tot Lering en Vermaak: Betekenissen van Hollandse genrevoorstellingen uit de zeventiende eeuw* (Amsterdam: Rijksmuseum, 1976).

26. Recent scholars in Revolutionary American history have considered the effect of domestic situations on men's political choices. See Jane Kamenksy, *A Revolution in Color: The World of John Singleton Copley* (New York: Norton, 2017), and Kathleen DuVal, *Independence Lost: Lives on the Edge of the American Revolution* (New York: Random House, 2015).

1. *"Una Casa, Dos Mujeres"*

1. The rebellion was centered on northern pueblos. Carroll L. Riley, *The Kachina and the Cross: Indians and Spaniards in the Early Southwest* (Salt Lake City: University of Utah Press, 1999), 222–23. See also Opinion of the Cabildo of Santa Fe, La Salineta, October 3, 1680, in *Revolt of the Pueblo Indians of New Mexico and Otermin's Attempted Reconquest 1680–1682*, trans. Charmion Clair Shelby, ed. Charles Wilson Hackett, 177–83 (1942; Albuquerque: University of New Mexico Press, 1970), 177–78, as well as Ramón A. Gutiérrez, *When Jesus Came, the Corn Mothers Went Away: Marriage, Sexuality, and Power in New Mexico, 1500–1846* (Stanford, CA: Stanford University Press, 1991); David Weber, *The Spanish Frontier in North America* (New Haven: Yale University Press, 1994); and Andrew Knaut, *The Pueblo Revolt of 1680: Conquest and Resistance in Seventeenth-Century New Mexico* (Norman: University of Oklahoma Press, 1995), 134.

2. Buenaventura, from Tolomato, blamed the friars for having "prevented the having of many wives." Others, such as Lucas from Tupiqui, claimed that the friars prevented men from having "more than one wife." See also the testimony of Bartolomé from Tolomato, Alonso from Ospo, and Pedro from Asao. "Información sobre el levantamiento de indios en Florida," AGI PATRONATO, 19, R. 28, 1–22: esp. pp. 6, 7, Archivo General de Indias, Seville, Spain (hereafter AGI). Luis Gerónimo de Oré, *Relación Histórica De La Florida, Escrita En El Siglo Xvii.*, ed. Atanasio López, facsimile (Madrid: Imprenta de Ramona Velasco, 1931), 9, and Luis Jerónimo de Oré, *The Martyrs of Florida, 1513–1616*, ed. and trans. Maynard Geiger, (New York: J. F. Wagner, 1937). I have translated this material from a rare Spanish edition at the Newberry Library (based on an exceptionally rare original), but I have used the Geiger translation for reference. Account of Fray Pedro Fernández de Chozas [October 1597], "Cartas de Gobernadores de Florida," AGI SANTO DOMINGO 224, R. 5, N 31, p. 160.

3. Michael V. Wilcox, *The Pueblo Revolt and the Mythology of Conquest: An Indigenous Archaeology of Contact* (Berkeley: University of California Press, 2009), 19. Another scholar contends that rebels wanted to "resurrect local

spiritual traditions"; Robert C. Galgano, *Feast of Souls: Indians and Spaniards in the Seventeenth-Century Missions of Florida and New Mexico* (Albuquerque: University of New Mexico Press, 2005), 8. Ramón Gutiérrez emphasizes the gulf between Christian Indians and "traditionalists," arguing that "within weeks of the Spaniards' defeat, the indigenous sacral topography was restored"; *When Jesus Came*, 123, 136. This trope appears in many discussions of Native American cultures and rebellions. Even James F. Brooks, who has attended gracefully to "the multivalent issue of men's control over their own (and others') women and children," has suggested that the rebels, in making the call for four wives for four dead Spaniards, were replicating "an indigenous pattern: Spanish men and their subordinated male Indian *servientes* would die, while their spouses and children were assimilated by marriage and adoption into victorious Indian families"; *Captives and Cousins: Slavery, Kinship, and Community in the Southwest Borderlands* (Chapel Hill: University of North Carolina Press for the Omohundro Institute of Early American History and Culture, 2002), 54. Brooks has recently contended that "pushing a program of nativist purification and return to the 'state of their antiquity,' the rebels urged the complete destruction of the mission churches and their liturgical paraphernalia as well as the rejection of the Spanish-influenced lifeways of livestock herding, wheat farming, tools, and architecture"; "AHR Forum: Women, Men, and Cycles of Evangelism in Southwest Borderlands, A.D. 750 to 1750," *American Historical Review* 118, no. 3 (2013): 738–64, 755. See also James F. Brooks, *Mesa of Sorrows: A History of the Awat'ovi Massacre* (New York: Norton, 2017).

4. As J. H. Elliott has observed, "For [King] Philip, heresy and rebellion were synonymous"; *Imperial Spain, 1469–1716* (London: Edward Arnold, 1963), 226. David Coleman argues that the frontier atmosphere of Granada led to a heightened emphasis on orthodoxy for figures such as Archbishop Guerrero; *Creating Christian Granada: Society and Religious Culture in an Old-World Frontier City, 1492–1600* (Ithaca, NY: Cornell University Press, 2003), 9–10, 145–47, 181.

5. Luis Marmol de Carvajal, as quoted in/translated by Coleman, *Creating Christian Granada*, 52, 63 (quotation). On these issues generally, see Bernard Vincent, "La Famille Morisque," *Historia. Instituciones. Documentos* 5 (1978): 469–83, esp. 477–78, https://dialnet.unirioja.es/descarga/articulo/669786.pdf and Yvette Cardaillac-Hermosilla, "Quand les Morisques Se Mariaint . . .," *Sharq al-Andalus* 12 (1995): 477–505. "The basic structure of the Jewish family in Muslim Spain was monogamous, but . . . there were also cases of polygamy";

Avraham Grossman, *Pious and Rebellious: Jewish Women in Medieval Europe*, trans. Jonathan Chipman (Waltham, MA: Brandeis University Press, 2004), 79 (quotation), 87, 97–101. "Jews in the Christian kingdoms of Spain continued to marry second wives as was practised under Muslim rule, and the *Reconquista* did not eradicate such behaviour"; Yom Tov Assis, "Sexual Behaviour in Mediaeval Hispano-Jewish Society," in *Jewish History: Essays in Honour of Chimen Abramsky*, ed. Ada Rapoport-Albert and Steven J. Zipperstein, 25–60 (London: P. Halban, 1988), 30. "Polygamy appeared to be even more depraved. . . . Critics . . . condemned polygamy and other Morisco marriage traditions that increased their birthrate, comparing their 'very great multiplication' to that of 'bad weeds' "; Mary Elizabeth Perry, *The Handless Maiden: Moriscos and the Politics of Religion in Early Modern Spain* (Princeton: Princeton University Press, 2005), 49–50. See also Manuela Marín, "Marriage and Sexuality in Al-Andalus," in *Marriage and Sexuality in Medieval and Early Modern Iberia*, ed. Eukene Lacarra Lanz (London: Routledge, 2002), 3–20.

6. Eukene Lacarra Lanz, "Changing Boundaries of Licit and Illicit Unions: Concubinage and Prostitution," in Lanz, *Marriage and Sexuality*, 158–94, 159, 161 (quotations). Bigamists were rarely punished with death; most were sent to the galleys, as decreed by Philip in 1562 (though this sentence often amounted basically to a death sentence). William Monter, *Frontiers of Heresy: The Spanish Inquisition from the Basque Lands to Sicily* (Cambridge: Cambridge University Press, 1990), 34 and appendix 2, 328. On prosecutions for bigamy in Spanish colonial contexts, see Alexandra Parma Cook and Noble David Cook, *Good Faith and Truthful Ignorance: A Case of Transatlantic Bigamy* (Durham, NC: Duke University Press, 1991); Richard Boyer, *Lives of the Bigamists: Marriage, Family, and Community in Colonial Mexico* (Albuquerque: University of New Mexico Press, 1995); and Gutiérrez, *When Jesus Came*, 246–47. On other punishments, see André Fernandez, "The Repression of Sexual Behavior by the Aragonese Inquisition between 1560 and 1700," *Journal of the History of Sexuality* 7 (1997): 469–501. For the prevalence of bigamy proceedings elsewhere, see also Solange Alberro, "El discurso inquisitorial sobre los delitos de bigamia, poligamia y de solicitación," in *Seis ensayos sobre el discurso colonial relativo a la comunidad doméstica: matrimonio, familia y sexualidad a través de los cronistas del siglo XVI, el Nuevo Testamento y el Santo Oficio de la Inquisición*, ed. Solange Alberro, 215–26 (Mexico City: INAH, 1980), and Allyson M. Poska, "When Bigamy Is the Charge: Gallegan Women and the Holy Office," in *Women in the Inquisition: Spain and the New World*, ed. Mary Giles, 189–205 (Baltimore:

Johns Hopkins University Press, 1998). A similar trajectory characterized Portugal. See Isabel M. R. Mendes Drumond Braga, *A Bigamia Em Portugal Na Época Moderna* (Lisbon: Hugin, 2003).

7. Sarah Cline, "The Spiritual Conquest Reexamined: Baptism and Christian Marriage in Early Sixteenth-Century Mexico," *Hispanic American Historical Review* 73, no. 3 (1993): 453–80, 479–80. See also James Lockhart, *The Nahuas after Conquest: A Social and Cultural History of the Indians of Central Mexico, Sixteenth through Eighteenth Centuries* (Stanford: Stanford University Press, 1992), 205, and Boyer, *Lives of the Bigamists.* The Inquisitorial trial of Don Carlos of Texcoco, an indigenous leader, combined charges of bigamy and heresy. See Patricia Lopes Don, "The 1539 Inquisition and Trial of Don Carlos of Texcoco in Early Mexico," *Hispanic American Historical Review* 88, no. 4 (2008): 573–606. See also Patricia Lopes Don, *Bonfires of Culture: Franciscans, Indigenous Leaders, and the Inquisition in Early Mexico, 1524–1540* (Norman: University of Oklahoma Press, 2010). One scholar of indigenous society in Peru has contended: "Wealth in this context might be defined as effective kin ties or the ability to mobilize the assistance of one's kind"; Karen Spalding, "Social Climbers: Changing Patterns of Mobility among the Indians of Colonial Peru," *Hispanic American Historical Review* 50, no. 4 (1970): 645–64, 654. See, for instance, Brooks, *Captives and Cousins,* and his " 'This Evil Extends Especially . . . to the Feminine Sex': Negotiating Captivity in the New Mexico Borderlands," *Feminist Studies* 22, no. 2 (1996): 279–309; Juliana Barr, *Peace Came in the Form of a Woman: Indians and Spaniards in the Texas Borderlands* (Chapel Hill: University of North Carolina Press, 2007), and her "From Captives to Slaves: Commodifying Indian Women in the Borderlands," *Journal of American History* 92, no. 1 (2005): 19–46; Brian DeLay, *War of a Thousand Deserts: Indians Raids and the U.S.-Mexican War* (New Haven: Yale University Press, 2008), 38–44; Pekka Hämäläinen, *The Comanche Empire* (New Haven: Yale University Press, 2008); and Kathleen DuVal, "Indian Intermarriage and Métissage in Colonial Louisiana," *William and Mary Quarterly* 65, no. 2 (2008): 267–304.

8. See Amy Turner Bushnell, " 'These people are not conquered like those of New Spain': Florida's Reciprocal Compact," *Florida Historical Quarterly* 92, no. 3 (2014): 524–53, 533. See also John H. Hann, *A History of the Timucua Indians and Missions* (Gainesville: University Press of Florida, 1996), 55. His full name was Pedro Menéndez Marqués de Avilés, but he introduced himself as Pedro Menéndez. Alejandra Dubcovsky, *Informed Power: Communication in the Early American South* (Cambridge: Harvard University Press, 2016), 45.

9. Rebecca Saunders, *Stability and Change in Guale Indian Pottery, A.D. 1300–1702* (Tuscaloosa: University of Alabama Press, 2000), 19. Information about micos' behavior comes from the first recording of a Native language in what is now the United States: the 1613 *Confessionario,* or confessional, of Francisco Pareja. It is centered on Timucua speakers in a slightly later period. Nevertheless, it is as close as we can get to a literary source on these individuals in this period. Francisco Pareja, *Francisco Pareja's 1613 Confessionario: A Documentary Source for Timucuan Ethnography,* trans. Emilio F. Moran, ed. Jerald T. Milanich and William C. Sturtevant (Tallahassee: Florida Division of Archives, 1972), 34–35, 67–70. As Margaret Holmes Williamson notes of Powhatans: "Undoubtedly, plural marriages, however brief, conferred political benefits"; *Powhatan Lords of Life and Death: Command and Consent in Seventeenth-Century Virginia* (Lincoln: University of Nebraska Press, 2004), 163. See also William Strachey, *The First Booke of the First Decade Contayning the Historie of Travaile into Virginia Britania (or the Historie of Travell into Virginia Britania, 1612),* Ashmole MS 1758, p. 26, Bodleian Library, Oxford University; William Strachey, *The Historie of Travell into Virginia Britania (1612),* ed. Louis B. Wright and Virginia Freund (1612; London: Hakluyt Society 1953), 64; Edward Bland, *The Discovery of New Brittaine Began August 27, Anno Dom. 1650* (London: Thomas Harper for John Stephenson, 1651), 8–9. On Florida rivalries, Elliot Hampton Blair, "Making Mission Communities: Population Aggregation, Social Networks, and Communities of Practice at Seventeenth-Century Santa Catalina de Guale," Ph.D. diss., University of California—Berkeley, 2015, 3. One friar reported: "There is [room] for all, even though they may amount to two thousand Indians, because they are very large and ample"; Francisco Alonso de Jesus and John H. Hann, "1630 Memorial of Fray Alonso de Jesus on Spanish Florida's Missions and Natives," *The Americas* 50, no. 1 (1993): 85–105, 94. See also David Hurst Thomas, "The Life and Times of Fr. Junípero Serra: A Pan-Borderlands Perspective," *The Americas* 71, no. 2 (2014), 185–225, 207.

10. Alonso de Jesus and Hann, "1630 Memorial," 94–96; "Información sobre el levantamiento de indios en Florida," AGI PATRONATO, 19, R. 28, 1–22, p. 5; Amy Turner Bushnell, *Situado and Sabana: Spain's Support System for the Presidio and Mission Provinces of Florida* (Athens: University of Georgia Press, 1995), 106. Cacicas included "doña maría cacica desta tierra" and "la cacica de aquera." Gonzalo Méndez de Canzo, "Cartas de Gobernadores de Florida," AGI SANTO DOMINGO 224, R. 5, N 31, pp. 155, 156.

11. Oré, *Relación Histórica,* 106.

12. Grant Jones contends: "Sororal polygyny was reportedly practiced. . . . There is little doubt that [Franciscan] active opposition was one factor in the 1597 rebellion"; Grant D. Jones, "The Ethnohistory of the Guale Coast through 1684," *American Museum of Natural History Anthropological Papers* 55, no. 2 (1978): 178–210, 202. Sororal polygamy was fairly common among southeastern matrilineal cultures, and it is one in which the women exert a fair amount of control. The editors/translators of the *Confessionario* explain this sentence about the mistress: "The Spanish says simply *alguna esclava o criada,* some slave or servant (both feminine). However, the Timucuan equivalent *inihimichu* is literally "one's black consort/spouse." This passage indicates that the Timucua were keeping black slaves by 1612." Pareja, *Pareja's Confessionario,* 47–48. Elsewhere, Jones notes that "the Guale were in close contact with related peoples," including Timucua speakers. Jones, "Ethnohistory of the Guale Coast," 186. As Alejandra Dubcovsky and George Aaron Broadwell have observed, "the different ways in which the Spanish author and the Timucua authors approached this topic underscore the dissimilar and at times conflicting understandings, projects, and even writing styles that uneasily cohabit the same text"; "Writing Timucua: Recovering and Interrogating Indigenous Authorship," *Early American Studies* 15, no. 3 (2017): 409–41, 437.

13. Jones, "Ethnohistory of the Guale Coast," 183; Pareja, *Confessionario,* 33–39, 110–18.

14. Oré, *Relación Histórica,* 93–94. Continued rebelliousness plagued this Spanish colony. There had already been major Guale rebellions, most notably the Guale-Orista Rebellion of 1576. The Guales continued to rebel through the seventeenth century (especially in the 1640s and the 1680s), and these rebellions helped to weaken the Spanish colonies, allowing an English takeover of the area of South Carolina. Weber, *The Spanish Frontier,* 143.

15. Lewis H. Larson, Jr., contends that polygamy "was one of the Indian customs which the priests regarded with unfriendly eyes, and their interference with the practice contributed to the 1597 revolt"; "Historic Guale Indians of the Georgia Coast and the Impact of the Spanish Mission Effort," in *Tacachale: Essays on the Indians of Florida and Southeastern Georgia during the Historic Period,* ed. Jerald T. Milanich and Samuel Proctor, 120–40 (Gainesville: University Press of Florida, 1978), 125. A similar emphasis can be found in Daniel S. Murphree, *Constructing Floridians: Natives and Europeans in the Colonial Floridas, 1513–1783* (Gainesville: University Press of Florida, 2006), 60, though he does acknowledge that tribute and leadership

were also factors (147n32). See also Jerald T. Milanich, *Laboring in the Fields of the Lord: Spanish Missions and Southeastern Indians* (Gainesville: University Press of Florida, 1999), 112–13. Elsewhere, Milanich and Paul Hoffman emphasize concerns over tribute and friars' interference in leadership as key causes, though they do acknowledge polygamy as a factor. Jerald T. Milanich, *Florida Indians and the Invasion from Europe* (Gainesville: University Press of Florida, 1995), 172–73, and Paul E. Hoffman, *Florida's Frontiers* (Bloomington: Indiana University Press, 2002), 82–83. Joseph M. Hall, Jr., stresses that "Franciscans had already stacked ample tinder by attacking important Guale traditions and restricting converts' movements among the province's towns. Disputes about marriage and authority provided the incendiary spark"; *Zamumo's Gifts: Indian-European Exchange in the Colonial Southeast* (Philadelphia: University of Pennsylvania Press, 2009), 47–48. Grant Jones contends, "The 1597 revolt was the climax of 27 years of constant rebellion against heavy-handed Spanish control"; "The Ethnohistory of the Guale Coast," 183. David Hurst Thomas states it plainly: "The Guale uprising of 1597 was not an indigenous rebellion against Spanish authority at all. Instead, the root cause of the unrest was underlying tension and conflict between indigenous chiefdoms"; "Life and Times," 208. The authors of the most thorough recent treatment of this rebellion summarize: "Most modern interpretations of the 1597 uprising agree that Franciscan interference in Guale political and religious affairs, most notably their efforts to abolish the Guale practice of polygamy, provided the incendiary spark for the 1597 uprising. This volume does not aim to dispute such claims"; J. Michael Francis and Kathleen M. Kole, "Murder and Martyrdom in Spanish Florida: Don Juan and the Guale Uprising of 1597," *American Museum of Natural History Anthropological Papers* 95 (2011): 1–156, 13.

16. Clark Spencer Larsen, Dale L. Hutchinson, Margaret J. Schoeninger, and Lynette Norr, "Food and Stable Isotopes at La Florida: Diet and Nutrition before and after Contact," in *Bioarchaeology of Spanish Florida: The Impact of Colonialism*, ed. Clark Spencer Larsen, 52–81 (Gainesville: University Press of Florida, 2001). There was probably "an increase in relatively static work"; Christopher B. Ruff and Clark Spencer Larsen, "Reconstructing Behavior in Spanish Florida: The Biomechanical Evidence," in Larsen, *Bioarchaelogy of Spanish Florida*, 113–45, 141. "The opportunity for diarrheal diseases to increase their prevalence in a population overworked and subject to dietary compromise, result[ed] in higher rates of morbidity and mortality"; Scott W. Simpson, "Patterns of Growth Disruption in La Florida: Evidence from

Enamel Microstructure," in Larsen, *Bioarchaeolgy of Spanish Florida,* 146–80, 175. See also Michael Schultz, Clark Spencer Larsen, and Kerstin Kreutz, "Disease in Spanish Florida: Microscopy of Porotic Hyperostosis and Cribra Orbitalia," in Larsen, *Bioarchaelogy of Spanish Florida,* 207–25.

17. See, for instance, Steve J. Stern, *Peru's Indian Peoples and the Challenges of Spanish Conquest,* 2nd ed. (Madison: University of Wisconsin Press, 1993), especially 102–13. As Rebecca Saunders observes, "Prior to contact, male involvement in cultivation was restricted to the heaviest clearing." However, men came to do more agricultural work because of tribute demands; *Stability and Change,* 34. "Repartimiento draft labor practice required able-bodied males to contribute labor with very little compensation"; Larsen, Hutchinson, Schoeninger, and Norr, "Food and Stable Isotopes," 75.

18. Guale ceramics, produced by women, bear witness to considerable changes in this period. One archaeologist concludes that this shift makes "Guale pottery one of the few demonstrable examples of ceramic change correlating with historic change." Unusually, among the Guale, something occurred to alter Irene phase pottery to distinctly different Altamaha forms around the year 1600. Saunders, *Stability and Change,* 8, 34. Cacicas included "doña maría cacica desta tierra" and "la cacica de aquera." Gonzalo Méndez de Canzo, "Cartas de Gobernadores de Florida," AGI SANTO DOMINGO 224, R. 5, N 31, pp. 155, 156. Oré, *Relación Histórica,* 76.

19. Katherine A. Spielmann, Tiffany Clark, Diane Hawkey, Katharine Rainey, and Suzanne K. Fish, " '. . . being weary, they had rebelled': Pueblo Subsistence and Labor under Spanish Colonialism," *Journal of Anthropological Archaeology* 28 (2009): 102–25, 122.

20. After the rebellion, the tribute level of corn was reduced. Gonzalo Méndez de Canzo, "Cartas de Gobernadores de Florida," AGI 22.2.448 SANTO DOMINGO 224, R. 5, N 31, p. 156. Hoffman, *Florida's Frontiers,* 885. Alonso Gregoria de Escobedo, *La Florida,* 350v.

21. Alonso de Jesus and Hann, "1630 Memorial," 94, 95, 99. Andrés de San Miguel, *An Early Florida Adventure Story,* trans. John H. Hann (Gainesville: University Press of Florida, 2001), 64, 65.

22. Bushnell, " 'These people,' " 542, 544; San Miguel, *Early Florida Adventure Story,* 70. The Mico Santamaría himself reported that gifts were the only way to entice the Native people to become Christian allies to the Spanish; Gonzalo Méndez de Canzo, "Cartas de Gobernadores de Florida," AGI SANTO DOMINGO, 224, R. 5, N 31, p. 156. Escobedo, *La Florida,* 352r. Francis and Kole, following the work of Joseph Hall, point out that Spanish goods were

prestige items among southeastern Indian chiefs, and could be used in trade for "enhancing a chief's authority"; "Murder and Martyrdom," 91. Oré, *Relación Histórica,* emphasizes this aspect. It also appears in the testimony of Francisco and others in "Información sobre el levantamiento de indios en Florida," AGI PATRONATO, 19, R. 28, 1–22. On the importance of clothing in the era more generally, see Ulinka Rublack, *Dressing Up: Cultural Identity in Renaissance Europe* (Oxford: Oxford University Press, 2010).

23. Oré never names this mico, but I identify him as Don Domingo because he was a Spanish ally and baptized Christian, who had become the mico mayor following the rebellion. Oré, *Relación Histórica,* 106. In their leniency, the friars may have been following precedent. Franciscans in Mexico had allowed polygyny to continue for some baptized, powerful Natives. Cline, "Spiritual Conquest Reexamined," 475.

24. "Los indios murmuraban diciendo: 'Hasta ahora el Cacique tenía en una casa dos mujeres y hijos, agora tiene dos casas, y en cada una tiene una mujer, como si fuera infiel' "; Oré, *Relación Histórica,* 106–8 (quotation 107). "This relationship is captured best by the concept of a fragile 'colonial bargain': a degree of native political and cultural autonomy in exchange for a grudging consent"; Yanna Yannakakis, *The Art of Being In-between: Native Intermediaries, Indian Identity, and Local Rule in Colonial Oaxaca* (Durham, NC: Duke University Press, 2008), 13.

25. Declaration of the Indian, Juan, Place on the Rio del Norte, Dec 18, 1681, in Hackett and Shelby, *Revolt of the Pueblo Indians,* 235. A later letter from the Franciscan *procurador general,* Fray Francisco de Ayeta, narrated the events, including the claim that Po'pay had instructed his followers to leave their Christian wives and take those whom they wanted. See Barbara De Marco, "Voices from the Archives, Part II: Francisco De Ayeta's 1693 Retrospective on the 1680 Pueblo Revolt," *Romance Philology* 53, no. 2 (2000): 449–508, 485. Declaration of Pedro Naranjo of the Queres Nation. Place on the Rio del Norte, Dec 19, 1681, in Hackett and Shelby, *Revolt of the Pueblo Indians,* 247; "que el Yndió que matare a un español cogerá una yndia por muger y el que matare quatro tendrá quatro mugeres y el que matare a diez o mas, tendrá a respecto otras tantas mujeres." Testimony of Pedro Garcia un Indio de nacíon tagno, AGI GUADALAJARA 138, f. 187, p. 288. See also Hackett and Shelby, *Revolt of the Pueblo Indians,* 24, and Brooks, *Captives and Cousins,* 54.

26. This is usually how scholars have treated it; see note 3. Even Matthew Liebmann, an archaeologist who otherwise largely rejects the idea that the Pueblo Revolt and its aftermath demonstrate simply a return to precolonial social

order, contends: "Finally, Po'pay proposed the dissolution of all Christian marriages, advocating a return to the traditional Puebloan practice of serial monogamy"; *Revolt: An Archaeological History of Pueblo Resistance and Revitalization in 17th Century New Mexico* (Tucson: University of Arizona Press, 2012), 72. Of these sources, Barbara De Marco notes: "All of the witnesses had been taken captive and were being interrogated as prisoners—even those who testified that they had joined up with the Spaniards of their own accord." She also contends that the statements are formulaic; "Voices from the Archives, Part I: Testimony of the Pueblo Indians in the 1680 Pueblo Revolt," *Romance Philology* 53, no. 2 (2000): 375–448, 378–79.

27. Riley, *The Kachina and the Cross*, 24. See also Wilcox, *Pueblo Revolt*, and Joe Sando, *Pueblo Nations: Eight Centuries of Pueblo Indian History* (Santa Fe, NM: Clear Light, 1998), 68; B. Sunday Eiselt, *Becoming White Clay: A History and Archaeology of Jicarilla Apache Enclavement* (Salt Lake City: University of Utah Press, 2012), 68; and Curtis F. Schaafsma, *Apaches De Navajo: Seventeenth-Century Navajos in the Chama Valley of New Mexico* (Salt Lake City: University of Utah Press, 2002).

28. "The Spanish presence in New Mexico disrupted the Pueblo people's way of life in many ways and, in so doing, led to large-scale population loss and forced abandonment of pueblos"; Elinore M. Barrett, *Conquest and Catastrophe: Changing Rio Grande Pueblo Settlement Patterns in the Sixteenth and Seventeenth Centuries* (Albuquerque: University of New Mexico Press, 2002), 67. See also Ross Frank, "Demographic, Social, and Economic Change in New Mexico" in *New Views of Borderlands History*, ed. Robert H. Jackson, 41–71 (Albuquerque: University of New Mexico Press, 1998). On matrilocal practices, see Riley, *The Kachina and the Cross*, 68–71, and Gutiérrez, *When Jesus Came*, 11. These practices varied between pueblos. Neighboring northern Apaches were also matrilocal. See Eiselt, *Becoming White Clay*, 37. "Seniors" appears in Gutiérrez, *When Jesus Came*, 12. By the early twentieth century, polygamy had largely ceased. Elsie Parsons wrote, "Monogamy prevails"; Elsie Clews Parsons, *Pueblo Indian Religion*, 2 vols. (1939; Lincoln: University of Nebraska Press, 1996), 1: 42. Gutiérrez may have overestimated the extent of polygyny among the Pueblo people. One source he uses is a problematic English translation of Gaspar Pérez de Villagrá's epic historical poem *Historia de la Nueva México, 1610*. This translation uses "wives" for a word, *hembras*, that means "women" or "females"; see Gaspar Pérez de Villagrá, *History of New Mexico*, trans. Gilberto Espinosa (Los Angeles: Quivira Society, 1933), 143. See Gaspar Pérez de Villagrá, *Historia de la*

Nueva México, 1610, trans. Miguel Encinias, Alfred Rodríguez, and Joseph P. Sánchez (Albuquerque: University of New Mexico Press, 1992). See also "hembra" in 1734 and 1780 dictionaries in Real Academia Española, *Nuevo Tesoro Lexicográfico de la Lengua Española,* at http://www.rae.es/rae.html. The other records of polygamy occur in an investigation conducted by the "Viceroy, Count of Monterrey, Regarding Conditions in the Provinces of New Mexico, July 1601," in *Don Juan de Oñate, Colonizer of New Mexico, 1595–1628,* 2 vols. ed. George P. Hammond and Agapito Rey, 2: 623–99 (Albuquerque: University of New Mexico Press, 1953). Sources that Gutiérrez cites as mentioning polygamy are Declaration of Joseph Brondate, 1601; Declaration of Marcelo de Espinosa, 1601; Declaration of Ginés de Herrera Horta; and Declaration of Captain Juan de Ortega, 1601, 2: 627, 636, 647, 663. These are formulaic responses (where men were asked "how many wives do the Indians have?") and are not therefore the most reliable sources. There is little evidence for widespread polygyny among the Pueblos; its use would have been restricted only to high-ranking leaders.

29. For general treatment of marriage among Plains Indians, see especially Collier, *Marriage and Inequality,* and Hämäläinen, *The Comanche Empire,* 247–50.

30. Spielmann et al., " '. . . being weary, they had rebelled,' " 107, 117, 119–22, 120, 125. Italics original.

31. "Letter of Fray Estevan de Perea, Cuarac, October 30, 1633," in *Historical Documents Relating to New Mexico, Nueva Vizcaya, and Approaches Thereto, to 1773,* 3 vols., ed. Charles Wilson Hackett, 3: 130 (Washington, DC: Carnegie Institution, 1937); Gutiérrez, *When Jesus Came,* 104; "Declaration of Captain Andrés Hurtado, Santa Fé, September 1661," and "Declaration of Andrés López Zambrano, Santo Domingo, February 20, 1664," in Hackett, *Historical Documents,* 3: 186, 244. Andrés Reséndez offers a significant recent interpretation of the importance of slavery in the Pueblo Revolt, though gender does not appear to be a major aspect of this compelling analysis; *The Other Slavery: The Uncovered Story of Indian Enslavement in America* (Boston: Houghton Mifflin, 2016), 149–71, especially 168–71; Eiselt, *Becoming White Clay,* 78, 84.

32. Stern, *Peru's Indian Peoples,* 104.

33. Gutiérrez, *When Jesus Came,* 131; Hackett and Shelby, *Revolt of the Pueblo Indians,* 1: 98–102; and Ned Blackhawk, *Violence over the Land: Indians and Empires in the Early American West* (Cambridge: Harvard University Press, 2006), 32.

34. "Testimony of Juan, Tewa from Tesuque," in De Marco, "Voices from the Archives, Part I," 389. As Gutiérrez has it, "The jubilation that swept the pueblos at the defeat of the Spaniards was short-lived. . . . Popé's alliance splintered. Civil war erupted. . . . In the midst of this chaos, ill-provisioned pueblos began to prey on the granaries of their neighbors. . . . The Tewa and Tanos deposed Popé as their leader because of his excessive demands for women, grain, and livestock"; *When Jesus Came,* 139. Brooks writes: "The alliance seems to have quickly unraveled as interpueblo friction grew and assaults by freshly mounted Apaches and Navajos haunted their days. Popé . . . now acted as the tyrant himself. . . . He instituted a reign of terror by which even use of the Castilian tongue could lead to execution. Concurrently he made heavy demands for women, grain, and livestock. In 1681, he was deposed"; *Captives and Cousins,* 54–55.

35. Andrew O. Wiget, "Truth and the Hopi: An Historiographic Study of Documented Oral Tradition concerning the Coming of the Spanish," *Ethnohistory* 29, no. 3 (1982): 181–99, 183, 186. Some of these issues echoed in Hopi communities after the rebellion: Brooks, *Mesa of Sorrows,* passim; "Hearing of February 21, 1661, Mexico, Fray Nicolás de Freitas," and "Reply of Mendizábal," in Hackett, *Historical Documents,* 3: 134, 216. This document was generated by the complicated show trial of Governor Bernardo López de Mendizábal and his wife for their alleged crypto-Judaism (among other accusations). See Frances Levine, *Doña Teresa Confronts the Spanish Inquisition: A Seventeenth-Century New Mexican Drama* (Norman: University of Oklahoma Press, 2016).

36. Matthew Liebmann, looking at Pueblo art combining indigenous and European motifs on canyon walls from the post–Pueblo Revolt period, argues that there was a process of "Pueblofication" in which there was a "contemporary construction of new identities, based in notions of traditional Pueblo practice; "Signs of Power and Resistance: The (Re)Creation of Christian Imagery and Identities in the Pubelo Revolt Era," in *Archaeologies of the Pueblo Revolt: Identity, Meaning, and Renewal in the Pueblo World,* ed. Robert W. Preucel, 132–44 (Albuquerque: University of New Mexico Press, 2002). More recently, Liebmann has termed this process "creation of tradition," which he describes as follows: "Pueblo people—and particularly the Jemez—constructed new forms of material culture in the wake of the revolt that resourced and referenced their perceptions of pre-Hispanic times but did not replicate them"; "The Innovative Materiality of Revitalization Movements: Lessons from the Pueblo Revolt of 1680," *American Anthropologist*

110, no. 3 (2008): 360–72, 364. There are no written sources for the period from 1680 to 1693, and earlier records, which might have provided some clues, were destroyed.

37. See Aimee Villareal, "Sanctuaryscapes in the North American Southwest," *Radical History Review* (forthcoming, 2019); Liebmann, "Innovative Materiality," 367. On the meanings of this dual form, see Robert W. Preucel, *Archaeological Semiotics* (Malden, MA: Wiley, 2010), ch. 9; Liebmann, "Signs of Power and Resistance," 132–44.

38. Patricia W. Capone and Robert W. Preucel, "Ceramic Semiotics: Women, Pottery, and Social Meanings at Kotyiti Pueblo," in Preucel, *Archaeologies of the Pueblo Revolt*, 99–113; Barbara J. Mills, "Acts of Resistance: Zuni Ceramics, Social Identity, and the Pueblo Revolt," in Preucel, *Archaeologies of the Pueblo Revolt*, 85–98; and Liebmann, "Innovative Materiality," 366.

39. It has also been called the Great Southwestern Revolt. See Brooks, *Captives and Cousins*, 52; Susan M. Deeds, *Defiance and Deference in Mexico's Colonial North: Indians under Spanish Rule in Nueva Vizcaya* (Austin: University of Texas Press, 2003), 86; and Reséndez, *The Other Slavery*, 169–71. Declaration of Tadeo, Papigochi, May 25, 1697, in AGI GUADALAJARA, 156, 206. Testimony of Pablo el Júmari, gobernador pima, reported in letter from Don Marcos Fernández de Castañeda, alcalde mayor de Santa Rosa de Cusihuiríachi, to the governor of Nueva Vizcaya en Parral, Don Juan Isidro de Pardiñas, rpt. in Luis González Rodríguez, "Testimonios Sobre La Destrucción De Las Misiones Tarahumaras Y Pimas En 1690," *Estudios de Historia Novohispana* 10 (1991): 189–235, 196–97. Joseph Neumann, *Révoltes Des Indiens Tarahumars (1626–1724)*, trans. Luis Rodríguez González (Paris: Institut des Hautes Études de l'Amérique latine, 1969), 25, 57–59. I have not been able to consult the original Latin so I have used this French translation.

2. *"Poligamie/Nintiouiouesaïn"*

1. "Il est homme fort & hardy, bon guerrier, a la langue asses bien penduë"; Reuben Gold Thwaites, ed., *The Jesuit Relations and Allied Documents: Travels and Explorations of the Jesuit Missionaries in New France, 1610–1791*, 73 vols. (Cleveland: Burrows Brothers, 1901), 11: 148–49 (hereafter *JR*). As a 1606 French-Latin dictionary had it: "*Estre fort hardi*, Audacia abundare." As a 1694 dictionary put it, "On dit, Avoir la langue bien penduë, pour dire, Avoir une grande facilité de bien parler." See Jean Nicot, *Le Thresor de la langue francoyse* (1606) and *Dictionnaire de l'Académie française*, 1st ed. (1694), at *The Project for American and French Research on the Treasury of the*

French Language (ARTFL) at http://artfl-project.uchicago.edu/node/17 (hereafter ARTFL). *JR* 11: 178–79.

2. *JR* 7: 36–37, 40–41, 42–43.

3. *JR* 11: 178–79, 18: 132–33. Makheabichtichiou is sometimes identified as "Montagnais chief." However, baptismal entries for his children list him as "Algonquin" or "La Petite Nation." He was a leader of Algonquin and Montagnais refugees. There is no further elucidation in Lucien Campeau, ed. *Monumenta Novae Franciae*, 9 vols. (Quebec: Presses de l'Université Laval, 1967–2003), especially vol. 2 (1979): *Établissement à Québec (1616–1634)* and vol. 4 (1989): *Les Grandes Épreuves (1638–1640)*, or in Thomas Grassman, "MAKHEABICHTICHIOU (Makhatewebichtichi)," *Dictionary of Canadian Biography/Dictionnaire biographique du Canada (DCB/DBC)*, University of Toronto/the Université Laval (1959), vol. 1 (1000–1700), online.

4. "La polygamie et l'instabilité des unions conjugales sont des obstacles à la conversion"; Dominique Deslandres, *Croire et Faire Croire: Les Missions Françaises au XVIIe Siècle* (Paris: Fayard, 2003), 261. Jesuit Sébastien Rasles "thought the biggest obstacle to their [Illinois men] conversion was their continuing attachment to polygamy"; Tracy Neal Leavelle, *The Catholic Calumet: Colonial Conversions in French and Indian North America* (Philadelphia: University of Pennsylvania Press, 2012), 174. "Polygamy was also a particular target of Jesuit missionaries"; Richard White, *The Middle Ground: Indians, Empires, and Republics in the Great Lakes Region, 1650–1815*, (Cambridge: Cambridge University Press, 1991), 65. "Indian premarital sexual experimentation . . . polygyny . . . and divorce therefore made many Europeans see Indian marital practices as disorderly"; Jennifer M. Spear, *Race, Sex, and Social Order in Early New Orleans* (Baltimore: Johns Hopkins University Press, 2009), 28. "Colonial officials invested indissoluble monogamous union with a power to . . . mark the boundaries between civilization and savagery"; Leslie Tuttle, *Conceiving the Old Regime: Pronatalism and the Politics of Reproduction in Early Modern France* (Oxford: Oxford University Press, 2010), 97. French colonial historians have debated whether indigenous women in the Great Lakes region had greater freedom in precolonial societies or in Catholic ones. For those taking the former position, polygamy was a Native "freedom"; for those arguing the latter, women became Catholic in part to avoid the exploitation of polygyny. For the former argument, see Karen Anderson, *Chain Her by One Foot: The Subjugation of Women in Seventeenth-Century New France* (London: Routledge, 1991), especially 75–76, 102; and Carol Devens, *Countering Colonization: Native American Women and*

Great Lakes Missions, 1630–1900 (Berkeley: University of California Press, 1992), 26–27. For the latter, see White, *The Middle Ground*, ch. 2; Susan Sleeper-Smith, *Indian Women and French Men: Rethinking Cultural Encounter in the Western Great Lakes* (Amherst: University of Massachusetts Press, 2001), especially 23–24; Allan Greer, *Mohawk Saint: Catherine Tekakwitha and the Jesuits* (Oxford: Oxford University Press, 2004), 140–45; and Leavelle, *The Catholic Calumet*, ch. 7. Although Robert Michael Morrissey disagrees with Sleeper-Smith on assimilation, he likewise argues that Native women converted to Christianity to escape "unfavorable" polygamy; "Kaskaskia Social Network: Kinship and Assimilation in the French-Illinois Borderlands, 1695–1735," *William and Mary Quarterly* 70, no. 1 (2013): 103–46, 117, and *Empire by Collaboration: Indians, Colonists, and Governments in Colonial Illinois Country* (Philadelphia: University of Pennsylvania Press, 2015). On relations between indigenous people, see, among others, Gilles Havard, *Empire et Métissages: Indiens et Français dans le Pays d'En Haut, 1660–1715* (Paris: Septentrion, 2003), 636–39. Michael Witgen, *An Infinity of Nations: How the Native New World Shaped Early North America* (Philadelphia: University of Pennsylvania Press, 2012. On "nindoodemag," Heidi Bohaker, "'Nindoodemag': The Significance of Algonquian Kinship Networks in the Eastern Great Lakes Region, 1600–1701," *William and Mary Quarterly* 63, no. 1 (2006): 23–52.

5. "Ils sont jaloux: et si la femme est trouvée faisant la bête à deux dos, elle sera repudiée, ou en danger d'estre tuée par son mary"; Marc Lescarbot, *Histoire de la Nouvelle France*, 3 vols. (Paris: Librairie Tross, 1866), 1: 716–17. See also Marc Lescarbot, *The History of New France* (Toronto: Champlain Society, 1907–11), 165–66.

6. On gestures, Céline Carayon, "Touching on Communication: Visual and Textual Representations of Touch as Friendship in Early Colonial Encounters," in *Empire of the Senses: Sensory Practices of Colonialism in Early America*, ed. Daniela Hacke and Paul Musselwhite, 33–66 (Leiden: Brill, 2017). On officials who recorded to obliterate, see Carlo Ginzburg, "The Inquisitor as Anthropologist," in *Clues, Myths, and the Historical Method* (Baltimore: Johns Hopkins University Press, 1989) 156–64, and Jill Lepore, "Historians Who Love Too Much: Reflections on Microhistory and Biography," *Journal of American History* 88, no. 1 (2001): 129–44. The *Jesuit Relations'* original title was *"Relation de ce qui s'est passé en la Nouvelle France en l'annee . . .,"* published by Sebastien Cramoisy in Paris from 1632 to 1672. Gordon M. Sayre, *Les Sauvages Américains: Representations of Native*

Americans in French and English Colonial Literature (Chapel Hill: University of North Carolina Press, 1997), 88.

7. There was the case of Nzinga Nkuwu, later João I, baptized by Portuguese clergy. "Within three years, however, the king had found intolerable his new religion's demand that he give up polygamy, and he lapsed"; Wyatt MacGaffey, "Dialogues of the Deaf: Europeans on the Atlantic Coast of Africa," in *Implicit Understandings: Observing, Reporting, and Reflecting on the Encounters between Europeans and Other Peoples in the Early Modern Era*, ed. Stuart B. Schwartz, 249–67 (Cambridge: Cambridge University Press, 1994), 254. They also occurred in the Mughal court of Jahangir; Muzaffar Alam and Sanjay Subrahmanyam, "Frank Disputations: Catholics and Muslims in the Court of Jahangir (1608–11)," *Indian Economic and Social History Review* 46, no. 4 (2009): 457–511, 458, 480–82. On issues of missionary energy, see Deslandres, *Croire et Faire Croire*, 288, and Leslie Choquette, " 'Ces Amazones du Grand Dieu': Women and Mission in Seventeenth-Century Canada," *French Historical Studies* 17, no. 3 (1992): 627–55. On French state building through marriage, see Sarah Hanley, "Engendering the State: Family Formation and State Building in Early Modern France," *French Historical Studies* 16, no. 1 (1989): 4–27, and Matthew Gerber, "Family, the State, and Law in Early Modern and Revolutionary France," *History Compass* 7, no. 2 (2009): 474–99, 479–80. According to Tuttle, the French crown "considered marriage and reproduction essential to rebuilding monarchical authority and creating a glorious and powerful France"; *Conceiving the Old Regime*, 14. Marie de l'Incarnation as quoted in Natalie Zemon Davis, *Women on the Margins: Three Seventeenth-Century Lives* (Cambridge: Harvard University Press, 1995), 98. On the dictionaries, "The missionaries produced, with essential assistance from Native people, hybrid religious texts . . . infused with Illinois cultural concepts and sensibilities"; Leavelle, *The Catholic Calumet*, 98. On kinship in these dictionaries, see David J. Costa, "The Kinship Terminology of the Miami-Illinois Language," *Anthropological Linguistics* 41, no. 1 (1999): 28–53. I consulted a range of dictionaries, either in original or in photocopies at the Powell Library of Anthropology, Smithsonian Institution in Washington, D.C. (except where noted otherwise, below). They are all manuscript materials, usually giving the French translation (though occasionally Latin). They include a variety of languages, ranging from the 1660s to the 1760s. Dictionaries from later western missions reflect cultures more hierarchical than earlier, eastern ones, but there are certain commonalities. Many thanks to

John Bishop and Bob Morrissey for sharing some of this material with me. Dictionaries used include Anon., *French-Algonkin Dictionary* (1662); Anon., *Racines de la Langue Outaouaise* (1669); Louis André, *Dictionnaire Algonquin* (1688–1691); Jacques Largillier [and Jacques Gravier], *Dictionnaire Illinois-Français* (ca. 1690s), Watkinson Library, Trinity College, Hartford, Connecticut. (This last item was previously identified as the work of Jacques Gravier, but now is generally identified as that of Jacques Largillier, or of them both. I have used "Largillier" for simplicity.) Also see Jacques Gravier, *Kaskaskia Illinois-to-French Dictionary*, trans. and ed. Carl Masthay (St. Louis: Carl Masthay, 2002); Antoine Silvy, *Dictionnaire Montagnais-Français (ca. 1678–1684)* (Quebec: Presses de l'Université du Québec, 1974); Bonaventure Fabvre, *Racines Montagnaises* (Quebec: Université Laval, 1970); Antoine-Robert Le Boullenger, *Dictionnaire Français-Illinois* (1704–44?), John Carter Brown Library; Pierre Du Jaunay, *Dictionarium Gallico-Outaouakum* (1748), McGill Library, photocopy; Jean Claude Mathevet, *Vieux Dictionnaire Algonquin-Français*, 1750; Guichard, *French-Algonkin Dictionary (1760)*; Jean-Baptiste de la Brosse, *Radicum Montanarum Silva (1766–1772)* (Ottawa: Deschâtelets Archives, unpublished, transcription by John Bishop). I have also made use of the list for "femme" included in David J. Costa, "The St-Jérôme Dictionary of Miami-Illinois," in *Papers of the 36th Algonquian Conference*, ed. H. C. Wolfart, 107–33 (Winnipeg: University of Manitoba, 2005), 120–21. Two of the dictionaries used here, those by Le Boullenger and Largillier, are now searchable online (not so when I did the research) at the wonderful Miami-Illinois Digital Archive at https://ilaatawaakani.org/index.php. I have therefore used the page numbers listed in the database for those two dictionaries, as they are the most accessible versions (and in the case of Largillier, there are no page numbers on the original). Throughout this chapter, I have changed the letter "8" in the originals to an "ou," which most closely approximates the sound indicated by this notation.

8. Anthropologists have contended that "such a set of regional groups shared a sense of common identity, language, and culture; exploited contiguous hunting ranges; and was linked by ties of kinship and marriage"; Edward S. Rogers and James G. E. Smith, "Environment and Culture in the Shield and Mackenzie Borderlands," in *Handbook of North American Indians*, ed. William C. Sturtevant, vol. 6, *Sub-Arctic*, ed. June Helm, 130–45 (Washington, DC: Smithsonian Institution, 1981), 141. Sleeper-Smith also emphasizes the importance of marriage; *Indian Women and French Men*, 4. Bohaker, "'Nindoodemag,'" 26, 46, 47.

9. "De trois femmes que j'ay espousées, je n'en ayme qu'une, que je veux retenir avec moy, je congedie les deux autres, mais elles retournent malgré que j'en aye, si bien qu'il faut que je les souffre ou que je les tuë; j'espere neantmoins que dans quelque temps, je les feray retourner en leur pays." / "Of the three women [Thwaites: wives] I have married, I love only one, whom I wish to keep with me; I dismiss the other two [Thwaites: send the other two away], but they return in spite of me, so that I must either suffer [Thwaites: endure] them or kill them. I hope, however, that in a little while I will make them [Thwaites: they will] return to their own country"; *JR* 11: 176–77.

10. "Jay deux femmes/ninrioukoueoue"; "la femme de mon mary/nikik pl. kouek; poligamie/nintiouiouesaïn"; *French-Algonkin Dictionary* (1662). See also, André, *Dictionnaire Algonquin;* Du Jaunay, *Dictionarium Gallico-Outaouakum;* Silvy, *Dictionnaire Montagnais-Français;* Fabvre, *Racines Montagnaises;* de la Brosse, *Radicum Montanarum Silva;* Largillier, *Dictionnaire Illinois-Français;* Le Boullenger, *Dictionnaire Français-Illinois.*

11. Later dictionaries from Illinois country include the phrase for "I am the second wife" as well as "she is the second wife of my husband." Le Boullenger has phrases such as: "the sister wives of the same husband" ("les soeurs femmes d'un meme mari/ecaperi mintchiki anicouapitchiki"); "marriage with two sisters" ("mariage de ces deux soeurs/anicouapiouni"); and "etre 2. femme c est mal/aouicoussiouni"; Le Boullenger, *Dictionnaire Français-Illinois,* 220. Largillier has "deux soeurs maries au mesme [mary]/anicouapitchiki." Largillier, *Dictionnaire Illinois-Français,* 34. Similar words appear in the St-Jérôme dictionary; see Costa, "The St-Jérôme Dictionary," 120–21. "La pluralité des Femmes est établie dans plusieurs Nations de la Langue Algonquine, et il est assez ordinaire d'épouser toutes les Sœurs; cet usage est fondé sur ce qu'on se persuade, que des Sœurs s'accommoderont mieux entre elles, que des Etrangeres. Dans de cas, toutes les Femmes sont sur le même pied, mais parmi les vrais Algonquins, il y en a de deux ordres, & celles du second sont les Esclaves des autres"; P.-F. X. d. Charlevoix, *Histoire et Description Generale de la Nouvelle France, Avec Le Journal Historique d'un Voyage fait par order du Roi dans l'Amérique Septentrionnale* (Paris: Pierre-François Giffart, 1744), 283–84. Pierre-François Xavier de Charlevoix, *Journal of a Voyage to North America,* 2 vols., trans. and ed. Louise Phelps Kellogg, (Chicago: Caxton Club, 1923), 2: 45–46.

12. "La 1ere. femme celle qui est plus aimée/nikitassicouo niouiouo"; Le Boullenger, *Dictionnaire Français-Illinois,* 220. "Premiere femme la plus aimée, qui est maitresse de tout/kitachioueta" and "l'autre femme, co[m]me la

seconde, f. terme de mepris/noukiouiouagana"; Largillier, *Dictionnaire Illinois-Français*, 225, 357. "Je suis 2e femme/kitaouicouissi"; Du Jaunay, *Dictionarium Gallico-Outaouakum*. See also "jaloux, jalousie/ensamoueta"; "C'est celle de [mes] ses femmes [que j] qu'il ayme la plus/nikitassata"; and "elle luy defend d'aller a sa rivale, a sa seconde femme/ensamouiroutama-ouata aouicoussari)"; Largillier, *Dictionnaire Illinois-Français*, 35, 226.

13. "Les marier se quittent/pakivinan ouasuintigue"; André, *Dictionnaire Algonquin*. "La femme que i'ay quittée/niouiouinaby" and "ie change de femme/nit'aratchououeou oui"; *French-Algonkin Dictionary* (1662). Similar phrases appear in Largillier, *Dictionnaire Illinois-Français*; Silvy, *Dictionnaire Montagnais-Français*; and Du Jaunay, *Dictionarium Gallico-Outaouakum*. Examples include: "il course apres les femmes/nousoukouesp? ninoupinara," *French-Algonkin Dictionary* [1662]); "qui court les femmes, va toujours les chercher it[em] (also) femme qui cherche les hom[m]es/mattamecoua," Largillier, *Dictionnaire Illinois-Français, 258;* "il aime les femmes/acouessiriouo," "il les court/nouticoueoueoua merateskita," and "courreur de femmes/mereouite-hekita," Le Boullenger, *Dictionnaire Français-Illinois*, 220, 162; "ni kichatau iskoueoua/j'aime les femmes, elles m'arrêtent," Silvy, *Dictionnaire Montagnais-Français*, 48. "Elle n'ayme pas son mary/ko ousabewimassour ouna-pénar" and "les femmes n'aymens pas leur maris, voila pourquoy les marier se quittens/ouinsk pauinitousch? Ouaningan"; André, *Dictionnaire Algonquin*. "Femme separee d'avec son mary qui ne veut plus le voir quoyq[ue] dans le mesme village/kissabamigouta"; Largillier, *Dictionnaire Illinois-Français*, 221.

14. Louis Armand de Lom d'Acre baron de Lahontan, *Nouveaux Voyages de Mr Le Baron de Lahontan dans l'Amérique Septentrionale* (The Hague: Les Frères l'Honoré, 1703), 2: 135, and *New Voyages to North-America*, 2 vols. (London: H. Bonwicke, 1703), 2: 37–38.

15. "Une ame quasi de chair"; *JR* 11: 176–77 and 12: 178–81.

16. Lahontan, *Nouveaux Voyages*, 2: 134. [Pierre Deliette], "Memoire concernant le pays d'Illinois" (1721), Memoranda on French Colonies in America, including Canada, Louisiana, and the Caribbean, 4 vols., VAULT, Ayer MS 293, Newberry Library, Chicago, 3: 264–362, 319. See also Antoine Laumet de Lamothe Cadillac and Pierre Deliette, *The Western Country in the 17th Century: The Memoirs of Lamothe Cadillac and Pierre Liette* (Chicago: Lakeside, 1947), 87–171, 134.

17. On looking and desiring: "I look at the woman with lust," "lascive de puella cogitate/nahte teicoueta"; "I look at the woman with lust, I gaze at her genitals," "lascive mulierem aspicio, pudenda intueor/nimacoungoue"; and "she

lies naked, legs apart," "nude jacet crurib[us] distantibus/Eiacaretichinoua";
Le Boullenger, *Dictionnaire Français-Illinois*, 322, and Largillier, *Dictionnaire
Illinois-Français*, 234, 149. On engorgement, "often touched her breasts so
that they swelled"/"ita saepe tetigit manu mammas ut creveint/nima acoun-
goue"; "one with an erect penis," "virgam inflatus/Pakimpeoua"; "he makes
himself erect by touching himself," "[virgam erigit] tangendo de luxuriose/
chipaoueoua"; and "I pull on his penis with great force so that he reaches
orgasm," "summa vi membrum ejus virile attraho quo moriatur/nirara-
coutchina"; Largillier, *Dictionnaire Illinois-Français*, 234, 123, 49. On the last
point here, "A woman taken from the rear, but preserving her vessel,"
"mulier a tergo cognita servato tn [tamen] vas/aremicoucshounta"; Largillier, *Dictionnaire Illinois-Français*, 59. In the classical period, at least, *uas* or
vas had sexual connotations, usually male but occasionally female. "Vas
('vessel, container') is used suggestively with the womb in mind by Julius
Valerius"; J. N. Adams, *The Latin Sexual Vocabulary* (London: Duckworth,
1982), 82, 219, quotation on 88.

18. *JR* 6: 251; "I burn with lust," "mali deciderii ardore flagravi/nimessa-
ouinaki"; "I desire him, the one that I see," "je le desire ce que je voy/nobile
sumitur in malam partram/nimessaouinaoua"; Largillier, *Dictionnaire Illinois-Français*, 230, 276. "Prostitutée, qui a plusieurs maris/missetunapeuet
and prostitué, qui a plusieurs femmes/missetuskuet"; Pierre Laure, *Apparat
français-montagnais* (Sillery, Quebec: Presses de l'Université du Québec,
1988), L638. "Verenda inflatus: *femina*/pakiheoua/*masculus* pakinpeoua";
Largillier, *Dictionnaire Illinois-Français*, 419. On mutual activities, "They sin
together, one with another, and mutually defile themselves," "peccant simul,
alter in alterum, fedant [foedant] se invicem/emareroutatitchik"; "touching
each other's gentials," "tetigit illus partes naales de utroq sexu/Regouneoua"
and "se mutuo tangent impudice/Regounitiouaki"; and "when two people
suck each other's private parts," "q[uan]do sibi duo invicem partes inhon-
estas sugunt/sousoupihepoutinghi"; Largillier, *Dictionnaire Illinois-Français*,
491, 504, 533.

19. *JR* 11: 264–65. "She arouses lust with her breasts," "sinu detecto ad libidinem
inducere cogitat/messainagoupareouita" as well as "sinu nudo ad libidinem
provocat/missaouinacoupareoua"; Largillier, *Dictionnaire Illinois-Français*,
298.

20. "Je desire à la verité d'embrasser vostre creance, mais vous me faites deux
commandemens qui se choquent l'un l'autre vous me deffendez d'un costé de
tuër, de l'autre vous me deffendez d'avoir plusieurs femmes, cela ne s'accorde

pas"; *JR* 11: 176–77. I have altered the Thwaites translation slightly to reflect the parallel of negatives in the original. Mughal kings who disputed Jesuits over monogamy also joked: "The Mughals . . . dealt with [Europeans] playfully, as powerful monarchs could in the face of what they imagined were quite minor interlocutors"; Alam and Subrahmanyam, "Frank Disputations," 507. *JR* 6: 241–43.

21. *JR* 5: 132–33. "Je me moque de luy, luy pete au nez plusieures/nipepekitira"; Largillier, *Dictionnaire Illinois-Français*, 458. James H. Merrell, "'The Customes of our Countrey': Indians and Colonists in Early America," in *Diversity and Unity in Early North America*, ed. Philip D. Morgan, 76–112 (London: Routledge, 1993).

22. The Mughal king Jahangir used a similar tactic with the Jesuits: "The King received all this well. What made him afraid was the fact of not having an exception (even for kings) in order to have many wives."; Jerónimo Xavier, as quoted in Alam and Subrahmanyam, "Frank Disputations," 481. Bruce G. Trigger, "Ontario Native People and the Epidemics of 1634–1640," in *Indians, Animals, and the Fur Trade: A Critique of* Keepers of the Game, ed. Shepard Krech III, 19–38 (Athens: University of Georgia Press, 1981), 31.

23. *JR* 14: 130–31; Day and Trigger, "Algonquin," 792–93; Eleanor Leacock, "Montagnais Women and the Jesuit Program for Colonization," in *Women and Colonization: Anthropological Perspectives*, ed. Mona Etienne and Eleanor Leacock (New York: Praeger, 1980), 25–42, 29; Peter Cook, "Onontio Gives Birth: How the French in Canada Became Fathers to Their Indigenous Allies, 1645–73," *Canadian Historical Review* 96, no. 2 (2015): 186.

24. Alan McPherron, "On the Sociology of Ceramics: Pottery Style Clustering, Marital Residence, and Cultural Adaptions of an Algonkian-Iroquoian Border," in *Iroquois Culture, History, and Prehistory*, ed. Elisabeth Tooker, 101–7: (Albany: University of the State of New York/New York State Museum and Science Service, 1967), 106. Corroboration on patrilocality comes from dictionary phrases such as "elle demeure chez les parens de son mari/nahanganacoueouo" and "elle est chez les parens de son mari/nahanganaeoua," Le Boullenger, *Dictionnaire Français-Illinois*, 312, 220; and St-Jérôme, in Costa, "The St-Jérôme Dictionary," 120. Gordon M. Day and Bruce G. Trigger, "Algonquin," in Sturtevant, *Handbook of North American Indians*, vol. 15, *Northeast*, ed. Bruce G. Trigger, 792–97 (Washington, DC: Smithsonian Institution, 1978), 795. Bilateral kinship, in which kinship ties through the father and the mother were socially significant, provided the foundation for political and economic structuring, though descent was

predominantly patrilineal. Bohaker argues, "In this cultural tradition, people inherited their *nindoodemag* [kinship networks] identities from their fathers"; "'Nindoodemag,'" 25–26. From the dictionaries: "femme de mon pays nit'egikoue; d'autre pays huronne outegabon; du pays des Guvons nadou-etegabon," Anon., *French-Algonkin Dictionary;* "je suis mariée hors du pays, en autre nation/ni nahatchichiouin," Silvy, *Dictionnaire Montagnais-Français*, 82; "je suis hors de mon païs, de mon village/nikiousi," and "(vo[us] ne me traites pas en parent/raragoui nikiousi)"; Largillier, *Dictionnaire Illinois-Français*, 143. See also "nabankihiouï/elle est mariee a ma nation," André, *Dictionnaire Algonquin*; "femme du pays," Du Jaunay, *Dictionarium Gallico-Outaouakum*; and "femme étrangère mariée en ce pays/nahahiskoueu," Silvy, *Dictionnaire Montagnais-Français*, 82.

25. Lescarbot, *Histoire de la Nouvelle France*, 1: 716–17; Louis Hennepin, *Nouvelle Découverte d'un tres grand Pays Situé dans l'Amérique* (Utrecht: Guillaume Broedelet, 1697), trans. as *A New Discovery of a Vast Country in America* (1698; Chicago: A. C. McClurg, 1903, rpt. of the 2nd London ed.), 483; Nicolas Perrot, *Memoire sur les Moeurs, Coustumes, et Religion des Sauvages de l'Amérique Septentrionale* (Leipzig: Librarie A. Franck, 1864), 70, 71; trans. Emma Helen Blair as *Indian Tribes of the Upper Mississippi Valley and Region of the Great Lakes,* 2 vols. (Cleveland: Arthur H. Clark, 1911), 64–65.

26. "Alles moy querir ma femme et amenes la moy bongré malgré elle, qui en suivy un autre qu elle aime/natchipataouicou niouioua," Largillier, *Dictionnaire Illinois-Français*, 330. A seventeenth-century English usage of this phrase, "he commanded her will'd she nill'd she to go to bed with her," also indicated coercion and implied the threat of violence. See John Josselyn, *John Josselyn, Colonial Traveler: A Critical Edition of Two Voyages to New-England*, ed. Paul J. Lindholdt (Hanover, NH: University Press of New England, 1988), 24. "F[emme] qui quit son m[ari]. et va a un autre que son m[ari] fache menace de lui couper le nez/kikiteherimegousiouo," Le Boullenger, *Dictionnaire Français-Illinois*, 220. Pierre Esprit Radisson reported of the "Nation of Beef," "Those have as many wives as they can keepe. If any one did trespasse upon the other, his nose was cutt off, and often the crowne of his head"; *Voyages of Peter Esprit Radisson*, ed. Gideon D. Scull (Boston: Prince Society, 1885), 219–20. Antoine Laumet de Lamothe Cadillac observed of the *pays d'en haut* that adulterous wives would have their heads shaved, have their noses cut off, and be turned out of the house; he also detailed the gang rapes such wives could suffer. "The Miami cut off their noses. Others inflict another punishment. They post about thirty young men on a road along which they

know their wives must pass in going to the woods. As soon as they see her, the husband issues from the abuscade and says to his wife: As I know that you are fond of men, I offer you a feast of them—take your fill. Her cries are futile; several of them hold her, and they enjoy her one after the other"; see "Memoire concernant le pays d'Illinois" and "Relation du sieur de La Mothe Cadillac Capitaine en pied ayant une Compagnie de La Marine en Canada, y devans Commandant de Missilimakinak et autres Postes dan le Pays Eloigné, ou il a esté pendant trois années," "Memoranda on French Colonies in America, Including Canada, Louisiana, and the Caribbean," VAULT, Ayer MS 293, 4 vols., Newberry Library, [1702–1750], 3: 300, 334–37. See also Cadillac and Deliette, *Western Country in the 17th Century*, 69–70, 117–18, and Havard, *Empire et Métissages*, 638–39.

27. Brett Rushforth has argued that only enslaved wives provoked this kind of aggressive behavior, in part because they lacked the protection of kin. Discussing the gang rapes, Rushforth contends that "the ritual language suggests the victim's status as a slave. It also seems unlikely that this level of violence would be tolerated against an Illinois woman, whose kin could have come to her aid"; *Bonds of Alliance: Indigenous and Atlantic Slaveries* (Chapel Hill: University of North Carolina Press for the Omohundro Institute of Early American History and Culture, 2012), 68, 69. "Le Sauvage luy repliqua en cholere. Et quoy? Mais as-tue que voir dans ma maison, si je bats mon chien? La comparaison estoit mauvaise, la response estoit aiguë"; *JR* 3: 102–4. For a masterful exposition of the ways in which slaves and dogs were compared linguistically and culturally, see Rushforth, *Bonds of Alliance*, ch. 1. Rushforth's work covers the period from 1660 on. The word used here, *oster*, implies that she was taken hostage. "D'un jeune homme qui s'estoit empoisonné du déplaisir qu'il avoit conceu, à raison qu'on luy avoit osté sa femme"; *JR* 8: 121. *Dictionnaire de l'Académie française*, 1st ed. (1694) notes that *oster* means "prendre par force ou par authorité" (ARTFL).

28. Karen M. Van Wagenen and Richard G. Wilkinson, "Violence against Women: Prehistoric Skeletal Evidence from Michigan," *Midcontinental Journal of Archaeology* 18, no. 2 (1993): 190–216, 203.

29. White, *The Middle Ground*, 62.

30. *JR* 11: 176–78. "Je luy fais sa cabanne, c est mon mary/niouikiha," and "c'est ma femme, elle fait ma cabanne, elle me loge, a soin de moy, me donne a manger/niouikicgoua"; Largillier, *Dictionnaire Illinois-Français*, 390.

31. "De vivre parmy nous sans femme, c'est vivre sans secours, sans mesnage, & tousiours vagabond"; *JR* 16: 160–63. Thwaites reads: "To live among us

without a wife is to live without help, without home, and to be always wandering." This translation seems to me to obscure the labor women did in terms of housekeeping. See *mesnage* and *feu*. "On dit prov. & par mespris, d'Un homme qui n'a rien, qu'*Il n'a ny feu ny lieu*"; *Dictionnaire de l'Académie française* (1694) (ARTFL). "The value system emphasized generosity, sharing, and hospitality among kinsmen and related groups"; Rogers and Smith, "Environment and Culture," 144. "Vagabond, sans lieu, sans feu hors de son païs/kiouiriniouita" and "vagabond mais dans son païs/kiouiouit-chikita"; Largillier, *Dictionnaire Illinois-Français*, 211.

32. "J'epouse sa femme, je la luy pille/niouikintamaoua aouiouari," Largillier, *Dictionnaire Illinois-Français*, 390; "Je ravis le bien, la femme d'autrui/ni maskataouan," Silvy, *Dictionnaire Montagnais-Français*, 68. "As tu pillé la femme d'autrui/koutaki riniouo aouiouari kiouikitamaouamingano," and "estre 2e femme/kitaouicoussi kiraouicoussinti mingano"; Le Boullenger, *Dictionnaire Français-Illinois*, 220. The St-Jérôme Dictionary, which dates from ca. 1700, has a similar phrase. See Costa, "The St-Jérôme Dictionary," 120.

33. *JR* 5: 132–33.

34. Canadian Skin Shirt ("A Match-coat from Virginia of Deer-skin, or, A Match-coat from Canada"), ID AN1685.B.209, description from Ashmolean website, http://collections.ashmolean.org/object/403868.

35. Susan Sleeper-Smith and Sylvia Van Kirk have stressed that European fur traders and *coureurs de bois* benefited from marriage with Native women, who often provided access to networks of indigenous hunters. See Susan Sleeper-Smith, *Indian Women and French Men*, especially chs. 1–3, and "Women, Kin, and Catholicism: New Perspectives on the Fur Trade," *Ethnohistory* 47, no. 2 (2000): 423–52; as well as Sylvia Van Kirk, *"Many Tender Ties": Women in Fur-Trade Society in Western Canada, 1670–1870* (Winnipeg: Watson and Dwyer, 1980). *JR* 5: 132–33, and Havard, *Empire et Métissages*, 639–51. Susan McKinnon, "On. Kinship and Marriage: A Critique of the Genetic and Gender Calculus of Evolutionary Psychology," in *Complexities: Beyond Nature and Nurture*, ed. Susan McKinnon and Sydel Silverman, 106–31 (Chicago: University of Chicago Press, 2005), 122.

36. *JR* 5: 165.

37. Pekka Hämäläinen, *The Comanche Empire* (New Haven: Yale University Press, 2008), 247–50.

38. McKinnon, "On Kinship and Marriage," 124. Similarly, Jane Fishburne Collier observes: "In societies without classes or estates, where kinship organizes people's rights and obligations, marriage, as the basis of kinship,

organizes social inequality"; *Marriage and Inequality in Classless Societies* (Palo Alto: Stanford University Press, 1988), vii. *JR* 9: 268–69.

39. *JR* 3: 98–100. "Mes filles, mes femmes, mes servants," Silvy, *Dictionnaire Montagnais-Français*, 37.

40. Tracy Leavelle details parallel encounters in the Great Lakes area in the late seventeenth century and early eighteenth centry, as do, to a lesser extent, Richard White, Susan Sleeper-Smith, and Robert Morrissey. Jennifer Spear recounts similar situations in colonial Louisiana, where polygamy was also fiercely defended.

41. *JR* 11: 176–77, 20: 209–11.

42. Gaetan Morin, ed., RAB du PRDH (CD-ROM), records 86685, 73912, but also see 86790, 86797, 89292, 86831, 89294, 82293, 73962, 74008. This CD-ROM is an improved electronic version of a printed collection, Programme de Recherche en Démographie Historique, *Répertoire des actes de baptême, mariage, sépulture, et des recensements du Québec ancien*, 47 vols. (Montreal, 1980–90). Many thanks to Brett Rushforth for help in navigating this material. I have cross-checked these references with images of the original manuscript registers, which can be found in familysearch.org. Also see Bohaker, " 'Nindoodemag.' " Iroquoian languages such as Mohawk have many words beginning with *kane/gane*, which is less common in Algonquin, Innu, and related languages. See Jacques Bruyas, *Radical Words of the Mohawk Language, with Their Derivatives* (Albany, NY: Comstock and Cassidy, 1863). In the absence of further evidence, though, this is speculation. *JR* 9: 264–67.

43. *JR* 14: 142–45.

44. "Je ne marie pas un homme marié/nama ni ouishoun"; Silvy, *Dictionnaire Montagnais-Français*, 111 and "ie ne mariray pas Luy qu a desia femme/ououiskoun," Fabvre, *Racines Montagnaises*, 244. See also "A compagne, l'autre femme de mon mari/niiskou," Silvy, *Dictionnaire Montagnais-Français*, 39, and "compagne. s. f. Fille ou femme qui a quelque liaison d'amitié, de familiarité, ou de service avec une autre fille ou femme, de pareille condition, ou approchant," *Dictionnaire de l'Académie française*, 1st ed. (1694) (ARTFL).

45. Sarah Blaffer Hrdy, *Mothers and Others: The Evolutionary Origins of Mutual Understanding* (Cambridge: Harvard University Press, 2009); Costa, "Kinship Terminology," 32; *JR* 11: 158–61.

46. As David Costa observes, "It has long been recognized that Algonquian languages possess two coexisting ways of classifying siblings—by relative

age and by relative sex"; "Kinship Terminology," 43; on Miami-Illinois relationships in particular see 33–35.

47. "Aretoue/vox injuriosa a nitaretoui; aretouiououa enfent abandoné de son pere," Largillier, *Dictionnaire Illinois-Français*, 61. In other settings, "kinlessness was often not so much a literal fact as a popular shorthand for someone whose lack of full personhood blocked her from being a sister or daughter in any socially meaningful sense"; Dylan C. Penningroth, "The Claims of Slaves and Ex-Slaves to Family and Property: A Transatlantic Comparison," *American Historical Review* 112, no. 4 (2007): 1039–69. [Deliette], "Memoire," 3: 264–362; Cadillac and Deliette, *Western Country in the 17th Century*, 117.

48. [Deliette], "Memoire," 3: 264–362; Cadillac and Deliette, *Western Country in the 17th Century*, 117. "He is prohibited from marrying again save with the knowledge and consent of his mother-in-law"; Perrot, *Memoire due les Moeurs*, 70, 71; Blair, trans., *Indian Tribes*, 73.

49. With Kanerouik, Makheabichtichiou had Claude (baptized in 1635, at age thirteen) and Robert (baptized in 1639, around age two). With Ousaoumoukoueou, Makheabichtichiou had Therese Kanigamouehet, who was around two years old when she was baptized at Sillery in 1638. With Oupououkoue, he had a girl named Paule who was baptized and died in early 1639, as well as a son named Ouampsonen who was also baptized in 1639 (no ages given). The children whose mothers were not listed were Agathe Khisipikiouan, who was around two in late 1639, and two children whose deaths only are recorded: Ouamgouon, who was five, and Antoinedepadou, who was twenty-five. They died sometime between early 1639 and the end of 1640. RAB du PRDH (CD-Rom), records 86685, 73912, 86790, 86797, 89292, 86831, 89294, 82293, 73962, 74008.

50. Bruce G. Trigger, "Ontario Native People and the Epidemics of 1634–1640," in *Indians, Animals, and the Fur Trade: A Critique of* Keepers of the Game, ed. Shepard Krech III (Athens: University of Georgia Press, 1981), 19–38, 34–35. *JR* 12: 164–65, 168–69, 184–85.

51. *JR* 6: 253, 12: 40–41.

52. *JR* 6: 130–31.

53. See Greer, *Mohawk Saint*, introduction and ch. 1.

54. "Depuis que j'ay presché parmy eux, qu'un homme ne devoit tenir qu'une femme, je n'ay pas esté bien venu des femmes, lesquelles estant en plus grande nombre que les hommes, si un homme n'en peut espouser qu'une, les autres sont pour souffrir; c'est pourquoy cette doctrine n'est pas conforme a leur affection"; *JR* 12: 164–65.

55. "Louis Nicolas depicted the Illinois chief with military accessories and smoking the calumet, a western diplomatic tradition, while wearing what is probably a painted bison robe"; Morrissey, *Empire by Collaboration*, 13.

56. *JR* 20: 210–11. Biblical quotation is from King James Version.

3. "Christians Have Kept 3 Wives"

1. Mary Rowlandson, *A True History of the Captivity and Restoration of Mrs. Mary Rowlandson* (London: Joseph Poole, 1682), 22. "The pattern [for wampum] was always one of contrasts, dark and bright"; Patricia E. Rubertone, *Grave Undertakings: An Archaeology of Roger Williams and the Narragansett Indians* (Washington, DC: Smithsonian Institution Press, 2001), 138. Nathaniel Saltonstall, *The Present State of New-England, with respect to the Indian War* (London: Dorman Newman, 1676), 3, 4. "Now it appears that *Squaw-Sachem* of *Pocasset* her men were conjoyned with the *Womponoags* (that is Philips men) in this Rebellion"; Increase Mather, *A Brief History of the Warr with the Indians in New-England* (Boston: John Foster, 1676), 4. On naming aspects, Lisa Brooks, *Our Beloved Kin: A New History of King Philip's War* (New Haven: Yale University Press, 2018), 168. See also Jill Lepore, *The Name of War: King Philip's War and the Origins of American Identity* (New York: Knopf, 1998), especially the introduction.

2. R. Todd Romero, *Making War and Minting Christians: Masculinity, Religion, and Colonialism in Early New England* (Amherst: University of Massachusetts Press, 2011), 63; Edward Winslow, *Good Newes from New England* (London: J.D. for William Bladen and John Bellamie, 1624), 57; and Kathleen J. Bragdon, *Native People of Southern New England, 1650–1775* (Norman: University of Oklahoma Press, 2009), 106.

3. Jacopo Sadoleto to the Genevans (1539), as quoted in John L. Thompson, "Patriarchs, Polygamy, and Private Resistance: John Calvin and Others on Breaking God's Rules," *Sixteenth-Century Journal* 25, no. 1 (1994), 3–27, 3.

4. The classic account remains Lepore, *The Name of War*. There are important analyses in Jenny Hale Pulsipher, *Subjects unto the Same King: Indians, English, and the Contest for Authority* (Philadelphia: University of Pennsylvania Press, 2005); Daniel R. Mandell, *King Philip's War: Colonial Expansion, Native Resistance, and the End of Indian Sovereignty* (Baltimore: Johns Hopkins University Press, 2010); and Michael Leroy Oberg, *Dominion and Civility: English Imperialism and Native America, 1585–1685* (Ithaca, NY: Cornell University Press, 1999). Significant recent treatments include Margaret Ellen Newell, *Brethren by Nature: New England Indians, Colonists,*

and the Origins of American Slavery (Ithaca, NY: Cornell University Press, 2015); David J. Silverman, *Thundersticks: Firearms and the Violent Transformation of Native America* (Cambridge: Harvard University Press, 2016); Brooks, *Our Beloved Kin;* Christine M. DeLucia, *Memory Lands: King Philip's War and the Place of Violence in the Northeast* (New Haven: Yale University Press, 2018); and Gina M. Martino-Trutor, " 'As Potent a Prince as Any Round About Her': Rethinking Weetamoo of the Pocasset and Native Female Leadership in Early America," *Journal of Women's History* 27, no. 3 (2015): 37–60, and Gina M. Martino, *Women at War in the Borderlands of the American Northeast* (Chapel Hill: University of North Carolina Press, 2018). On indigenous marriage and gender, the classic treatment remains Ann Marie Plane, *Colonial Intimacies: Indian Marriage in Early New England* (Ithaca, NY: Cornell University Press, 2000). See also Jean M. O'Brien, " 'Divorced' from the Land: Resistance and Survival of Indian Women in Eighteenth-Century New England," in *After King Philip's War: Presence and Persistence in Indian New England*, ed. Colin G. Calloway, 144–61 (Hanover, NH: University Press of New England for Dartmouth College, 1997); Ann Little, *Abraham in Arms: War and Gender in Colonial New England* (Philadelphia: University of Pennsylvania Press, 2007); and Romero, *Making War and Minting Christians.* Lisa Brooks does consider kinship in valuable ways; *Our Beloved Kin.*

5. John Cotton, "Sermons preached by Mr John Cotton pastor of the first Church in Boston," sermon 15, vol. 4, Cotton Papers, American Antiquarian Society (hereafter AAS). This sermon is briefly but usefully discussed in Plane, *Colonial Intimacies,* 56–57. The farewell sermon was published as John Cotton, *Gods Promise to His Plantation* (London, 1630), 19, in Reiner Smolinski, ed., *University of Nebraska Digital Commons: Electronic Texts in American Studies,* online at http://digitalcommons.unl.edu/cgi/view content.cgi?article=1022&context=etas.

6. Heather Miyano Kopelson notes of the Anglophone Atlantic: "The distinctive culture [was] influenced by 'hot' Protestants"; *Faithful Bodies: Performing Religion and Race in the Puritan Atlantic* (New York: New York University Press, 2014), 10. John Cotton, *Milk for Babes. Drawn out of the Breasts of Both Testaments* (London: J Coe, 1646), 10, online at Digital Commons, University of Nebraska, Lincoln, http://digitalcommons.unl .edu/cgi/viewcontent.cgi?article=1018&context=etas; and Little, *Abraham in Arms,* 1.

7. This appeared in the *Wittenberg Rathschlag,* as quoted in Thompson, "Patriarchs, Polygamy, and Private Resistance," 10.

8. "Ames's *Marrow* and *Cases of Conscience* were the standard manuals . . . for decades."; Keith L. Sprunger, *The Learned Doctor William Ames: Dutch Backgrounds of English and American Puritanism* (Eugene, OR: Wipf and Stock, 1972), 255. John Weemes, *An Exposition of the Morall Law, or Ten Commandements of Almightie God, Set downe by way of Exercitations* (London: T. Cotes, 1632), 178, 173, 174. Milton also pointed to "the procreation of children"; see John Milton, *The Complete Works of John Milton*, vol. 8, *De Doctrina Christiana*, ed. John K. Hale and J. Donald Cullington (Oxford: Oxford University Press, 2012), 231. William Ames, *Conscience with the Power and Cases Thereof* (n.p., 1639), 198–99. These points receive attention in Edmund Leites, *The Puritan Conscience and Modern Sexuality* (New Haven: Yale University Press, 1986), 82–84.

9. Ames, *Conscience with the Power*, 199, and Weemes, *Exposition of the Morall Law*, 175–76. "Sometimes a comment on polygamy comes in so irrelevantly as to suggest that the idea is somehow haunting the speakers." Leo Miller, *John Milton among the Polygamophiles* (New York: Loewnthal, 1974), 54. John Goodwin, *Anti-Cavalierisme, or Truth Pleading as well the Necessity* (London: Henry Overton, 1642), 9.

10. Milton died before he could publish this lengthy treatise in Latin; see Milton, *De Doctrina Christiana*, 377–99, especially 381, 369, 377. It was not published until the early nineteenth century, when it was translated into English. On Milton and polygamy, see Miller, *Milton among the Polygamophiles*, passim.

11. Cotton, sermon 13, vol. 4, AAS. Robert Sanderson, *Nine Cases of Conscience* (London: H. Brome, J. Wright and C. Wilkinson, 1678), 29.

12. A major issue of the era was "the problem of how change over time affects supposedly timeless law"; Richard J. Ross, "Distinguishing Eternal from Transient Law: Natural Law and The Judicial Laws of Moses," *Past and Present* 217 (2012): 79–115, 93, 111, 82. John Cotton, "Cotton's 'Moses His Judicials,'" *Massachusetts Historical Society Proceedings*, 2nd ser., 16 (1902): 274–84, 280. "The duties of civil rulers during the millennium were to protect the restored apostolic church and to administer 'the judicial laws of Moses that are built upon moral equity'—a provision that for Cotton included the capital laws of ancient Israel and excluded circumcision, diet, jubilee years, polygamy, and certain other matters"; Richard W. Cogley, *John Eliot's Mission to the Indians before King Philip's War* (Cambridge: Harvard University Press, 1999), 14. Charles Chauncy, "The Answer of Mr. Charles Chauncy," in William Bradford, *A History of Plymouth Plantation, 1620–1647*, 2 vols. (Boston: Massachusetts Historical Society, 1912), 2: 321–28, 321.

13. Ralph Partridge, "Mr Partrich his writing, in ans to the questions" (2: 319–21, 320); John Reynor, "The Answer of Mr Reynor" (2: 315–19, 315); Chauncy, "The Answer of Mr. Charles Chauncy" (2: 327, 325, 323), in Bradford, *Plymouth Plantation*.

14. Reynor, "The Answer of Mr Reynor," 316, 315. The passages cited are Leviticus 18:22 and 20:13 (abomination) as well as the story of Lot in Genesis 19:5. According to Richard Godbeer, both men executed had had sex with boys; *Sexual Revolution in Early America* (Baltimore: Johns Hopkins University Press, 2002), 105–6, 110.

15. Ross, "Distinguishing Eternal from Transient Law," 88; Cotton, "Cotton's 'Moses His Judicials,'" 284. "New Haven Colony came close to establishing a single standard for men and women in the areas of sexual and moral conduct"; Cornelia Hughes Dayton, *Women before the Bar: Gender, Law, and Society in Connecticut, 1639–1789* (Chapel Hill: University of North Carolina Press for the Institute of Early American History and Culture, 1995), 10. John Cotton, *An Abstract of the Lawes of New England [Massachusetts Body of Liberties]* (London: F. Coules and W. Ley, 1641), 14. Online copy at http://www.mass.gov/anf/docs/lib/an-abstract-of-the-laws-of-new-england-cotton.pdf. Quoted in Godbeer, *Sexual Revolution in Early America*, 106. "The law code and system of justice [of New Haven] owed more to the Mosaic law than did those of any other colony"; Francis J. Bremer, *Building a New Jerusalem: John Davenport, a Puritan in Three Worlds* (New Haven: Yale University Press, 2012), 3.

16. Cotton, "Moses His Judicials," *MHS Proceedings*, 282.

17. Cotton, *Gods Promise*, 19; Godbeer, *Sexual Revolution in Early America*, 88; and Faramerz Dabhoiwala, "Lust and Liberty," *Past and Present* 207 (2010): 89–179, see especially 99–114. Also see his *The Origins of Sex* (London: Penguin, 2012). John Winthrop, *A Short Story of the Rise, Reign, and Ruine of the Antinomians, Familists, and Libertines*, rpt. in *The Antinomian Controversy, 1636–1638: A Documentary History*, 2nd ed., ed. David D. Hall, 199–310 (Durham, NC: Duke University Press, 1990), 201, 275–76. Mary Beth Norton, *Founding Mothers and Fathers: Gendered Power and the Forming of American Society* (New York: Knopf, 1996), 397. The best treatments of Anne Hutchinson's trial, as well as that of Ann Hibbens, are by Mary Beth Norton and Jane Kamensky. Norton, *Founding Mothers and Fathers*, ch. 8. Kamensky linked the two, connecting them to larger concerns about women's speech; *Governing the Tongue: The Politics of Speech in Early New England* (Oxford: Oxford University Press 1997), ch. 3, especially 73. "A Report of

the Trial of Mrs. Ann Hutchinson before the Church in Boston, March, 1638," in Hall, *Antinomian Controversy*, 349–88, 372.

18. Cotton, *Gods Promise*, 19. William Hubbard, *A General History of New England, From the Discovery to 1680*, 2nd ed. (Boston: Charles C. Little and James Brown, 1848), 175. The first statement connected Cotton's behavior with lack of self-control as well as physical desecration. Godbeer, *Sexual Revolution in Early America*, 87–88. This episode, and Cotton's mission among the Wampanoag, receives helpful treatment in Plane, *Colonial Intimacies*, 55–59, and David Silverman, *Faith and Boundaries: Colonists, Christianity, and Community among the Wampanoag Indians of Martha's Vineyard, 1600–1871* (Cambridge: Cambridge University Press, 2007), ch. 2. John Cotton to John Winthrop Jr, 8 Mar 1664, in *The Correspondence of John Cotton Junior*, ed. Sheila McIntyre and Len Travers, 48–51 (Boston: Colonial Society of Massachusetts/University Press of Virginia, 2009), 51.

19. John Cotton, Jr., *The Diary of John Cotton Jr*, Massachusetts Historical Society (hereafter MHS). The diary without the dictionary is transcribed in John Cotton, Jr., "The Missionary Journal of John Cotton, Jr., 1666–1678," ed. Len Travers, *Proceedings of the Massachusetts Historical Society* 109 (1997): 52–101. The dictionary remains in manuscript: *John Cotton, Jr. diary and Indian vocabulary, 1666–1678*, Special Collections, ms. N-1042, MHS. Many of the issues of the war itself swirled around Christian Indians, most notably John Sassamon, a "praying Indian," whose murder, and the hasty trial and execution of three Wampanoags for it, was one of the reasons the war started.

20. Cotton, *Diary*, 71, 90, 87. George had become a "praying Indian" on February 27, 1671. Robin and George's wife had converted on March 29. The reconciliations took place on May 10. Thomas Gataker, *Marriage Duties Briefly Couched Together* (London: William Jones, 1620).

21. Cotton, *Diary*, 79. "What did native men and women think of these interventions? Only in the grumbling by 'the body' that 'did manifest their dislike' . . . or Wattapahtahinnit's difficult questions are there suggestions that they offered their own challenge to the Christian project"; Plane, *Colonial Intimacies*, 59.

22. Cotton, *Diary*, 81.

23. Ibid., 80–81.

24. Ibid., 80.

25. Ibid., 71, 80.

26. Roger Williams, *A Key into the Language of America* (London: Gregory Dexter, 1643), 176, 35. Cotton, *Diary*, 78, 89, 91. Increase Mather described an incident

involving "a bloody Indian called *Tuckpoo* (who the last summer murdered a man of *Boston* at *Namasket*)." Mather, *A Brief History of the Warr*, 40.

27. William Harris, *A Rhode Islander Reports on King Philip's War: The Second William Harris Letter of August, 1676*, ed. Douglas Edward Leach (Providence: Rhode Island Historical Society, 1963), 82. Metacom's surviving wife and son became significant diplomatic challenges for settlers at the end of the war. The English were not sure whether they were justified in executing the son. He was nine years old. Solicited for his opinion, John Cotton argued that it was congruent with the Bible to kill him. In the end, the English, hesitant to do so, decided on a dire compromise, selling the son into slavery. The silence around the wife suggests that she had perished in prison, though she too may have been sold. Lepore, *The Name of War*, 150–54.

28. Ethel Boissevain, *The Narragansett People* (Phoenix: Indian Tribal Series, 1975), 14; and Michael Nassaney, "Native American Gender Politics and Material Culture in Seventeenth-Century Southern New England," *Journal of Social Archaeology* 4, no. 3 (2004): 334–67, 343. Winslow, *Good Newes*, 56. "Those sachem women we know of were related by blood or marriage to powerful male sachems, but we cannot be sure that their own matrilineages . . . were not significant as well"; Kathleen J. Bragdon, *Native People of Southern New England, 1500–1650* (Norman: University of Oklahoma Press, 1996), 159. O'Brien, " 'Divorced' from the Land," 146.

29. "Though sachems were born into their positions as village leaders, their power and following depended on their charisma, power of persuasion, and demonstrated skill. . . . Sachems with rich networks of relatives could display power through their ability to mobilize kin support; they married into other groups and sometimes practiced polygyny to enhance kin connections"; Jean M. O'Brien, *Dispossession by Degrees: Indian Land and Identity in Natick, Massachusetts, 1650–1700* (Cambridge: Cambridge University Press, 1997), 20. On the general importance of kinship, see Brooks, *Our Beloved Kin*. Winslow, *Good Newes*, 59.

30. "Since polygynous marriage had played an important role in consolidating native elites . . . the missionaries' goal of eradicating polygyny carried important implications for indigenous politics"; Plane, *Colonial Intimacies*, 43. Roger Williams related these marriages to "5 or 6 wives" in his letters to Governor John Winthrop, of February 18, 1638, July 23, 1638, and July 21, 1640. Roger Williams, *The Correspondence of Roger Williams*, 2 vols., ed. Glenn W. LaFantasie (Hanover, NH: Brown University Press/University Press of New England, 1988), 1: 147–48, 168, 202. Eric S. Johnson, "Uncas

and the Politics of Contact," in *Northeastern Indian Lives, 1636–1816,* Robert S. Grumet, 29–47 (Amherst: University of Massachusetts Press, 1996), 40.

31. Bragdon, *Native People, 1500–1650,* 160, 244; Bragdon, *Native People, 1650–1775,* 91; and Rubertone, *Grave Undertakings,* 131, 133.

32. Williams, *Key into the Language,* 176; Pulsipher, *Subjects unto the Same King,* 103.

33. There was an "increased presence of female sachems after the mid-seventeenth century"; Nassaney, "Native American Gender Politics," 344. Plane notes, "Access to powerful, public leadership roles for southern New England's native women decreased with the establishment of English dominion in 1676." For Awashunkes's trajectory, see Ann Marie Plane, "Putting a Face on Colonization: Factionalism and Gender Politics in the Life History of Awashunkes, the 'Squaw Sachem' of Saconet," in Grumet, *Northeastern Indian Lives,* 140–65, 141. Rubertone, *Grave Undertakings,* 153, 159, 140.

34. Rowlandson, *True History,* 19, 22, 12. Thomas Foster asserts that "Mary Rowlandson, in a vehemently anti-Indian account of her captivity, highlighted her Indian master's polygamous marriage as a way of underscoring his status as a 'savage'"; *Sex and the Eighteenth-Century Man: Massachusetts and the History of Sexuality in America* (Boston: Beacon, 2007), 44. Daniel Gookin, *Historical Collections of the Indians in New England* (Boston: Apollo by Belknap and Hall, 1792), 9. The word she used was *squaws,* a common epithet for Indian wives then but now inappropriate and offensive. I have therefore not quoted this word in the main text.

35. As Kathleen Bragdon has observed, "those ties that lay at the center of Native social life during the colonial period were not marriage ties, but the ties between siblings, parents, and others"; *Native People, 1650–1775,* 85. James D. Drake, *King Philip's War: Civil War in New England, 1675–6* (Amherst: University of Massachusetts Press, 1999), 98; Martino-Trutor, "'As Potent a Prince as Any Round About Her,'" 47.

36. Bragdon, *Native People, 1650–1775,* 106.

37. Mandell, *King Philip's War,* 95–96.

38. Rowlandson, *True History,* 22.

39. Bragdon, *Native People, 1650–1775,* 104, 114.

40. Rowlandson, *True History,* 21. These actions were "appropriate to a wealthy sachem of the Pocasset with dynastic ties to the Wampanoag and Narragansett, revealing a woman aware of her important position"; Martino-Trutor, "'As Potent a Prince as Any Round About Her,'" 48.

41. Rowlandson, *True History*, 28. There is a long history of these kinds of strategies in wars against Native Americans. See Wayne Lee, *Barbarians and Brothers: Anglo-American Warfare, 1500–1865* (Oxford: Oxford University Press, 2011), ch. 8.

42. Rubertone, *Grave Undertakings*, 140, 159, 153.

43. Rowlandson, *True History*, 17.

44. "This abundance may have contributed to the territoriality that was becoming increasingly evident"; Bragdon, *Native People, 1500–1650*, 98; Johnson, "Uncas and the Politics of Contact," 44. "Native participation in the fur trade . . . potentially restructured the division of labor along gender lines"; Nassaney, "Native American Gender Politics," 345. There is consensus on the economic woes of Native Americans in this area in the later seventeenth century. Oberg, *Dominion and Civility*, 152; Pulsipher, *Subjects unto the Same King*, 103; Newell, *Brethren by Nature*, 125.

45. Rowlandson, *True History*, 22. Wampum "circulated largely among sachem families and was a sign of rank"; Bragdon, *Native People, 1650–1775*, 104. One archaeologist has found that the colonial period brought "increasing ornamentation and marking of dominant individuals" and suggests that this situation "may indicate the use of such imports as markers of political roles in a time of instability and competition"; Elise M. Brenner, "Sociopolitical Implications of Mortuary Ritual Remains in 17th-Century Native Southern New England," in *The Recovery of Meaning: Historical Archaeology in the Eastern United* States, ed. Mark P. Leone and Parker B. Potter, 147–81 (Washington: Smithsonian Institution Press, 1988), 174. "The sachems needed wampum and European manufactured goods for distribution in order to rally indigenous political support"; Julie A. Fisher and David J. Silverman, *Ninigret, Sachem of the Niantic and Narragansetts* (Ithaca, NY: Cornell University Press, 2014), 90. As Brooks puts it, "this 'work' signaled the highest status in Algonquian society. . . . Weetamoo was entwining the bonds between nations, weaving a multifaceted tapestry of northeastern political networks"; *Our Beloved Kin*, 264.

46. Fisher and Silverman, *Ninigret*, 90. "These technological changes had important ramifications for the organization of labor as women were drawn into a new form of commodity production"; Nassaney, "Native American Gender Politics," 348.

47. Silverman, *Thundersticks*, 104, 105, 112.

48. Rowlandson, *True History*, 14; Lepore, *The Name of War*, xviii, 26.

49. "In throwing the bible to the ground, Weetamoo rejected that belief system and all that it justified"; Brooks, *Our Beloved Kin*, 278.

50. Silverman, *Thundersticks*, 104. Thomas Wheeler, *A Thankefull Remembrance of Gods Mercy* (Cambridge: Samuel Green, 1676), 6.

51. Rubertone, *Grave Undertakings*, 140.

52. Rowlandson, *True History*, 18; Williams, *Key into the Language*, 194. "Although such disparities [in grave goods] might be taken as evidence of . . . social inequalities . . . an alternative interpretation considers the role of maternal expectations concerning a child's survival"; Rubertone, *Grave Undertakings*, 145. On Rowlandson's indifference, see Mitchell Breitwieser, *American Puritanism and the Defense of Mourning: Religion, Grief, and Ethnology in Mary White Rowlandson's Captivity Narrative* (Madison: University of Wisconsin Press, 1990), esp. 115; Julia Stern, "To Represent Afflicted Time: Mourning as Historiography," *American Literary History* 5, no. 2 (1993): 378–88; and Tiffany Potter, "Writing Indigenous Femininity: Mary Rowlandson's Narrative of Captivity, " *Eighteenth-Century Studies* 36, no. 2 (2003): 153–67, 160. The most persuasive reading belongs to Lisa Brooks: "Both women lost children to the violence of colonization. . . . Had she acknowledged Weetamoo's pain, Rowlandson might have recognized their mutual suffering, and been compelled to question the divinity of the colonial project"; Brooks, *Our Beloved Kin*, 282.

53. Rowlandson, *True History*, 33; Mather, *A Brief History of the Warr*, 46.

54. Mather, *A Brief History of the Warr*, 46.

55. Ibid., 47. "Hunger drove others to surrender themselves or their children"; Newell, *Brethren by Nature*, 156.

56. Williams, *Key into the Language*, 35.

4. *"Negroe Mens Wifes"*

1. On such terror, see John M. Murrin, "Beneficiaries of Catastrophe: The English Colonists in America," in *Diversity and Unity in Early North America*, ed. Philip D. Morgan, 259–82 (London: Routledge, 1993). On slave suicides, see Terri L. Snyder, "Suicide, Slavery, and Memory in North America," *Journal of American History* 97, no. 1 (2012): 39–62, 50, and her *The Power to Die: Slavery and Suicide in British North America* (Chicago: University of Chicago Press, 2015). "Inventory of Ripon Hall Plantation," January 1712, Francis Porteus Corbin Papers, Duke University, North Carolina. Consulted on Microfilm 36.3 at Colonial Williamsburg.

2. Snyder, "Suicide, Slavery, and Memory," 57.

3. Vincent Brown discusses the ubiquity of suicide in colonial Jamaica, arguing that masters attempted to prevent it through mutilation, terror, and display (including of heads on poles); *The Reaper's Garden: Death and Power in the*

World of Atlantic Slavery (Cambridge: Harvard University Press, 2008), 131–37, 131. "To understand both dimensions of this story—the impediments to family life and the slaves' spirited commitment to overcoming them—must be our goal"; Philip D. Morgan, *Slave Counterpoint: Black Culture in the Eighteenth-Century Chesapeake and Lowcountry* (Chapel Hill: University of North Carolina Press for the Institute of Early American History and Culture, 1998), 501.

4. Amy Dru Stanley, "Instead of Waiting for the Thirteenth Amendment: The War Power, Slave Marriage, and Inviolate Human Rights," *American Historical Review* 115, no. 3 (2010): 732–65, 749. Historians of colonial slavery have considered the issue of slavery and marriage mainly as a problem of definition; Morgan, *Slave Counterpoint*, 499. More recent, excellent treatment occurs in Tera Hunter, *Bound in Wedlock: Slave and Free Black Marriage in the Nineteenth Century* (Cambridge: Harvard University Press, 2017). Herbert Gutman and Brenda Stevenson, among others, have argued for the continuation of domestic practices: Herbert G. Gutman, *The Black Family in Slavery and Freedom, 1750–1925* (Oxford: Basil Blackwell, 1976), and Brenda Stevenson, "Black Family Structure in Colonial and Antebellum Virginia: Amending the Revisionist Perspective," in *The Decline in Marriage among African Americans: Causes, Consequences, and Policy Implications,* ed. M. Belinda Tucker and Claudia Mitchell-Kernan, 27–56 (New York: Russell Sage Foundation, 1995). Most works on marriage focus on the nineteenth century: Brenda Stevenson, *Life in Black and White: Family and Community in the Slave South* (Oxford: Oxford University Press, 1996); Ann Patton Malone, *Sweet Chariot: Slave Family and Household Structure in Nineteenth-Century Louisiana* (Chapel Hill: University of North Carolina Press, 1992); Wilma Dunaway, *The African-American Family in Slavery and Emancipation* (Cambridge: Cambridge University Press, 2003); Larry E. Hudson, Jr., *To Have and Hold: Slave Work and Family Life in Antebellum South Carolina* (Athens: University of Georgia Press, 1997); Emily West, *Chains of Love: Slave Couples in Antebellum South Carolina* (Urbana: University of Illinois Press, 2004); Rebecca J. Fraser, *Courtship and Love among the Enslaved in North Carolina* (Jackson: University of Mississippi Press, 2007); and Francis Smith Foster, *'Til Death or Distance Do Us Part: Love and Marriage in African America* (Oxford: Oxford University Press, 2010). Many debates on African polygamy have centered on whether higher rates of polygyny, and the higher prices enslaved women commanded in areas where it was more common, tended to mean fewer women were exported from certain areas to

the Atlantic slave trade. Paul Lovejoy, *Transformations in Slavery: A History of Slavery in Africa,* 2nd ed. (1983; Cambridge: Cambridge University Press, 2000); Patrick Manning, *Slavery and African Life: Occidental, Oriental, and African Slave Trades* (Cambridge: Cambridge University Press, 1990); and G. Ugo Nwokeji, *The Slave Trade and Culture in the Bight of Biafra: An African Society in the Atlantic World* (Cambridge: Cambridge University Press, 2010). Also see Jennifer L. Morgan, *Laboring Women: Reproduction and Gender in New World Slavery* (Philadelphia: University of Pennsylvania Press, 2004). A classic example of this claim: "Despite severe dislocation, they [Africans] retained many elements of traditional culture"; Barbara Bush, " 'The Family Tree Is Not Cut': Women and Cultural Resistance in Slave Family Life in the British Caribbean," in *In Resistance: Studies in African, Caribbean, and Afro-American History,* ed. Gary Okihiro, 117–32 (Amherst: University of Massachusetts Press, 1986), 121.

5. "African-American culture . . . was less an achieved state . . . than an ongoing argument about what elements of a shared past were relevant to a current situation"; Walter Johnson, "On Agency," *Journal of Social History* 37, no. 1 (2003): 113–24, 119, and Morgan, *Laboring Women,* 66.

6. Morgan, *Laboring Women,* 66; Dylan C. Penningroth, "The Claims of Slaves and Ex-Slaves to Family and Property: A Transatlantic Comparison," *American Historical Review* 112, no. 4 (2007): 1039–69, 1069; James H. Sweet, "Defying Social Death: The Multiple Configurations of African Slave Family in the Atlantic World," *William and Mary Quarterly* 70, no. 2 (2013): 251–72, 253.

7. Penningroth, "Claims of Slaves and Ex-Slaves," 1053; Hunter, *Bound in Wedlock,* 7.

8. Morgan, *Laboring Women;* Marisa J. Fuentes, *Dispossessed Lives: Enslaved Women, Violence, and the Archive* (Philadelphia: University of Pennsylvania Press, 2016); Sasha Turner, *Contested Bodies: Pregnancy, Childrearing, and Slavery in Jamaica* (Philadelphia: University of Pennsylvania Press, 2017). Hope Masterton Waddell, *Twenty-Nine Years in the West Indies and Central Africa* (1863), 147, as quoted in B. W. Higman with contributions by George A. Aarons, Karlis Karklins, and Elizabeth J. Reitz, *Montpelier, Jamaica: A Plantation Community in Slavery and Freedom, 1739–1912* (Kingston: University Press of the West Indies, 1998), 145. Dylan C. Penningroth, *The Claims of Kinfolk: African American Property and Community* (Chapel Hill: University of North Carolina Press, 2003), 9. Stephanie Smallwood, *Saltwater Slavery: A Middle Passage from Africa to American Diaspora* (Cambridge:

Harvard University Press, 2007); Marcus Rediker, *The Slave Ship: A Human History* (New York: Penguin, 2007); and Sowande' M. Mustakeem, *Slavery at Sea: Terror, Sex, and Sickness in the Middle Passage* (Urbana: University of Illinois Press, 2016).

9. "There is an old American tradition of seizing on black people's disputes with each other in order to put down blacks as a people"; Penningroth, *The Claims of Kinfolk*, 12. See also Daniel Moynihan et al., "The Negro Family: The Case for National Action" (1965); Daniel Geary, *Beyond Civil Rights: The Moynihan Report and Its Legacy* (Philadelphia: University of Pennsylvania Press, 2015); and Ta-Nehisi Coates, "The Black Family in the Age of Mass Incarceration," *Atlantic*, October 2015.

10. See, among others, Amy Dru Stanley, "Conjugal Bonds and Wage Labor: Rights of Contract in the Age of Emancipation," *Journal of American History* 75, no. 2 (1988): 471–500, and her "Instead of Waiting"; Laura F. Edwards, "'The Marriage Covenant Is at the Foundation of All Our Rights': The Legal and Political Implications of Marriage in Post-Emancipation North Carolina," *Law and History Review* 14 (1996): 81–124, and her *Gendered Strife and Confusion: The Political Culture of Reconstruction* (Urbana: University of Illinois Press, 1997); Noralee Frankel, *Freedom's Women: Black Women and Families in Civil War Era Mississippi* (Bloomington: Indiana University Press, 1999); Katherine M. Franke, "Becoming a Citizen: Reconstruction Era Regulation of African American Marriages," *Yale Journal of Law and the Humanities* 11, no. 2 (1999): 251–309; and Megan J. McClintock, "The Impact of the Civil War on Nineteenth-Century Marriages," in *Union Soldiers and the Northern Home Front: Wartime Experiences, Postwar Adjustments*, ed. Paul A. Cimbala and Randall M. Miller, 395–416 (New York: Fordham University Press, 2002). Pieter de Marees, *Description and Historical Account of the Gold Kingdom of Guinea* (1602), trans. and ed. by Albert van Dantzig and Adam Jones (Oxford: Oxford University Press, 1987), 37, 23. Willem Bosman, *A New and Accurate Description of the Coast of Guinea* (London: James Knapton and Dan Midwinter, 1705), 198–99, 206. Polygamy supposedly also rendered women infertile. See Katherine Paugh, *The Politics of Reproduction: Race, Medicine, and Fertility in the Age of Abolition* (Oxford: Oxford University Press, 2017).

11. "The strong attachment of the Blacks to *Polygamy*, is curiously illustrated by the following story"; *Massachusetts Gazette*, October 14, 1788, p. 4. Charles Cocock Jones, "Suggestions on the Religious Instruction of the Negroes in the Southern States," *Princeton Review* 20, no. 1 (1848), 1–30, 9. Making of

America Database, University of Michigan. Stanley, "Instead of Waiting," 749.

12. Marees, *Description and Historical Account*, 29, 31, 38.

13. "Ils ont autant de femmes qu'ils en peuvent nourrir"; Père Godefroy Loyer (1714), as quoted in *L'établissement D'issiny, 1687–1702*, ed. Paul Roussier (Paris: Librairie Larousse, 1935), 145. A French manuscript version and a (posthumous) English printed version of Jean Barbot's account of Guinea are extant. The modern English translation of the French is the more reliable. P. E. H. Hair, Adam Jones, and Robin Law, eds., *Barbot on Guinea: The Writings of Jean Barbot on West Africa, 1678–1712*, 2 vols. (London: Hakluyt Society, 1992), 2nd ser., vols. 175–76, 175: 86. Jean Barbot, *A Description of the Coast of North and South-Guinea* (London: John Walthoe, Thomas Wotton, Samuel Birt, and Daniel Browne et al., 1732), 36. William Smith, *A New Voyage to Guinea* (London: John Nourse, 1744), 145.

14. Bosman, *New and Accurate Description*, 347, 24, 52, 206, 344.

15. William Pietz, "The Problem of the Fetish, IIIa: Bosman's Guinea and the Enlightenment Theory of Fetishism," *RES: Anthropology and Aesthetics* 16 (1988): 105–24, 116.

16. Olaudah Equiano, *The Interesting Narrative of the Life of Olaudah Equiano, Written by Himself*, ed. Robert J. Allison (1789; Boston: Bedford, 1995), 48; Venture Smith, *A Narrative of the Life and Adventures of Venture, a Native of Africa* (New London, CT: C. Holt, 1798), 5, http://docsouth.unc.edu/neh/venture/venture.html.

17. Edna Bay, *Wives of the Leopard: Gender, Politics, and Culture in the Kingdom of Dahomey* (Charlottesville: University of Virginia Press, 1998), 3, 8–9, 18–20, 68–69, 152.

18. Garrett R. Fesler, "Living Arrangements among Enslaved Women and Men at an Early-Eighteenth-Century Virginia Quartering Site," in *Engendering African American Archaeology: A Southern Perspective*, ed. Jillian E. Galle and Amy L. Young, 177–236 (Knoxville: University of Tennessee Press, 2005), 182; Allan Kulikoff, *Tobacco and Slaves: The Development of Southern Cultures in the Chesapeake, 1680–1800* (Chapel Hill: University of North Carolina Press for the Institute of Early American History and Culture, 1986), 321; Morgan, *Slave Counterpoint*, 321; Lorena S. Walsh, *Motives of Honor, Pleasure, and Profit: Plantation Management in the Colonial Chesapeake, 1607–1763* (Chapel Hill: University of North Carolina Press for the Omohundro Institute of Early American History and Culture, 2010), 55; Douglas B. Chambers, *Murder at Montpelier: Igbo Africans in Virginia* (Oxford: University Press of Mississippi,

2005), and his "Tracing Igbo in the African Diaspora," in *Identity in the Shadow of Slavery*, ed. Paul E. Lovejoy, 55–71 (New York: Continuum, 2000). As Eugenia Shanklin wryly observes, "Africans hate all generalizations about Africa"; "Family and Kinship," in *Understanding Contemporary Africa*, 4th ed., ed. April A. Gordon and Donald L. Gordon, 265–92 (Boulder, CO: Lynne Rienner, 2007), 274–75. On Igbo diversity and also polygamy, Don C. Ohadike, *Anioma: A Social History of the Western Igbo People* (Athens: Ohio University Press, 1994), 27, 207.

19. Ohadike, *Anioma*, 71. "Wealth, power, and prestige were measured primarily in people, not land or money"; James H. Sweet, *Domingos Álvares, African Healing, and the Intellectual History of the Atlantic World* (Chapel Hill: University of North Carolina Press, 2011), 33. On lineage, see Ohadike, *Anioma*, 69–71, and Elechukwu Nnadibuagha Njaka, *Igbo Political Culture* (Evanston: Northwestern University Press, 1974), 27.

20. Augustine Konneh, "Life and Work in West Africa," in *A Companion to African American History*, ed. Alfred Hornsby, Jr., 5–22 (Oxford: Blackwell, 2005), 7. "Marriage was also a means of tapping new sources of knowledge"; Jane I. Guyer and Samuel M. Eno Belinga, "Wealth in People as Wealth in Knowledge: Accumulation and Composition in Equatorial Africa," *Journal of African History* 36 (1995): 91–120, 115. Egodi Uchendu, "Woman-Woman Marriage in Igboland," in *Critical Essays on Gender and Sexuality in African Literature and Film*, ed. Ada Uzoamaka Azodo and Maureen Eke, 1–16 (Trenton, NJ: Africa World, 2007), 5.

21. Uchendu, "Woman-Woman Marriage," 1, 2, 7.

22. Such seems to have been the case in Anlo in the early eighteenth century, as detailed by Sandra E. Greene, *Gender, Ethnicity, and Social Change on the Upper Slave Coast: A History of the Anlo-Ewe* (Portsmouth, NH: Heinemann, 1996), 38–39.

23. Marees, *Description and Historical Account*, 22; Hair et al., ed. *Barbot on Guinea*, 1: 504; Chike Aniakor, "Household Objects and the Philosophy of Igbo Social Space," in Mary Jo Arnoldi and Kris L. Hardin, *African Material Culture* (Bloomington: Indiana University Press, 1996), 214–42, 220; and Joseph Thérèse Agbasiere, *Women in Igbo Life and Thought* (London: Routledge, 2000), 41.

24. Njaka, *Igbo Political Culture*, 59, 155; Ohadike, *Anioma*, 72–73, 92; Smith, *New Voyage*, 145–46; Hair, Jones, and Law, *Barbot on Guinea*, 1: 504. On this point for other areas, see Nakanyike B. Musisi, "Women, 'Elite Polygyny,' and Buganda State Formation," *Signs* 16, no. 4 (1991): 757–86, 778; Bay, *Wives of the Leopard*,

8; and Victoria B. Tashjian and Jean Allman, "Marrying and Marriage on a Shifting Terrain: Reconfigurations of Power and Authority in Early Colonial Asante," in *Women in African Colonial Histories*, ed. Susan Geiger, Nakanyike Musisi, and Jean Marie Allman, 237–60 (Bloomington: Indiana University Press, 2002), 244. Elizabeth Isichei, *A History of the Igbo People* (New York: St. Martin's, 1976), 102–4, 102, and Lovejoy, *Transformations in Slavery*, 183–84.

25. Shanklin, "Family and Kinship," 271.

26. Nwokeji, *Slave Trade and Culture*, 26–27, 148; Ohadike, *Anioma*, 27. On the political import of sacrifice of captives, Bay, *Wives of the Leopard*, 66.

27. Musisi, "Women," passim; Greene, *Gender, Ethnicity, and Social Change*, passim; and Bay, *Wives of the Leopard*, 143.

28. Nwokeji, *Slave Trade and Culture*, 27, and Roquinaldo Ferreira, *Cross-Cultural Exchange in the Atlantic World: Angola and Brazil during the Era of the Slave Trade* (Cambridge: Cambridge University Press, 2012), 55.

29. Peter P. Ekeh, "Social Anthropology and Two Contrasting Uses of Tribalism in Africa," *Comparative Studies in Society and History* 32, no. 4 (1990): 660–700, 661, 682, and Ferreira, *Cross-Cultural Exchange*, 55.

30. Kulikoff, *Tobacco and Slaves*, 354, and Shanklin, "Family and Kinship," 274.

31. Sweet, "Defying Social Death," 254. "The greater distribution of men . . . gave women more options for choosing and rejecting partners for sex and enjoying the full panoply of heterosexual relationships"; Hunter, *Bound in Wedlock*, 33.

32. Walsh, *Motives*, 251. In Philip Morgan's analysis of the Carter inventory, 57 percent of African men lived alone or with other men in small quarters; *Slave Counterpoint*, 502, 503, 512.

33. Garrett R. Fesler and Matthew R. Laird, "A Phase I Cultural Resources Survey of 9 Acres Located along York River Road . . .," unpublished report, VDHR File Number: 2010–1637 (2010), 7.

34. "Inventory of Ripon Hall Plantation," December 1712. The use of poison may also suggest connections with West African practices. See Chambers, *Murder at Montpelier*, 67. Henry Laurens to Elias Ball, Wambaw, May 2, 1766, in *The Laurens Papers*, 16 vols., vol. 5, *Sept 1, 1765–July 31, 1768*, ed. David R. Chesnutt, (Columbia: University of South Carolina Press, 1974), 123–24.

35. Darrett B. Rutman and Anita H. Rutman, *A Place in Time: Middlesex County, Virginia, 1650–1750* (New York: Norton, 1986).

36. Walsh, *Motives*, 262; Fesler, "Living Arrangements," 193; Elizabeth Isichei, *A History of Nigeria* (London: Longman, 1983), 192; and Ohadike, *Anioma*, 90.

37. Unlike the other two cabins, Structure 10, the central and largest one in the northern position, "has the strongest association with women's activity." Yet at the same time "men may have asserted a more prominent role in Structure 10"; Fesler, "Living Arrangements, 205, 212–13, 215.

38. Garrett Randall Fesler, "From Houses to Homes: An Archaeological Case Study of Household Formation at the Utopia Slave Quarter, ca. 1675 to 1775," Ph.D. diss., University of Virginia, 2004, 283; Patricia M. Samford, *Subfloor Pits and the Archaeology of Slavery in Colonial Virginia* (Tuscaloosa: University of Alabama Press, 2007), ch. 8.

39. At New Kent, there were eight women, and three men; at Bridges, ten women, three men; Fesler "Living Arrangements," 189, 191, 192. Robert Carter, neighboring planter, described renaming new arrivals; Walsh, *Motives*, 259.

40. Nwokeji, *Slave Trade and Culture*, 145–77 esp. 147.

41. "In one quarter, one of the foremen had two wives, a common custom in Africa but unusual in the Chesapeake"; Walsh, *Motives*, 258, 262, 261. Carter quotation from Robert Carter Inventory, Virginia Historical Society inventory at http://carter.lib.virginia.edu/html/C33inven.mod.html. Walsh, *Motives*, 258. "The numbers of individuals encompassed in two-parent units detracts from the fact that the real strength of the slave community was its multiplicity of forms, its tolerance for a variety of slave families and households, its adaptability, and its acceptance of all types of families and households as functional and contributing"; Malone, *Sweet Chariot*, 258.

42. Walsh, *Motives*, 262.

43. "Even though Carter apparently encouraged marriage and family life . . . over half the men and a similar proportion of boys age ten to fourteen lived with unrelated men"; Kulikoff, *Tobacco and Slaves*, 356.

44. Hilary D. Beckles, "Female Enslavement and Gender Ideologies in the Caribbean," in Lovejoy, *Identity in the Shadow of Slavery*, 163–82, 169–70, and Nwokeji, *Slave Trade and Culture*, 153.

45. On age-grades, see Ohadike, *Anioma*, 72–73.

46. Richard Ligon, *A True & Exact History of the Island of Barbadoes* (London, 1673), 47. Peter Thompson, "Henry Drax's Instructions on the Management of a Seventeenth-Century Barbadian Sugar Plantation," *William and Mary Quarterly* 66, no. 3 (2009): 565–604. Quotations and discussion, 577, 600. Rawlinson Agreement MSS A348, fol. 10v. Jennifer Morgan recognizes that *wifes* refers to polygamy and how "Nocco's family's African past is made visible"; *Laboring Women*, 120. Higman, *Montpelier, Jamaica*, 122–23.

47. Fesler, "Living Arrangements," 198.

48. Nwokeji, *Slave Trade and Culture*, 171. See, among others, Thelma Jennings, " 'Us Colored Women Had to Go Through a Plenty': Sexual Exploitation of African-American Slave Women," *Journal of Women's History* 1, no. 3 (1990): 45–74; Morgan, *Laboring Women;* Kathleen M. Brown, *Good Wives, Nasty Wenches, and Anxious Patriarchs: Gender, Race, and Power in Colonial Virginia* (Chapel Hill: University of North Carolina Press, 1996); Edward E. Baptist, " 'Cuffy,' 'Fancy Maids,' and 'One-Eyed Men': Rape, Commodification, and the Domestic Slave Trade in the United States," *American Historical Review* 106, no. 5 (2001): 1619–50; Wendy Warren, " 'The Cause of Her Grief': The Rape of a Slave in Early New England," *Journal of American History* 93, no. 4 (2007): 1031–49; Thomas A. Foster, "The Sexual Abuse of Black Men under American Slavery," *Journal of the History of Sexuality* 20, no. 3 (2011): 445–64. There are also rich treatments of these issues for the Anglophone Caribbean. See, among others, Fuentes, *Dispossessed Lives;* Turner, *Contested Bodies*; Trevor Burnard, *Mastery, Tyranny, and Desire: Thomas Thistlewood and His Slaves in the Anglo-Jamaican World* (Chapel Hill: University of North Carolina Press, 2004); Daniel Livesay, *Children of Uncertain Fortune: Mixed-Race Jamaicans in Britain and the Atlantic Family, 1733–1833* (Chapel Hill: University of North Carolina Press for the Omohundro Insitute of Early American History and Culture, 2018); and Brooke N. Newman, *A Dark Inheritance: Blood, Race, and Sex in Colonial Jamaica* (New Haven: Yale University Press, 2018).

49. Nwokeji, *Slave Trade and Culture*, 175. "Although there were known incidents of plural marriages in which partners knew about and agreed to the arrangement, they were unusual"; Hunter, *Bound in Wedlock*, 33.

50. "If slavery bred strong women, however, it hardly emasculated black men"; Morgan, *Slave Counterpoint*, 533.

51. Sarah M. S. Pearsall, *Atlantic Families: Lives and Letters in the Later Eighteenth Century* (Oxford: Oxford University Press, 2008), introduction; Faramerz Dabhoiwala, *The Origins of Sex: A History of the First Sexual Revolution* (London: Penguin, 2012); and David Herlihy, "Family," *American Historical Review* 96, no. 1 (1991): 1–16, 2.

52. See, for instance, Brown, *Good Wives;* Kulikoff, *Tobacco and Slaves;* Rhys Isaac, *Landon Carter's Uneasy Kingdom: Revolution and Rebellion on a Virginia Plantation* (Oxford: Oxford University Press, 2004); Emory G. Evans, *A "Topping People": The Rise and Decline of Virginia's Old Political Elite, 1680–1790* (Charlottesville: University of Virginia Press, 2009); and

Matthew Kruer, "Bloody Minds and Peoples Undone: Emotion, Family, and Political Order in the Susquehannock-Virginia War," *William and Mary Quarterly* 74, no. 3 (2017): 401–36.

53. Walsh, *Motives*, 256, and Virginia Foundation for the Humanities/Library of Virginia, *Encyclopedia Virginia*, http://encyclopediavirginia.org/Carter_Robert_ca_1664-1732#start_entry, accessed February 20, 2015.

54. Appendix A of Fesler, "From Houses to Homes."

55. Evans, *A "Topping People,"* 127, 123, 16–17. See also Kulikoff, *Tobacco and Slaves*, 252–53. See William Byrd, *The Secret Diary of William Byrd of Westover, 1709–1712*, ed. Louis B. Wright and Marion Tinlin (Richmond, VA: Dietz, 1941).

56. Chernoh M. Sesay, Jr., "The Revolutionary Black Roots of Slavery's Abolition in Massachusetts," *New England Quarterly* 87, no. 1 (2014): 99–131, 100, and "Petition for freedom to Massachusetts Governor Thomas Gage, His Majesty's Council, and the House of Representatives, May 25, 1774," MHS Online.

57. Hunter, *Bound in Wedlock*, 33, 38. Declaration of 16 Sept 1780 (wigs) and Dec 15 1810 (carnal), Upper King & Queen Church (Rappahannock) 1774–1815; Case of Negro Daniel, 19 Dec 1789, in Buck Marsh (Now Berryville) 1785–1803; Label inside: "The Records of the Church of Christ at Buck Marsh" 1786 (uncleanness), The Case of Fanny, 6 Feb 1808, 5 Mar 1808, Apr 2 1808, "The Records of the Church of Christ at Buck Marsh," second book, 1804–41; Query, Decr 18 1797, and Jan 1826, Upper King & Queen Church (Rappahannock) 1774–1815; Virginia Baptist Historical Society, University of Richmond (hereafter VBHS). For a general discussion of these records, see Sylvia Frey and Betty Wood, *Come Shouting to Zion: African American Protestantism in the American South and the British Caribbean to 1830* (Chapel Hill: University of North Carolina Press, 1998). See also Jewel L. Spangler, *Virginians Reborn: Anglican Monopoly, Evangelical Dissent, and the Rise of the Baptists in the Late Eighteenth Century* (Charlottesville: University Press of Virginia, 2008).

58. Hunter, *Bound in Wedlock*, 10. Theodore Parker to David Wasson, December 12, 1857, Theodore Parker Papers, Massachusetts Historical Society. Many thanks to Ben Park for this reference.

59. According to one historian of the Igbo people, "a man without a title was like a child without a face. . . . When he died, he was not mourned with much grieving, nor was his corpse buried with dignity. . . . The Igbo believed that a man who died before acquiring the higher titles had failed to secure

immortality and therefore would not join the ancestors, . . . instead his sprit would roam the universe, aimlessly, sometimes causing mischief and pain to the living"; Ohadike, *Anioma*, 90.

5. *"The Natural Violence of Our Passions"*

1. Letter from Abigail Adams to John Adams, June 17, 1782, Adams Papers Online, Massachusetts Historical Society, https://www.masshist.org/digitaladams/archive/doc?id=L17820617aa.

2. On storytelling, as one historian has phrased it, in a quite different context, "The inaccuracies in these stories make them exceptionally reliable historical sources as well: they offer historians a way to see the world the way story-tellers did"; Luise White, *Speaking with Vampires: Rumor and History in Colonial Africa* (Berkeley: University of California Press, 2000), 5. On "logic of elimination" and settler colonialism, see Patrick Wolfe, "Land, Labor, and Difference: Elementary Structures of Race," *American Historical Review* 106, no. 3 (2001): 866–905; Daiva Stasiulis and Nira Yuval-Davis, eds., *Unsettling Settler Societies: Articulations of Gender, Race, Ethnicity, and Class* (London: Sage, 1995); Margaret D. Jacobs, *White Mother to a Dark Race: Settler Colonialism, Maternalism, and the Removal of Indigenous Children in the American West and Australia, 1880–1940* (Lincoln: University of Nebraska Press, 2009); and Ann Laura Stoler, *Carnal Knowledge and Imperial Power: Race and the Intimate in Colonial Rule* (2002; Berkeley: University of California Press, 2010). On gender, family, and Enlightenment, see Sylvana Tomaselli, "The Enlightenment Debate on Women," *History Workshop Journal* 20 (1985): 101–24, and her "The Most Public Sphere of All: The Family," in *Women, Writing, and the Public Sphere, 1700–1830*, ed. Elizabeth Eger, Charlotte Grant, Cliona O. Gallchoir, and Penny Warburton, 239–56 (Cambridge: Cambridge University Press, 2001); Sarah Maza, *Private Lives and Public Affairs: The Causes Célèbres of Prerevolutionary France* (Berkeley: University of California Press, 1995); Nicholas B. Miller, *John Millar and the Scottish Enlightenment: Family Life and World History* (Oxford: Voltaire Foundation, 2017); and Meghan K. Roberts, *Sentimental Savants: Philosophical Families in Enlightenment France* (Chicago: University of Chicago Press, 2016). On Enlightenment, empire, and slavery, see Caroline Winterer, *American Enlightenments: Pursuing Happiness in the Age of Reason* (New Haven: Yale University Press, 2016); Sankar Muthu, *Enlightenment against Empire* (Princeton: Princeton University Press, 2003); Jennifer Pitts, *A Turn to Empire: The Rise of Imperial Liberalism in Britain and France* (Princeton: Princeton

University Press, 2005); T. Carlos Jacques, "From Savages and Barbarians to Primitives: Africa, Social Typologies, and History in Eighteenth-Century French Philosophy," *History and Theory* 36, no. 2 (1997): 190–215; Laurent DuBois, "An Enslaved Enlightenment: Rethinking the Intellectual History of the French Atlantic," *Social History* 31 (2006): 1–14; Justin Roberts, *Slavery and the Enlightenment in the British Atlantic, 1750–1807* (Cambridge: Cambridge University Press, 2013); David Allen Harvey, *The French Enlightenment and Its Others: The Mandarin, the Savage, and the Invention of the Human Sciences* (Basingstoke: Palgrave Macmillan, 2012); and Silvia Sebastiani, *The Scottish Enlightenment: Race, Gender, and the Limits of Progress,* trans. Jeremey Carden (Basingstoke: Palgrave Macmillan, 2013). Quotation from Carol Blum, *Strength in Numbers: Population, Reproduction, and Power in Eighteenth-Century France* (Baltimore: Johns Hopkins University Press, 2002), 81.

3. William Alexander, *The History of Women, from the Earliest Antiquity, to the Present Time,* 2 vols. (London: W. Strahan and T. Cadell, 1779), 2: 220.

4. Terryl L. Givens long ago identified what he calls "the Orientalization of Mormonism"; *The Viper on the Hearth: Mormons, Myths, and the Construction of Heresy* (Oxford: Oxford University Press, 1997), 130. Yet in fact it might make more sense to think about the "Mormonization of Orientalism." Christine Talbot acknowledges the importance of "Orientalism" in anti-Mormonism, but she focuses on literature about Muslims in the early American republic; *A Foreign Kingdom: Mormons and Polygamy in American Political Culture, 1852–1890* (Urbana: University of Illinois Press, 2013), 130–31. Paul Reeve contends that "Mormonism's founding decades coincided with a period in which whiteness itself came under question." He points to the worries attendant on race in this period, including nativism and immigration concerns. While Reeve's argument is powerful, these complications over whiteness and race had long preexisted the nineteenth century. W. Paul Reeve, *Religion of a Different Color: Race and the Mormon Struggle for Whiteness* (Oxford: Oxford University Press, 2015), 7, 8. See also J. Spencer Fluhman, *"A Peculiar People": Anti-Mormonism and the Making of Religion in Nineteenth-Century America* (Chapel Hill: University of North Carolina Press, 2012), 117, 119. All these authors link these negative stereotypes with the alleged inferiority of women in polygamy, but less consideration is given to the male-male relations invoked by these "Orientalist" tropes.

5. Since the key point here is how Tournefort got picked up by Anglophone authors, I have used the contemporary translation: Joseph Pitton de

Tournefort, *A Voyage into the* Levant, 2 vols. (London: D. Browne et al., 1718), 2: 248–49.

6. Ibid., 2: 248.

7. Ibid., 2: 72–73.

8. Ibid., 2: 324.

9. Christopher Levett (1628) quoted in George Parker Winship, ed., *Sailors' Narratives of Voyages along the New England Coast, 1524–1624* (New York: Burt Franklin, 1905), 284.

10. Louis Hennepin, *Nouvelle Découverte d'un très grand Pays Situé dans l'Amérique* (Utrecht: Guillaume Broedelet, 1697), 219–20, trans. as *A New Discovery of a Vast Country in America* (1698; Chicago: A. C. McClurg, 1903, rpt. of the 2nd London ed.), 167–68.

11. Barbot borrowed from many other writings, most notably Pieter de Marees, *Description and Historical Account of the Gold Kingdom of Guinea* (1602), trans. and ed. by Albert van Dantzig and Adam Jones (Oxford: Oxford University Press, 1987), and Willem Bosman, *A New and Accurate Description of the Coast of Guinea* (London: James Knapton and Dan Midwinter, 1705). See P. E. H. Hair, Adam Jones, and Robin Law, eds., *Barbot on Guinea: The Writings of Jean Barbot on West Africa, 1678–1712*, 2 vols., *Works Issued by the Hakluyt Society*, 2nd ser. nos. 175–76 (London: Hakluyt Society, 1992), 1: ix, xii, xxi–lvi, and Jean Barbot, *A Description of the Coast of North and South-Guinea* (London: John Walthoe, Thomas Wotton, Samuel Birt, and Daniel Browne et al., 1732), 36, 84–85, 87, 53, 56, 88. Francis Moore, *Travels into the Inland Parts of Africa* (London, 1755), 60–61, 91.

12. François Pyrard, *The Voyage of François Pyrard of Laval to the East Indies, the Maldives, the Moluccas, and Brazil*, trans. Albert Gray, ed. H. C. P. Bell (1897; Cambridge: Cambridge University Press, 2010), 162–63. As Carmen Nocentelli rightly notes, "early modern representations of nonmonogamy assisted in the construction of domestic heterosexuality"; *Empires of Love: Europe, Asia, and the Making of Early Modern Identity* (Philadelphia: University of Pennsylvania Press, 2014), ch. 4, 94. Pyrard, *Voyage*, 163. "Comment ils se marient" and "La Polygamie en usage"; Martin Martinivsi, "Description Geographique de la l'Empire de la Chine," in Melchisédech Thévenot, *Recueil de voyages de M Thevenot* (Paris: Estienne Michallet, 1681). John Locke owned a copy of this work. See Bodleian Library Locke 8.196. See also François Bernier, *History of the Late Revolution of the Empire of the Great Mogol*, 4 vols. (London: Moses Pitt, Simon Miller, and John Starkey, 1671). For a useful discussion of these authors, see Nicholas Dew, "Reading Travels

in the Culture of Curiosity: Thévenot's Collection of Voyages," *Journal of Early Modern History* 10, nos. 1–2 (2006): 39–59, and his *Orientalism in Louis XIV's France* (Oxford: Oxford University Press, 2009), esp. chs. 2–3. Shannon Lee Dawdy, *Building the Devil's Empire: French Colonial New Orleans* (Chicago: University of Chicago Press, 2008).

13. Miller, *John Millar and the Scottish Enlightenment*, 47; Joanna de Groot, "Oriental Feminotopias? Montagu's and Montesquieu's 'Seraglios' Revisited," *Gender and History* 18, no. 1 (2006): 66–86, 77, and Joseph Allen Boone, *The Homoerotics of Orientalism* (New York: Columbia University Press, 2014), 96. See also Perrin Stein, "Exoticism as Metaphor: Turquerie in Eighteenth-Century France," Ph.D. diss., New York University, 1997, and Alexander Bevilacqua and Helen Pfeifer, "Turquerie: Culture in Motion, 1650–1750," *Past and Present*, no. 221 (2013): 75–118.

14. This vision "represents a powerful strategy for making the erotic, as well as the domestic, constituent signifiers of the political and of power relations in general"; De Groot, "Oriental Feminotopias?" 68. Montesquieu, *The Complete Works of M. de Montesquieu*, 4 vols. (London: T. Evans and W. Davis, 1777), 3: 216–17, 268, 299. I have used a contemporary English translation as its circulation in this era was significant.

15. Helen Berry, *The Castrato and His Wife* (Oxford: Oxford University Press, 2011), especially ch. 1; Thomas Foster, "Deficient Husbands: Manhood, Sexual Incapacity, and Male Marital Sexuality in Seventeenth-Century New England," *William and Mary Quarterly* 56, no. 4 (1999): 723–44; and Ali Behdad, "The Eroticized Orient: Images of the Harem in Montesquieu and his Precursors," *Stanford French Review* 13, nos. 2–3 (1989), 109–26, 119. Montesquieu, *Complete Works*, 3: 216–17, 219–20.

16. Jean-François Melon, *Mahmoud le Gasnevide: Histoire Orientale* (Rotterdam: Jean Hofhoudt, 1729), 1, 12, 78 (translation mine). Jean-François Melon, *Essai Politique sur le Commerce* (n.p., 1736).

17. Montesquieu, *The Complete Works of M. de Montesquieu*, 4 vols. (London: T. Evans and W. Davis, 1777), 1: 332–33, 335 (italics mine).

18. Ibid., 1: 336, 330. David M. Turner, *Fashioning Adultery: Gender, Sex, and Civility in England, 1660–1740* (Cambridge: Cambridge University Press, 2002). Boone contends that eunuchs "represented a disturbing anomaly in European conceptions of racialized heterosexual masculinity"; *The Homoerotics of Orientalism*, 96–100, 99.

19. Montesquieu, *Complete Works*, 1: 338–39. On these themes, see Tobias Smollett, *The Adventures of Roderick Random*. This phrase also appears in letters of

the period, as in that of John Tharp about his son's preference for sex with men. See Sarah M. S. Pearsall, *Atlantic Families: Lives and Letters in the Later Eighteenth Century* (Oxford: Oxford University Press, 2008), ch 7. On rape and its political valence in this era, see Sharon Block, "Rape without Women: Print Culture and the Politicization of Rape, 1765–1815," *Journal of American History* 89, no. 3 (2002): 849–68.

20. Montesquieu, *Complete Works*, 1: 330, 336–38.

21. David Hume, "Of Polygamy and Divorces," in *Essays, Moral and Political,* 3rd ed. (London: A. Millar and A. Kincaid, 1748), 247–59, 258, 249, 247.

22. Ibid., 250, 252–53. Montesquieu, *Complete Works*, 3: 299. On Scottish marriage and divorce practices, see Leah Leneman, *Alienated Affections: Divorce and Separation in Scotland, 1684–1830* (Edinburgh: Edinburgh University Press, 1998), and Katie Barclay, *Love, Intimacy, and Power: Marriage and Patriarchy in Scotland, 1650–1850* (Manchester: Manchester University Press, 2011). On Hume's ideas about women and gender, see, for instance, Anne Jaap Jacobson, ed., *Feminist Interpretations of David Hume* (University Park: Pennsylvania State University Press, 2000). On control of passions, see Nicole Eustace, *Passion Is the Gale: Emotion, Power, and the Coming of the American Revolution* (Chapel Hill: University of North Carolina Press for the Omohundro Institute of Early American History and Culture, 2008).

23. Hume, "Of Polygamy and Divorces," 251. Elaine Forman Crane, "Political Dialogue and the Spring of Abigail's Discontent," *William and Mary Quarterly* 56, no. 4 (1999), 745–74.

24. Hume, "Of Polygamy and Divorces," 252, 259. On the political import of relations between men, see Mark Kann, *Republic of Men: The American Founders, Gendered Language, and Patriarchal Politics* (New York: New York University Press, 1998), and Richard Godbeer, *The Overflowing of Friendship: Love between Men and the Creation of the American Republic* (Baltimore: Johns Hopkins University Press, 2009).

25. André-Pierre le Guy de Prémontval, *La Monogamie, ou L'Unité dans le Mariage* (The Hague: Pierre van Cleef, 1751), 227–28, 231–32 (translation mine).

26. Adam Smith, *Lectures on Justice, Police, Revenue, and Arms* (1763), ed. Edwin Cannan (Oxford: Clarendon, 1896), 75.

27. For Smith, according to David Lieberman, "natural jurisprudence had an explicitly normative and universalistic orientation." Smith emphasized the "rudeness and barbarism" of earlier stages of human development; he placed polygamy in these early, "rude" stages. David Lieberman, "Adam Smith on Justice, Rights, and Law," in *The Cambridge Companion to Adam Smith*, ed.

Knud Haakonssen, 214–45 (Cambridge: Cambridge University Press, 2006), 224, 228. Smith, *Lectures on Justice*, 80–81. See also Adam Smith, *The Theory of Moral Sentiments* (London: A. Millar, A. Kincaid, and J. Bell, 1759), part I, 82–83.

28. Smith, *Lectures on Justice*, 81–83.

29. Antoine Léonard Thomas, *An Essay on the Character, the Manners, and the Understanding of Women, in Different Ages*, trans. Jemima Kindersley (London: J. Dodsley, 1781), 6.

30. *The Independent Chronicle and the Universal Advertiser* (Boston), October 4, 1779, p. 4, Early American Newspapers Database. Thomas, *An Essay on Women*, 1, 3, 4, 6. I have also checked the 1773 translation, which has some minor differences. Antoine Léonard Thomas, *Essay on the character, manners, and genius of womens in different ages. Enlarged from the French of M. Thomas, by Mr. Russell*, 2 vols. (London: G. Robinson, 1773). The discussion here is focused on the Kindersley translation. Thomas, *An Essay on Women*, 4.

31. Thomas, *An Essay on Women*, 8, 220–21.

32. "Introduction by Mrs. Kindersley," in Thomas, *An Essay on Women*, iv, vi.

33. On women and history writing in the Scottish Enlightenment, see Jane Rendall, "Clio, Mars, and Minerva: The Scottish Enlightenment and the Writing of Women's History," in *Eighteenth-Century Scotland: New Perspectives*, ed. T. M. Devine and J. R. Young, 134–51 (East Linton: Tuckwell, 1999), as well as Sebastiani, *The Scottish Enlightenment*. Alexander, *The History of Women*, 1: 1, 140, 2: 221. An American edition appeared in 1796; William Alexander, *The History of Women, from the Earliest Antiquity, to the Present Time*, 2 vols. (Philadelphia: J. H. Dobelbower, 1796). See also Adam Ferguson, *An Essay on the History of Civil Society*, ed. Fania Oz-Salzberger (Cambridge: Cambridge University Press, 1996).

34. Alexander, *The History of Women*, 2: 122, 149, 215, 219–20.

35. "As men were almost every where the lawgivers, most of the legal advantages of matrimony were also on their side"; Alexander, *The History of Women*, 2: 218, 219, 222, 223; 1: 3, 173.

36. William Paley, *The Principles of Moral and Political Philosophy*, ed. D. L. De Mahieu (Indianapolis: Liberty Fund, 2002). American authors also worried over these issues. As one scholar observes, "The fact that men's natural sexual desire was aimed at women out of convenience and culture left the door open to a number of circumstances in which men might turn to other men for gratification"; Jen Manion, *Liberty's Prisoners: Carceral Cultures in Early America* (Philadelphia: University of Pennsylvania Press, 2015), 159.

37. "Thoughts on the STATE OF AMERICAN INDIANS," *Gazette of the United States* (Philadelphia), May 29, 1793, Early American Newspapers Database.

38. "On Love," *New York Magazine, or Literary Repository*, June 1791, Early American Newspapers Database.

39. Anon., *The Lustful Turk* (1828; London: W. H. Allen, 1985), 14, 57.

40. Craig L. Foster, "Victorian Pornographic Imagery in Anti-Mormon Literature," *Journal of Mormon History* 19 (1993): 115–32, 121; Ann Eliza Young, *Wife Number 19, or The Story of a Life in Bondage* (Hartford, CT: Dustin, Gilman, 1876), 433. Paul Reeve's helpful discussion of race and polygamy attends only to the nineteenth century; *Religion of a Different Color*, 220.

41. Increase Van Deusen and Maria Van Deusen, *Spiritual Delusions: Being a Key to the Mysteries of Mormonism, exposing the Particulators of that Astounding Heresy, The Spiritual-Wife System, as Practiced by Brigham Young, of Utah* (New York: Tuttle and Moulton, 1854), 39, 8, 9–10, 30–31, 19, 17, 30.

42. *Crimes and Mysteries,* as quoted in Foster, "Victorian Pornographic Imagery," 121.

43. John Marchmont [pseud.], *An Appeal to the American Congress: The Bible Law of Marriage against Mormonism* [n.p., 1873], 7.

6. *"Such a Revolution as This"*

1. Connecticut Church Records Reel #315 LDS#0005182/Norfolk/Church of Christ (Cong) 1760–1948, v. 5, 1–4, 6–8, Connecticut State Archives (hereafter CSA), October 6, 1780, 1: 109–18.

2. Debate for December 11, 1780, Robin Hood, Butcher Row, Temple bar: "Whether any encrease of population on the Rev. Mr. Madan's plan would compensate for the confusion, Polygamy would create in society? And (if time permits) Would not the present aspect of American affairs justify Parliamentary thanks to the Ministry for the PERSEVERANCE in the national cause?" *Morning Chronicle,* http://www.british-history.ac.uk/london-record-soc/vol30/pp64-124#s1.

3. Susan Juster, *Disorderly Women: Sexual Politics and Evangelicalism in Revolutionary New England* (Ithaca, NY: Cornell University Press, 1996).

4. John Miner, *Dr. Miner's Defense* (Hartford: Hudson and Goodwin, 1781), 15, 17, 33, 46, 50, 56–58.

5. Martin Madan, *Thelyphthora; or, a Treatise on Female Ruin*, 2 vols. (London: J. Dodsley, 1780), 1: vii–viii, 182–84; 2: 186, 192, 195–96. Madan's arguments against polyandry are enumerated in 1: 295–99.

6. On dissenting networks of this era, and the loss of communication between them during the Revolutionary War, see Katherine Carté Engel, "Connecting Protestants in Britain's Eighteenth-Century Atlantic Empire," *William and Mary Quarterly* 75, no. 1 (2018): 37–70.

7. On the American side of this historiography, there is an emphasis on the causal force of the American Revolution. Richard Godbeer, *Sexual Revolution in Early America* (Baltimore: Johns Hopkins University Press, 2002), 15; Clare A. Lyons, *Sex among the Rabble: An Intimate History of Gender and Power in the Age of Revolution, Philadelphia, 1730–1830* (Chapel Hill: University of North Carolina Press for the Omohundro Institute of Early American History and Culture, 2006), 3; Susan Klepp, *Revolutionary Conceptions: Women, Fertility, and Family Limitation in America, 1760–1820* (Chapel Hill: University of North Carolina Press for the Omohundro Institute of Early American History and Culture, 2009), 5–6. On the British side, Dror Wahrman has also argued that the Revolution changed much; *The Making of the Modern Self: Identity and Culture in Eighteenth-Century England* (New Haven: Yale University Press, 2004), 247. By contrast, historians of the English "sexual revolution," such as Henderson, Hitchcock, and Dabhoiwala, do not give much weight to the American Revolution. Tim Hitchcock, *English Sexualities, 1700–1800* (Basingstoke: Macmillan, 1997); Tony Henderson, *Disorderly Women in Eighteenth-Century London: Prostitution and Control in the Metropolis, 1730–1830* (London: Longman, 1999); Faramerz Dabhoiwala, *The Origins of Sex: A History of the First Sexual Revolution* (London: Penguin, 2012). Treatments of Madan include John Cairncross, *After Polygamy Was Made a Sin: The Social History of Christian Polygamy* (London: Routledge and Kegan Paul, 1974), 157–65; John Witte, Jr., *The Western Case for Monogamy over Polygamy* (Cambridge: Cambridge University Press, 2015), 349–56, Nicholas B. Miller, *John Millar and the Socttish Enlightenment: Family Life and World History* (Oxford: Voltaire Foundation, 2017), ch. 1. See also Oscar Sherwin, "Madan's Cure-All 1," *American Journal of Economics and Sociology* 22, no. 3 (1963): 427–43, and "Madan's Cure-All 2," *American Journal of Economics and Sociology* 22, no. 4 (1963): 543–49. There are also brief discussions in Vern Bullough, "Prostitution and Reform in Eighteenth-Century England," in *'Tis Nature's Fault: Unauthorized Sexuality during the Enlightenment*, ed. Robert Purks Maccubbin, 61–74 (Cambridge: Cambridge University Press, 1988), 68; Hitchcock, *English Sexualities*, 105–6; Henderson, *Disorderly Women*, 99; Arianne Chernock, *Men and the Making of Modern British Feminism* (Stanford: Stanford University Press, 2010), ch. 4; Laura J. Rosenthal, *Infamous Commerce: Prostitution in*

Eighteenth-Century British Literature and Culture (Ithaca, NY: Cornell University Press, 2006), conclusion; and Dabhoiwala, *The Origins of Sex*, ch. 4.

8. Ammi Ruhamah Robbins, *Baptisms, marriages, burials and list of members taken from the church records of the Rev. Ammi Ruhamah Robbins, first minister of Norfolk, Connecticut, 1761–1813* (n.p.: Carl and Ellen Battelle Stoeckel, 1910), 35–36.

9. Theron Wilmot Crissey and Joseph Eldridge, *History of Norfolk, Litchfield County, Connecticut, 1744–1900* (Everett: Massachusetts Publishing Company, 1900), 14, 15, 69.

10. Ibid., 23.

11. Robbins, *Baptisms*, 39–40. Samuel Richardson, *Pamela; or, Virtue Rewarded*, 2nd ed., 2 vols. (London: C. Rivington and J. Osborn, 1741), and his *Clarissa; or, the History of a Young Lady*, 7 vols. (London: S. Richardson, 1748). [Johann Wolfgang von Goethe], *The Sorrows of Werter: A German Story*, 2 vols. (London: J. Dodsley, 1779)—an early English edition, by Madan's own publisher; [Susanna Rowson], *Charlotte [Temple]: A Tale of Truth* (London: Minerva, 1791). Godbeer, *Sexual Revolution in Early America*, 263, and Ruth H. Bloch, "Changing Conceptions of Sexuality and Romance in Eighteenth-Century America," *William and Mary Quarterly* 60, no. 1 (2003): 13–42, 26.

12. Franklin Bowditch Dexter, *Biographical sketches of the graduates of Yale College*, 6 vols. (New York: Holt, 1885–1912). There is no listing for John Miner in relevant volumes, 2–4. I also checked the records for every plausible John Miner in the Connecticut State Archives, as well as familysearch.org. Henry P. Johnston Eldridge, ed., *The Record of Connecticut Men in the Military and Naval Service During the War of the Revolution, 1775–1783*, in *Record of Service of Connecticut Men in I. War of the Revolution, II. War of 1812, and III. Mexican War* (Hartford: Adjutants-General of Connecticut, 1889), 227–28; from "Connecticut, Deaths and Burials, 1772–1934," index, FamilySearch (https://familysearch.org/pal:/MM9.1.1/F7XQ-ZZ5, accessed June 24, 2014), John Miner (born 1752, died in 1813, age sixty-one), March 23, 1813; reference 7643; FHL microfilm 3170. Robbins's original manuscript records show merely a dash where her name should be. While women often lost their names in colonial New England records, it is odd that her name consistently does not appear in this record. 1773 Apri 4th Elizabeth Miner Dar of Dr John & ___Miner; 1776 Decr 29th Amos Miner Son of Dr John & ___ Miner, Robbins, *Baptisms, marriages, burials and list of members taken from the church records of the Rev. Ammi Ruhamah Robbins, first minister of Norfolk, Connecticut, 1761–1813*, online through www.archive.org, 32, 35–36. I checked the manuscript version at CSA as well.

13. Miner, *Defense*, 5–6. Eldridge, *Record of Connecticut Men*, 61–62, 91.

14. CSA, 1: 109.

15. Ibid., 1: 109–10.

16. Ibid., 1: x.

17. Ibid., 1: 36, 109–10, 112, 114, 36, 117.

18. Miner, *Defense*, 25, 26, 22, 58, 59.

19. Ibid., 6. CSA, 1: 112.

20. Miner, *Defense*, 6. Samuel Johnson, *Samuel Johnson. President of King's College His Career and Writings*, ed. Herbert and Carol Schneider, 4 vols. (New York: Columbia University Press, 1929), 1: 11–12. Richard L. Bushman, *From Puritan to Yankee: Character and the Social Order in Connecticut, 1690–1765* (New York: Norton, 1967), 161.

21. William E. Bassett, "The Pastors and the Spiritual Progress of the Church," in [Norfolk Centennial 1776–1876], *Historical Discourses Preached in the Congregational Church*, Norfolk Conn, July 9, 1876 (Hartford: Press of the Case, Lockwood, and Brainard Company, 1876), 3–21, 5; Bushman, *From Puritan to Yankee*, 159; Jared Abernethy marched to the "Lexington alarm," spent a year in Canadian campaigns, and was injured. Jesse Tobey served at Fort Clinton on the Hudson in 1778. Miner served in the Hudson Highlands in 1780. Eldridge, *Record of Connecticut Men*, 86–87. As Robert A. Gross has observed "From 1777 on, the Continental ranks were manned largely by the lower social orders"; *The Minutemen and Their World*, 25th anniv. ed. (1976; New York: Hill and Wang, 2001), 150. Alfred F. Young, *The Shoemaker and the Tea Party: Memory and the American Revolution* (Boston: Beacon, 1999), 66.

22. Christopher Grasso, *A Speaking Aristocracy: Transforming Public Discourse in Eighteenth-Century Connecticut* (Chapel Hill: University of North Carolina Press for the Omohundro Institute of Early American History and Culture, 1999), 2. On New Haven, see Cornelia Hughes Dayton, *Women before the Bar: Gender, Law, and Society in Connecticut, 1639–1789* (Chapel Hill: University of North Carolina Press for the Institute of Early American History and Culture, 1995).

23. John Rogers, *A Looking-Glass for the Presbyterians at New-London* (Providence: "Printed for the Author," 1767), 15, 27, 33–36. *Pennsylvania Journal* (Philadelphia), April 10, 1766, p. 2, Early American Newspapers Database.

24. CSA, 1: 117–18.

25. Madan added a third volume a year after the initial two-volume treatise: Martin Madan, *Thelyphthora; or, a Treatise on Female Ruin*, 3 vols. (London: J. Dodsley, 1781); subsequent citations are to this 1781 edition. Up to 1786,

there were at least seventeen pamphlets published about Madan's ideas. These include H.W., *The Unlawfulness of Polygamy Evinced [or, Observations Occasioned by the Erroneous Interpretations of the Passages of the New Testament, respecting the Laws of Marriage, Lately published in a Treatise on Female Ruin]* (London: G. Kearsly, 1780); "A Layman," *A Letter to the Rev. Mr. Madan, concerning the chapter on polygamy, in his late publication, entitled Thelyphthora* (London: Fielding and Walker, 1780); John Smith, *Polygamy Indefensible* (London: Alexander Hogg, 1780); John Towers, *Polygamy Unscriptural* (London: Alex. Hogg, 1780); Anon., *A Letter to Dr. P—y, in answer to a discourse of his, lately published; in which are also some observations on Dr. M—n's treatise on polygamy* (London: n.p., 1781); Anon., *Martin's Hobby Houghed and Pounded, or Letters on Thelyphthora* (London: J. Buckland, 1781); Edward Burnaby Greene, *Whispers for the Ear of the Author of Thelyphthora in favor of Reason and Religion* (London: H. Payne, 1781), and *Sweets for the tooth of the author of Thelyphthora: occasioned by that writer's Five letters to Abraham Rees, D.D.* (London: H. Payne and C. Dilly, 1784); Thomas Haweis, *A Scriptural Refutation of the Arguments for Polygamy* (London: Charles Dilly, J. Matthews, and T. Wilkins, 1781); Richard Hill, *The Blessings of Polygamy Displayed* (London: J. Mathews, C. Dilly, and J. Eddowes, 1781), and *The Cobler's Letter to the Author of Thelyphthora* (London: J. Mathews, C. Dilly, and J. Eddowes, 1781); Henry Moore, *A Word to Dr. Madan* (Bristol: n.p., 1781); John Palmer, *An Examination of Thelyphthora, on the Subject of Marriage* (Birmingham: Pearson and Rollason for J. Johnson, 1781); James Penn, *Remarks on Thelyphthora* (London: Bladon, Deane, and Froud, 1781); Thomas Wills, *Remarks on Polygamy* (London: T. Hughes, F. Walsh, R. Baldwin, and W. Otridge, 1781); James Cookson, *Thoughts on Polygamy* (Winchester: J. Wilkes, T. Cadell, and J. Debrett, 1782); and James Edward Hamilton, *A Short Treatise on Polygamy* (Dublin: n.p., 1786). There were also five significant and lengthy poems published on the topic: Anon., *An Heroic Epistle to the Rev. Martin M—d—n, author of a late treatise on polygamy* (London: R. Faulder, 1780); "Married Woman," *Political Priest, A Satire Dedicated to a Reverend Polygamist* (London: J. Stockdale, 1781); "A Nymph of King's-Place," *A Poetical Epistle to the Reverend Mr. Madan* (London: Fielding and Walker, 1781); Anon., *Polygamy, or Mahomet the Prophet to Madan the Evangelist, an heroic poem* (n.p., 1782?); and William Cowper, "Anti-Thelyphthora," in *The Works of William Cowper, Esq., Comprising His Poems, Correspondence and Translations. With a Life of the Author by the Editor, Robert Southey* (London: Baldwin and Cradock,

1836–37), 112–19. There were two plays performed about it: Frederick Pilon, *Thelyphthora, a farce* (London: n.p., 1781), and B. Walwyn, *The Farce of Chit Chat, or the Penance of Polygamy* (Dublin: n.p., 1792). There were also at least a dozen magazine reviews in periodicals such as the *Monthly Review* and the *Critical Review.* There were several cartoons about it, as well as scores of newspaper stories. It did not receive the kind of coverage that the Revolution or the Gordon Riots did, but it nevertheless formed a significant source of discussion in especially the winter of 1780–81. In her work on London debating societies in 1780, Donna T. Andrew terms Madan's work "much discussed," and highlights at least ten separate debates in late 1780; "Popular Culture and Public Debate: London 1780," *Historical Journal* 39, no. 2 (1996): 405–23, 411. For instance, the Westminster Forum considered the proposition "Would it not be prudent to suffer the Convocation to sit, in order to consider the dangerous Doctrines contained in the late Publication of the Rev. Mr. Madan?" while the all-female La Belle Assemblée pondered: "Can the Rev. Mr Madan's doctrine of a plurality of wives be justified either by the laws of policy or religion?" Donna T. Andrew, "London Debating Societies, 1766–1799," London Record Society, 1994, in British History Online, http://www.british-history.ac.uk/source.aspx?pubid=238. Wills, *Remarks on Thelyphthora,* vi. Smith, *Polygamy Indefensible,* 7.

26. Madan, *Thelyphthora,* 1: 36, 48; 2: 21–22. On evangelical domesticity, see Leonore Davidoff and Catherine Hall, *Family Fortunes: Men and Women of the English Middle Class, 1780–1850* (Chicago: University of Chicago Press, 1987). It is difficult to escape the conclusion that Madan's own marriage was not an especially happy one. His wife may not have been keen on her husband's hearty evangelicalism. Falconer Madan, *The Madan Family and Maddens in Ireland and England: A Historical Account* (Oxford: Oxford University Press, 1933), 107.

27. Madan, *Thelyphthora,* 1: 295–99.

28. Greene, *Whispers for the Ear,* xxiii. Madan, *The Madan Family,* ch. 8. "A Layman," *A Letter to the Rev. Mr. Madan,* 71.

29. Paul Langford, *A Polite and Commercial People: England, 1727–1783* (Oxford: Oxford University Press, 1989), 254. The hospital governors reported that visiting patient wards "became so exceedingly offensive, that . . . Mr. Madan found it impracticable"; [Anon.], *An Address to the President, VPs, and the other Governors of the Lock Hospital near Hyde park Corner on behalf of that Charity* (London, 1781), 20–21. See Kevin P. Siena, *Venereal Disease, Hospitals, and the Urban Poor: London's "Foul Wards," 1600–1800* (Rochester:

University of Rochester Press, 2004), 181–205. Judith Madan, letter to daughter, November 15, 1757, as quoted in Falconer Madan, *The Madan Family,* 111. "Lent-Preachers appointed to preach at his Majesty's Chapel at Whitehall, on Wednesdays and Fridays, for the year 1780," *London Evening Post,* January 15, 1780. Martin Madan, *A Collection of Psalms and Hymns, extr. from various authors, and publ. by Mr. Madan* (London, 1760).

30. Admittedly, Edward Burnaby Greene did claim: "He was in earlier youth a professed 'bon-vivant' of the libertine cast"; *Whispers for the Ear,* xxiii. One poem derided Madan, "Whose youthful days (if loud Report says true) / Own to more vices, riot, and excess, / Than man *should* know, or language *can* express!"; "Married Woman," *Political Priest,* 19. Still, if he had rioted in his youth, it was long ago and much repented. Martin Madan, *A New and Literal Translation of Juvenal and Persius; with notes by M. Madan* (London, 1787). He is one of the gender-panicked translators of Juvenal in Wahrman, *The Making of the Modern Self.* Wills, *Remarks on Polygamy,* iv. Haweis, *Scriptural Refutation,* viii. Robert Dodsley, joined later by brother James, published major works of the eighteenth century. Charles Henry Timperley, *A Dictionary of Printers and Printing* (London: H. Johnson, 1839).

31. David Lemmings, "Introduction: Law and Order, Moral Panics, and Early Modern England," in *Moral Panics, the Media and the Law in Early Modern England,* ed. David Lemmings and Claire Walker, 1–21 (Basingstoke: Palgrave/Macmillan, 2009), 6. Donna T. Andrew and Randall McGowen, *The Perreaus and Mrs. Rudd: Forgery and Betrayal in Eighteenth-Century London* (Berkeley: University of California Press, 2001), 67, 59.

32. See debates of January 5, 1780, at Coachmakers Hall; March 16, 1780, at the Carlisle House School of Eloquence; and March 24, 1780, at La Lycée Français ("La poligamie est-elle d'aucun advantage dans un Gouvernment & son utile l'emporte t-elle sur ses abus?"), in http://www.british-history.ac.uk/source.aspx?pubid=238. "The rhetoric of marriage, much like that of politics, served both to expose underlying fears and to legitimate and encourage patterns which had already come to prevail"; Jan Lewis, "The Republican Wife: Virtue and Seduction in the Early Republic," *William and Mary Quarterly* 44, no. 4 (1987): 689–721, 695. Edwin Welch, *Spiritual Pilgrim: A Reassessment of the Life of the Countess of Huntingdon* (Cardiff: University of Wales Press, 1995), 102. See also Alan Harding, *The Countess of Huntingdon's Connexion: A Sect in Action in Eighteenth-Century England* (Oxford: Oxford University Press, 2003).

33. The limits of reformation of marriage receive attention in Eric Josef Carlson, *Marriage and the English Reformation* (London: Wiley-Blackwell, 1994), 3. See also Bernard Capp, "Bigamous Marriages in Early Modern England," *Historical Journal* 52, no. 3 (2009): 537–56; R. H. Helmholz, *Roman Canon Law in Reformation England* (Cambridge: Cambridge University Press, 1994); Ralph Houlbrooke, *Church Courts and the People during the English Reformation, 1520–1570* (Oxford: Oxford University Press, 1979); Martin Ingram, *Church Courts, Sex, and Marriage in England, 1570–1640* (Cambridge: Cambridge University Press, 1990); Ronald A. Marchant, *The Church under the Law: Justice, Administration, and Discipline in the Diocese of York, 1560–1640* (Cambridge: Cambridge University Press, 1969); and R. B. Outhwaite, *Clandestine Marriage in England, 1550–1850* (London: Hambledon, 1995). On the 1753 act, see David Lemmings, "Marriage and the Law in the Eighteenth Century: Hardwicke's Marriage Act of 1753," *Historical Journal* 39, no. 2 (1996): 339–60, and Rebecca Probert, "The Judicial Interpretation of Lord Hardwicke's Act 1753," *Journal of Legal History* 23, no. 2 (2002): 129–51; her "The Impact of the Marriage Act of 1753: Was It Really 'a Most Cruel Law for the Fair Sex'?" *Eighteenth-Century Studies* 38, no. 2 (2005): 247–62; and her *Marriage Law and Practice in the Long Eighteenth Century: A Reassessment* (Cambridge: Cambridge University Press, 2009). Outhwaite, *Clandestine Marriage in England*, 116. Also Langford, *A Polite and Commercial People*, 111. Madan's theories were mentioned in the 1781 debate. "Debate on Mr. Fox's Bill, 21 George III," *Cobbett's Parliamentary History of England from the Norman conquest, in 1066, to the year, 1803*, 36 vols. (London: T. C. Hansard, 1806–12), 22: 390–92. March 16, 1780, Carlisle House School of Eloquence, *Gazetteer*, March 13, 1780, https://www.british-history.ac.uk/london-record-soc/vol30/pp64-124#p243.

34. Madan had already courted controversy for Methodism in the 1760s, when charges of simony were leveled against him and his assistant, Thomas Haweis, for their involvement in obtaining a clerical living for Haweis. The situation was resolved only with the intervention of the countess of Huntingdon, whose patronage Madan had enjoyed since the 1750s; Welch, *Spiritual Pilgrim*, 102. A thousand-page treatise does not get written overnight. Hill, *Blessings of Polygamy Displayed*, 167. Henry Abelove, *Evangelist of Desire: John Wesley and the Methodists* (Stanford: Stanford University Press, 1990), 49, 54, 65, 72, and Dee Andrews, *The Methodists and Revolutionary America, 1760–1800: The Shaping of an Evangelical Culture* (Princeton: Princeton University Press, 2000), 114. [George Lavington], *The Enthusiasm of*

Methodists and Papists Compared, 3 vols. (London: J. and P. Knapton, 1754), 1: 119. There were Methodist women preachers, but they were controversial figures. In its early years, Methodism was riven with theological and leadership disputes. On the radical appeal of Methodism, see David Hempton, *Methodism: Empire of the Spirit* (New Haven: Yale University Press, 2005). As Emma Major observes, "The image of Methodist women was not helped by high-profile scandals involving followers such as the Methodist Lady Margaret Hastings (the Countess of Huntingdon's sister-in-law), who not only married a Methodist preacher, Benjamin Ingham, but cohabited with him before they married"; *Madam Britannia: Women, Church, and Nation, 1712–1812* (Oxford: Oxford University Press, 2011), 143. Dee Andrews also highlights these tensions on the American side: *Methodists and Revolutionary America*, 103. Most religious historians of Madan and his circles pass over this polygamy controversy. See Welch, *Spiritual Pilgrim*, and Harding, *The Countess of Huntingdon's Connexion*.

35. These included concerns over the 1774 Québec Act. Ian Haywood and John Seed, eds., *The Gordon Riots: Politics, Culture, and Insurrection in Late Eighteenth-Century Britain* (Cambridge: Cambridge University Press, 2012). See also Owen Stanwood, *The Empire Reformed: English America in the Age of the Glorious Revolution* (Philadelphia: University of Pennsylvania Press, 2013). Madan, *Thelyphthora*, 3: 301. One satire mocked him as the new "Martin": "Thou second bold Reformer of the name!"; *Heroic Epistle to the Rev. Martin M—d—n*, 15. On Luther's defense of the bigamy of Philip of Hesse, see Miller, *John Millar and the Scottish Enlightenment*, ch. 2, and Cairncross, *After Polygamy Was Made a Sin*, ch. 2.

36. Hill, *Blessings of Polygamy Displayed*, 38–39, 68, 155; Towers, *Polygamy Unscriptural*, 5; Miner, *Defense*, 69.

37. Madan, *Thelyphthora*, 1: 8, 39; Martin Madan, *An Account of the Triumphant death of F.S. a Converted Prostitute, who Died April 1763, aged Twenty-Six* (London: Z. Fowle, 1763), 4. Martin Madan, *Every Man our Neighbour. A Sermon Preached at the Opening of the Chapel, of the Lock-Hospital near Hyde-Park Corner, March 28, MDCCLXII*, 3rd ed. (London: For the Benefit of Charity, 1762), 10.

38. Richardson, *Pamela* and *Clarissa*. E. A. Wrigley and R. S. Schofield, *The Population History of England, 1541–1871: A Reconstruction* (Cambridge: Harvard University Press, 1981), 266; Lawrence Stone, *The Family, Sex, and Marriage in England, 1500–1800* (New York: Harper and Row, 1977), 607–15; Peter Laslett, Karla Oosterveen, and Richard M. Smith, eds., *Bastardy and Its*

Comparative History: Studies in the History of Illegitimacy and Marital Nonconformism in Britain (London: Edward Arnold, 1980); and Alysa Levene, Thomas Nutt, and Samantha Williams, eds., *Illegitimacy in Britain, 1700–1920* (Basingstoke: Palgrave Macmillan, 2005), introduction. Henderson, *Disorderly Women*, passim, and Dabhoiwala, *Origins of Sex*, passim.

39. By 1790, "premarital pregnancy was common throughout New England"; Laurel Thatcher Ulrich, *A Midwife's Tale: The Life of Martha Ballard, Based on Her Diary, 1785–1812* (New York: Knopf, 1990), 157. See also Godbeer, *Sexual Revolution in Early America*, ch. 7. Dayton, *Women before the Bar*, 227, 229. Lyons, *Sex among the Rabble*, 126. Miner, *Defense*, 56.

40. Dabhoiwala, *Origins of Sex*, 201–11; March 16, 1778, Robin Hood [Society], *Chronicle*, 1778; December 5, 1777, Society for Free Debate, Horn, Doctors-Commons, *Gazeteer*. For an excellent discussion of the trope of "lords of creation," see Klepp, *Revolutionary Conceptions*, 99–106. November 11, 1776, Robin Hood, *Morning Chronicle*, http://www.british-history.ac.uk/report .aspx?compid=38841.

41. January 20, April 28, August 11, and December 15, 1774, Pantheon Society Minutes 1773–1779, MS Gen 1283, Special Collections, Glasgow University Library (hereafter Pantheon Minutes).

42. January 3, 12, and 26, 1775, February 15 and July 1776, ibid.

43. June 20 and July 6, 20, 1775, and January 8, 1778, ibid.

44. December 10 and 17, 1778, ibid.

45. This ad appeared in both the *Pennsylvania Packet*, November 22, 1773, and the *Boston Newsletter*, January 13, 1774. See Kirsten Denise Sword, "Wayward Wives, Runaway Slaves, and the Limits of Patriarchal Authority in Early America," Ph.D. diss., Harvard University, 2002, 187–91. Such ads are also discussed in Lyons, *Sex among the Rabble*, 237–38. Anon., *A Letter to Those Ladies Whose Husbands Possess a Seat in Either House of Parliament* (London: J. Almon, 1775), 9. A wife could not in fact be sure of redress from the law in the eighteenth century, even in cases of marital cruelty.

46. John Cartwright, *A Letter to Edmund Burke, Esq.* (London: H.S. Woodfall, 1775), 26–27.

47. See, for instance, the debate on population that occurred in 1780–81. Richard Price, *An Essay on the Population of England, from the Revolution to the Present Day*, 2nd ed. (London: T. Cadell, 1780), and John Howlett, *An Examination of Dr. Price's Essay on the Population of England and Wales* (Maidstone: J. Blake and T. Payne, 1781). Also see Dabhoiwala, *Origins of Sex*, 224, and Miller, *John Millar and the Scottish Enlightenment*, ch. 2. Britain had long used

foreign mercenaries, but the reliance on them was striking in this war. Madan contended that "passing such a law as this, in a maritime and commercial *island*, whose . . . strength . . . must depend on the numbers of its people, is surely a capital *solecism*"; Madan, *Thelyphthora*, 2: 60, 275–85. Richard Hill contended that women would be so fearful that their future husbands would adopt polygyny that they would refuse to marry altogether; *Blessings of Polygamy Displayed*, 44–46.

48. James Graham, *A Lecture on the Generation, Increase and Improvement of the Human Species* (London: M. Smith, 1780?), 7. On Graham, see Roy Porter, "The Sexual Politics of James Graham," *British Journal for Eighteenth-Century Studies*, 5, no. 2 (1982): 199–206, especially 203, and his "Sex and the Singular Man: The Seminal Ideas of James Graham," *Studies on Voltaire and the Eighteenth Century* 228 (1984): 3–24; Roy Porter and Lesley Hall, *The Facts of Life: The Creation of Sexual Knowledge in Britain, 1650–1950* (New Haven: Yale University Press, 1995), ch. 5; Barbara Brandon Schnorrenberg, "A True Relation of the Life and Career of James Graham, 1745–1794," *Eighteenth-Century Life* 15 (1991): 58–75; James Delbourgo, *A Most Amazing Scene of Wonders: Electricity and Enlightenment in Early America* (Cambridge: Harvard University Press, 2006), 117–18; and Peter Otto, "The Regeneration of the Body: Sex, Religion, and the Sublime in James Graham's *Temple of Health and Hymen*," *Romanticism on the Net*, Érudit, http://www.erudit.org/revue/ron/2001/v/n23/005991ar.html. Edward Burnaby Greene, invoking "celestial beds," declared: "A similarity of character is obvious between this man and Dr. Graham, with a preference to the latter, who presumes not to introduce Scripture, but *necessity,* as a supporter of his immoralities"; *Whispers for the Ear*, xxvii. See also *Polygamy, or Mahomet the Prophet to Madan the Evangelist*, 69–94, 76, and Hill, *The Cobler's Letter*, 53–56.

49. Graham, *A Lecture*, 4–5, 59. Karen Harvey, *Reading Sex in the Eighteenth Century: Bodies and Gender in English Erotic Culture* (Cambridge: Cambridge University Press, 2004), 132–33.

50. In 1779, Franklin's essay was reprinted in a general collection of his writings. Benjamin Franklin, *Political, Miscellaneous, and Philosophical Pieces* (London: J. Johnson, 1779), 1–23. In the 1781 discussion of the possible repeal of Hardwicke's 1753 Marriage Act, one speaker contended that America had no marriage act and hence greater population growth; "Debate on Mr. Fox's Bill, 21 George III," *Cobbett's Parliamentary History*, 22: 392. See Bernard Bailyn, *Voyagers to the West: A Passage in the Peopling of America*

on the Eve of the Revolution (New York: Vintage, 1986). *Polygamy, or Mahomet the Prophet to Madan the Evangelist,* 93.

51. Richard Wells, *A Few Political Reflections Submitted to the Consideration of the British Colonies* (Philadelphia: John Dunlap, 1774), 33; "Cosmopolitan," in *Massachusetts Spy,* December 1, 1775, as quoted in Edwin G. Burrows and Michael Wallace, "The American Revolution: The Ideology and Psychology of National Liberation," *Perspectives in American History* 6 (1972): 167–308, 213; *New York Journal,* May 25, 1775, as quoted ibid., 202.

52. Samuel Seabury, *A View of the Controversy Between Great-Britain and her Colonies* (London: Richardson and Urguhart, 1775), 77; Anon., *The Justice and Necessity of Taxing the American Colonies, Demonstrated* (London: J. Almon, 1766), 25; Anon., *The Constitutional Right of the Legislature of Great Britain to Tax the British Colonies in America, Impartially Stated* (London: J. Ridley, 1768), 35; Anon., *The Case Stated on Philosophical Ground, between Great Britain and her Colonies: or the Analogy between States and Individuals, Respecting the Term of Political Adultness, Pointed Out* (London: G. Kearsley, [1778]), 56.

53. *Polygamy, or Mohomet the Prophet to Madan the Evangelist,* 71, 79; Hill, *Blessings of Polygamy Displayed,* 41; "A Traveller," "To the Editor of the MORNING POST. POLYGAMY," *Morning Post and Daily Advertiser,* November 21, 1780. Nicholas Miller argues that the Madan controversy shows how dominant the "Oriental other" was; *John Millar and the Scottish Enlightenment,* 32.

54. Madan, *Thelyphthora,* 2: 188–89; "Married Woman," *Political Priest,* 17; Hill, *Blessings of Polygamy Displayed,* 57–58, 44; *Martin's Hobby Houghed and Pounded,* 25–26. On this issue, see Philip Carter, "Men about Town: Representations of Foppery and Masculinity in Early Eighteenth-Century Urban Society," in *Gender in Eighteenth-Century England: Roles, Representations, and Responsibilities,* ed. Hannah Barker and Elaine Chalus, 31–57 (London: Longman, 1997). See also Wahrman, *The Making of the Modern Self,* 60–65; "Character of a Macaroni," *Town and Country Magazine,* May 1772, 242–43; Andrew and McGowen, *The Perreaus and Mrs. Rudd,* 132–33.

55. Dabhoiwala, *Origins of Sex,* 142, 179. Wahrman, *The Making of the Modern Self,* passim; Lyons, *Sex among the Rabble,* 188.

56. [Anon.], *The Parliament of Women* (London: W. Wilson, 1646), A4, A3.

57. [Anon.], *Now or Never: or A New Parliament of Women* (London: George Horton, 1656), A2, A3; [Anon.], *The London Ladies Petition* (London: F. Baker, 1710).

58. Barbara Clark Smith, "Food Rioters and the American Revolution," *William and Mary Quarterly* 51, no. 4 (1994): 3–38, 29, 27; *Philadelphia Evening Post,*

September 30, 1780, Early American Newspapers Database; [Esther Reed], *The Sentiments of an American Woman* (Philadelphia: John Dunlap, 1780), online at American Memory Project, Library of Congress.

59. Towers, *Polygamy Unscriptural*, 56. After noting this debate, Donna Andrew concludes: "The mere fact that such things could be publicly discussed by both men and women, in a formal, accessible setting, and could meet with any support at all, is of considerable interest"; "Popular Culture and Public Debate," 413–14. *Morning Post*, April 11, 1780, Oratorical Society, Old Theatre, http://www.british-history.ac.uk/source.aspx?pubid=238.

60. *St. James Chronicle*, May 11, 1780, http://www.british-history.ac.uk/source .aspx?pubid=238.

61. Mary Cawthorne to [John Newton], June 3, 1780, MS Hyde 76 1.6.522.4, Houghton Library, Harvard University; Elizabeth Carter to Elizabeth Robinson Montagu, May 8, 1780, in Elizabeth Carter, *Letters from Mrs. Elizabeth Carter to Mrs. Montagu between the Years 1755 and 1800*, vol. 3 (London: F. C. and J. Rivington, 1817), 128–30, from British and Irish Women's Letters and Diaries database. Many thanks to Felix Waldmann for the Cawthorne reference.

62. Janet Polasky tracks a number of these voices in the wider Atlantic world; *Revolutions without Borders: The Call to Liberty in the Atlantic World* (New Haven: Yale University Press, 2015).

63. *The Massachusetts Centinel and the Republican Journal* (Boston), June 12, 1784, Early American Newspapers Database.

7. "The Repugnance Inherent in Having Multiple Wives"

1. Junípero Serra to Felipe de Neve, Monterey, January 7, 1780, in Junípero Serra, *Writings of Junípero Serra*, ed. Antonine Tibesar, 4 vols. (Washington, DC: Academy of American Franciscan History, 1956–66), 3: 406–17. These volumes display the Spanish and the English translation side by side.

2. As Christina Snyder puts it, "The debate over the place of 'civilized' Indians demonstrates that many whites disagreed with inclusive ideals, doubting that Indians and African Americans, in particular, could ever overcome their 'heathen' backgrounds or the stain of slavery to become citizens in a free republic"; *Great Crossings: Indians, Settlers, and Slaves in the Age of Jackson* (Oxford: Oxford University Press, 2017), 11. Brendan C. Lindsay has argued that this process was essential to dehumanizing Indians in the nineteenth century; *Murder State: California's Native American Genocide, 1846–1873* (Lincoln: University of Nebraska Press, 2012), 66.

3. On sex and gender in early California, see Antonia Castañeda, "Sexual Violence in the Politics and Poetics of Conquest: Amerindian Women and the Spanish Conquest of Alta California," in *Building with our Hands: New Directions in Chicana Studies,* ed. Adela de la Torre and Beatriz M. Pesquera, 15–33 (Berkeley: University of California Press, 1993), especially 29; Miroslava Chávez-García, *Negotiating Conquest: Gender and Power in California, 1770s to 1880s* (Tucson: University of Arizona Press, 2004), ch. 1; Virginia M. Bouvier, *Women and the Conquest of California, 1542–1840* (Tucson: University of Arizona Press, 2004); Steven W. Hackel, *Children of Coyote, Missionaries of Saint Francis: Indian-Spanish Relations in Colonial California, 1769–1850* (Chapel Hill: University of North Carolina Press for the Omohundro Institute of Early American History, 2005); and Erika Pérez, *Colonial Intimacies: Interethnic Kinship, Sexuality, and Marriage in Southern California, 1769–1885* (Norman: University of Oklahoma Press, 2018), ch. 1. For a broad coverage of sex and conquest, see Antonia Castañeda, Susan H. Armitage, Patricia Hart, and Karen Weathermon, eds., *Gender on the Borderlands: The Frontiers Reader* (Lincoln: University of Nebraska Press, 2007), and Elizabeth D. Heineman, ed., *Sexual Violence in Conflict Zones: From the Ancient World to the Era of Human Rights* (Philadelphia: University of Pennsylvania Press, 2011). Important work on the Utes includes Ned Blackhawk, *Violence over the Land: Indians and Empires in the Early American West* (Cambridge: Harvard University Press, 2008), and Natale A. Zappia, *Traders and Raiders: The Indigenous World of the Colorado Basin, 1540–1859* (Chapel Hill: University of North Carolina Press, 2014). For the wider context, see also James F. Brooks, *Captives and Cousins: Slavery, Kinship, and Community in the Southwest Borderlands* (Chapel Hill: University of North Carolina Press for the Omohundro Institute of Early American History and Culture, 2002); Juliana Barr, *Peace Came in the Form of a Woman: Indians and Spaniards in the Texas Borderlands* (Chapel Hill: University of North Carolina Press, 2007); Brian DeLay, *War of a Thousand Deserts: Indians Raids and the U.S.-Mexican War* (New Haven: Yale University Press, 2008); and Pekka Hämäläinen, *The Comanche Empire* (New Haven: Yale University Press, 2008). For the Cherokees, the classic account of gender remains Theda Perdue, *Cherokee Women: Gender and Culture Change, 1700–1835* (Lincoln: University of Nebraska Press, 1998). For general context, see also Tom Hatley, *The Dividing Paths: Cherokees and South Carolinians through the Revolutionary Era* (Oxford: Oxford University Press, 1998); William G. McLoughlin, *Cherokee Renascence in the New Republic* (Princeton: Princeton

University Press, 1986); Theda Perdue and Michael D. Green, *The Cherokee Nation and the Trail of Tears* (New York: Viking, 2007); Tiya Miles, *The House on Diamond Hill: A Cherokee Plantation Story* (Chapel Hill: University of North Carolina Press, 2010); and Gregory D. Smithers, *The Cherokee Diaspora: An Indigenous History of Migration, Resettlement, and Identity* (New Haven: Yale University Press, 2015).

4. Christina Snyder, *Slavery in Indian Country: The Changing Face of Captivity in Early America* (Cambridge: Harvard University Press, 2012), 210.

5. Albert L. Hurtado, *Indian Survival on the California Frontier* (New Haven: Yale University Press, 1988), 17–18; Lowell John Bean, *Mukat's People: The Cahuilla Indians of Southern California* (Berkeley: University of California Press, 1972); Hackel, *Children of Coyote*, especially 187–89, where he details the varieties of polygamy, monogamy, and divorce among California natives. Also see Steven W. Hackel, *Junípero Serra: California's Founding Father* (New York: Hill and Wang, 2013), 164, and Erika Pérez, "Family, Spiritual Kinship, and Social Hierarchy in Early California," *Early American Studies* 14, no. 4 (2016): 661–87, 674. Pedro Fages, *A Historical, Political, and Natural Description of California*, trans. and ed. Herbert Ingram Priestley (Berkeley: University of California Press, 1937), 21.

6. This kind of repudiation was sometimes required before baptism. In one church register from the 1820s, one wife was listed as " 'segunda mug[e]r repudiada haora' (second wife now repudiated) of the village chief (capitán)"; Pérez, "Family, Spiritual Kinship, and Social Hierarchy," 674. Hugo Reid, *The Indians of Los Angeles County: Hugo Reid's Letters of 1852*, ed. Robert E. Heizer, Southwest Museum Papers, no. 21 (Highland Park, CA: Southwest Press, 1968), 25, 27. Fages, *A Historical, Political, and Natural Description of California*, 12, 58. Historians of the period after 1846, such as Benjamin Madley, have tended to emphasize the harmonious and thriving nature of California Indian life before the establishment of the missions; *An American Genocide: The United States and the California Indian Catastrophe, 1846–1873* (New Haven: Yale University Press, 2016), 16–41, especially 25.

7. The nine missions were San Diego, San Juan Capistrano, San Gabriel, San Buenaventura, San Luis Obispo, San Antonio de Padua, San Carlos Borromeo, Santa Clara, and San Francisco; Hackel, *Junípero Serra*, xii. On Franciscan training and trajectories generally, see David Rex Galindo, *To Sin No More: Franciscans and Conversion in the Hispanic World, 1683–1830* (Stanford: Stanford University Press, 2018), and David Hurst Thomas, "The Life and Times of Fr. Junípero Serra: A Pan-Borderlands Perspective," *The*

Americas 71, no. 2 (2014): 185–225. On this enlightened Bourbon restructuring, see David Weber, *Bárbaros: Spaniards and Their Savages in the Age of Enlightenment* (New Haven: Yale University Press, 2006).

8. "Judicial proceedings against Silberio and Rosa at San Luís Obispo," in *Lands of Promise and Despair: Chronicles of Early California, 1535–1846*, ed. Rose Marie Beebe and Robert M. Senkewicz, 250–59 (Santa Clara: Heyday, 2001), 256. See also Brian T. McCormack, "Conjugal Violence: Sex, Sin, and Murder in the Mission Communities of Alta California," *Journal of the History of Sexuality* 16, no. 3 (2007): 391–415, and Steven W. Hackel, "Sources of Rebellion: Indian Testimony and the Mission San Gabriel Uprising of 1785," *Ethnohistory* 50, no. 4 (2003): 643–69, 646.

9. Serra to Father Fermin Francisco Lasuen, Monterey, March 29, 1779, *Writings*, 3: 292–301, 294–95, 296–97; Serra to Father Rafael Verger, Monterey, August 15, 1779, ibid., 3: 48–51. For the complicated dynamics of indigenous rebellions, Bourbon reform, and Franciscan responses, see Hackel, *Children of Coyote*, and Cameron D. Jones, *In Service of Two Masters: The Missionaries of Ocopa, Indigenous Resistance, and Spanish Governance in Bourbon Peru* (Stanford: Stanford University Press, 2018).

10. Serra to Father Fermin Francisco Lasuen, Monterey, August 16, 1779; Serra to Felipe de Neve, Monterey, January 7, 1780; Serra to Father Fermin Francisco Lasuen, January 12, 1780, *Writings*, 3: 362–69; 410–11; and 418–27, 421.

11. "Desertor, amancebado, embiando recados a la gente de acá"; Serra to Felipe de Neve, Monterey, January 7, 1780, *Writings*, 406–17, 408–9. *Amancebado* was translated by Tibesar as adulterer, but this does not quite capture its meaning of keeping a long-term concubine or cohabiting partner. See RAE-NTLLE. The English translator was Stevens (1706). Hackel convincingly argues that this alcalde was the one involved in the 1785 rebellion; "Sources of Rebellion," 652.

12. See accounts by Nikolay Rezanov (1806), Semyon Yakovlevich Unkovsky (1815), and Otto von Kotzebue (1816 and 1824), in *California Through Russian Eyes, 1806–1848*, trans. and ed. James R. Gibson, with assistance of Alexi A. Istomin (Norman, OK: Arthur H. Clark, 2013), 67, 68, 81, 89, 286.

13. José María Fernández, as quoted in Beebe and Senkewicz, *Lands of Promise and Despair*, 262; Serra to Father Rafael Verger, Monterey, August 8, 1772; Serra to Antonio Maria de Bucareli y Ursua, Mexico City, May 21, 1773; Serra to Bucareli, May 21, 1773, *Writings*, 1: 256–59, 260–65, 356–57, 362–63.

14. Letter of Luís Jayme, San Diego, October 17, 1772, trans. and ed. Maynard Geiger, *Letter of Luís Jayme, O.F.M.* (Los Angeles: Published for San Diego

Public Library by Dawson's Book Shop, 1970), 38, 46. Pedro Fages to Antonio Bucareli y Orsúa, June 2, 1773, Presidio of San Carlos de Monte Rey, AGN, Calif., vol. 2, part 1, exp. 8–9, fols. 251–52, 287, 291, as quoted in Bouvier, *Women and the Conquest of California*, 197; Serra to Bucareli, Mexico City, March 13, 1773, *Writings*, 1: 304–5; Serra to Father Rafael Verger, Monterey, August 15, 1779, ibid., 3: 348–49.

15. Fray Francisco Palóu, *Historical Memoirs of New California*, 4 vols., ed. Herbert Eugene Bolton (Berkeley: University of California Press, 1926), 4: 62–71, 66, and "Compadre y señor don Raphael digo Joseph Francisco de Ortega," in *Diario del Capitán Comandante Fernando de Rivera y Moncada*, 2 vols., ed. Ernest J. Burrus, 2: 433–55 (Madrid: Ediciones Jose Porrúa Turanzas, 1967), 2: 434. "Most accounts of this uprising neglect to analyze the immediate causes of the revolt or the context presented by Father Jayme's concerns"; Bouvier, *Women and the Conquest of California*, 47–48, 140. Castañeda, Bouvier, and Chávez-García have emphasized the political importance of sexual assault in these moments. Two recent treatments do not consider at length the issue of sexual violence; Claudio Saunt, *West of the Revolution: An Uncommon History of 1776* (New York: Norton, 2014), ch. 2, and Hackel, *Junípero Serra*, 206–9.

16. Castañeda, "Sexual Violence," 26. Palóu, *Historical Memoirs*, 4: 156–58, and "Investigations of Occurrences at Mission San Gabriel on the Night of October 25, 1785," in Beebe and Senkewicz, *Lands of Promise and Despair*, 247–49, 248. Steven Hackel rightly notes that her testimony "reflects the Indian-Indian tensions that were exacerbated by Spanish colonization"; "Sources of Rebellion," 656.

17. Palóu, *Historical Memoirs*, 158.

18. The original, based on the copy at the Newberry Library, reads: "De que se infiere tener estos bárbaros noticia o conocimiento de la repugnancia que incluye la multiplicidad de mujeres a un mismo tiempo. De aquí tomó ocasíon el Padre para instruirlos sobre el punto, y exhortarlos a que no tuviesen más que una"; 149. Silvestre Vélez de Escalante and Francisco Atanasio Domínguez, *The Domínguez-Escalante Journal: Their Expedition through Colorado, Utah, Arizona, and New Mexico in 1776*, trans. Angelico Chavez, ed. Ted J. Warner (Provo: Brigham Young University, 1976), 31. Ned Black-hawk discusses the names of various groups like the Sabuaganas; *Violence over the Land*. Bianca Premo, *The Enlightenment on Trial: Ordinary Litigants and Colonialism in the Spanish Empire* (Oxford: Oxford University Press, 2017).

19. On the effects of horse culture, see Robert W. Delaney, *The Southern Ute People* (Phoenix: Indian Tribal Series, 1974), 11–12 and Pekka Hämäläinen, "The Politics of Grass: European Expansion, Ecological Change, and Indigenous Power in the Southwest Borderlands," *William and Mary Quarterly* 67, no. 2 (2010): 173–208. On leadership through talents and martial prowess, see James Jefferson, Robert W. Delaney, and Gregory C. Thompson, *The Southern Utes: A Tribal History*, ed. Floyd A. O'Neil (Ignacio, CO: Southern Ute Tribe, 1972), 48; and DeLay, *War of a Thousand Deserts*, 45. On the rise of raiding, see ibid., 38–44.

20. Brooks, *Captives and Cousins;* and Barr, *Peace Came in the Form of a Woman*, and her "From Captives to Slaves: Commodifying Indian Women in the Borderlands," *Journal of American History* 92, no. 1 (June 2005): 19–46. For the specific connections of hide processing, slavery, and polygamy, see DeLay, *War of a Thousand Deserts*, 93, and Hämäläinen, *The Comanche Empire*, 247–50.

21. "Arrival of the Utahs!" / "An Indian Wedding," *Deseret News*, April 4, 1855.

22. Ibid.

23. For the classic account, see Brooks, *Captives and Cousins*, and his " 'This Evil Extends Especially . . . to the Feminine Sex': Negotiating Captivity in the New Mexico Borderlands," *Feminist Studies* 22, no. 2 (1996): 279–309. On the rise in captivity and violence in this larger area, see Zappia, *Traders and Raiders*. Daniel Jones, *40 Years among Indians*, and interview conducted by William R. Palmer, as quoted in LeRoy R. Hafen and Ann W. Hafen, *Old Spanish Trail: Santa Fé to Los Angeles* (Glendale, CA: Arthur H. Clark, 1954), 268, 281–82.

24. "At his death the Indians killed two Piute [wives], three children, and twenty horses. They also buried an Indian boy of twelve years in the same grave, telling him to take care of Wakara"; LDS "Journal History, January 29, 1855," as quoted in Hafen and Hafen, *Old Spanish Trail*, 257. His attempt to gain a Utah settler wife is detailed in Kathryn M. Daynes, *"More Wives than One": Transformation of the Mormon Marriage System, 1840–1910* (Urbana: University of Illinois Press, 2001); 43–44. Stephen C. Foster (prefect of Los Angeles) to Bennett Riley (military governor of California), September 29, 1849, and Parley P. Pratt, LDS "Journal History, Sept 5, 1848," as quoted in Hafen and Hafen, *Old Spanish Trail*, 236, 237, 253, 254.

25. Daniel Jones, *40 Years among Indians*, as quoted in Hafen and Hafen, *Old Spanish Trail*, 268, and "Southern Indian Mission (Fort Harmony)," *Deseret News*, March 6, 1855, April 4, 1855.

26. Solomon Nunes Carvalho, *Incidents of Travel and Adventure in the Far West* (New York: Derby and Jackson, 1857), 158, 189–93.

27. Joseph Williams, *Narrative of a Tour From the State of Indiana to the Oregon Territory, 1841–2*, introduction by James C. Bell, Jr. (New York: Cadmus Book Shop, 1921), 74–76, 80–81.

28. Daniel S. Butrick et al. to J. H. Payne, December 15, 1835, vol. 4, folder 2, bound volume, pp. 120, 116, Payne Papers, Ayer Collection, Newberry Library (hereafter Payne Papers). Perdue, *Cherokee Women*, 44.

29. The laws passed were: "New Town, Cherokee Nation, November 2nd, 1819"; "An Act Relative to Breach of Marriage . . . Piney, Sept. 24, 1824"; "New Town, Cherokee Nation, November 10th 1825," in *Laws of the Cherokee Nation: Adopted by the Council at Various Periods* (Tahlequah, Cherokee Nation: Cherokee Advocate Office, 1852). The 1826 law code is the same.

30. Letter to Lewis Cass, "Washington City Brown's Hotel Feb 14 1835," vol. 7, folder 11, p. 198, Payne Papers. Elias Boudinot, *Cherokee Editor: The Writings of Elias Boudinot*, ed. Theda Perdue (Knoxville: University of Tennessee Press, 1983), 68–69, 75. On his own marriage to a non-Cherokee named Harriett Gold, see Theresa Strouth Gaul, ed., *To Marry an Indian: The Marriage of Harriett Gold and Elias Boudinot in Letters, 1823–1839* (Chapel Hill: University of North Carolina Press, 2005), as well as Ann McGrath, *Illicit Love: Interracial Sex and Marriage in the United States and Australia* (Lincoln: University of Nebraska Press, 2015), 35–86, and Nicholas Guyatt, *Bind Us Apart: How Enlightened Americans Invented Racial Segregation* (New York: Basic, 2016), 151–58. The hostility this marriage provoked was an indication of the deep-set racism of even sympathetic white Americans.

31. William McLoughlin, *Cherokees and Missionaries, 1789–1839* (Norman: University of Oklahoma Press, 1995). "Elizabeth Taylor to Abigail Williams, Brainerd Cherokee Nation June 26, 1828"; "Lucy McPherson to Mary Coe, Brainerd Cherokee Nation July 23, 1828"; "Sally M. Reece to Rev Daniel Campbell, Brainerd Cherokee Nation July 25 1828," in "Letters from Brainerd Missionary Station, May 16, 1828–July 16, 1828," vol. 8, folder 1, pp. 11, 30, 31, Payne Papers. See also Rowena McClinton, Introduction to *The Moravian Springplace Mission to the Cherokees*, 2 vols., ed. Rowena McClinton, 1–40 (Lincoln: University of Nebraska Press, 2007), 21; McLoughlin, *Cherokees and Missionaries*.

32. Daniel Butrick to Samuel Worcester, January 1, 1819, ABC 18.3.1. vol. 3, no. 114, American Board of Commissioners for Foreign Missions, Houghton Library, Harvard University. See also "Entry for Jan 25 1817," in *The Brainerd*

Journal: A Mission to the Cherokees, 1817–1823, ed. Joyce B. Phillips and Paul Gary Phillips (Lincoln: University of Nebraska Press, 1998), 28.

33. "National Committee Oct 28–29, 31 1829," vol. 7, folder 7, Payne Papers.

34. John Ridge to Albert Gallatin, February 27, 1826, vol. 8, folder 4, Payne Papers.

35. McLoughlin, *Cherokee Renascence,* 333.

36. On Cherokees and slavery, see especially Theda Perdue, *Slavery and the Evolution of Cherokee Society, 1540–1866* (Knoxville: University of Tennessee Press, 1987); Snyder, *Slavery in Indian Country;* Cleia E. Naylor, *African Cherokees in Indian Territory: From Chattel to Citizens* (Chapel Hill: University of North Carolina Press, 2008); Tiya Miles, *Ties that Bind: The Story of an Afro-Cherokee Family in Slavery and Freedom* (Berkeley: University of California Press, 2005), and her *House on Diamond Hill.*

37. Perdue, *Cherokee Women,* 41, 146. Snyder, *Slavery in Indian Country,* 209.

38. Petition, in Theda Perdue, *The Cherokee Removal: A Brief History with Documents,* 3rd ed. (Boston: Bedford, 2016), 126. As Christina Snyder puts it, "This dispersal reflected—and reinforced—the erosion of clan power"; *Slavery in Indian Country,* 193–208, 208.

39. Butrick et al. to Payne, 94, Payne Papers. On some of these trajectories, see Hatley, *The Dividing Paths,* 52–63. John Ridge to Albert Gallatin, "No. 1. Washington City, 27 Feb 1826," vol. 8, folder 4, pp. 67–68, Payne Papers.

40. See McLoughlin, *Cherokee Renascence,* 326–49; Snyder, *Slavery in Indian Country,* 182–212; Miles, *Ties that Bind,* and her *House on Diamond Hill.*

41. Petition, in Perdue, *The Cherokee Removal,* 125.

42. As Perdue has noted, "Although the Cherokee elite accepted many tenets of western 'civilization,' some balked at abandoning the practice of polygamy. The chief justice of the Cherokee Supreme Court was only one of the several Cherokee leaders who had more than one wife"; *Cherokee Women,* 198. McClinton, *Moravian Springplace Mission,* 1: 251, 302. McLoughlin, *Cherokee Renascence,* 73, 151–52.

43. As Rowena McClinton puts it, "The Cherokees' subsistence-level economy and nonexploitative worldview militated against accumulation"; Introduction to *Moravian Springplace Mission,* 1: 29. Miles, *House on Diamond Hill,* 109.

44. McClinton, *Moravian Springplace Mission,* 1: 62, 65. Among others, see incidents recorded for January and June 1805, January 1808; ibid., 1: 43, 57, 245. The situation with the theft is detailed in September–November 1805; ibid., 1: 64–72, especially 66. Ibid., 1: 57. As Christina Snyder observes, "Rates of

alcohol consumption surged during the removal era, as Indians sought relief—however temporary—from their waking nightmare"; *Great Crossings,* 159.

45. McClinton, *Moravian Springplace Mission,* 1: 304–6, 375, 461, 494, and 2: 229, 274.

46. Ibid., 1: 57, 77, 114, 291. Perdue contends that "few Cherokees seem to have resorted to this traditional practice [polygamy], however, because the disruption of hunting by war, land cessions, and game depletion made the male contribution to more than one wife or household very difficult"; Perdue, *Cherokee Women,* 98. As Tiya Miles puts it, "His rapid accumulation of capital, the foundation of his mounting success, depended on the subjugation of two groups: Cherokee women, whose wealth he pilfered, and African slaves, whose bodies and labors made up much of that wealth"; *House on Diamond Hill,* 55.

47. See Julie L. Reed, *Serving the Nation: Cherokee Sovereignty and Social Welfare, 1800–1907* (Norman: University of Oklahoma Press, 2016).

48. On the complications of even powerful masters and households imposing their will on subordinates, see Rhys Isaac, *Landon Carter's Uneasy Kingdom: Revolution and Rebellion on a Virginia Plantation* (Oxford: Oxford University Press, 2004). Opinion of Daniel Dulany, esq., Dec 16, 1767 in Thomas Harris Jr and John McHenry, *Maryland Reports: Being a Series of the Most Important Law Cases, Argued and Determined in the Provincial Court . . . of Maryland* (New York: L Riley, 1809), 560. Lydia Maria Child, *An Appeal on Behalf of That Class of Americans Called Africans* (Boston: Allen and Ticknor, 1833), 200; Tera W. Hunter, *Bound in Wedlock: Slave and Free Black Marriage in the Nineteenth Century* (Cambridge: Harvard University Press, 2017), 50, 71; Herbert G. Gutman, *The Black Family in Slavery and Freedom, 1750–1925* (Oxford: Basil Blackwell, 1976), 284; James H. Hammond, *Plantation Manual of James H. Hammond,* typed transcription, Hammond Collection, South Carolina Collection, University of South Carolina Library (Columbia, 1934). H. N. McTyeire, *Duties of Masters to Servants: Three Premium Essays* (Charleston, SC: Southern Baptist Publication Society, 1851), 28–29.

49. McClinton, *Moravian Springplace Mission,* 1: 100, 108, 113–14.

50. Ibid., 1: 113–14, 392.

51. Ibid., 1: 392–93, 435.

52. Ibid., 1: 435, 437, 492.

53. Charles Colcock Jones, *The Religious Instruction of the Negroes, in the United States* (Savannah: Thomas Purse, 1842), 132, 233, 134, 137, 147. Online at

Documenting the American South, University of North Carolina at Chapel
Hill Library, https://docsouth.unc.edu/church/jones/jones.html.

54. Hunter, *Bound in Wedlock*, 30–32.

8. *"Defence of Polygamy by a Lady"*

1. Belinda Marden Pratt, "Belinda M. Pratt, Autobiography, 1884," MS19225,
   Church of Jesus Christ of Latter-day Saints Church History Library, Salt
   Lake City (hereafter Church History Library).

2. Ibid.

3. Laurel Thatcher Ulrich, *A House Full of Females: Plural Marriage and
   Women's Rights in Early Mormonism, 1835–1870* (New York: Knopf, 2017),
   267. Article VIII, *North American Review*, July 1, 1862, 189–227, 192. See
   Sarah Barringer Gordon, *The Mormon Question: Polygamy and Constitutional
   Conflict in Nineteenth-Century America* (Chapel Hill: University of North
   Carolina Press, 2002), especially 19–54, as well as her " 'Our National
   Hearthstone': Anti-Polygamy Fiction and the Sentimental Campaign against
   Moral Diversity in Antebellum America," *Yale Journal of Law and the
   Humanities* 8 (1996): 295–350. It was so unusual for a woman to publish a
   piece like this one that some have even questioned whether Belinda Pratt
   wrote it, assuming she must have been a mouthpiece for her husband, Parley,
   or his brother Orson, admittedly gifted writers. I can find no evidence to
   support this idea. While Parley surely edited it, I believe it is Belinda's own
   writing, given its unusual emphasis on women and children (not found in the
   published work of Parley or Orson); her time as a schoolteacher (thus
   showing her educational abilities); and her own memoir and eloquent public
   pronouncements on polygamy, decades after Parley's death.

4. There is no mention of the tract in Merina Smith's account and in Talbot a
   very brief one, to the effect that the purpose of marriage was children, not sex;
   Christine Talbot, *A Foreign Kingdom: Mormons and Polygamy in American
   Political Culture, 1852–1890* (Urbana: University of Illinois Press, 2013), 45.
   Ulrich includes the fullest and most recent analysis, but it is still fairly limited;
   House Full of Females, 267–68. See also B. Carmon Hardy, *Doing the Works of
   Abraham: Mormon Polygamy; Its Origins, Practice, and Demise* (Norman, OK:
   Arthur Clark, 2007), 95–97, 122, 194. It is a perennial debate, summarized in
   Sarah M. S. Pearsall, "Polygamy and Bigamy," *Oxford Bibliographies Online:
   Atlantic History*, ed. Trevor Burnard (Oxford: Oxford University Press, 2013).
   Classic statements include Joan Iversen, "Feminist Implications of Mormon
   Polygyny," *Feminist Studies* 10, no. 3 (1984): 505–22, and Jessie L. Embry,

"Effects of Polygamy on Mormon Women," *Frontiers: A Journal of Women Studies* 7, no. 3 (1984): 56–61. Kathryn Daynes, Christine Talbot, Lauren Thatcher Ulrich, and especially Paula Harline have stressed the constraints on polygamous wives, though all of them, especially Daynes and Ulrich, have also considered some of its benefits. Kathryn M. Daynes, *"More Wives than One": Transformation of the Mormon Marriage System, 1840–1910* (Urbana: University of Illinois Press, 2001); Paula Kelly Harline, *The Polygamous Wives Writing Club: From the Diaries of Mormon Pioneer Women* (Oxford: Oxford University Press, 2014); Talbot, *A Foreign Kingdom*; and Ulrich, *House Full of Females*. Leo Miller, John Cairncross, and John Witte, Jr., do not spend time on the tract.

5. See Dirk Hartog, *Man and Wife in America: A History* (Cambridge: Harvard University Press, 2000); Norma Basch, *Framing American Divorce: From the Revolutionary Generation to the Victorians* (Berkeley: University of California Press, 2001); and Robert Abzug, *Cosmos Crumbling: American Reform and the Religious Imagination* (Oxford: Oxford University Press, 1994).

6. As Nancy Cott observes of the state, "marriage was their political creation"; *Public Vows: A History of Marriage and the Nation* (Cambridge: Harvard University Press, 2000), 54. See Hartog, *Man and Wife*, and Basch, *Framing American Divorce*, as well as Beverly Schwartzberg, "'Lots of Them Did That': Desertion, Bigamy, and Marital Fluidity in Late-Nineteenth-Century America," *Journal of Social History* 37 (2004): 573–600. George Elliott Howard, *A History of Matrimonial Institutions (Chiefly in England and the United States with an Introductory Analysis of the Literature and the Theories of Primitive Marriage and Family)*, 3 vols. (Chicago: University of Chicago Press, 1904), 3: 11–13.

7. On the complex relationship between state and states, and coercion, Gary Gerstle, *Liberty and Coercion: The Paradox of American Government from the Founding to the Present* (Princeton: Princeton University Press, 2015), and Margot Canaday, *The Straight State: Sexuality and Citizenship in Twentieth-Century America* (Princeton: Princeton University Press, 2011). Lydia Maria (Mrs. D. L.) Child, *The History of the Condition of Women, in Various Ages and Nations*, 2 vols. (Boston: John Allen, 1835). Frances Peters to Robert Peters, February 22, 1851, quoted in Cott, *Public Vows*, 66. Sarah H. Crowell, toast, "The New Year," *Communitist*, January 15, 1846, as quoted in Thomas D. Hamm, *God's Government Begun: The Society for Universal Inquiry and Reform, 1842–1846* (Bloomington: Indiana University Press, 1995).

8. [Anon.], *A Brief exposition of the established principles and regulations of the United Society of Believers called Shakers* (New York: E. O. Jenkins, 1851),

4–6, 21. The classic account is Lawrence Foster, *Religion and Sexuality: The Shakers, the Mormons, and the Oneida Community* (1981; Urbana: University of Illinois Press, 1984), esp. chs. 1–2; quotation 74. See also Julie Dunfey, "'Living the Principle' of Plural Marriage: Mormon Women, Utopia, and Female Sexuality in the Nineteenth Century," *Feminist Studies* 10, no. 3 (1984): 523–36.

9. John Humphrey Noyes, *"The Way of Holiness,"* A series of papers formerly published in The Perfectionist, at New Haven (Putney, VT: H. H. Noyes, 1838), 52, 34, and John Humphrey Noyes, *Male Continence: Or, Self-Control in Sexual Intercourse. A Letter of Inquiry Answered* (Oneida, NY: Oneida Community Collection, Department of Special Collections, Syracuse University, 1867, rpt. 2000 digital edition), 3.

10. Mary Kelley, *Learning to Stand and Speak: Women, Education, and Public Life in America's Republic* (Chapel Hill: University of North Carolina Press for the Omohundro Institute of Early American History and Culture, 2006), 51.

11. Sarah Moore Grimké, *Letters on the Equality of the Sexes, and the Condition of Woman* (Boston: Isaac Knapp, 1838), 12, and Elizabeth Cady Stanton to Susan B. Anthony, 1853, as quoted in Cott, *Public Vows*, 67.

12. Carolyn L. Karcher, *The First Woman in the Republic: A Cultural Biography of Lydia Maria Child* (Durham, NC: Duke University Press, 1994), 231. Most controversially, Child argued against legislation stopping interracial marriages, though she knew it would make her the target of "gross ridicule"; Lydia Maria Child, *An Appeal on Behalf of That Class of Americans Called Africans* (Boston: Allen and Ticknor, 1833), 200, 209.

13. Margaret M. R. Kellow, "The Divided Mind of Antislavery Feminism: Lydia Maria Child and the Construction of African American Womanhood," in *Discovering the Women in Slavery: Emancipating Perspectives on the American Past*, ed. Patricia Morton, 107–26 (Athens: University of Georgia Press, 1996), 108. Child, *History*, 1: 9. "But the seraglios of the Sultan and his grandees do not furnish a true picture of the character and condition of the Turkish women"; ibid., 1: 63. She also averred that Turkish slavery was the mildest in the world; ibid., 1: 71.

14. "Notwithstanding the universal practice of polygamy, there are instances of very strong domestic attachment in the South Sea islands"; ibid., 2: 205, 224, 284–85.

15. Grimké, *Equality of the Sexes*, 11, 21, 37, 45, 33, 48, 49, 85–86.

16. Margaret Fuller, *Woman in the Nineteenth Century*, ed. Larry J. Reynolds (1845; New York: Norton, 1998), 46. Fuller wanted women to have "a much

greater range of occupation than they have, to rouse their latent powers";
78–79, 102.

17. This European system privileged finances and family over "genuine
marriage, (the mutual choice of souls inducing a permanent union)"; ibid.,
82. Mary S. Gove (Mary Sargeant Gove Nichols), *Lectures to Ladies on
Anatomy and Physiology* (Boston: Saxton and Peirce, 1842), 89.

18. Edgar A. Poe, "The Literati of New York City IV, Some Honest Opinions at
Random Respecting Their Authorial Merits, With Occasional Words of
Personality," *Godey's Lady Book*, August 1846, 72. Sophia Peabody Hawthorne
to Mrs. Elizabeth Palmer Peabody, March 6, 1845, and Lydia Maria Child,
February 8, 1845, as quoted in Charles Capper, *Margaret Fuller: An American
Romantic Life*, 2 vols., vol. 2, *The Public Years* (Oxford: Oxford University
Press, 2007), 186, 186–87.

19. Fuller, *Woman in the Nineteenth Century*, 103.

20. Susan Klepp, *Revolutionary Conceptions: Women, Fertility, and Family Limitation in America, 1760–1820* (Chapel Hill: University of North Carolina
Press for the Omohundro Institute of Early American History and Culture,
2009), and Will of John Marden, Merrimack County Probate Department,
item 1040, vol. 8.272, vol. 5.567.

21. Belinda Pratt, "Autobiography." Also see marriage of John Marden with
Rachel Shaw, 4 Jan 1792, "New Hampshire, Marriage Records, 1637–1947."
"New Hampshire, Marriages, 1720–1920," index, FamilySearch. The 1840
census for Goffstown, New Hampshire, shows a household with Benjamin
and Belinda, and one male between fifteen and nineteen years old. In her
memoirs, Belinda recalled the date of the marriage as 1839, but in fact it
was 1840. The first listing of Benjamin Hilton in a Boston city directory is
from 1843, where he is listed as " "Hilton Benjamin A. cabinetmaker, h.
Silver n. Turnpike"; *Stimpson's Boston Directory* (Boston: Charles Stimpson,
1843), 35. Within a year, they had moved to a house at Kneeland and Washington. "Hilton Benj. A. pattern maker, h. Kneeland cor. Wash"; *Stimpson's
Boston Directory* (Boston: Charles Stimpson, 1844), 286. Nathan Hatch,
Democratization of American Christianity (New Haven: Yale University Press,
1991).

22. Ronald J. Zboray and Mary Saracino Zboray, "Women Thinking: The Inter-
national Popular Lecture and Its Audience in Antebellum New England," in
*The Cosmopolitan Lyceum: Lecture Culture and the Globe in Nineteenth-Century
America*, ed. Tom F. Wright, 42–66 (Amherst: University of Massachusetts
Press, 2013).

23. April Haynes, *Riotous Flesh: Women, Physiology, and the Solitary Vice in Nineteenth-Century America* (Chicago: University of Chicago Press, 2015), 81.

24. Gove, *Lectures to Ladies,* 126, 157, 165, 234.

25. Ibid., 218, 220, 222, 225, 226, 227–28, 234. Gove's admiration for Fuller is mentioned in Capper, *Margaret Fuller,* 2: 180. Ulrich mentions the friendship between Gove and Cobb; *House Full of Females,* 106. On Mary Gove's trajectory, see Jean L. Silver-Isenstadt, *Shameless: The Visionary Life of Mary Gove Nichols* (Baltimore: Johns Hopkins University Press, 2002). Maine woman quoted in Haynes, *Riotous Flesh,* 40.

26. The controversies surrounding Frances (Fanny) Wright, and the shock her reform ideas provoked are ably covered in Lori D. Ginzberg, " 'The Hearts of Your Readers Will Shudder': Fanny Wright, Infidelity, and American Freethought," *American Quarterly* 46, no. 2 (1994): 195–226; Helen Lefkowitz Horowitz, *Rereading Sex: Battles over Sexual Knowledge and Suppression in Nineteenth-Century America* (New York: Knopf, 2002), ch. 3; and Carolyn Eastman, *A Nation of Speechifiers: Making an American Public after the Revolution* (Chicago: University of Chicago Press, 2009), ch. 6. "Fanny Wrightism," reprinted from *Belfast* (Maine) *Journal, Boston Investigator,* September 14, 1842; issue 19, 19th Century U.S. Newspapers database.

27. See Hamm, *God's Government Begun.* "Social Reform Convention," *Boston Investigator,* June 12, 1844, 19th Century U.S. Newspapers.

28. "Morals of the East," *Boston Courier,* April 25, 1844, and "Verdict of the Coroner's Jury in the Case of Eliza Ann Munson," reprinted from *New-York Express, Boston Courier,* April 25, 1844, 19th Century U.S. Newspapers.

29. David Henkin, *City Reading: Written Words and Public Spaces in Antebellum New York* (New York: Columbia University Press, 1998), ch. 4, especially 72–73.

30. Parley P. Pratt, *The Autobiography of Parley P. Pratt* (Chicago: Law, King, and Law, 1888), 186–88, 330. On Joseph Smith's trajectory, see Richard Lyman Bushman, *Joseph Smith: Rough Stone Rolling* (New York: Knopf, 2005).

31. Belinda Pratt, "Autobiography." On Cobb, Ulrich, *House Full of Females,* 85, 131, 105–7, 213–21, and podcast "The Lioness of the Lord: The Letters of Augusta Adams Cobb to her Husband, Brigham Young," January 1, 2012, at https://www.sunstonemagazine.com/the-lioness-of-the-lord-the-letters-of-augusta-adams-cobb-to-her-husband-brigham-young-2/.

32. Nancy Cott argues that the difficulty of traveling alone is one reason women stayed in unhappy marriages; *Public Vows,* 38. Belinda Pratt, "Autobiography."

33. "Record of the Deaths and Burials in the City of Boston, for the year 1844," Massachusetts Vital Records, Boston Public Library.

34. Parley P. Pratt to William Patterson, 9 May 1853, Parley P. Pratt Collection, Church History Library, as quoted in Terryl L. Givens and Matthew J. Grow, *Parley P. Pratt: The Apostle Paul of Mormonism* (Oxford: Oxford University Press, 2011). "Two of his books . . . attained near-canonical status"; ibid., 6, see also 3, 178. Orson Pratt to "The Saints in the Eastern and Middle States," August 25, 1845, in *New York Messenger* 2 (August 30, 1845): 71, as quoted in David J. Whittaker, "Early Mormon Pamphleteering," *Journal of Mormon History* 4 (1977): 35–49.

35. Parley Pratt, *Autobiography*, 329. On these points, see Daynes, *"More Wives than One,"* 55–56, especially 60, and 158–60; Merina Smith, *Revelation, Resistance, and Mormon Polygamy: The Introduction and Implementation of the Principle, 1830–1853* (Logan: Utah State University Press, 2013), 37; and Ulrich, *House Full of Females*, 16.

36. Kathleen Flake, "The Development of Early Latter-day Saint Marriage Rites, 1831–1853," *Journal of Mormon History* 41, no. 1 (2015): 77–103, 79, 90; Smith, *Revelation, Resistance, and Mormon Polygamy*, 88. "Persons, *male as well as female,* not married for eternity by being sealed on earth have no possibility of being exalted"; Kathryn Daynes, "Celestial Marriage (Eternal and Plural)," in *Oxford Handbook of Mormonism*, ed. Terryl L. Givens and Philip L. Barlow, 334–48 (Oxford: Oxford University Press, 2015), 5, italics original. Joseph Smith, "Blessing to Sarah Ann Whitney, [Nauvoo,] 23 March 1843," Whitney Family Documents, Church History Library. A full image and transcript can be found in Joseph Smith Papers online, http://www.josephsmithpapers.org/paper-summary/blessing-to-sarah-ann-whitney-23-march-1843/1. On this document and its context, see Benjamin Park, "Joseph Smith, Sarah Ann Whitney, and the Familial Dynamics of Nauvoo Polygamy," online blog at https://professorpark.wordpress.com/2017/10/16/sarah-ann-whitney-blessing/.

37. As Christine Talbot has noted, "Almost all Church leaders practiced polygamy"; Talbot, *A Foreign Kingdom*, 38–39. "A Special Conference of the elders of the Church of Jesus Christ of Latter-day Saints assembled in the Tabernacle, Great Salt Lake City, August 28th, 1852," *Deseret News Extra,* September 14, 1852; "The Smiths' bitter differences over polygamy" receive attention in Richard S. Van Wagoner, *Mormon Polygamy: A History,* 2nd ed. (Salt Lake City: Signature, 1989), 52. *The Doctrine and Covenants of the Church of Jesus Christ of Latter-day Saints* 132: 19–20, 32–39, 54, online at https://

www.lds.org/scriptures/dc-testament/dc/132 (hereafter *Doctrine and Covenants*).

38. Givens and Grow, *Parley P. Pratt*, 227–29. Daynes notes the uptick in plural marriages after Smith's assassination; *"More Wives than One,"* 35. David J. Whittaker, "Early Mormon Polygamy Defenses," *Journal of Mormon History* 11 (1984): 43–63, 54n37.

39. Susanna Musser Sheets Journal in Elijah Funk Sheets, Journals, 1843–1904, vol. 1, online at https://history.lds.org/overlandtravel/sources/6414/sheets -susanna-musser-journal-in-elijah-funk-sheets-journals-1843-1904-vol-1 [1847], and Susanna Musser Sheets to Anna Bitner, August 1847, in Musser family, letters, 1847–49, online at https://history.lds.org/overlandtravel/ sources/18259/sheets-susanna-musser-to-anna-bitner-aug-1847-in -musser-family-letters-1847-1849-1877. Parley Pratt, Jr. [Reminiscences], in Arthur D. Coleman, compiler, Pratt Pioneers of Utah, xxviii–xxix, online at https://history.lds.org/overlandtravel/sources/6407/pratt-parley-p-jr -reminiscences-in-arthur-d-coleman-comp-pratt-pioneers-of-utah-1967 -xxviii-xxix. Givens and Grow, *Parley P. Pratt*, 266.

40. Whittaker, "Early Mormon Polygamy Defenses." Fawn Brodie, *No Man Knows My History: The Life of Joseph Smith*, 2nd ed. (1945; New York: Knopf, 1995), 187. Ulrich, *House Full of Females*, xxiv.

41. Whittaker notes: "Her eleven-page pamphlet was in fact a letter to Lydia dated Salt Lake City, January 12, 1854. Printed as a *Defence of Polygamy, by a Lady of Utah, in a Letter to Her Sister in New Hampshire*, this work was a specific reply to Lydia's October 2, 1853 letter which Belinda had received on January 11, 1854." He also notes: "Belinda Pratt's pamphlet reached a wider audience in the nineteenth century than any other Mormon exposition on the subject, with the exception of Orson Pratt's works"; "Early Mormon Polygamy Defenses," 54, 57. Peter Crawley, ed., *A Descriptive Bibliography of the Mormon Church*, 3 vols., vol. 3, item 875, article VIII; *North American Review*, July 1, 1862, pp. 189–227, 191.

42. As quoted in Haynes, *Riotous Flesh*, 107; see also 85. By contrast, an actual letter to a disapproving sister back east, inquiring about polygamy, received a curt response from recipient Vilate Kimball, who omitted mentioning her own plural marriage; Ulrich, *House Full of Females*, 231–33.

43. Pratt, *Defence*, 4.

44. *Doctrine and Covenants* 132: 65, and Pratt, *Defence*, 2.

45. Pratt, *Defence*, 3. *Doctrine and Covenants* 132: 30. Brodie, *No Man Knows My History*, 279. Ulrich, *House Full of Females*, 267. Parley P. Pratt, *An Appeal to*

the inhabitants of the State of New York . . . Intelligence and Affection (Nauvoo: John Taylor, 1844), 38–39, published online by Brigham Young University, http://contentdm.lib.byu.edu/cdm/compoundobject/collection/NCMP1820-1846/id/2814/rec/1. "The Saints' ideology and practice of 'plurality' expressed a positive ethic and religious identity related to their priestly ideals"; Kathleen Flake, *The Emotional and Priestly Logic of Plural Marriage*, Leonard J. Arrington Mormon History Lecture Series, no. 15 (Logan: Utah State University Press, 2010), 3.

46. Pratt, *Defence*, 3.

47. Ulrich notes that there was a belief that men should not indulge in sex too often. "Others accepted the notion that respectable women were essentially passionless. Even those who challenged this idea believed that sexual arousal during pregnancy and lactation might affect the character as well as the health of the child"; *House Full of Females*, 96. Sylvester Graham, *A Lecture to Young Men on Chastity*, 10th ed. (Boston: Charles H. Peirce, 1848), 47–50. Noyes, *Male Continence*, 3. "About female pleasure Noyes was silent"; Horowitz, *Rereading Sex*, 255.

48. T. L. Nichols and M. G. Nichols, *Esoteric Anthropology (The Mysteries of Man): A Comprehensive and Confidential Treatise on the Structure, Functions, Passional Attractions, and Perversions, True and False Physical and Social Conditions, and the Most Intimate Relations of Men and Women* (London: Nichols, 1853; rpt. New York: Arno, 1972), 98, 137, 141.

49. Klepp, *Revolutionary Conceptions*, and Ulrich, *House Full of Females*, 267–73.

50. John Miner, *Dr. Miner's Defense* (Hartford: Hudson and Goodwin, 1781), 46, 17, 50, 56–57, 57–58. Pratt, *Defence*, 5.

51. Anon., *Martin's Hobby Houghed and Pounded, or Letters on Thelyphthora* (London: J. Buckland, 1781), 86. Martin Madan, *Thelyphthora; or, a Treatise on Female Ruin*, 2 vols. (London: J. Dodsley, 1780), 2: 188–89. See also Miner, *Defense*, 57–58. Pratt, *Defence*, 6.

52. Belinda Pratt, "Autobiography," 11, and Ulrich, *House Full of Females*, 85.

53. Austin N. Ward, with Maria Ward, *The Husband in Utah; or, Sights and Scenes among the Mormons* (New York: Derby and Jackson, 1857), 195.

54. Parley P. Pratt to Belinda Marden Pratt, San Francisco, California, 17 January 1855, Church History Library. I have checked every court in several relevant counties of Massachusetts (Suffolk, Norfolk, Middlesex, Essex) and New Hampshire (Merrimack, Hillsborough, Rockingham, Strafford, Belknap) in the relevant period and can locate no record. It is possible that there was such a divorce and the paperwork has been lost. On the other hand,

it is also possible that there was never any legal divorce. Givens and Grow, *Parley P. Pratt,* 231. The *Voree Herald,* a publication vociferously anti–Brigham Young, claimed in 1846 that Parley had had to leave Boston abruptly because of "notes for borrowed money, writs for seducing wives, and warrants for adultery"; *Voree Herald,* September 1846, vol. 1, no. 9. Benjamin married Jane Hancock in Massachusetts in February 1846, suggesting that he and Belinda had legally divorced. Benjamin and Jane went on to have at least five children, moving in the 1850s to Alabama, where Benjamin continued to work as a "pattern maker"; Marriage records, February 1846, Boston, Boston City Records. "Free Inhabitants in the 1st District in the County of Montgomery State of Alabama," June 8, 1860, p. 25, Alabama Census of 1860.

55. Klepp, *Revolutionary Conceptions,* passim. Ulrich notes that there was a three-year gap, on average, between the births of each of Parley's wives. She concludes: "The Pratt family was a reproductive collective that produced an impressively large number of children for the father while making fewer demands on the mothers than was the case with the Woodruffs"; *House Full of Females,* 271.

56. Daynes, *"More Wives than One,"* 141–72. Around 1840, the "church was in a position to institute radical changes in forms of marriage"; Smith, *Revelation, Resistance, and Mormon Polygamy,* 37.

57. Gordon identifies this patriarchal marriage as having a "commitment to male supremacy"; *Mormon Question,* 105.

58. "Parley's own letters fizz with enthusiasm for all kinds of love"; Ulrich, *House Full of Females,* 271. Parley P. Pratt, Ship "Queen of the West," to Belinda Marden Pratt, n.d. and October 14, 1846. Parley P. Pratt Collection, Church History Library.

59. Mrs. Benjamin Ferris, *The Mormons at Home: with some incidents of travel from Missouri to California, 1852–3. In a series of letters* (New York: Dix and Edwards, 1856), 169, and John Humphrey Noyes, "Bible Argument," in *Bible Communism: A Compilation from the Annual Reports and Other Publications of the Oneida Association and Its Branches; Presenting, in Connection with Their History, a Summary View of Their Religious and Social Theories* (Brooklyn, NY: Oneida Community Collection, Department of Special Collections, Syracuse University, 1853; rpt. 2000).

60. Paula Harline has stressed the negative aspects of polygamy for especially more rank-and-file plural wives; *Polygamous Wives Writing Club,* 79.

61. Givens and Grow, *Parley P. Pratt,* 478. There are several relevant documents at https://clmroots.blogspot.com/2008/07/thomas-box-early-mormon-convert

-from.html. See also Belinda M. Pratt Diary, 1877–October 1885, May 13, 1881, p. 68, Church History Library.

62. See Daynes, *"More Wives than One,"* and Ulrich, *House Full of Females,* 84–107, especially 91–93 on Smith. Ulrich considers this issue as well with William Clayton.

63. As quoted in Givens and Grow, *Parley P. Pratt,* 278; Ward, *The Husband in Utah,* 194; Ferris, *Mormons at Home,* 166–67.

64. Maria Ward's *Female Life among the Mormons* also contains a tale of a man buying wives in exchange for livestock; Maria Ward, *Female Life among the Mormons: A Narrative of Many Years' Personal Experience* (New York: J. C. Derby. 1855), 322–28.

65. Benjamin G. Ferris, *Utah and the Mormons: The History, Government, Doctrines, Customs, and Prospects of the Latter-Day Saints* (New York: Harper and Brothers, 1854), 247; and Anne F. Hyde, *Empires, Nations, and Families: A New History of the North American West, 1800–1860* (Lincoln: University of Nebraska Press, 2011), 358.

66. As Gordon has put it, "Most antipolygamists made a counterargument, claiming that Mormon polygamy demonstrated that traditional marriage protected and respected women. . . . By enacting laws to prohibit the 'enslavement of women in Utah,' congressmen could deflect attention from domestic relations in their own states and direct it toward a rebellious territory"; *Mormon Question,* 53–54.

67. As W. Paul Reeve has helpfully detailed in *Religion of a Different Color: Race and the Mormon Struggle for Whiteness* (Oxford: Oxford University Press, 2015). See also J. Spencer Fluhman, *"A Peculiar People": Anti-Mormonism and the Making of Religion in Nineteenth-Century America* (Chapel Hill: University of North Carolina Press, 2012), 117; and Gordon, *Mormon Question,* especially 171–81, and her " 'The Liberty of Self-Degradation': Polygamy, Woman Suffrage, and Consent in Nineteenth-Century America," *Journal of American* History 83 (1996): 815–47. As Patrick Q. Mason observes, "anti-Mormonism provided one set of bonds that helped reforge national unity after the Civil War and Reconstruction, and gave southerners common cause with northern reformers and politicians who had been their bitter enemies only a few years earlier"; Patrick Q. Mason, *The Mormon Menace: Violence and Anti-Mormonism in the Postbellum South* (Oxford: Oxford University Press, 2011), 14.

68. Ward, *The Husband in Utah,* 210. The best treatment of these campaigns is Gordon, *Mormon Question,* passim. On these issues, see, among many

others, Hyde, *Empires, Nations, and Families;* Karl Jacoby, *Shadows at Dawn: A Borderlands Massacre and the Violence of History* (New York: Penguin, 2008); Ari Kelman, *A Misplaced Massacre: Struggling over the Memory of Sand Creek* (Cambridge: Harvard University Press, 2013); and Andrew Graybill, *The Red and the White: A Family Saga of the American West* (New York: Norton, 2013).

69. Gordon concludes, "Almost 100 novels and many hundreds of magazine and newspaper stories . . . built on the market for antipolygamy fiction" from 1850 to 1900; *Mormon Question,* 29. Both Gordon and Talbot offer useful analysis of the cultural work of novels and other antipolygamy publications. Francis Lieber, "Shall Utah be Admitted to the Union?" *Putnam's Monthly Magazine of American Literature, Science, and Art* 5, no. 27 (1855): 10, in American Periodicals Database.

70. Gordon, *Mormon Question,* 119–45, 134. U.S. Supreme Court, *Reynolds v. United States,* 98 U.S. 145, January 1879, at https://supreme.justia.com/cases/federal/us/98/145/case.html.

71. Wilford Woodruff, "Manifesto: Official Declaration 1," *Doctrine and Covenants.* See Kathleen Flake, *The Politics of American Religious Identity: The Seating of Senator Reed Smoot, Mormon Apostle* (Chapel Hill: University of North Carolina Press, 2004), 27–30.

72. "The Mormon question" was "a contest over the very meaning of Americanness"; Talbot, *A Foreign Kingdom,* 1. Gordon, *Mormon Question,* passim. Speech of Belinda Marden Pratt, January 1879, and Belinda M. Pratt Diary, 1877–October 1885, Papers of Belinda Marden Pratt, Church History Library.

Conclusion

1. https://en.wikipedia.org/wiki/Romney_family#Family_members; http://news.byu.edu/byu-numbers; http://www.city-data.com/city/Provo-Utah.html. Of all people, it is 89 percent LDS. Emma Kerr, "Inside Gay Students' Fight to be Heard at BYU," *Chronicle of Higher Education,* May 22, 2018, online at https://www.chronicle.com/article/Inside-Gay-Students-Fight/243487.

2. Annie Clark Tanner, *A Mormon Mother: An Autobiography by Annie Clark Tanner* (Salt Lake City: Tanner Trust Fund, University of Utah Library, 1983), 16–17, 24, 130, 132, 152, 269.

3. On the controversies surrounding his seating in the Senate, see Kathleen Flake, *The Politics of American Religious Identity: The Seating of Senator Reed*

Smoot, Mormon Apostle (Chapel Hill: University of North Carolina Press, 2004). Ann Eliza Young, *Wife Number 19, or The Story of a Life in Bondage* (Hartford, CT: Dustin, Gilman, 1876), 307, 601.

4. Mari Sandoz and Evelyn Oppenheimer, *The Beaver Men: Spearheads of Empire* (New York: Hastings House, 1964), and Robert M. Utley, *A Life Wild and Perilous: Mountain Men and the Paths to the Pacific* (New York: Henry Holt, 1997). See Sylvia Van Kirk, *"Many Tender Ties": Women in Fur-Trade Society in Western Canada, 1670–1870* (Winnipeg: Watson and Dwyer, 1980); Susan Sleeper-Smith, *Indian Women and French Men: Rethinking Cultural Encounter in the Western Great Lakes* (Amherst: University of Massachusetts Press, 2001), especially chs. 1–3, and "Women, Kin, and Catholicism: New Perspectives on the Fur Trade," *Ethnohistory* 47, no. 2 (2000): 423–52; Lucy Eldersveld Murphy, *Great Lakes Creoles: A French-Indian Community on the Northern Borderlands, Prairie du Chien, 1750–1860* (Cambridge: Cambridge University Press, 2014), and "To Live among Us: Accommodation, Gender, and Conflict in the Western Great Lakes Region, 1760–1832" in *Contact Points: American Frontiers from the Mohawk Valley to the Mississippi, 1750–1830*, ed. Andrew R. L. Cayton and Fredrika J. Teute, 270–303 (Chapel Hill: University of North Carolina Press for the Omohundro Institute of Early American History and Culture, 1998); Anne F. Hyde, *Empires, Nations, and Families: A New History of the North American West, 1800–1860* (Lincoln: University of Nebraska Press, 2011); Andrew R. Graybill, *The Red and the White: A Family Saga of the American West* (New York: Norton, 2013); Ann McGrath, *Illicit Love: Interracial Sex and Marriage in the United States and Australia* (Lincoln: University of Nebraska Press, 2015); and Gilles Havard, *Histoire des Coureurs de Bois* (Paris: Les Indes Savants, 2016).

5. David Jackson, "Obama, Romney Both Have Family Histories with Polygamy," *USA Today*, April 13, 2012.

6. A classic statement is Cheshire Calhoun, "Who's Afraid of Polygamous Marriage? Lessons for Same-Sex Marriage Advocacy from the History of Polygamy," *San Diego Law Review* 42, no. 3 (2005): 1023–42. As Andrew F. March observes, "In a large, morally diverse society during reasonably prosperous times it may indeed be fantastical to argue that legalizing polygamy would have recognizable deleterious effects on society"; "Is There a Right to Polygamy? Marriage, Equality and Subsidizing Families in Liberal Public Justification," *Journal of Moral Philosophy* 8, no. 2 (2009): 246–72, 271.

7. See Clare Chambers, *Against Marriage: An Egalitarian Defense of the Marriage-Free State* (Oxford: Oxford University Press, 2017), esp. ch. 1 for a

useful overview of discussions both about feminist and queer critiques of marriage and the relationship of arguments for same-sex marriage and polygamy.

8. As Ara Wilson has suggested, binaries shape more than gender: "Critical transnational scholarship has analyzed the binary logic in hegemonic demarcations of territory and time: in the categories of developed/underdeveloped, modern/traditional"; "The Infrastructure of Intimacy," *Signs: Journal of Women in Culture and Society* 41, no. 2 (2016): 247–80, 271.

Index

Abernethy, Jared, 183–84, 186, 188, 189

Abraham: as Old Testament patriarch and polygamist, 86, 93, 273, 274

Adam and Eve: as examples of monogamy, 88

Adams, Abigail: on women's position in society, 153–54, 170, 171

Adams, John, 153

adultery: associated with polygamy, 11, 97, 160; justifications for, 199; punishments for, 64–66, 157; and sexual exploitation, 142, 258–59; as sin, 88–90, 96, 98

Africa. *See* slavery; West Africa

African Americans: monogamy among, 142–43; polygamy among (in slavery), 116–17, 119–20, 129–30; stereotypes regarding, 148. *See also* slaves/enslaved people

Akins, Henry, 186–87

Akpa people, 128–29

Alexander, William: *History of Women*, 171–72

Algonquian language: subgroups of, 55

Algonquian people, 50, 55; children of, 76–77; clothing worn by, 68; division of labor among, 67–71; family structure in households of, 71, 79–80; and the fur trade, 63, 68–69; kinship systems among, 73–75; mockery and wit among, 61–62; polygamy among, 57, 62, 66–67, 70–71; widows in, 74–75. *See also* Makheabichtichiou

Alpujarras rebellion, 24–25, 39

America: as emblematic of manhood, in the eyes of the British, 204–5

American Revolution: as analogous to marriage between the British and their colonies, 201–2; as manifestation of

cultural transformation, 179–80, 182, 213–14

Ames, William, 87, 88

Anabaptists: polygamy as advocated by, 5–8, 93

Anthony, Susan B., 12, 256

Apaches, 40, 42, 43

Armistead, Judith, 145

Athapaskan societies, 44, 46. *See also* Pueblo Revolt

Atlantic slave trade, 116

Awashunkes, 104

Baltasar: as alcalde at the San Carlos Mission, 215, 221; polygamy of, 220–21, 222, 247

baptism: forced, 24; of Native peoples' children, 75–76, 77; during the Revolutionary era, 182–83

Barbados: slavery in, 139

Barbot, Jean, 121, 126

Baudier, Michel, 158

Benavides, Alonso de, 5

Benin empire, 127

Biard, Pierre, 65, 70

Bible, the: English veneration for, 110–11; passages from, relating to polygamy, 5, 7, 8, 84, 88–91, 98, 187; as source of conflict and confusion for Native people, 84–85, 94–98

bigamy: during the Spanish Inquisition, 25, 26. *See also* polygamy

birth control, 13–14; lactation as, 59–60, 279; nonprocreative sex as, 60–61

Bland, Edward, 28

Bosman, Willem, 121–22, 128

Boston Female Moral Reform Society, 261